Investigations in Healthcare Interpreting

Studies in Interpretation

Melanie Metzger and Earl Fleetwood, General Editors

Investigations in Healthcare Interpreting

*Brenda Nicodemus
and Melanie Metzger,
Editors*

GALLAUDET UNIVERSITY PRESS

Washington, DC

Gallaudet University Press
Washington, DC 20002
http://gupress.gallaudet.edu

ISBN 1-56368-612-0; 978-1-56368-612-2
ISSN 1545-7613

♾ This paper meets the requirements of ANSI/NISO Z39.48-1992 (Permanence of Paper).

Contents

Introduction

During the fall that we were reviewing and editing this volume, Melanie's seven-year-old daughter Bonnie Rose ended up in the emergency room late at night, the evening before the American Thanksgiving holiday. Bonnie Rose had been suffering from a cold and cough, and woke up at 10:00 P.M. unable to stop coughing, and unable, really, to breathe. Concerned that she might have pneumonia, Melanie and her husband called their pediatrician, who recommended an immediate visit to an urgent care clinic for a chest x-ray. In route from the car, they called to request an appointment, only to discover they were being re-routed to the hospital for emergency room care.

In the emergency room they were fortunate—the waiting room was not crowded and there were intake and insurance experts available to acquire the needed legal information, medical history, and to check Bonnie Rose's pulse oxgen level (which was very low) simultaneously. Within the next three hours, their young daughter had blood tests, chest x-rays, nebulizer treatments, IV fluids, and was diagnosed as having not only walking pneumonia, but also her first-ever asthmatic reaction as well. After some discussion about antibiotics and related medications, they were sent home at 2:00 A.M. with prescriptions, medications, and instructions to address both their daugher's diagnosed problems.

Across North America, this type of medical experience is relatively common for many families, though the age, gender, and diagnoses of the patient vary greatly. Navigating the complex tapestry of healthcare professionals via a home phone, cell phone while driving, and face-to-face in the emergency room, while experiencing the emotional distress of having a loved one struggling with her health, raises a number of communicative challenges. All the factors that impact people's ability to coconstruct meaningful discourse, including gender, education, regional variation in language, conversational style, and so forth, are at play as always, but within a context of increased risk and tension. In the situation above, all the participants shared a common language. Added complexities are faced when healthcare interactions are mediated through an interpreter and a new set of issues comes into play with the discourse.

Early studies of doctor-patient discourse focused on a variety of issues, including the complex process of eliciting adequate medical history to accurately diagnose a patient (Shuy, 1972, 1976, 1983). Research that examined the discourse of medical interviews (even without the stress of emergency care) identified numerous problems including language use differences, cultural differences, and divergent goals between doctors and patients. Further, healthcare providers often use medical jargon and specialized vocabulary that created challenges for patients' comprehension, despite sharing a common language (Shuy, 1972, 1976, 1979, 1983; Ford, 1976; Fisher, 1983).

Research also revealed that doctor-patient communication was hampered by different backgrounds, lifestyles, and world experiences (Cicourel, 1983; Mishler, 1984; Tannen & Wallat, 1983, 1993). Moreover, studies pointed out that the communication situation itself occurs in a place and with topics very familiar to the healthcare practitioner (e.g., the environment, the symptoms, and health issues), whereas the patient is often in a weakened state, in an unfamiliar place, and facing decisions that could impact their life routines or even whether they will live or die (Bonanno, 1995; Fisher, 1983).

The critical importance of successful healthcare interaction, as well as the implications should communication go awry, may well account for its ongoing study, even in communicative events that take place with a shared language. Studies continue to this day, focused on the complex communication that occurs in monolingual healthcare situations, updating earlier findings and examining the more current uses of eHealth technology, including doctor-patient communication via electronic messaging (see, for example, Leong et al., 2005; Wallwiener et al., 2009).

Given the documented challenges faced by healthcare practitioners and patients, it is not surprising that a growing body of evidence-based research focuses on bilingual or multilingual healthcare contexts, and issues of accessibility and communication when healthcare is mediated through interpreters. As Pöchhacker and Shlesinger's (2007) volume on discourse-based research in healthcare interpreting brings to light, the issues faced by interpreters, patients, and healthcare providers include not only the communication issues common in a monolingual healthcare discourse encounter, but also interpreters' performance standards and issues related to the participation framework and alignment of participants in medical encounters.

The current volume is intended to add to the dialogue about medical interpreting by providing evidence-based studies of interpreted health care on several critical issues. In Chapter 1, Angelelli reports on an ethnographic examination of the coconstruction of understanding between Spanish-speaking healthcare patients and English-speaking healthcare providers in a public hospital in California, in the United States. Her study has practical and theoretical implications for interpreting studies in general and for the education of healthcare interpreters and healthcare providers in particular.

Extending previous studies that suggest the importance of an interpreter's interactional skills for accurate communication in medical settings, Major's study in c Chapter 2 examines interpreters' requests for clarification, and their interpretation of requests for clarification by the interlocutors.

Based on 15 years of data and the growing literature on bilingual health communication, Hsieh provides a description of emerging trends on interpreter-mediated healthcare in Chapter 3. Her chapter focuses on four trends: (a) recognizing interpreters as active participants in medical encounters, (b) examining medical interpreting as a coordinated accomplishment, (c) identifying the complexity of clinical demands, and (d) exploring contextual factors in bilingual health care.

Swabey, Nicodemus, and Moreland look at deaf bilingual physicians discourse in Chapter 4. This investigation focuses on how typical medical questions are translated into ASL, while also providing an overview of the current state of ASL-English healthcare interpreting. The authors examine the linguistic challenges in creating ASL translations of common medical interview questions, provide descriptions and samples of the ASL translations, and discuss patterns in the data as a step toward the ultimate goal of improving healthcare communication for deaf patients.

In Chapter 5, Brueck, Rode, Hessmann, Meinicke, Unruh, and Bergmann offer insights of five practicing signed language interpreters into the conditions and factors that characterize medical interpreting in Austria and Germany. One hundred and forty two healthcare assignments, delivered by the five interpreters in 2012, were documented and analyzed. After considering general challenges offered by the medical setting and outlining field-specific conditions in the two countries, recurrent features of medical encounters between deaf patients and hearing doctors that involve a signed language interpreter are discussed in detail with reference to the data.

Leeson, Sheikh, Rozanes, Grehan and Matthews' work on healthcare interpreting stems from cooperation in a European Commission funded project called Medisigns (2010–2012), and is addressed in Chapter 6.

Medisigns is an award-winning project that represents a ground-breaking initiative focused on providing a better understanding of the impact that interpreted interaction in medical contexts within the framework of a blended learning program for deaf people, interpreters, and those in the medical profession.

Driven by studies that document miscommunication and misunderstandings among monolingual healthcare patients and practitioners, and given that Deaf patients often lack access to healthcare information in an accessible form, In Chapter 7, Napier and Sabolcec report on a qualitative examination of access to healthcare information for deaf people in Australia.

In Chapter 8, Smeijers, van den Bogaerde, Ens-Dokkum, and Oudesluys-Murphy introduce guidelines for adapting internationally validated questionnaires found in specialized psychological and psychiatric health care and translating them into Sign Language of the Netherlands (*Nederlandse Gebarentaal*, NGT). The authors describe the selection and translation process of research instruments for use with deaf and hard of hearing individuals. The problems, dilemmas and ethical issues encountered are also discussed.

In Austria, amid a persistent lack of policy on reliable communication support services for patients with an insufficient command of German, an initiative was taken to jump-start professional interpreting service provision by harnessing videoconferencing technology. In Chapter 9, Pöchhacker describes and analyzes a field test carried out in preparation for a pilot project on video interpreting for Austrian healthcare institutions. The discussion of the field test data links up various dimensions, highlighting how social forces such as public and professional attitudes and policy considerations are as critical to successful project implementation as human and technological resources.

In Chapter 10, in an exploratory study, van den Bogaerde and de Lange, questioned deaf clients ($n=276$) as well as medical healthcare workers ($n=445$) about their experiences about accessibility of healthcare for patients. The authors also present the results for a subgroup of eight sign language interpreters (SLIs) and four deaf communication experts that were involved in the survey and relate their results to the answers provided by deaf clients and hearing medical professionals. Their results indicate a discrepancy between groups, and therefore add support to previous calls for deaf awareness training for hearing healthcare staff as a necessary part of accessibility.

Our hope for the current volume is to bring together these empirical studies of healthcare interpretation in deaf and hearing bilingual or multilingual encounters that incorporate interpreters, to address the ongoing issues faced by all of us as we negotiate the complexities of communication in healthcare settings.

REFERENCES

Bonanno, M. (1995). Hedges in the medical intake interview: Discourse task, gender, and role. PhD diss., Georgetown University.

Cicourel, A. (1983). Hearing is not believing: Language and the structure of belief in medical communication. In S. Fisher & A. D. Todd (Eds.), *The social organization of doctor-patient communication*. Washington, DC: Center for Applied Linguistics.

Fisher, S. (1983). Doctor talk/patient talk: How treatment decisions are negotiated in doctor-patient communication. In S. Fisher & A. D. Todd (Eds.), *The social organization of doctor-patient communication* (pp. 135–157). Washington, DC: Center for Applied Linguistics.

Ford, J. (1976). A linguistic analysis of doctor-patient communication problems. PhD diss., Georgetown University.

Leong, S., Gingrich, D., Lewis, P., Mauger, T., & George, J. (2005). Enhancing doctor-patient communication using email: A pilot study. *Journal of the American Board of Family Medicine 18*(3) 180–188.

Mishler, E. (1984). *The discourse of medicine: Dialects of medical interviews.* Norwood, NJ: Ablex.

Pöchhacker, F., & Shlesinger, M. (Eds.). (2007). *Healthcare interpreting: Discourse and interaction.* Amsterdam, the Netherlands: John Benjamins.

Shuy, R. (1972). Sociolinguistics and the medical history. Paper presented at the Third International Conference of Applied Linguistics.

Shuy, R. (1976). The medical interview: Problems in communication. *Primary Care 3*(3), 375–386.

Shuy, R. (1979). Language policy in medicine: Some emerging issues. In J. Alatis & G. Tucker (Eds.), Language in public life (pp. xxx–xxx). Washington, DC: Georgetown University Press.

Shuy, R. (1983). Three types of interference to an effective exchange of information in the medical interview. In S. Fisher & A. Todd (Ed.), *The social organization of doctor-patient communication* (pp. 189–202). Washington, DC: Center for Applied Linguistics.

Tannen, D., & Wallat, C. (1983). Doctor/mother/child communication: Linguistic analysis of pediatric interaction. In S. Fisher & A. Todd (Ed.), *The social organization of doctor-patient communication* (pp. 203–219). Washington, DC: Center for Applied Linguistics.

Tannen, D., & Wallat, C. (1993).Interactive frames and knowledge schemas in interaction: Examples from a medical examination/interview. In D. Tannen (Ed.), *Framing in discourse* (pp. 57–76). New York: Oxford University Press.

Wallwiener, M. C., Wallwiener, J., Kansy, H., Seegar, & Rajab, T. (2009). Impact of electronic messaging on the patient-physician interaction. *Journal of Telemedicine and Telecare 15*(5) 243–250.

Contributors

Claudia V. Angelelli
School of Management and
    Languages
Heriot-Watt University
Edinburgh, Scotland, United Kingdom

Anja Bergmann
Professional Signed Language Interpreter
Karlsruhe, Germany

Beppie van den Bogaerde
Department of Deaf Studies
Utrecht University of Applied Sciences
Utrecht, Netherlands

Patricia Brueck
Professional Signed Language Interpreter
Vienna, Austria

M. Ens-Dokkum
Medical Department
Kentalis School for the Deaf
Zoetermeer, Netherlands

Carmel Grehan
Centre for Deaf Studies
School of Linguistic, Speech and
    Communication Sciences
Trinity College Dublin (University of
    Dublin)
Dublin, Ireland

Jens Hessmann
Department of Health and Social
    Sciences
Magdeburg-Stendal University of
    Applied Sciences
Magdeburg, Germany

Elaine Hsieh
Department of Communication
University of Oklahoma
Norman, OK

Rob de Lange
Research Unit Deaf Studies
Utrecht University of Applied Sciences
Utrecht, Netherlands

Lorraine Leeson
Centre for Deaf Studies, School
    of Linguistic, Speech and
    Communication Sciences, Trinity
    College Dublin (University of
    Dublin)
Dublin, Ireland

George Major
School of Language and Culture
Auckland University of Technology
Auckland, New Zealand

Patrick A. Matthews
Centre for Deaf Studies
School of Linguistic, Speech and
    Communication Sciences
Trinity College Dublin (University
    of Dublin)
Dublin, Ireland

Britta Meinicke
Professional Signed Language
    Interpreter
Cologne, Germany

Christopher Moreland, MD
Department of Medicine
The University of Texas Health
    Science Center
San Antonio, TX

Jemina Napier
Heriot-Watt University
School of Management and
    Languages
Heriot-Watt University
Edinburgh, Scotland, United Kingdom

Brenda Nicodemus
Department of Interpretation
Gallaudet University
Washington, DC

A. M. Oudesluys-Murphy
Department of Paediatrics
Leiden University Medical Centre
Leiden, the Netherlands

Franz Pöchhacker
Center for Translation Studies
University of Vienna
Vienna, Austria

Juliane Rode
Professional Signed Language
    Interpreter
Munich, Germany

Ilana Rozanes
School of Computer Science and
    Statistics
Trinity College Dublin (University of
    Dublin)
Dublin, Ireland

Joseph Sabolcec
Northern Melbourne Institute of TAFE
Melbourne, Australia

Asim A. Sheikh
Barrister-at-Law
Four Courts, Dublin and Forensic
    and Legal Medicine
School of Medicine and Medical Science
University College Dublin
Dublin, Ireland

Anika S. Smeijers, MD
Department of Paediatrics
Leiden University Medical Centre
Leiden, the Netherlands

Laurie Swabey
School of Humanities, Arts, and
    Sciences
St. Catherine University
Minneapolis, MN

Daniela Unruh
Professional Signed Language Interpreter
Munich, Germany

Investigations in Healthcare Interpreting

"Uh . . . I Am Not Understanding You at All": Constructing (Mis)Understanding in Provider/Patient-Interpreted Medical Encounters

Claudia V. Angelelli

ABSTRACT

In multilingual societies, patients seeking health care and the health-care professionals who serve them often do not speak the same language. In a healthcare encounter, in both urban and rural areas, effective communication between these providers and patients is enabled by interpreters. Interpreters vary in their abilities and qualifications; moreover, for some language combinations there simply are as yet no professional interpreters. In this chapter I present a transcript of a typical healthcare provider–patient conversation about the patient's current health concern contextualized in her medical history and medicine intake. I examine the co-construction of understanding among the interlocutors and the way in which they work together in an attempt to communicate. The data are part of a larger ethnographic study (Angelelli, 2001 & 2004a) conducted in a public hospital in California, where interpreters work for Spanish-speaking patients and English-speaking healthcare providers in both face-to-face and over-the-speakerphone interpreted communicative events (ICEs). This study has practical and theoretical implications for interpreting studies in general and for the education of health-care interpreters and healthcare providers in particular.

The need for communication between speakers of the more dominant and less dominant languages is constant. Providing reliable services for linguistically and culturally diverse linguistic minorities has proven to be a challenge all over the world. In multilingual societies, patients seeking health care and the healthcare professionals who serve them often do not speak the same language. In both urban and rural areas, communication between healthcare providers and patients who do not share a language is enabled by interpreters (professionals or ad hoc). Interpreters vary in their abilities and qualifications, and for some language combinations there simply are as yet no professional interpreters.[1]

In this chapter I discuss the challenges faced in the United States as an example of a country in which multilingualism is the norm rather than the exception. I present a transcript of a typical healthcare provider–patient conversation about the patient's current health concern contextualized in her medical history and medicine intake. I examine the co-construction of (mis)understanding among the interlocutors and the way in which they work together in an attempt to communicate. I analyze an interaction that is part of a larger ethnographic study (Angelelli, 2001, 2004a) conducted in a public hospital in California. Interpreters work for Spanish-speaking patients and English-speaking healthcare providers in face-to-face and over-the-speakerphone interpreted communicative events (ICEs).

Accessing information during a medical encounter is essential to understanding conditions and making decisions. As the transcript presented here shows, interpreting and communication about illness and disease, diagnosis and treatment, caring and curing are often complicated by the collision of discourse and cultural communities. In addition, as in any ICEs because there are three participating interlocutors with specific communicative goals, the potential for such as collision increases.

LINGUISTIC DIVERSITY AND ACCESS TO HEALTH CARE

In many countries, populations of speakers of majority languages coexisting with indigenous languages have been augmented by waves of immigrants (e.g., refugees) who bring with them their own languages and traditions as they contribute to the economy of their new country. The nature of these waves has changed over time. Therefore, the linguistic needs of such geographically displaced people have also changed over time. To illustrate this, consider the United States, which has 60,577,020 speakers (age 5 and over) of languages other than English at home (U.S. Census Bureau's American Community Survey, 2013). This accounts for 20.1% of the total U.S. population (see Figure 1).

Statistics from the 2010 census illustrate that of the countries with the largest populations of citizens who have emigrated to the United States, Mexico ranks eighth. Mexican-born immigrants (such as Joaquín, the interpreter, and Filomena, the patient) accounted for 30.1% of all

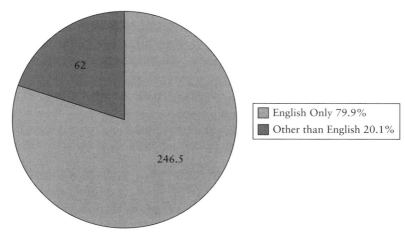

62

246.5

English Only 79.9%
Other than English 20.1%

FIGURE 1. *Multilingualism in the US (2010 Census Bureau).*

foreign-born residents in the United States and are by far the largest immigrant group in that country. Before 2008 no single country accounted for more than 15% of the total of foreign-born population. In 2010, 62% of foreign-born immigrants were reported to be of Hispanic or Latino origin. That same year 79% of the total U.S. population age 5 and older were reported to speak only the societal language, English, at home. When asked to assess their ability to speak English as "very well," "well," "not well," and "not at all" (see Figure 2), 15.4% of the 60,557,020 speakers of all languages other than English reported they did not speak it well, and another 7% said they spoke no English at all (U.S. Census Bureau's American Community Survey, 2013). Most important, "people speaking at a level below the 'very well' category are thought to need English assistance in some situations" (Shin & Kominski, 2010). This means that a significant part of the population is unable to fully and responsibly participate in interactions conducted in English and therefore needs interpreting into/from a language other than English in order to access services.

Of the 37,579,787 speakers of Spanish (62% of the total number of speakers of languages other than English at home), 16.9% reported they were unable to speak English well, and another 9% said they spoke no English at all (U.S. Census Bureau's American Community Survey, 2013).

In certain cases (e.g., the aforementioned study conducted in a public hospital in California) the diversity in population is such that it challenges existing conceptualizations of linguistic minorities, linguistic participation, or accommodation (Berk-Seligson, 2011; Edaes, 2003). More than

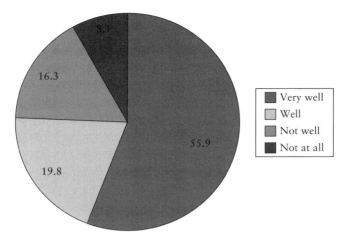

FIGURE 2. *English language ability of speakers in the US (2010 Census).*

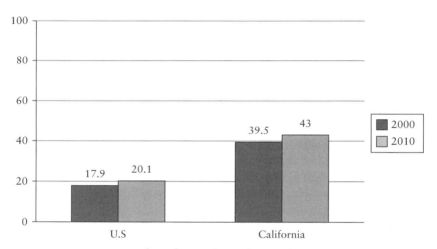

FIGURE 3. *Increase in number of Spanish speakers in the US.*

100 languages are spoken in the state of California (Modern Language Association, 2005). Among these linguistic groups, Hispanics (focus of this research) are the fastest growing, with an increase of 58% between 1990 and 2000 (Ramírez & de la Cruz, 2003; [see Figure 3]). According to projections (Tienda & Mitchell, 2005, p. 3), by 2030, 25% of U.S. residents will be of Hispanic origin/heritage. These changes in demographics have affected all aspects of U.S. society, especially the delivery of services (e.g., health care [Angelelli, 2004a]) to members of linguistic minorities.

HEALTHCARE (MEDICAL) INTERPRETING: A REVIEW
OF RELEVANT LITERATURE

This study is informed by research on interpreted communicative events (Angelelli, 2000, adapted from Hymes, 1974), which has established that when members of linguistic minorities need to access services by means of translation or interpreting, the interpreter's role is to facilitate communication in real time. The two monolingual parties interacting in any ICE belong to two distinct discourse communities. They not only do not share a linguistic code but also have very different social statuses (Angelelli, 2004a, 2004b, 2012; Baraldi & Gavioli, 2012; Davidson, 2001; Metzger, 1999). An ICE, then, is much more complex than a monolingual interaction between members of different social groups in which power differentials are salient. Interpreters facilitate specialized, dynamic, multifaceted interactions. They comprehend and produce language of various degrees of complexity, alternating between target and source languages, for rural and urban speakers whose levels of education range from second grade to graduate school, and in speech communities to which they do not necessarily belong. All of this occurs under extreme pressure (Angelelli, 2004a, 2004b).

Research on the challenges embedded in interpreted communicative events is informed by foundational work in sociolinguistics (Gumperz, 1982; Hymes, 1974) and qualitative sociology (Goffman, 1981) and, in the case of healthcare interpreting, draws from studies on cross-cultural communication, within which language use is viewed as both presupposing and creating social relations in specific communicative contexts (Blommarert, 1999; Heller, 1999; Rampton, 2005). Also relevant is relatively recent research on critical discourse analysis (Toolan, 2002; Van Leuven, 2002a, 2002b; Wodak, 2002).

This examination of interpreter-mediated healthcare communication is also informed by the literature on bilingual medical encounters, which considers language as one of the most salient factors in determining the success of communication and one of the most important barriers to accessing healthcare services (Moreno, Tarn, & Morales, 2009; Jiménez, Moreno, Leng, Buchwald, & Morales, 2012). This chapter also looks at the literature that considers the traditional focus on information-processing and problem-solving skills used in interpreter preparation (e.g., Bell, 1991; Dollerup & Lodegaard, 1992; Gile, 1994; Kalina, 2000; Lorscher, 1992; Shreve, Schäffner, Danks, & Griffin, 1993; Shreve &

Angelone, 2010) to be inadequate for preparing interpreters whose role is to broker communication between linguistic minorities and speakers of societal languages (Angelelli, 2004b, 2006; Hsieh, this volume; Metzger, 1999; Wadensjö, 1998).

When members of linguistic minorities need to access health services, for example, a language interpreter is called to bridge the communication gap. It is important to note that, in addition to language gaps, healthcare interpreting generally occurs across gulfs of culture, education, and socio-economic levels (Kaufert & Putsch, 1997) and that power differentials between interlocutors are usually quite salient (Angelelli, 2004b, 2011).

Since the two monolingual parties that take part in an interpreted communicative event not only do not share either their linguistic code or social status but also belong to two distinct discourse communities (e.g., the communities of healthcare providers and administrators and the communities of patients seeking health care), an ICE is much more complex than a monolingual interaction between members of any given linguistic group in which the power differentials are evident. What makes healthcare interpreting even more challenging is that, as I argue elsewhere (Angelelli, 2000), interpreters are not necessarily full "residents" of either of the two speech communities (Hymes, 1974) in which they work. They are, instead, temporary guests. They do not necessarily belong to the community of either of the monolingual interlocutor (e.g., the healthcare provider who is performing a test and the patient who requires it), yet they must be able to navigate both as if they belonged. Additionally, many times healthcare interpreters navigate speech communities in which asymmetrical relations exist between speakers of more and less privileged societal groups. Therefore, the job of healthcare interpreters who facilitate those interactions is specialized, dynamic, and highly complex.

As the data presented here demonstrate, in the course of doing their jobs, healthcare interpreters comprehend and produce language of various degrees of complexity, alternating between target and source languages, rural and urban speakers whose level of education ranges from second grade to graduate school, all of which takes place in speech communities to which they do not necessarily belong. In addition, all of this occurs under extreme pressure and critical conditions. To add to the complexity of the job, it is generally the case that medical interpreters have limited opportunities for professional development and education. Therefore, they may not always be aware of their own professional responsibilities and limitations (Angelelli, 2004a, 2004b). It has been established that in monolingual interactions between healthcare providers and patients, providers ask the majority of questions, and patients are mostly limited to supplying answers (Prince, 1986; Swabey, Nicodemus, & Moreland, this volume). In an interpreted communicative event, this pattern of conversation is not entirely obvious. In addition to the phenomenon of adjacent pairs (Davidson, 1998), even when providers do ask the majority of the questions, many times interpreters dive into a line of questions in which they either let patients verify the information, clarify answers, and add information or prevent patients from doing any of this (Angelelli 2004a, 2011, 2012; Davidson, 2000, 2001). Providers need to obtain some information from the patient that, in the provider's mind, is important. They generally ask closed questions (Prince, 1986). Most of the time the patients do not answer these questions directly. They tell stories and embed in them information that is valuable to the provider. In addition to telling stories while answering questions, patients seek information that will help them make vital decisions.

In a cross-linguistic encounter, when taking a patient's medical history and exploring chronic illnesses (Angelelli, 2011) or when discussing and measuring pain (Angelelli, 2012), providers need to access specific information with the interpreters' help. This information is crucial in that it helps providers make subsequent decisions on treatment. In the interaction presented in this chapter, we will see that the pain that causes the patient to call the clinic is not discussed immediately (i.e., as soon as the provider asks about it). Even though the provider's request for information about the pain is interpreted, it is not necessarily going to be addressed right away. Both patients and interpreters introduce other elements that may change the course of the conversation. Researchers have agreed that ethnic background affects pain perception and that pain is a complex, culturally defined, multifactorial experience (Bates, 1987; Greenwald, 1991; Ramer et al., 1999; Rollman, 1998; Strelzer, 1997). Each culture has its own language describing the experience of pain (Callister, 2003; Zborowski, 1952). Members of a shared culture may understand the meaning of the pain and suffering of another member of the same culture, whereas someone from outside that culture may not understand them in the same way.

Focusing on interpreters' behaviors during provider/patient interactions, other studies (Angelelli, 2004a; Baraldi & Gavioli, 2012; Bolden, 2000; Cambridge, 1999; Davidson, 1998, 2000, 2001; Metzger, 1999; Prince, 1986) have established that, as interpreters become the "owners" of text, their visibility increases. When this happens, the interpreter's role is highly consequential as it influences the medical or personal information exchanged during an ICE (Angelelli, 2004a). This has consequences for the provider-patient relationship and the outcomes of the medical consultation (Moreno et al., 2009; Jiménez et al., 2012). In the interaction discussed here we will see examples of this impact.

In addition to the interplay of the aforementioned social factors, the interpreter's own agency, and the interlocutor's differences, recent technological developments coupled with high demands for service and an insufficient number of educated professionals willing to work under the current state of affairs (e.g., low salary, limited conditions of workplace [working long hours, feeling the pressure of short and infrequent breaks, receiving no extra remuneration/recognition for doing translations in addition to interpreting]) have complicated the interpreters' job even more. Nowadays, rather than brokering communication during traditional face-to-face encounters and observing beneficial workplace practices (e.g., taking breaks after every 30 minutes of uninterrupted work), many healthcare interpreters perform their roles via teleconference or videoconference, during which they work for extended periods of time without breaks (Angelelli, 2004a) while healthcare organizations are becoming more "productive." These sources of stress and constant change in technology only increase the difficulty of the task at hand.

Monolingual interlocutors have to resort to interpreting services to meet their communicative needs. Since the number of bilingual encounters requiring the assistance of a healthcare interpreter constantly exceeds the supply of professional interpreters, many times linguistic minorities are forced either to make decisions based on their limited proficiency in the societal language (this occurs not only in healthcare settings; see, for example, Berk-Seligson [2007, 2009] on police investigations) or to resort to whatever means are available to them. Some examples in health care include janitors being called upon to interpret in medical settings (Cambridge, 1999), nurses playing the dual role of healthcare provider and interpreter (CHIA, 2002). At other times, having experienced the frustration of such situations, if allowed, members of linguistic minorities bring their relatives or friends to the medical appointments to interpret for them. These bilinguals (whether adults or youngsters) step up to the plate and perform with varying degrees of success. They are drawn into situations in which choices are limited and for which no one is responsible. They can either refuse to act as interpreters and merely witness how the minority-language speaker is deprived of the right to communicate or do their best to assist the individual, with whom they identify. In either case, the success of the communicative outcome is uncertain.

THE STUDY

This chapter investigates the co-construction of (mis)understanding among patients, healthcare providers, and interpreters as they communicate about health concerns. Specifically, it aims to shed light on the issues that arise when providers lose control of the medical consultation to the hands of the interpreter. The data presented here are a subset of the data from an ethnography conducted on interpreting in healthcare settings.[2] The goal of the larger study was to investigate the role of healthcare interpreters in a public hospital in the United States.

The Site

California Hope[3] is a public hospital. Located in the Bay Area of California, it has established a strong foundation as the premier healthcare provider within the community. At the time the ethnography was conducted it was the only hospital in the county with an open-door policy that guarantees access to needed medical care regardless of a patient's ability to pay. The population served by California Hope (CH) ranges from middle class to working class, but the average patient falls below the socioeconomic poverty line. The residents of the area speak more than 40 different languages. When the ethnography was conducted, the population served by California Hope was white (49.6%), Hispanic (26.6%), Asian or Pacific Islander (18.6%), African American (4.4%), and other (0.8%).

Data Collection

Observing the principles of ethnographic study (Le Compte & Schensul, 2010), before I started recording I had spent a significant amount of time getting acquainted with the site, shadowing interpreters, and building trust. By the time the data collection started I had already shadowed and monitored Joaquín (as well as the other Spanish interpreters) for more than 9 months. Two to three times per week I arrived

TABLE 1. *Inventory of All ICEs according to Modality and Those Involving Joaquín*

Total Number of ICEs	392	Percentage	Percentage of Total Involving Joaquín
Face-to-face	11	2.81	9
Speakerphone	381	97.19	11

at Interpreting Services at 8:30 a.m. and spent the day with Joaquín. I hooked a headset to his telephone and walked with him to face-to-face interviews, and he interacted with me as he did with other new interpreters in training.

At CH interpreted communicative events vary widely in terms of length, time of the day, and so on. Tables 1 and 2 illustrate the variety of the 392 ICEs collected for the larger study (2004a) for ten interpreters and those produced by Joaquín.

During the data collection, I made an effort to minimize my intrusion into the interaction. Interpreters at CH were used to having others listening to their interpretations (but never recording) or going with them for a face-to-face interview with a patient because that is the way in which new interpreters learn while on the job. Interpreters in training observed and asked questions, and so did I. Consent for recording and observing was requested immediately before the interpreting started (see turns 2, 3, 11, and 12 in the transcript).

The Participants

The healthcare ICE I am about to analyze involved three participants: Filomena, the patient, who is a middle-aged Hispanic woman born in Mexico. Catherine is a Caucasian English-speaking nurse in her midthirties and has worked at CH for more than 7 years. Joaquín, the interpreter, also in his midthirties, was born and raised in Mexico and is one of the ten full-time English/Spanish interpreters working at Interpreting Services at CH. Joaquín interprets between 9:00 a.m. and 5:00 p.m. Monday through Friday. At the time the study was conducted Joaquín had nine years of seniority at California Hope, and his terminal degree was a high school diploma. To join the staff of interpreters in the Interpreting Services department at CH, Joaquín met three out of three of the following requirements (as stated by the manager of CH Interpreting Services):

he had passed the interpreting test given by Interpreting Services (the test was designed as an in-house instrument, and at the time the study was conducted no information on the validity or reliability of the test was available); he had demonstrated bilingual ability; he had a minimum of two years of experience in a related job in the field (Joaquín had worked as bilingual medical assistant).

The Encounter

Filomena had called CH to complain about pain from a bump on her head. Catherine, the nurse, wanted to explore Filomena's medical history (turns 10–23) and medicine intake (turns 24–38) first to contextualize Filomena's concern (turns 39–40). During the conversation we see some of the issues and complexities of communication as the interlocutors co-construct a story and eventually interpret the conversation between the patient and the nurse. We then observe that the distance between Filomena and Catherine seems to increase even when Joaquín attempted to bridge the linguistic and cultural differences between them. Although his role was to bring them closer together, he unintentionally distanced them. I explore the reasons for this in the analysis following the transcript.

The Data

We enter the conversation as Joaquín, the interpreter, and Catherine, the nurse, are exchanging greetings after Joaquín has been called to the CH nurse line. Catherine is on the line with Filomena, who does not speak English. Catherine needs Joaquín's assistance to communicate with her patient.

TAPE 34. *Joaquín. Side B, Call 3 (91–215)*
DURATION: 12 MINUTES
SEGMENT 1. *N = Nurse; I = Interpreter; P = Patient*

1	N	I'm fine, and you?
2	I	I'm okay. We're supposed to be recording this . . . this conversation for research purposes.
3	N	All righty. Okay, I have, Filo . . . Filomena Machado, who is here on the line.
4	I	Okay, okay.

5	N	Okay, her medical number is 2-1-1-1-1-1-2-1.
6	I	*Señora, buenos días.*
		/Good morning, ma'am/
7	P	*Buenos días,*
		/Good morning/
8	I	*Tengo en la línea a la enfermera*
		/I have the nurse on the line/
9	P	*Ajá, sí.*
		/Uh-uhmm, yes/
10	N	[Okay, the first thing I need to know is if she has, uh, um, chronic health problems, not the problems she's going for today?
11	I	*Eh, eh, estamos grabando esta conversación por un estudio que están haciendo, señora.*
		/Uh-uhh, ma'am, we are recording this conversation for a study that they're doing/
12	P	*Sí.*
		/Yes/

After greeting Catherine, Joaquín immediately alerts her to the fact that the conversation is being recorded (turn 2). The nurse consents verbally but does not ask for the patient's consent. Catherine starts to give Joaquín the patient's information (turns 3–5). As soon as Joaquín greets Filomena, Catherine asks her first question about Filomena's medical history (turn 10) and clearly distinguishes between the medical history and the issue that caused Filomena to call today. By following her protocol she needs Filomena's medical history first. Joaquín, however, does not interpret that information to Filomena right away (turn 11); rather, he uses that turn to alert Filomena that the conversation is being recorded. After Filomena consents (turn 12) Joaquín goes back to the "enfermedades crónicas" (chronic illnesses) question, and, at that point, Catherine is not made aware that Filomena has just expressed her consent to be recorded. Although not highly consequential for the quantity and quality of technical information shared, the behaviors of both the nurse and the interpreter in segment 1 illustrate differences in goals. The nurse needed to follow protocol and goes directly into business. The interpreter is aware of this. The interpreter, not the nurse, asks the patient for consent. The nurse is not aware that this exchange took place.

13	I	Ok, *uhhh, y la pregunta que si usted tiene alguna enfermedad. No, no el problema que tiene hoy sino si tiene una enfermedad como diabetes, alta presión, enfermedad del corazón, de la tiroides, alguna cosa de esas.* /Ok, Uh-uhh, and she asks you whether you have any illness. No, not the problem that you have today, but whether you have any illness like diabetes, high blood pressure, heart problems, thyroid, any of that?/
14	P	*Sí tengo diabetis* [sic] /Yes, I have diabetes/
15	I	She has diabetes, *¿y qué más?* /Yes, she has diabetes, and what else?/
16	P	*Y tengo algo alta presión* /and I have high blood pressure/
17	I	High blood pressure.
18	N	Uh-uhhmm . . .
19	P	*Ajá, nada más y*[/Uh-uhmm, anything else? and/[
20	N	[What about high cholesterol?
21	I	*¿Tiene colesterol elevado?* /Do you have high cholesterol?/
22	P	*Sí, pues ahorita no sé cómo lo tenga, pero sí tengo también colesterol* /Yes, well, I don't know whether I have it right now, but, yes, I also have cholesterol/
23	I	Okay, okay.
24	N	Okay, and medicines that she uses for those [
25	I	[*¿Y qué medicamentos toma usted para sus enfermedades?* [/And what medications do you take for your illnesses?/
26	P	*Pues estoy tomando ahorita pastillas para la presión, para el colesterol*[/Well, right now I'm taking pills for the blood pressure, for cholesterol/[
27	I	[*¿No sabe cómo se llaman?* /And you don't know the names?/
28	P	*Sí, sé cómo se llaman, nada más que como no veo muy bien de los ojos*[/Yes, I know the names, but because I don't see very well with my eyes/
29	I	[Oh, thank God!!!!! Okay, she's taking medication for cholesterol, for high blood pressure, but she says she doesn't see well enough to read the names.

30	N	Okay [
31	P	[Y *me estaba inyectando insulin*
		/And I was getting a shot of insulin/
32	I	And she gets a shot of insulin
33	N	Okay, okay, is she allergic to any medicines that she's aware of?
34	I	*¿Es alérgica a algún medicamento?*
		/Are you allergic to any medication?/
35	P	*¿Mande?*
		/Excuse me?/
36	I	*¿Es alérgica a algún medicamento?*
		/Are you allergic to any medication?/
37	P	*No, a ninguno.*
		/No, to none/
38	I	No.

When Joaquín asks Filomena about chronic illnesses, he does not use the term "enfermedades crónicas" in Spanish but rather uses (limited) examples of chronic conditions. As the patient starts answering, he reports to Catherine, and in the same turn he keeps asking Filomena for more information (turns 13–19). Joaquín is the one doing the probing, not Catherine. When Filomena states that she has no other condition, Catherine takes back the control of the line of questions on chronic illnesses by adding "high cholesterol" to the list Joaquín had started. After Filomena replies, the "chronic illnesses" exploration ends as Catherine turns to medicine intake (turn 24). However, once again Catherine does not directly ask Filomena the complete question for Joaquín to interpret. Instead, she turns to Joaquín and asks him to do it without—for the second time—providing him with the exact wording of the question. Based on his experience working at California Hope (as revealed by subsequent interviews, which are part of the larger study; see Angelelli 2004a, pp. 114–118), Joaquín considers himself cognizant of interview protocol and does not hesitate to decide on questions and construct them in the way he believes patients understand better. This accounts for his changing a technical term such as "chronic illness" for a set of examples (turn 13), as well as for his clarifying and anticipating information providers may need (see later examples). At every turn he reports to Catherine, and by turn 38 the medicine-intake exploration also ends. So far we have seen Joaquín taking the lead in asking questions only when Catherine asks him to do so. This is not the pattern seen in the rest of the interview.

In turn 10 Catherine seems to have obtained the information she needed for the medical history and now is ready to discuss Filomena's current health concern, the one that made her call CH.

In turn 40 Joaquín asks Filomena to explain why she had called CH today. Filomena does not answer the question directly. Rather, she begins to tell a story about what had happened to her: how she hit her head, causing the bump that now hurts (the reason for her call).

SEGMENT 3.

39	N	Okay, and why is she calling today?
40	I	*¿Y por qué habla hoy? ¿Qué le pasa?*
		/And why are you calling today? What's going on?/
41	P	*Mire yo, este, fui a tose, fui o sea a escupir afuera y así cuando me salió la flema, me dio como asco. Así como que me dio asco y ya de ahí ya no supe, ya perdí el conocimiento y ya cuando sentí ya me di, ya me estaban levantando.*
		/Look, umm, I went to cough, I mean, I went to spit outside and . . . when I was spitting out the phlegm, it made me nauseated. So I was kind of nauseated, and then I lost it, I lost consciousness, and when I felt I was coming to, they were picking me up/
42	I	*¿Se desmayó?*
		/Did you pass out?/
43	P	*Me desmayé, perdí el conocimiento. Sí, me desmayé y me golpeé la cabeza, y ahorita nada más el dolor no me duele por dentro, sino que me duele el golpe.*
		/I passed out, I lost consciousness. Yes, I passed out and I hit my head, and right now it does not hurt inside, but the bump hurts/
44	I	*¿Cuándo se cayó?*
		/When did you fall?/
45	P	*Orita [sic], apenas tiene como una hora.*
		/Right now, like an hour ago/
46	I	*¿No sabe cuánto tiempo pasó de desmayada?*
		/Do you know how long you were unconscious?/
47	P	*Desmayada no, fueron . . . fue como fracciones de segundo*
		/Unconscious no . . . it was like . . . like fractions of a second/
48	I	Ok, she says she was going outside, spitting outside, but then she got nauseated, and then by the time she came back she was, uh, waking up from passing out.
49	N	When was this? . . . Uh, I'm not understanding you at all.

Filomena told the story with Joaquín's help (asking for more details between turns 41 and 47). Catherine could neither share the story nor probe for more details because Joaquín was not interpreting. He was co-constructing Filomena's story without Catherine's input. So when in turn 48 he summarizes the story for Catherine, it is not surprising that Catherine cannot see the connection of the story to her question in line 40. The distance between the interlocutors is beginning to grow.

Catherine cannot understand Spanish. Since she did not hear Filomena's story (turns 41–48), which contains the information requested (turn 39), Joaquín now has to take 11 turns to explain what he has just learned from Filomena. During this time it is Filomena who is prevented from clarifying, responding, and adding other relevant information. Catherine now directs all of her follow-up or clarifying questions to Joaquín (turns 51, 53, 55, 57, 59), who is responding from memory and from his own reconstruction of Filomena's story. Catherine is surprised when she learns that Filomena walked outside of the house to spit up phlegm (turn 59) and, while doing so, became nauseated and passed out. Catherine had not gotten this information during Filomena's initial explanation because it was not interpreted. Her confusion and frustration are evident in her rising intonation (turn 59) and her exclamation "Uhhhhh" (turn 61). The distance between the interlocutors continues to widen.

SEGMENT 4.

50	I	She passed out.
51	N	Passed out?
52	I	Yeah.
53	N	Oh, passed out. Did she fall down when she passed out?
54	I	Yeah, yeah, she hit her head.
55	N	Ooohhh, and what was she doing when she passed out?
56	I	She was spitting outside.
57	N	Spitting?
58	I	Yeah.
59	N	She walked outside of the house to spit saliva?
60	I	Yes, and she got nauseated, then passed out.
61	N	Uhhhhh. Ok, hold on while I write this down, okay?
62	I	Okay.
63	N	Thanks.

64	I	*¿Señora, no sangró?*
		/Ma'am, didn't you bleed?/
65	P	*No, no me salió sangre, para nada, se me hizo una bola, nada más, se me siente une bola.*
		/No, I wasn't bleeding at all, I suddenly could feel a bump, that's all, it feels like I have a bump/
66	I	*¿Qué parte de la cabeza?*
		/What part of your head?/
67	P	*Para el lado izquierdo.*
		/On the left side/
68	N	How long was she unconscious when she passed out?
69	I	She said just seconds.
70	N	Just seconds?
71	I	Yeah, she hit the back of her head.
72	N	Okay.
73	I	*¿Y usted se levantó solita o alguien la levantó?*
		/And did you get up by yourself or did someone pick you up?/
74	P	*Sí, no, aquí estaba mi cuñada y otros muchachos que estaban aquí, me levantaron ellos.*
		/Yes, no, my sister-in-law and other young men were here, they picked me up/
75	I	*Ah, okay.*
		/Ah, okay/
76	N	What did you ask her?
77	I	Whether she got up by herself or somebody picked her up, and she said that there were people there who picked her up.

Joaquín continues eliciting information from Filomena (e.g., whether she had bled, what part of her head was hit). Catherine does not provide him with this line of questions. Once again she is not aware of Joaquín's exploration of Filomena's fall. Once again the nurse's and the interpreter's paths diverge, and the distances between the interlocutors increase. As Catherine is making sense of what was discussed in the previous ten turns or so and requesting new information (e.g., how long Filomena was unconsciousness) she is falling behind in the new path set by the interpreter. Clearly Joaquín, not Filomena, is answering Catherine's questions. Moreover, although Filomena stated that she hit the left side of her head (turn 67), Catherine is told that she hit the back part of her head (turn 71) as Joaquín is participating in parallel conversations (Metzger, 1999) that he has created. Once again Joaquín, not Catherine, has decided what information is relevant and worth pursuing. Instead of having the nurse guide the interpreter in the questioning, it is the interpreter who is leading, and the nurse is obtaining only partial (and at times erroneous) information. When Catherine realizes that she is missing information and that the interpreter is directing the line of questions, she tries to regain control of the interview (turn 76). Perhaps keeping close to the interpreter and the patient (instead of letting the interpreter embark on an independent exploration) will help decrease the divide between the interlocutors, and we will see a pas de trois (Wadensjö, 1998).

SEGMENT 6.

78	N	Okay, ask her, I guess I'm, I'm really confused at the beginning. Why would she walk outside to spit?
79	I	Right, because you don't want to spit on your floor or carpet.
80	N	Oh, so you don't spit in the garbage or a cup or the sink?
81	I	I guess.
82	N	Oookay, all right. And then, why did she become nauseous? Does she, does she have any idea?
83	I	*¿Usted sabe por qué le daría la náusea?* /Do you know why you were nauseated?/
84	P	*Pues últimamente me están dando las náuseas, cada vez que voy así, este a toser algo así, me dan nauseas.* /Well, lately I have been nauseated . . . every time I'm gonna cough or something like that, I get nauseated/
85	I	I don't know, she says, but I think I've been getting nauseated lately every time I, I have to cough.
86	N	Okay, ask her if, uhhmm, she's coughing so hard that she is like, uhhmm, you know, feeling short of breath and maybe that's causing her nausea[
87	I	[*¿Está tosiendo tanto que se le va la respiración y se marea o?*[/Are you coughing so hard that you get out of breath and you get dizzy, or/[
88	P	[*Ándele, como que . . . no, no toso mucho fíjese nada más una vez que voy a escupir siento que me hace en el pescuezo acá adentro, una, una cosquillita, una flema y eso es lo que me provoca el mareo, el desmayo*[[/ Yeah, like . . . no, I don't cough a lot, you know, but when I'm going to spit, I feel like tickles in my neck, a phlegm, and that's what causes the dizziness and the passing out/[
89	I	[*¿Pero no tiene mucha tos?* [/But do you cough a lot?/
90	P	*No, no tengo mucha tos.* /No, no I don't cough a lot/

91	I	[She says that she feels like she has some phlegm in her throat, and when she's, uhhh, when she feels it, that's when she gets nauseated.
92	N	Really? Okay, when she gets nauseous, does she feel like she's gonna pass out every time, if she gets nauseous every time she coughs, does she feel like she's gonna pass out every time she feels nauseous?
93	I	*¿Cada vez, cada vez que le da esa náusea, siente que se va a desmayar?* /Every time you get nauseated, do you feel like you're going to pass out?/
94	P	*Sí.* /Yes/
95	I	*¿Cada vez?* /Every time?/
96	P	*Cada vez que voy así, a escupir al baño, siento que hasta me hace la cabeza "tuuuuuuuuuuuu," así como siento que si me fuera a desmayar.* /Every time I go to the bathroom to spit, it feels like my head is going "tuuuuuuuuuuuuu," [and] I feel like I'm going to pass out/
97	I	Yeah, she says every time I go out to spit, she also goes to spit in the toilet.
98	N	And so she feels like she's gonna pass out every time she spits?

In trying to make sense of the information she has received, Catherine suggests changing the course of the conversation to go back to the story she missed (turn 78). Joaquín does not convey Catherine's request for clarification to Filomena but answers it himself. His response is not based on previous information related by Filomena, however. It is the interpreter's own reply. Joaquín makes his own guess as to why Filomena walked outside to spit (turn 79). Catherine challenges that response (turns 80 and 82: "Oookay . . . all right"), reclaims control of the interview, and keeps it until turn 88, when Joaquín takes a couple of turns to explore Catherine's questions (turns 87–91) but does not immediately relay Filomena's answers to her. Catherine needs to understand the connection between coughing, spitting, and passing out. Joaquín explores those incidents for Catherine (turns 93–97). Interestingly, when he reports to Catherine, he adds that the patient does spit in the toilet. He does this to correct his previous assumption (turns 79–80) that she might not want to spit on the carpet or the floor. The nurse does not acknowledge this correction. She is concentrating on the relationship between spitting and losing consciousness. Interlocutors have different needs and different agendas in this interaction (as in many). While Joaquín still has his comment on not spitting on the carpet fresh in his mind and wants to clarify the misunderstanding his statement may have caused, Catherine is focusing on understanding connections. She plays with the control of the interview, giving it and taking it back at times. Filomena is completely unaware of this tension, of the competing agendas, and needs an answer for her pain. The distances widen.

Once more Catherine does not request information about either the clinic or Filomena's doctor, but Joaquín asks about them. This generates another parallel conversation (Metzger, 1999). While the nurse con-

SEGMENT 7.

99	I	*Yeah. ¿Y a qué clínica va oiga?*
		/Yeah, and which clinic do you go to?/
100	P	*A la Mortov. Con, con me, medicina general ahí tengo mi médico general.*
		/To Mortov. To me, general medicine, I have my family doctor there/
101	N	Is this the first time she has actually passed out when this happens?
102	I	*¿Pero esta es la primera vez que así se desmaya?*
		/But is this the first time you passed out?/
103	P	*No, si me había desmayado, pero nunca me he caído.*
		/No, yes, I have passed out before, but I have never fallen down/
104	I	*Oh, y de las veces que se ha desmayado ehh ¿qué hace para no caerse, en qué . . .[*
		/Oh, and those times when you passed out, umm, so, what do you do . . . so that you don't fall down?/
105	P	*[Me siento, me siento . . . tengo tiempo para sentarme o para[*
		[/I sit down, I sit down . . . I have enough time to sit down or to[
106	I	[She says this is the first time I fall down all the way down because usually she has enough time to sit down or[
107	N	[Okay, okay. Does she have a fever?
108	I	*¿Tiene fiebre?*
		/Do you have a fever?/
109	P	*No. No, nada, ahorita me acabo de tomar dos Tylenol.*
		/No. No, nothing, I just took two Tylenol/
110	I	No.

tinues to pursue the connection between passing out and spitting, the interpreter and patient are discussing the clinic where Filomena's family doctor works. These two conversations converge when Catherine asks more questions, thus interrupting Joaquín's new exploration. Joaquín resumes the lead (turn 104) to explore the new information that the patient not only passed out but also fell down. After doing so (turns 102–105) he reports the news to Catherine (turn 106). Thus Joaquín creates questions of his own, departs from the nurse's original request, clarifies, repairs, and so on. He also decides which information to relay to the nurse. For example, in turn 109, Filomena volunteers that she has taken Tylenol. Perhaps Catherine would have found that information important since painkillers can suppress fever, which might account for Filomena's lack of a high temperature. But Catherine did not have access to that information because it was not interpreted. Distances are not shrinking.

Segment 8.

111	N	Okay, and what color is she spitting up?
112	I	*¿De qué color es la flema que le sale?* /What color is the phlegm that you're spitting?/
113	P	*Blanca.* /White/
114	I	White.
115	N	In which clinic is she seen . . . ? Ohhh, Mortov, I believe.
116	I	Yes, she goes to Mortov.
117	N	Okay.
118	I	Second floor.
119	N	Uh-uhhmm. And, uhhmm, she just fell and hit her head . . . uhh, is she feeling dizzy or walking funny or, you know, feeling like she's not quite right with her injury?
120	I	*¿Se siente ahorita como que está mareada o como que se va a caer o está tambaleando o no?* /Right now, do you feel nauseated or like you're going to fall down or wobbling or not?/
121	P	*No, orita [sic] ya me siento bien, nada más que llamé por el golpe que tengo en la cabeza[* /No, right now I feel well; I only called because of the bump on my head/[
122	I	[No, she feels fine; she called because of her bump she has in her head.
123	N	She's calling because of her bump?

124	I	Yeah.
125	N	Uh, what about the passing out every time she coughs and spits?
126	I	*¿Entonces le preocupa más el chichón que tiene en la cabeza, señora, que los mareos, señora, o los desmayos?* /So, ma'am, are you more concerned with the bump you have on the head than the dizziness or the passing out?/
127	P	*¿Mande? El desmayo orita [sic] ya no lo tengo.* /Excuse me? Passing out, now . . . no that's gone/
128	I	*Pues sí, pero dijo ahorita que le está dando.* /Well, yes, but . . . what are you feeling right now?/
129	P	*¿Si me está dando otro desmayo? ¿Perdón, qué me dijo?* /If I'm feeling like I'm going to pass out now? Excuse me, what did you tell me?/
130	I	*No, le pregunta la enfermera, le preocupa a usted el chichón que tiene en la cabeza, pero qué tal tos . . . los desmayos, ¿no le preocupan?* /No, the nurse is asking you if you are more concerned with the bump you have on the head, but what about the cough . . . the fainting, passing out, are you concerned about that?/
131	P	*Sí, me preocupan también, pero porque yo no sé por qué me están viniendo, nunca me habían dado[* /Yes, they worry me also, but because I don't know why am I having that, I never had that before/
132	I	[Yeah, she also worries about the passing out.

In turn 121 the patient reiterates the reason for her call. From then on we see another type of co-construction of understanding. As Joaquín interprets the nurse's surprise that Filomena is worrying about the bump rather than what caused it, he reproduces what the nurse said almost word for word. This confuses the patient. Filomena and Joaquín use six turns to co-construct an understanding of the question and to provide an answer. It seems that close renditions are not guaranteeing the interlocutors' understanding.

As Catherine explains to Filomena which symptoms of head injury she should look for, Catherine and Joaquín stay quite close. Catherine keeps control of the line of questions. That does not preclude Filomena from interpreting the advice/warning as a request for an answer regarding her present condition (turn 137), however, forcing Joaquín to clarify (turns 140–141). Both this segment and the previous one illustrate that distances between interlocutors may grow even when the interpreting occurs on a turn-by-turn basis.

133	N	Okay, okay. Uhhmm, I'm gonna be booking her appointment, but let me focus back on this head bump. Tell her, you know, I'm sure that's just a small bump, you know, [on] her head from falling, but she does need to watch for symptoms of the head injury.
134	I	*Uhmmm, dice . . . probablemente es nada más que un chichón ¿verdad? por el golpe que se dio al caerse, pero tiene que, tiene que fijarse si hay algún daño a la cabeza.* /Uh-uhhm, she says that . . . probably . . . it is only a bump, right? . . . as you fell down and hit your head . . . but . . . you have to check if there is any injury to your head/
135	N	Okay, so on the nausea problem, so, the signs of a head injury would be repeated vomiting, uhhmm, or walking like she's drunk, talking funny, not being able to do things, you know, use her hands . . .
136	I	*A usted ya le dan nauseas ¿no? pero señas de que se dañó más la cabeza sería que . . . le den vómitos, que sienta como que anda caminado borracha, ¿verdad? que tenga dificultad para controlar sus movimientos, sus manos.* /You get nauseated, right? But signs that you may have hurt your head more would be like . . . you feel like vomiting, or you feel like you are walking funny . . . or if you are having difficulties to control your movement, using your hands/
137	P	*No, no siento esas cosas.* /No, I don't feel those things/
138	I	She doesn't feel any of that[
139	N	[Okay, that's fine, she may not have them now, those can occur, you know, down the road. That's why I prefer to talk to her about them now.
140	I	*Sí, ehhh, yo le creo que ahorita no sienta nada de eso, pero nada más le estoy diciendo por si siente algo así más adelante, ya sabe, ¿verdad?* /Yes . . . umm . . . I believe you that you are not feeling any of those things now, but I am only telling you this just in case you feel them later, you know . . . right?/
141	P	*Sí, sí.* /Yes, yes/
142	N	Okay, okay, uhhmm, tell her I'm still looking for an appointment.
143	I	*Le están buscando una cita.* /They're looking for an appointment/
144	P	*Está bien.* /Okay/ (The call ended here, and the patient was transferred to the appointments line.)

DISCUSSION AND CONCLUSION

What is this interaction telling us about healthcare provider/patient communication when the parties do not share the same linguistic and cultural background? How much understanding can actually take place even when a language broker is present? At what point do distances between interlocutors begin to grow? How do they arise in the first place? The interaction among Filomena, Catherine, and Joaquín provides some insight into the complexities of constructing (mis)understanding among providers, patients, and interpreters. The nine segments presented here illustrate how the different strategies pursued by the interlocutors contribute to both increasing and decreasing the distances that separate them. Over the course of this 12-minute interaction we see a wide range of behaviors that affect the construction of (mis)understanding among the patient, nurse, and interpreter:

- The nurse and the interpreter communicate without involving the patient (turns 78–83).
- The patient and the interpreter communicate without involving the nurse (turns 99–100).
- The nurse questions the interpreter's renditions. She seems to have lost partial control of the interview (e.g., turns 49, 59, 76, 78, 92).
- The nurse challenges the interpreter to render closer renditions (e.g., turns 48–60).
- The nurse does not understand how the interpreter's renditions assist her exploration of the situation (e.g., turns 48–60, 76).
- The interpreter goes back to repair misunderstanding and fill in gaps by exploring the patient's health concern (e.g., turns 64–67).
- The interpreter and the nurse do not share the exploratory path (i.e., the patient reports that she hit the left side of her head when she fell, whereas the interpreter tells the nurse that the patient hit the back of her head; turns 67, 71).
- The nurse asks the interpreter to clarify parts of the information that in her mind do not make sense (turn 78).
- The interpreter attempts to dispel the nurse's concern with the patient's behavior (going outside when she felt dizzy) with a culturally acceptable behavior (not spitting on the carpet) (turn 79).
- The nurse asks the interpreter for repetitions as she seems to have lost the thread of the story (turns 49, 76).

- The interpreter takes it upon himself to ask the patient questions to elicit more information (e.g., turn 98).
- The interpreter selectively interprets/omits what the patient says (e.g., turns 41–48; 107–110).
- The interpreter anticipates what he believes will be useful information for the nurse and explores the issue on his own initiative (e.g., turns 42–47).

One might believe that medical consultations are speech events in which healthcare conditions take center stage. One might also think that during these consultations patients provide information and look for answers and that providers ask questions to elicit information that will help them make decisions. Furthermore, one might believe that when medical consultations are mediated by an interpreter, healthcare conditions continue to hold center stage. The only difference, one may argue, is that there are three participants, that more time is required, that it is more costly than without an interpreter, and that explanations may at times be needed. A closer look at interpreter-mediated provider/patient consultations, however, allows us to see what the interaction focuses on, how the focus changes according to who is directing the line of questions, which elements have center stage, and how the focus shifts from medical condition to communication, trust, control, and so on. Many turns in this conversation were clearly more related to or triggered by the need to construct understanding or to deconstruct misunderstanding, repair talk, and teach "cultural" aspects than to answering questions. Many turns in this healthcare consultation were plainly related to issues that increased the distances between the interlocutors. Many times these issues are consequences of membership in different discourse communities, socioeconomic status, language, or culture as well as other social factors that affect such interactions (Angelelli, 2004b).

Implications for Practice

This study has implications for healthcare providers, policymakers, interpreter educators, and interpreters. Nearly every hospital in the United States receives patients with limited-English proficiency. As a result, we see an increasing need for professional interpreters in medical settings. In the absence of qualified interpreters, healthcare organizations in the United States have resorted to creative solutions in order to bridge the linguistic barrier between providers seeking to assist patients and patients seeking help. Further studies are necessary to determine whether the current methods are enabling linguistic minorities to have meaningful access to equal quality of health care.

As the earlier discussion shows, complex layers of meaning are embedded in conversations about pain, illness, and medicine. The complexity multiplies when interpreters are needed to bridge the cultural communities of the provider (and of the medical field) and the patient not only by interpreting the languages spoken but also by bridging cultures, coordinating and repairing talk, and seeking answers to questions that providers and patients raise as they communicate with one another.

Cross-linguistic communication in medical settings has been the focus of various studies discussed in this chapter. Interestingly, the results of empirical research still need to permeate the practice of both communication in medical settings and medical/healthcare interpreting (Angelelli, 2008; Valéro-Garcés & Martin, 2010).

In the United States, as in many other parts of the world, the education of healthcare providers provides little to no training in how to communicate with a population that is increasingly diverse. Neither language diversity nor the impact of language brokering during consultations is acknowledged. Policies regulating linguistic minorities' equal access to services as well as nonlinguistic discrimination need to account for the reality faced in the field. Interpreters currently working in medical settings range from certified professionals in areas related to language (e.g., court interpreting, translation, language teaching) to bilingual professionals in other areas who are assigned dual roles (e.g., a bilingual nurse or lab technician) to nonprofessionals or ad-hoc interpreters (patients' friends and family members, including children). Additionally, in the United States, healthcare interpreters have only limited educational opportunities to pursue. The need for qualified healthcare interpreters, however, is increasing exponentially. Fewer than 25% of U.S. hospitals are either staffed with skilled interpreters (Flores et al., 2003) or have adequate screening mechanisms in place to determine who can competently perform the job.

This chapter argues for both a conceptualization and an education/ assessment (including certification procedures) in healthcare interpreting that acknowledge the complex situated practice of healthcare interpreting, the management of power relations in cross-cultural interactions, and the responsibility of interpreters in brokering communication in interactions constrained by social factors such as gender, age, ethnicity, and socioeconomic status of the participants (Angelelli, 2004b).

Clearly, we all need to deepen our understanding of the interactions between and practices of individuals who participate in healthcare interpreted communication in order to determine whether speakers of nonsocietal languages enjoy equal access to health care. Nearly all examinations of health and culture reveal that "miscommunication, noncompliance, different concepts of the nature of illness and what to do about it, and above all different values and preferences of patients and their physicians limit the potential benefits of both technology and caring" (Payer, 1988, p. 10). Cross-cultural caring considers health care to be a social process in which professionals and patients each bring a set of beliefs, expectations, and practices to the medical encounter (Peña Dolhun, Muñoz, & Grumbach, 2003). Cross-cultural care, however, many times also entails cross-linguistic care. It is important to highlight the central role that language and interpreting play in cross-linguistic care in order to understand the complexities deriving from them. Evidently, as we have seen in the analysis of this transcript, the issues arising during interpreted, mediated provider/patient consultation illustrate clearly that the whole is greater than the sum of its parts. Negotiating understanding within and among these multicultural health and illness communities, amid their particular cultural and political systems, is complicated and challenging. Getting it right is, however, imperative if we believe in ensuring equal access to health care (as well as the legal system, education, and other services) to linguistic minorities.

NOTES

1. Many areas of the world still do not offer degrees in healthcare/medical interpreting or public-service interpreting. For further discussion on what constitutes professionalism and a professional healthcare interpreter see Angelelli (2005).
2. For more information see Angelelli (2004a).
3. To protect the identity of the participants, all names of organizations and persons are fictitious.

REFERENCES

Angelelli, C. (2000). Interpreting as a communicative event: A look through Hymes' lenses. *Meta: Journal des Traducteurs, 45*, 580–592.

Angelelli, C. (2001). Deconstructing the Invisible Interpreter: a study of the interpersonal role of the interpreter in a cross-linguistic/cultural communicative event. Unpublished doctoral dissertation. Stanford University.

Angelelli, C. (2004a). *Medical interpreting and cross-cultural communications.* Cambridge: Cambridge University Press.

Angelelli, C. (2004b). Revisiting the interpreter's role: A study of conference, court, and medical interpreters in Canada, Mexico, and the United States. Amsterdam: Benjamins.

Angelelli, C. (2005). Healthcare interpreting education: Are we putting the cart before the horse? *ATA Chronicle, 34*(11), 33–38, 55.

Angelelli, C. (2006). Designing curriculum for healthcare interpreter education: A principles approach. In C. Roy, (Ed.), *New approaches to interpreter education* (pp. 23–46). Washington DC: Gallaudet University Press.

Angelelli, C. (2008). The role of the interpreter in the healthcare setting: A plea for a dialogue between research and practice. In C. Valéro-Garcés and A. Martin (Eds.), *Building bridges: The controversial role of the community interpreter* (pp. 139–152). Amsterdam: Benjamins.

Angelelli, C. (2011). Can you ask her about chronic illnesses, diabetes, and all that? In C. Alvstad, A. Hild, & E. Tiselius (Eds.), *Methods and strategies of process research: Integrative approaches in translation studies* (pp. 231–246). John Benjamins Translation Library 94. Amsterdam: Benjamins.

Angelelli, C. (2012). Challenges in interpreters' coordination in the construction of pain. In C. Baraldi and L. Gavioli (Eds.), *Coordinating participation in dialogue interpreting* (pp. 251–268). Amsterdam: Benjamins.

Baraldi, C., & Gavioli, L. (2012). *Coordinating participation in dialogue interpreting.* Amsterdam: Benjamins.

Bates, M. (1987). Ethnicity and pain: A bio-cultural model. *Social Science Medicine, 24*, 47–50.

Bell, R. (1991). *Translation and translating: Theory and practice.* London: Longman.

Berk-Seligson, S. (2007). The elicitation of a confession: Admitting to murder but resisting an accusation of attempted rape. In J. Cotterill (Ed.), *The language of sexual crime* (pp. 16–41). London: Palgrave Macmillan.

Berk-Seligson, S. (2009). *Coerced confessions: The discourse of bilingual police interrogations.* Berlin: Mouton de Gruyter.

Berk-Seligson, S. (2011). Negotiation and communicative accommodation in bilingual police interrogations: A critical interactional sociolinguistic perspective. *International Journal of the Sociology of Language, 2011*(207), 29–58.

Blommaert, J. (Ed.). (1999). *Language ideological debates.* Berlin: Mouton de Gruyter.

Bolden, G. (2000). Toward understanding practices of medical interpreting: Interpreters' involvement in history taking. *Discourse Studies, 2,* 387–419.

Brewer, M. B. (1988). A dual process model of impression formation. In T. K. Srull & R. S. Wyer (Eds.), *Advances in Social Cognition* (Vol. 1, pp. 1–36). Hillsdale, NJ: Erlbaum.

Callister, L. (2003). Cultural influences on pain perceptions and behaviors. *Home Healthcare Management & Practice, 15,* 207–211.

Cambridge, J. (1999). Information loss in bilingual medical interviews through an untrained interpreter. *Translator, 5,* 201–219.

CHIA (California Healthcare Interpreters Association). (2002). *California standards for healthcare interpreters: Ethical principles, protocols, and guidance on roles and intervention.* Sacramento: California Endowment.

Davidson, B. (1998). *Interpreting medical discourse: A study of cross-linguistic communication in the hospital clinic.* Unpublished doctoral dissertation, Stanford University.

Davidson, B. (2000). The interpreter as institutional gatekeeper: The sociallinguistic role of interpreters in Spanish-English medical discourse. *Journal of Sociolinguistics, 4,* 379–405.

Davidson, B. (2001). Questions in cross-linguistic medical encounters: The role of the hospital interpreter. *Anthropological Quarterly, 74,* 170–178.

Dollerup, C., & Lodegaard, E. (Eds.). (1992). *Teaching translation and interpreting: Training, talent, and experience.* Amsterdam: Benjamins.

Duggleby, W. (2003). Helping Hispanic/Latino home health patients manage their pain. *Home Healthcare Nurse, 21,* 174–179.

Edaes, D. (2003). The politics of misunderstanding in the legal process: Aboriginal English in Queensland. In J. House, G. Kasper, and S. Ross (Eds.), *Misunderstanding in social life: Discourse approaches to problematic talk* (pp. 196–223). London: Longman.

Flores, G., Laws, M. B., Mayo, S. J., Zuckerman, B., Abreu, M., Medina, L., et al. (2003). Errors in medical interpretation and their potential clinical consequences in pediatric encounters. *Pediatrics, 111,* 6–14.

Gile, D. (1994). Methodological aspects of interpretation and translation research. In S. Lambert & B. Moser-Mercer (Eds.), *Bridging the gap: Empirical research in simultaneous interpretation.* Amsterdam: Benjamins.

Goffman, E. (1981). *Forms of talk.* Philadelphia: University of Pennsylvania Press.

Greenwald, H. (1991). Interethnic differences in pain perception. *Pain, 41,* 157–163.

Gumperz, J. (1982). *Discourse strategies.* Cambridge: Cambridge University Press.

Heller, M. (1999). Heated language in a cold climate. In J. Blommaert (Ed.), *Language ideological debates* (pp. 143–170). Berlin: Mouton de Gruyter.

Hymes, D. (1974). *Foundations in sociolinguistics: An ethnographic approach.* Philadelphia: University of Pennsylvania Press.

Jiménez, N., Moreno, G., Leng, M., Buchwald, D., and Morales, L. (2012). Patient-reported quality of pain treatment and use of interpreters in Spanish-speaking patients hospitalized for obstetric and gynecological care. *Journal of General Internal Medicine, 27*(12), 1602–1608.

Kalina, S. (2000). Interpreting competences as a basis and a goal for teaching. *Interpreters' Newsletter, 10,* 3–32.

Kaufert, J., and Putsch, R. (1997). Communication through interpreters in healthcare: Ethical dilemmas arising from differences in class, culture, language, and power. *Journal of Clinical Ethics, 8,* 71–87.

Le Compte, M., & Schensul, J. (2010). *Designing and conducting ethnographic research: An introduction.* Lanham, MD: AltaMira.

Lorscher, W. (1992). Process-oriented research into translation and implications for translation teaching. *TTR: Traduction, Terminologie, Rédaction, 5,* 145–161.

Metzger, M. (1999). *Sign language interpreting: Deconstructing the myth of neutrality.* Washington, DC: Gallaudet University Press.

Meyer, B. (2012). Ad-hoc interpreting for partially language-proficient patients: Participation in multilingual constellations. In C. Baraldi and L. Gavioli (Eds.), *Coordinating participation in dialogue interpreting* (pp. 99–114). Amsterdam: Benjamins.

Modern Language Association. (2010). *Most spoken languages in California in 2005.* Retrieved September 26, 2013, from http://www.mla.org/map_data

Moreno, G., Tarn, D., and Morales, L. (2009). Impact of interpreters on the receipt of new prescription medication information among Spanish-speaking Latinos. *Medical Care, 47*(12), 1201–1208.

Payer, L. (1988). *Medicine and culture: Notions of health and sickness in Britain, the U.S., France, and West Germany.* New York: Holt.

Peña Dolhun, E., Muñoz, C., & Grumbach, K. (2003). Cross-cultural education in U.S. medical schools: Development of an assessment tool. *Academic Medicine, 78*(6), 615–622.

Prince, C. (1986). *Hablando con el doctor: Communication problems between doctors and their Spanish-speaking patients.* Unpublished doctoral dissertation, Stanford University.

Ramer, L., Richardson, J. L., Cohen, M. Z., Bedney, C., Danley, K. L., & Judge, E. A. (1999). Multimeasure pain assessment in an ethnically diverse group of patients with cancer. *Journal of Transcultural Nursing, 10*(2), 94–101.

Ramírez, R. R., & de la Cruz, G. P. (2003). *The Hispanic population in the United Status: March 2002.* Current Population Reports, P20–545 (pamphlet). Washington, DC: U.S. Census Bureau.

Rampton, B. (2005). *Crossing: Language and ethnicity among adolescents.* Northampton, MA: St. Jerome.

Rollman, G. (1998). Culture and pain. In S. S. Kazarian & D. R. Evans (Eds.), *Cultural clinical psychology: Theory, research, and practice* (pp. 267–286). New York: Oxford University Press.

Roy, C. B. (2000). *Interpreting as a discourse process.* New York: Oxford University Press.

Shin, H. B., & Kominski, R. A. (2010). *Language use in the United States.* U.S. Census official website. Retrieved June 30, 2013, from http://www.census.gov/prod/2010pubs/acs-12.pdf

Shreve, G., & Angelone, E. (Eds.). (2010). *Translation and cognition.* American Translators Association Scholarly Monograph Series 15. Amsterdam: Benjamins.

Shreve, G., Schäffner, M. C., Danks, J. H., & Griffin, J. (1993). Is there a special kind of "reading" for translation? An empirical investigation of reading in the translation process. *Target, 5,* 21–41.

Strelzer, J. (1997). Pain. In W. S. Tseng & J. Strelzer (Eds.), *Culture and psychopathology* (pp. 87–100). New York: Brunner Mazel.

Tienda, M., & Mitchell, F. (Eds.). (2005). *Multiple origins, uncertain destinies: Hispanics and the American future.* National Research Council of the National Academies. Washington, DC: National Academies Press.

Toolan, M. (Ed.). (2002). *Critical discourse analysis: Critical concepts in linguistics* (Vol. 1, pp. xxi–xxvi). New York: Routledge.

U.S. Census Bureau's American Community Survey. (2013). *Language use in the United States: 2011.* Retrieved September 26, 2013, from www.census.gov/prod/2013pubs/acs-22.pdf

Valéro-Garcés, C. (2005). Doctor-patient consultations in dyadic and triadic exchanges. *Interpreting, 7,* 193–210.

Valéro-Garcés, C., & Martin, A. (Eds.). (2008). *Building bridges: The controversial role of the community interpreter.* Amsterdam: Benjamins.

Van Leuven, T. (2002a). Genre and field in critical discourse analysis: A synopsis. In M. Toolan (Ed.), *Critical discourse analysis: Critical concepts in linguistics* (Vol. 2, pp. 166–199). New York: Routledge.

Van Leuven, T. (2002b). The representation of social actors. In M. Toolan (Ed.), *Critical discourse analysis: Critical concepts in linguistics* (Vol. 2, pp. 302–339). New York: Routledge.

Wadensjö, C. (1998). *Interpreting as interaction.* London: Longman.

Wodak, R. (2002). Critical discourse analysis and the study of doctor-patient interaction. In M. Toolan (Ed.), *Critical discourse analysis: Critical concepts in linguistics* (Vol. 2, pp. 340–364). New York: Routledge.

Zborowski, M. (1952). Cultural components in response to pain. *Journal of Social Issues, 8,* 15–35.

"Sorry, Could You Explain That"? Clarification Requests in Interpreted Healthcare Interaction

George Major

ABSTRACT

Accuracy is crucial in the healthcare setting, given that wrongly conveyed information or misunderstandings could lead to very real and negative health outcomes for patients. In order to promote the accurate transfer of information, healthcare interpreters must possess the interactional skills to clarify when necessary, and they must also be able to recognize and effectively convey others' requests for clarification.

This chapter describes a study in which the clarification strategies of professional interpreters were examined, providing the first systematic description of this essential healthcare interpreting skill. Findings are drawn from a dataset of ten role-plays specifically designed to elicit clarification requests in a naturalistic interaction setting. Each of the ten role-plays depicted the same scenario, and involved a deaf patient, a practicing doctor, and an accredited Australian Sign Language (Auslan)/English interpreter.

The chapter begins by examining retrospective interviews with interpreter participants, focusing on their recollections of how they were taught to clarify during training and how they requested clarification within the role-plays. A descriptive analysis of clarification patterns within the dataset is then presented, and detailed discourse analyses of transcript excerpts are used to illustrate strategies used by interpreters to request clarification and to convey the clarification requests of others. The analysis highlights the fact that clarification request forms are highly context-bound, which has important implications for healthcare interpreter training.

The task of interpreting in healthcare settings presents a variety of challenges for interpreters, with potentially high stakes: "In medical interpreting situations, an incorrect explanation of symptoms to the practitioner or incomplete instructions to the patient can have serious ramifications: the wrong diagnosis or treatment can be life threatening" (Napier, McKee, & Goswell, 2006, p. 112). A fundamental aspect of healthcare interpreting, therefore, is being able to request an explanation or a repetition of information. That is, interpreters must possess the interactional skills, the interpersonal skills, and the judgment to clarify information when necessary, and they must also be able to recognize and effectively convey others' requests for clarification.

Although clarification has previously been observed in several empirical interpreting studies (e.g., Metzger, 1999; Wadensjö, 1998), no prior studies have been conducted in which this key skill has been systematically described with regard to a number of interpreters. The study outlined in this chapter addresses this gap by carefully examining clarification strategies used by professional interpreters working between Australian Sign Language (Auslan) and English.[1] Detailed discourse analyses of excerpts from healthcare role-play data are used to illustrate the sophisticated linguistic and nonlinguistic strategies employed by interpreters, and to highlight the context bound nature of clarification request forms.

BACKGROUND

Signed Language Interpreting in Australia

Auslan, the visual-gestural language of the Deaf community in Australia, is used by an estimated 6,500 deaf people (Johnston, 2006). Signed language interpreters in Australia are accredited under the same system as spoken language interpreters. This system is provided by the National Authority for the Accreditation of Translators and Interpreters (NAATI), and Auslan/English interpreters can currently achieve accreditation at either the paraprofessional or the professional level. "Paraprofessional" is generally regarded as an entry-level accreditation, while "professional" is the ideal accreditation that an interpreter should have for working in specialized areas, such as legal, educational, and healthcare settings. Note, however, that accreditation does not necessarily mean that an interpreter has completed formal interpreter training, as the accreditation exam can be taken by anyone regardless of the person's prior education or training (Napier, 2004). Healthcare interpreters are provided to deaf people in Australia through either the National Auslan Interpreter Booking and Payment Service (NABS) or the Healthcare Interpreting Service (HCIS) or its equivalents in different states (HCIS is the name of the New South Wales service, the state in which the current study was based).

RESEARCH ON HEALTHCARE INTERPRETING

The healthcare setting is one of the most prevalent settings for interpreters to work in (Napier, Major, & Ferrara, 2011; Pöchhacker & Shlesinger, 2005), and it is also one of the most demanding. To begin with, terminology is a potential source of difficulty, as practitioners' use of health terms occasionally impedes interpreter and patient understanding (Brown & Attardo, 2000; Napier et al., 2011). Practitioners frequently lack training in working with interpreters and deaf patients (Leeson, Sheikh, Rozanes, Grehan, & Matthews, this volume; van den Bogaerde & de Lange, this volume) and are often under pressure to complete the consultation in a certain amount of time (Coiera, Jayasuriya, Hardy, Bannan, & Thorpe, 2002; Davidson, 2000; Roberts, 2006; Roberts, Wass, Jones, Sarangi, & Gillet, 2003). In addition, serious power differences can arise between practitioners and patients, which can limit patients' ability to contribute to the conversation (Brown & Attardo, 2000; Meyer, Apfelbaum, Pöchhacker, & Bischoff, 2003; Todd, 1983).

It has been suggested that deaf patients tend to possess a lower "health literacy" than hearing people because they often miss out on the incidental information about health care that hearing people access daily through advertisements and the news media and by overhearing conversations (Harmer, 1999). In addition, many signed languages, including Auslan, can be considered languages of "limited diffusion." This means that they are used by a small number of people and have had limited exposure in technical domains, and as such, they have developed few signs to denote technical concepts, including health concepts (Napier et al., 2011). Interpreters are therefore often faced with the need to bridge lexical gaps in the signed language by using strategies such as fingerspelling, depiction, and negotiating the use of "one-off" signs with deaf patients (Major, Napier, Ferrara, & Johnston, 2012; Napier et al., 2011).

Healthcare interpreters also need to be skilled discourse managers, and research has shown that interpreters take responsibility for coordinating turn taking, getting participants' attention when needed, and generally managing the flow of interaction (e.g., Angelelli, 2004; Bot, 2005; Davidson, 2000; Merlini & Favaron, 2005; Metzger, 1999; Sanheim, 2003; see also Hsieh, this volume, for a more detailed review of this literature). In her 1999 study of both naturally occurring and role-play interpreted healthcare interaction, for example, Metzger identified a range of interactional management strategies used by interpreters. These "nonrenditions" (cf. Wadensjö, 1998) included introductions, responses to questions, clarification requests, and summonses (attention-getting strategies), all of which are evidence of interpreters taking responsibility for the structure and flow of interaction.

All interaction involves "relational work," which is "the 'work' individuals invest in negotiating relationships with others" (Locher & Watts, 2005, p. 10). Interpreted interaction is no exception, and Major (2013) shows that, in both naturally occurring and role-play Auslan/English healthcare interpreting, the development and maintenance of good doctor/patient/interpreter relationships are also integral parts of the healthcare interpreter's role. The experienced and professionally accredited interpreters in Major's study were seen to modify face threats, directly influence the flow of interaction, actively facilitate social talk and humor, and occasionally even engage in it themselves. Auslan/English healthcare interpreters have also been shown to consciously expand and modify the utterances of doctors and patients in order to promote accuracy, for example, by making implied information more explicit in the interpretation or by encoding extra visual information to clarify a potentially difficult concept (Major & Napier, 2012).

In terms of interpreter education, studies of terminology, discourse, and interpersonal aspects of healthcare interpreting are now beginning to provide a small but rich set of empirical findings that educators can draw upon. However, there is still a distinct lack of systematic description of several key healthcare interpreting skills, including the ways interpreters clarify information, suggesting that the teaching of this skill in educational programs is as yet unlikely to be based upon empirical evidence.

CLARIFICATION

Clarification involves both interactional and relational work. With regard to the interactional skills required, an interpreter who wishes to initiate clarification must create a new turn and become an active participant in the interaction. In monolingual dyadic conversation either the practitioner or the patient would have the next turn; the interpreter therefore potentially disrupts the usual sequence and makes a change in footing in order to take a turn in their own right (Metzger, 1999). This means that the interpreter needs to exercise a degree of control in managing this process, which can be in breach of the normative "interaction order" of a consultation, where the doctor by and large manages the agenda (Heritage & Clayman, 2010).

On an interpersonal level, clarification can also be challenging in that it potentially threatens a person's "face," which is understood as "the positive social value a person effectively claims for [himself/herself] by the line others assume [he/she] has taken during a particular contact" (Goffman, 1967, p. 5). We constantly work to maintain face—and the intrinsically linked concept of "self" (one's identity)—in interaction (Watts, 2003). A clarification request, then, might be perceived as "face threatening" if it promotes a perception that the interpreter is questioning the addressee's competence (Jacobsen, 2008).

Clarification has been the focus of analysis within the conversation analysis (CA) literature, typically as one type of repair (among several) performed in response to problematic talk (Ten Have, 1995). The seminal study on conversational repair was conducted by Schegloff, Jefferson, and Sacks (1977), who used a CA approach to outline the sequential organization of repairs based on a corpus of audio and video recorded, naturally occurring monolingual talk. Through microanalysis of transcript excerpts they illustrate that repair sequences frequently start with a "repairable," which is the trouble source itself. Repairs can then be self-initiated or other-initiated, with a general preference for the former.

Clarification has been noted within studies of courtroom interpreting (for example, Berk-Seligson, 1990; Napier, 2011). However, it has rarely been mentioned in the context of healthcare interpreting even though it is often cited as a crucial skill for healthcare interpreting students to master (Metzger, 2000, 2005; Napier et al., 2006). Two exceptions are Wadensjö's (1998) study of Russian/Swedish interpreting and Metzger's (1999) study of American Sign Language (ASL)/English interpreting. Wadensjö (1998) found evidence of an interpreter answering a patient's (implied) clarification request, then reporting to the nurse the reason it needed to be clarified. Similarly, Metzger (1999) noted instances of clarification in an interpreted pediatric consultation, although she did not describe them in detail as it was not the focus of her study. The current study takes a descriptive approach to investigating clarification in interpreted healthcare interaction in order to strengthen our understanding of this key interpreting skill.

METHOD

This study uses discourse analysis within a framework of interactional sociolinguistics (IS) (see Gumperz, 1982, 1999, 2001; Tannen, 2000) to explore the forms and functions of clarification requests produced and conveyed by professional signed language interpreters, elicited through semistructured role-plays. An IS analysis relies on fine-grained discourse analysis of cues within interactional sequences in order to provide evidence of the ways that speakers imply and listeners infer meaning—fundamental yet largely unnoticed interactional processes.[2] In this study, an IS analysis allows us to examine the forms and functions of clarification requests at a level of detail far beyond that which any interpreter might later recall or even notice at the time. The use of role-play data allows a systematic comparison of the clarification behavior of ten different interpreters in a semicontrolled environment.

PARTICIPANTS

Participants in the study were ten NAATI-accredited Auslan/English interpreters who were recruited through my personal networks and also by sending out a flyer through the Australian Sign Language Interpreters Association (ASLIA) New South Wales branch to Sydney-based interpreters. As this is not a quantitative study, I did not attempt to balance demographic characteristics, and the ten interpreters varied in age, gender, educational background, and interpreting experience. Four participants were male, and six were female. Three held NAATI professional accreditation, and seven held paraprofessional accreditation. The least experienced had been interpreting for 1 year, and the most experienced had been interpreting for 18 years. Table 1 presents demographic information about the role-play participants in more detail.

TABLE 1. *Role-Play Participant Background Information*

Pseudonym	Gender	Age Group	Highest Interpreting Qualification	Native or Nonnative Signer	Accreditation Level	Interpreting Experience (Years)
Amy	female	18–29	none	native	paraprofessional	8
Callum	male	18–29	diploma	nonnative	paraprofessional	2
Eva	female	18–29	diploma	nonnative	paraprofessional	6
Gabrielle	female	18–29	diploma	nonnative	professional	9
Hugo	male	18–29	diploma	nonnative	paraprofessional	3
Kate	female	40–49	postgraduate diploma	nonnative	professional	10
Katherine	female	30–39	diploma	nonnative	paraprofessional	4
Logan	male	40–49	master's degree	nonnative	professional	18
Madeleine	female	30–39	diploma	nonnative	paraprofessional	3
Oliver	male	18–29	none	native	paraprofessional	1

DATA AND ANALYSIS

Data collection was designed so that each interpreter was involved in the exact same scenario. It was important to select a topic that was likely to require some clarification, while still being relatively uncomplicated so as not to make the data collection an uncomfortable experience for the interpreters. Two paid actors were recruited to be the patient and the healthcare practitioner. It was very fortunate that a genuine practicing doctor (pseudonym = Dr. Bourke) agreed to play the part of the practitioner as it helped make the simulation more naturalistic. Doctor Bourke was female and had previous experience in real life working with signed language interpreters. A deaf person (pseudonym = Phoebe) was recruited to be the patient. Neither the doctor nor the patient were professional actors, but both prepared well and performed consistently in the ten role-plays.

In consultation with Dr. Bourke and Phoebe, it was decided that Phoebe would be visiting her doctor to ask for more pain medication for a very recently fractured ankle. In addition to discussing and prescribing pain medication, Dr. Bourke would also focus on a potential risk of osteoporosis and outline the need for further tests to either diagnose this condition or rule it out. Both actors were asked to encourage instances of clarification but to do so in a subtle way so that the analytical focus of the study would not be obvious to interpreters. The day before data collection, interpreters were sent a short briefing with information about the participants and the reason for the patient's visit to the doctor.

Data collection was conducted on a weekend day in a seminar room at a university. The space was set up to resemble a doctor's office as closely as possible, and two hard-drive video cameras were used to capture all three participants on screen. The researcher was not present in the "doctor's office" during filming. The total role-play footage collected was 2 hours, 29 minutes, 55 seconds long; the shortest role-play lasted 13 minutes, 21 seconds, and the longest, 16 minutes, 19 seconds. Debriefing interviews were conducted with all participants. Interpreters were asked to reflect on how they thought they had clarified in the consultation and were then given a chance to view the video footage and consider their interpreting choices. Although the interpreters were very aware that the interaction was a simulated appointment, the majority stated that the cameras did not bother them and that the role-play felt realistic. They particularly enjoyed being able to work with a real doctor rather than someone pretending to be a doctor.

Transcription and analysis involved a cyclic process of transcribing, observing, and conducting sequential analyses of the data at a microlevel. To begin with, all instances of clarification were identified and roughly transcribed. For the purposes of this study, a clarification request was defined as *a request for previously mentioned information to be repeated, expanded, or explained to aid understanding.* A clarification request was included in the dataset if it matched the definition and if there was also supporting evidence within the text (i.e., if the request resulted in a response offering clarification).[3] It is important to note that a "request" speech function may be realized in a number of different ways; that is, clarification requests are not only interrogative in form. For example, when the request was implied, it was identified from the interactional context. The sequences involving clarification were transcribed in technical detail (see Major, 2013, for a discussion of the transcription system developed for the study), and detailed IS analyses were conducted along with consideration of the reported data collected in the debriefing interviews. Both the English and the Auslan were transcribed; the Auslan signs are shown in the chapter in SMALL CAPITAL LETTERS. A full list of transcription conventions can be found in the appendix.

The technical transcripts presented in this chapter are often complicated, given that two languages are involved, and frequently three people are speaking at the same time. Rather than providing a translation of the

Auslan within the technical transcript, which would make it even more cluttered and difficult to read, a separate, "clean" version is provided for each excerpt. This is a version of the excerpt from which overlap has been removed, and the Auslan has been translated into English (indicated by underlined text), so that readers may quickly skim and understand the content of each exchange prior to focusing on a sequential analysis of the data. Before examining actual clarification sequences, however, I first examine interpreters' reports of how they were taught to clarify and how they believed they clarified in the role-play data.

INTERPRETERS' REFLECTIONS ON HOW THEY CLARIFY

Although clarification is certainly taught or at least discussed in many interpreter education programs, the literature review conducted for this study identified no information on how this is done, and so the interpreters were asked in the debriefing interviews to explain how they learned to clarify. Three reported that they picked up clarification skills on the job: two because they had never undergone formal interpreter training, and one because it was not a part of the training she had completed. Two interpreters reported that the course they had completed had dealt with clarification skills, but in a prescriptive manner that did not reconcile well with the realities of actual interaction. Gabrielle, for example, explained that she was taught to refer to herself in the third person:

> I was taught to [say] "Excuse me, the interpreter would like to clarify the situation" . . . or "I'm sorry, interpreter error." [I] hated it, hated it. But at the same time if you don't clarify that it's you who's made the error or you who's asked for clarification then it makes it look like the deaf person has made the error or yeah. So it's a fine line.

Six interpreters could not recall the exact techniques they had learned, although they could recall being taught that clarification is important. As Hugo explained, for example:

> I can't say that we had a whole class based on clarification . . . but we were taught and it was emphasized about clarity many times throughout the whole diploma of interpreting in particular. To ensure that we clarified, to ensure that we produced a clear message, to ensure we received a clear message.

Before interpreters were shown any video clips or transcript excerpts of the simulated consultation they had participated in, they were asked to report on strategies they had used to clarify information during the recording. Some of them offered examples of things that they had clarified, such as "paracetamol" (acetaminophen), "types of drugs," and "blood test," and in each case they recalled these correctly.

However, recall bias was clearly evident, as interpreters found it challenging to remember the exact phrases that they had used to clarify. For example, Logan said:

> I have no idea. If there was something I needed clarification about, and I think there was . . . it would depend on what it was and why I needed it and how flummoxed I was or how important I thought that information was so I don't know.

It is interesting that Logan's explanation contains many hedges ("I have no idea"; "I don't know") and conditional formulations ("if there was"; "it would depend on"). This illustrates the highly contingent and context-bound nature of interpreting, supporting the notion that descriptions of interpreting skills must be based upon interaction data rather than interpreters' recollections alone.

Clarification Requests in the Role-Play Data

Although this study does not aim to create generalizations about the ways all interpreters clarify, it does allow me to identify several salient features of interest. Because ten interpreters completed what was essentially the same role-play, the simulated consultations could be examined for common patterns.

A total of 105 instances of clarification requests were counted in the role-play data, as table 2 shows.

TABLE 2. *Number of Clarification Requests*

Initiator	Not interpreted	Interpreted into Auslan	Interpreted into English	Total
Interpreter	English: 15 Auslan: 26	-	-	41
Patient	Answered in Auslan: 1	-	45	46
Doctor	-	18	-	18
Total	42	18	45	105

Of the 41 interpreter-initiated clarification requests, 26 were directed at the patient, and 15 were directed at the doctor. Of the 64 other-initiated clarification requests, few were used to clarify directly with the interpreter. That is, most were used to clarify information given by the patient or the doctor rather than by the interpreter, for example, "so you just fell down and you broke your ankle?" (doctor clarifying patient's description of the accident). Although it is possible that the doctor's and the patient's clarification requests were not as naturalistic as they might otherwise have been (as actors, they knew the purpose of the study), they are nonetheless included for the purpose of analyzing how interpreters deal with such requests initiated by others.

Of the 64 other-initiated clarification requests, the majority were conveyed by the interpreter to the other participant. Only one was directly answered by an interpreter (Amy), this being a request from the patient to expand on the meaning of a pragmatic device ("all that sort of stuff"), which had been interpreted fairly literally from English into Auslan.

With regard to the 41 interpreter-initiated clarification requests, the number per individual interpreter range from 0 (Amy) to 11 (Madeleine), while the average was 4. Unfortunately, the small numbers make it impossible to draw solid conclusions based on demographic information. Having said that, there are no striking differences with regard to gender, age, or level of NAATI accreditation. Notably, the majority of clarification requests (40 out of 41) were produced by the eight participants who had completed interpreter training. Of the two untrained interpreters in the study (Amy and Oliver), only Oliver made a clarification request. Interpretation of this finding is complicated, however, because the eight trained interpreters are also nonnative signers, while the two untrained interpreters are native signers.[4] It is impossible to know whether Amy and Oliver produced few clarification requests because of a lack of formal training, their native fluency in Auslan, or some other contextually bound or more idiosyncratic reasons.

Participants' interpreting experience may also have an impact on the number of clarification requests produced. Those with more than 5 years of experience made fewer clarification requests (2 on average) than those with less than 5 years of experience (6 on average). It may be that the former understand the dialogue better, are more confident, and therefore feel less need to clarify information. It is interesting to note, however, that both the doctor and the patient actors reported that they appreciated the style of the interpreters who clarified more often.

Doctor Bourke explained that, even though it was troublesome for her when interpreters got too far behind, she understood the need to clarify information:

> Some of them stopped to ask me what to do or say and that was them being clear. I don't find that a problem, I'm happy to make it clear for them so they can make it clear for the [deaf] person.

The patient (Phoebe) also commented on clarification, specifically noting that a lack of clarification sometimes makes her suspicious about the quality of information being conveyed:

> I could see that some interpreters were very—well, some really worked to make sure that very accurate information was being conveyed. Whereas others were a lot more casual about it . . . these interpreters didn't clarify anything, except perhaps very small details here and there. So I'm finger-spelling away crazy fast and they are still not clarifying anything.

Although not specifically elicited during the postrecording interviews, both the doctor and the patient reported which interpreters they enjoyed working with the most. As implied by the preceding quotes, their favorite interpreters were not necessarily those with the most experience. The interpreter that Dr. Bourke named, for example, was a relative novice with only 3 years of interpreting experience (Hugo). She thought his style was "stunning" because he kept up with her and clarified when necessary, and she felt that Phoebe "seemed to follow him quite easily." This particular interpreter clarified six times during the role-play: once with the patient and five times with the doctor. This serves as a reminder to interpreters—experienced and novice alike—that the need to clarify does not always represent the need to repair problematic talk. Practitioners and patients expect interpreters to clarify, and clarification can help them feel confident that information is being conveyed accurately.

Inserting Clarification Requests into the Sequence of Talk

Prompted by the participants' reports that it can at times be difficult to take control and interrupt other speakers, an examination of strategies interpreters use to get a turn in order to clarify was conducted. Turn taking is an integral part of any face-to-face interaction, often signaled by speakers using a range of both linguistic and nonlinguistic cues. In signed languages, for example, turn allocation is often indicated by eye gaze (e.g., Smith & Ramsay, 2004; Van Herreweghe, 2002). Roy (1989, 2000) conducted the seminal study on turn taking within interpreted interaction involving a signed language (ASL) by conducting an IS analysis of a naturally occurring interpreted interview between a hearing professor and a deaf student at a university in the United States. She illustrated that interpreters constantly make complex and context-bound decisions in managing turn taking between deaf and hearing parties, considering factors such as the status of the speakers, as well as the intent and the desired outcome of an utterance. It is a crucial part of the interpreter's job, particularly given that turn taking can affect not only the quality and amount of information that is interpreted but also people's perceptions of each other—for better or worse (Sanheim, 2003).

The following discussion focuses mainly on interpreters' management of their *own* turns in order to request clarification or to interpret a clarification request. First, instances in which explicit turn getting was unnecessary are addressed, that is, when interpreters were not required to interrupt another speaker. This is followed by an analysis of strategies interpreters use in instances where the need to clarify (or to convey another's clarification request) did require them to interrupt another speaker and explicitly create a turn for themselves.

When a Turn Does Not Need to Be Created

In 76 of the 105 total clarification requests (72.3%) the interpreter did not need to interrupt another participant in order to get a turn. In many cases, the interpreter's clarification request (or interpretation of another's clarification request) occurred at a transition relevance place (see Ten Have, 1999). An example of a *transition relevance place* is the point at which the participant who had been speaking is coming to the end of an utterance, thus providing an opportunity to insert a clarification request as the next turn. Another frequent context in which the flow of talk is not interrupted by a clarification request occurs when the interpreter already has the floor and thus effectively only interrupts him- or herself. For example, in Excerpt 1 Dr. Bourke is explaining to Phoebe some types of medications that people with osteoporosis can take. A "clean" version is first provided, with overlap removed and the Auslan translated into English (indicated by underlined text). This is followed by the technical version of the transcript (please see the appendix for a description of all transcript conventions). The clarification request is indicated in bold text.

EXCERPT 1. *"can you spell fosomax for me?"*

D = Dr Bourke, P = patient (Phoebe), I = interpreter (Gabrielle)

D:	. . .and those tablets (.) um have names like (.) fosomax or (actonel)
I:	. . .group of medications call- they'll help you to get calcium into your bones
P:	((nods head))
D:	*((quietly)) i don't know if you've ever heard of those names*
I:	have you heard of tablets called- **can you spell fosomax for me?**
D:	i'll write it down for you
I:	she'll write it

EXCERPT 1. *Technical transcript (09:06-09:18)*

1	D	. . ..and those tablets (.) um have names like (.) fosomax or (actonel)=
2	I	. . .GROUP THOSE MEDICATIONS CALL- WILL HELP YOU=
3	D	=*((quietly)) i don't know if* [*you've ever heard of those names*]
4	P	[((nods head))
5	I	=IN BONES [C-A-L-C-I-U-M] IN BONES=
6	I	YOU HEARD NAME TABLETS CALLED- **can you spell fosomax for** =
7	I	=**me?**
8	D	i'll write it down [for you]
9	I	[WILL WRITE]

This excerpt begins as Dr. Bourke is explaining the use of certain medications in treating osteoporosis (line 1). The interpreter, Gabrielle, conveys to Phoebe: GROUP THOSE MEDICATIONS CALL- WILL HELP YOU IN BONES C-A-L-C-I-U-M IN BONES ("group of medications call- they'll help you to get calcium into your bones") (lines 2, 5). At this point Gabrielle has a slightly longer lag time than usual, so although her interpretation appears not to match the doctor's talk, it relates directly to the doctor's previous utterance (not shown in the transcript). In line 6 Gabrielle begins to convey the doctor's utterance from line 1, at which point she requires clarification on spelling one of the medication names and asks the doctor, "can you spell fosomax for me?" This clarification request does not require Gabrielle to interrupt anybody: the patient is watching the Auslan interpretation, and the doctor is also waiting for a response to her explanation. The interpreter indicates a footing shift (from that of interpretation to taking a turn in her own right for clarification) by using cues such as leaning toward and also directing her eye gaze toward Dr. Bourke. The doctor subsequently writes the word on a piece of paper and passes it to Gabrielle, who then fingerspells the word to Phoebe.

At other times, such as when the doctor had already interrupted the patient or vice versa, the interpreters did not need to create explicit turns for themselves. That is, although neither could understand the other's talk directly, they often noticed when the other had begun speaking or signing and sometimes reacted to it as if they had been interrupted, stopping their own contribution midutterance. In this type of sequence an interpretation of the interruption is the expected next turn.

When a Turn Needs to Be Explicitly Created

Although the majority of clarification-request sequences occurred as natural next turns (as in Excerpt 1), 29 (27.6%) of the clarification requests required the interpreters to create a turn for themselves in the discourse. In these 29 cases, the interactional challenge of interrupting another participant is evident in the interpreters' frequent use of discourse markers (particularly in English) and body movement (particularly in Auslan) to signal the upcoming interruption and at times to mitigate it.

Out of the 60 English clarification requests,[5] the interpreters interrupted the doctor on 13 occasions. Five out of the 13 interruptions were achieved with "sorry," a discourse device that, in these cases, functioned as both a turn-getting and a mitigating device and sometimes also as a shift-implicative device (discussed later in the chapter). Other discourse markers used to signal the interpreter's intention to take the floor included "oh," "and," a false start, and three instances of "so"; the latter is illustrated in Excerpt 2. This excerpt occurs as the doctor is explaining which pain medications she will prescribe to the patient.

EXCERPT 2. *"so there's another one"*

D = Dr Bourke, P = patient (Phoebe), I = interpreter (Callum)

D:	i can give you two tablets (.) one is a single tablet that you take at- that lasts for twenty four hours
I:	. . .<u>another one for pain relief</u>
P:	**<u>another one you mean five?</u>**
I:	so there's another one does that mean i will have a fifth?
D:	no no you just don't- you said you had no more left though
I:	<u>you said four had run out right?</u>
P:	((nods head))
I:	oh yes that's right

EXCERPT 2. *Technical transcript (11:52-12:04)*

1	D	i can give you two tablets (.) one is a single tablet that you take at- that]=
2	I	. . .EXTRA ANOTHER ONE FOR (.) PAIN REDUCE: (.) RELIEF]
3	D	=[lasts for twenty [four hours]
4	P	=[**ANOTHER ONE (MEAN)** [**FIVE?**
5	I	[so there's] another one does that mean i=
6	I	=will have a *((FIVE+))* fifth?
7	D	no no you just don't- you said you had no more [left though]
8	I	[YOU SAID FOUR]=
9	P	[((nods head))]
10	I	=RUN-OUT RIGHT [FOUR] *((nods head))* oh yes that's right

Excerpt 2 begins as Dr. Bourke begins her explanation (line 1), although in line 2, Callum is still interpreting a previous utterance by the doctor: EXTRA ANOTHER ONE FOR (.) PAIN REDUCE: (.) RELIEF ("another one for pain relief") (line 2). In direct response to this, Phoebe clarifies: ANOTHER ONE (MEAN) FIVE? ("another one do you mean five?") (line 4). Even though Phoebe's utterance occurs at a transition relevance place within the Auslan dyad, it overlaps the doctor's utterance, but the doctor continues speaking and does not react to Phoebe's signing as an interruption. This motivates Callum to interrupt the doctor in order to convey the clarification request. It is interesting to note that Callum prioritizes the patient's clarification request rather than the doctor's explanation in line 1, which is not interpreted until the doctor later repeats it. Within the context of the dataset as a whole, this seems not to represent an alliance with the patient but rather that interpreters tend to give priority to clarification requests. In other excerpts when the doctor clarified, her clarification requests were usually given priority also.

In lines 5 and 6 Callum indicates his intention to interrupt with the discourse marker "so," followed by the clarification request: "there's another one does that mean i will have a fifth?" He also leans toward the doctor, although this appears to be more for Phoebe's benefit, as the body movement (as well as the sign FIVE, which is simultaneously produced) indicates a shift in footing and informs the patient that her clarification request is being conveyed. When interrupted by the interpreter, Dr. Bourke does not immediately stop speaking but completes her utterance and then stops. In line 7 she responds to the misunderstanding: "no no you just don't- you said you had no more left though," confirming that it is not an extra tablet she is referring to but rather a replacement tablet.

Turning to Auslan clarification requests, 16 out of 44 required the interpreters to create a turn for themselves.[6] Given the fact that signed languages make much use of nonlinguistic cues, including body movement and facial expression (Hoza, 2007b; Johnston & Schembri, 2007), it had been expected that this would be the interpreters' main strategy to interrupt the patient. Certainly body movement was often used, but always in conjunction with lexical cues. Nine out of 16 occurrences included both body movement and lexical cues, and 7 out of 16 included lexical cues alone. Lexical cues prefacing Auslan clarification requests were either discourse devices (such as SORRY, WAVE, HOLD) or the core clarification request itself.

Excerpt 3 is a particularly interesting exchange as it illustrates an interpreter creating a turn in Auslan using SORRY, a discourse marker which Hoza (2007b) defines categorically as a bald on-record apology when used in ASL. Arguably, however, SORRY does not function primarily as a mitigating device in this excerpt. Excerpt 3 occurs as Phoebe is explaining about the different pain medication she has been taking.

EXCERPT 3. *"there's four different types"*

P = patient (Phoebe), I = interpreter (Madeleine)

I:	. . .for what?
P:	*((quickly)) i have four different ones*
I:	there's four different types
P:	*first one's for quick second's for slow third's for headache fourth's for pain*
I:	((nods head, raises hands)) <u>sorry</u> sorry doctor i'm just gonna clarify those **the four tablets please explain them again so the first one**
P:	the first one is for slow release . . .

EXCERPT 3. *Technical transcript (01:42-01:54)*

1	P	*((quickly)) ME FOUR DIFFERENT (.) FIRST] FOR QUICK FIRST=*
2	I	. . .FOR WHAT? there's four different types]
3	P	*SECOND FOR SLOW SECOND THIRD FOR [HEADACHE THIRD=*
4	I	[((nods head, raises hands))=
5	P	*=FOURTH FOR PAIN FOUR]* [((laughs))]
6	I	*=SORRY* sorry doctor] i'm just gonna [clarify those] **FOUR=**
7	P	[FIRST SLOW RELEASE FIRST . . .
8	I	**=EXPLAIN AGAIN PLEASE [FIRST**

In lines 1, 3, and 5 Phoebe summarizes her medication regimen, though she is signing quickly and in a slightly unclear manner. Madeleine begins to interpret: "there's four different types" (line 2), but is unable to keep up with the pace of Phoebe's explanation. In line 4 Madeleine begins to nod her head and raises her hands slightly, indicating that she is about to begin signing. She then interrupts Phoebe (in line 6) by signing SORRY, which is followed by a brief explanation to alert Dr. Bourke to the problem: "sorry doctor i'm just gonna clarify those." Madeleine then asks Phoebe to repeat her explanation: FOUR EXPLAIN AGAIN PLEASE FIRST ("the four tablets please explain them again so the first one") (lines 6, 8).

In this instance, SORRY appears to function primarily as a turn-getting device (to interrupt Phoebe), as well as to indicate the upcoming clarification request. It may also have a mitigating function, given that Madeleine has chosen this lexical item with which to interrupt rather than WAIT or HOLD, for example. The multifunctionality of this instance of SORRY and the fact that it functions primarily as a turn-getting device serves as a reminder that context is crucial to understanding the meaning of discourse devices.

Relational Work: Mitigating Clarification Requests

As discussed earlier, clarification requests have the potential to be perceived as face threatening either because of the content of the request (for example, if it is implied that the original speaker was unclear or not well informed) or because of a perceived imposition (for example, when an interruption occurs). The following discussion focuses on the possible reasons for interpreters' mitigation of clarification requests and ways in which they accomplish it. From the total of 105 clarification requests, mitigation was identified in 42 (40%).

Mitigating English Clarification Requests

Of the 15 interpreter-initiated clarification requests directed at the doctor, 12 (80%) were mitigated in some way. In one example, the interpreter mitigated an entire utterance by using a softened voice, leaning toward the doctor, and gesturing. In all other instances, however, the mitigation was achieved through the use of one or more lexical mitigating devices. The most common strategy was to use indirect questions (such as "could you"), which occurred seven times, followed by explicit apologies ("sorry"), which occurred six times, and softening devices (such as "just"), which occurred four times. Excerpt 4 illustrates a clarification request mitigated by Callum using all three of these strategies. Prior to this, Phoebe had informed Dr. Bourke that she had not brought any paperwork related to the initial treatment of her fractured ankle with her.

EXCERPT 4. *"just to clarify"*

D = Dr Bourke, I = interpreter (Callum)

D:	okay: that's unfortunate never mind are you gonna go and see them again?
I:	well that's unfortunate: in any case will you visit- i'm going to clarify who you will visit again **clarify- um could you- just to clarify visit who again sorry?**
D:	there's the hospital doctors or whoever it was that fixed her ankle
I:	the hospital or doctor who fixed your ankle who helped you before

EXCERPT 4. *Technical transcript (01:35-01:48)*

1	D	okay that's unfortunate [never mind are you gonna go and see them again?]
2	I	[WELL UNFORTUNATE: SO-ANYWAY]=
3	I	=(WILL-) VISIT CLARIFY WHO WILL VISIT AGAIN **clarify- um**=
4	I	=**could you- just to clarify visit who again sorry?**
5	D	there's the hospital [doctors or whoever it was that fixed her ankle]
6	I	[WHO HOSPITAL DOCTOR WHO ( ) FIX]=
7	I	BEFORE HELP-YOU . . .

In this example Callum clarifies who "them" (in line 1) refers to. He first informs the patient what he intends to do: CLARIFY WHO WILL VISIT AGAIN ("i'm going to clarify who you will visit again") (line 3). He then requests clarification from the doctor (lines 3 and 4). The English clarification request begins with a false start ("clarify-"), followed by a hesitation ("um") and a more "polite" reformulation ("could you"), which is cut short and then reformulated: "just to clarify visit who again." Here the softening device "just" mitigates the reason for Callum's request ("to clarify"). Finally, there is a postposed "sorry," used here as a mitigating device. Given that the core message in Callum's request could probably be paraphrased as "visit who?" it seems clear that this request involves substantial relational work in the form of mitigating devices used to minimize the imposition of clarifying with the doctor. There is also some dysfluency, which may relate to an online processing issue.

This redressive action may address a perceived threat to the doctor's face; that is, Callum may perceive that drawing attention to a lack of clarity in the doctor's utterance is not an appropriate way to address a health professional. If this is the case, however, the reason for the mitigation may not be a conscious decision on Callum's part. In the retrospective interview he found it difficult to explain his wording choices: "I think I always apologize 'cause it's more my error." This is particularly interesting given that the ambiguity in Excerpt 4 is created by the doctor, and the need to clarify is not related in any way to interpreter error.

In addition to interpreter-initiated English clarification requests, patient-initiated requests were also examined, with a focus on the strategies interpreters used to interpret these into English. From the 46 patient-initiated clarification requests, Phoebe mitigated 6, and in all 6, the corresponding English request involved a comparable level of mitigation. In 3 of the 6 requests, Phoebe mitigated her clarification request by using a speaker-oriented device such as ME NOT SURE ("i'm not sure"), which is likely mitigating as it places any blame for the lack of clarity on the patient and not the doctor. In all three instances, a fairly close rendition of this mitigation was provided in English.

In the other three instances in which the patient mitigated a clarification request, she did so by smiling. This nonlinguistic mitigation device was also reflected in the interpreters' Auslan clarification requests. As opposed to a phrase such as ME NOT SURE, however, there is no easy lexical equivalent of a smile, and so it was interesting to investigate how this was conveyed into English. In one instance, it was interpreted as an apology ("sorry"), and in two instances it was conveyed as a speaker-oriented device (for example, "i'm not quite sure"), as in Excerpt 5. This occurs at Dr. Bourke's first mention of a bone mineral density test, which she suggests Phoebe should do to find out whether she has osteoporosis.

EXCERPT 5. *"mm i'm not quite sure what that is"*

D = Dr Bourke, P = patient (Phoebe), I = interpreter (Eva)

D:	. . .we do a test called a bone mineral density test
I:	so i will do a test called a bone mineral density test
P:	((smiles, shakes head))
I:	mm i'm not quite sure what that is
D:	it's a kind of x-ray not very different to what you've had for your ankle
I:	she's saying like oh hmm it's er like ( ) the x-ray . . .

EXCERPT 5. *Technical transcript (08:34–08:51)*

1	D	. . .we do a test called a bone mineral density test]
2	I	. . .OR WEAK BONES: (.) SO ME WILL] DO TEST NAMED=
3	P	[((smiles, shakes head))]
4	I	=BONE M-I-N-E-R-A-L D-E-N-S-I-T-[Y TEST mm i'm not quite sure]=
5	D	[it's] a kind of x-[ray not very different to what you've had for=
6	I	=what that [is] [(SHE) HMM LIKE::: ER=
7	D	=your ankle]
8	I	=( )] X-RAY . . .

Eva's strategy for conveying this new concept is to sign BONE and fin-gerspell both "mineral" and "density." On seeing this, Phoebe smiles and shakes her head (line 3), and while doing so she quickly looks at Dr. Bourke and then back to Eva. Immediately Eva says, "mm i'm not quite sure what that is" (line 4). The speaker-oriented "i'm not sure" is further softened by the addition of "quite," and she also shakes her head very slightly, perhaps to indicate to Phoebe that the clarification request is being conveyed.

Of the 40 patient-initiated clarification requests that did not contain any type of mitigation in the Auslan original, interpreters *added* mitiga-tion to 13 (32.5%). This suggests that they sometimes judged the patient's clarification requests to require facework in English. Their strategies were similar to those already discussed; particularly frequent was the use of speaker-oriented devices (seven instances), as well as apologies and sof-tening devices (three instances each). Several excerpts in the dataset show that the patient is perfectly capable of mitigating her own requests when she wishes to, so the interpreters' behavior here is more than simply bridging sociolinguistic differences between Auslan and English. It is not possible to say with certainty, but the interpreters' actions may relate to perceived power differences between the patient and the doctor, and thus interpreters deem additional facework to be necessary. In any case it is clear that interpreters take responsibility for the way that the patient's talk is presented to the doctor, and this includes doing relational work on the patient's behalf.

Mitigating Auslan Clarification Requests

In examining the ways that interpreters mitigated Auslan clarifica-tion requests, it became immediately apparent that proportionally less such mitigation was directed at the patient than at the doctor. Of the 26 interpreter-initiated clarification requests directed at the patient, only nine (34.6%) were mitigated (as opposed to 80% of those directed at the doctor). Five included the apology SORRY, two of which coincided with smiling. Two requests included the use of PLEASE, and two included both SORRY and PLEASE (one of which also included smiling).

The doctor mitigated almost none of her 18 clarification requests, with the possible exception of one use of a speaker-oriented device ("let me get this right"), which was not conveyed in any form by the interpreter. It was not possible, therefore, to identify patterns with respect to the ways the interpreters conveyed English mitigation in original utterances into Auslan. However, two interpreters (Eva and Madeleine) added mitigation to two of the doctor's clarification requests, each time in the form of smiling, which served to soften an otherwise very direct request (Excerpt 6). This exchange occurred only 27 seconds into the consultation, as Dr. Bourke was questioning Phoebe about how she had fractured her ankle.

EXCERPT 6. *"i was walking along and fell over"*

D = Dr Bourke, P = patient (Phoebe), I = interpreter (Eva)

P:	i was walking along and fell over
I:	well i was walking and i just fell over
D:	**you were just walking along and you fell over?**
I:	you were just walking and fell over that's it nothing else?
P:	no i was bush walking and (in the bush) there was a hill which i was walking down then i slipped over
I:	well i was bush walking sorry ((inhales)) and there was like bit of a hill and i just fell down

EXCERPT 6. *Technical transcript (00:27-00:40)*

1	P	(ME) WALKING [FELL-OVER]
2	I	[well i was] walking and i just fell over
3	D	**you were just walking along [and you fell over?]**
4	I	[WALK FALL-OVER] THAT'S-ALL=
5	P	[NO ME BUSH] WALKING AND [(BUSH) ME HILL ME=
6	I	=[NOTHING?] [well i was bush walking sorry=
7	P	WALK-DOWN SLIP-OVER]
8	I	((inhales)) and there was like bit of a] hill and i just fell down

The excerpt begins as Phoebe is explaining ME WALKING FELL-OVER ("I was walking along and fell over") (line 1). After Eva conveys this, Dr. Bourke responds: "you were just walking along and you fell over?" (line 3). The slightly incredulous tone of the doctor's voice, along with a frown on her face and gestured movements toward Phoebe serve to render the clarification request even more direct than it may appear on paper. In lines 4 and 6 Eva signs WALK FALL-OVER THAT'S-ALL NOTHING? ("you were just walking and fell over that's it nothing else?"). As she begins the utterance, she sits up straight and raises her eyebrows markedly, conveying the incredulous tone of Dr. Bourke's request. However, as she signs THAT'S-ALL NOTHING? Eva's face relaxes into a subtle smile, which seemed to both a native signer and to me to soften the overall force of the entire clarification request. In a retrospective interview Eva confirmed this:

> I think a lot of the way I work, a lot of what I show, is in my face and in my expression. Like even my tone when I want to clarify something . . . it's not exactly what I say, it's the way I say it.

The data suggest that smiling is used as a mitigating strategy in Auslan, although clearly further research on naturally occurring monolingual Auslan interaction would be needed to investigate this further. Nevertheless, the data support Hoza's (2007a, 2007b) findings that ASL signers often mitigate requests by using nonlinguistic strategies. The reasons are less clear, however, for interpreters' relatively frequent use of SORRY in Auslan. Although Hoza (2007b) found this strategy in his ASL politeness data, he identifies only two instances of SORRY; also, the patient in the current study did not use SORRY even once. It is possible that the interpreters' use of this device is a transfer from English. The situation is also further complicated when we examine the multifunctionality of discourse devices that interpreters use; in five out of nine instances of the Auslan SORRY, for example, the device appeared to also serve other functions in addition to mitigation.

MULTITASKING INTERPRETERS: MULTIFUNCTIONALITY AND CLARIFICATION

The final role-play data excerpts in this chapter illustrate some of the sophisticated—and perhaps not even conscious—interactional multitasking performed by interpreters. Two discourse devices that frequently performed more than one action within clarification requests are discussed first: "sorry"/SORRY and "so." Finally, a small group of clarification requests that analysis revealed to be multifunctional in an overall sense is described.

The Multifunctionality of SORRY

As previously discussed, interpreters used "sorry"/SORRY with relative frequency (17 of the total 105 clarification requests). On all 17 occasions, "sorry"/SORRY either originated with or was added by the interpreter. We have already seen examples of it functioning primarily as both a turn-getting device (Excerpt 3) and a mitigation device (Excerpt 4). In some instances, "sorry"/SORRY was found to act simultaneously as a mitigating and turn-getting device and/or a shift implicative device. A *shift implicative device* can be used to signal some kind of trouble in understanding (Beach, 1993), which is often the case when it prefaces a clarification request. "Sorry"/SORRY is not the only mitigating device to also function as a shift implicative device; others include WAVE (also an attention-getting device) and smiling in Auslan, as well as words such as "so," "okay," and "yeah" in English.

Multifunctional "sorry" occurred seven times (used by three interpreters: Callum, Hugo, and Katherine[7]). Excerpt 7 clearly illustrates the difficulty some interpreters encounter in interrupting a doctor.

EXCERPT 7. *"a special test"*

D = Dr Bourke, I = interpreter (Hugo)

D:	. . .and you have a special test called a bone mineral density test
I:	. . .osteoporosis
D:	now that (.) ( )-
I:	if you ha- **sorry can you go back (.) if: the condition: for you- sorry just**
	( ) **for in- what you are saying is in order for you to find out**
D:	in order to find out . . .

EXCERPT 7. *Technical transcript (09:52-10:07)*

1	D	. . .and you have a special test called a bone mineral density test]	
2	I	O- S- T- E- O- P- E- R- O- S- I- S WELL	] IF=
3	D	[now that (.) ( )-]	
4	I	=[HA- **sorry**] **can you go back (.) if: the condition: for you- sorry**=	
5	I	=**just ( ) for in- what you are saying is in order for you to find out**	
6	D	in order to find out . . .	

In Excerpt 7 Dr. Bourke is again explaining the "special test called a bone mineral density test" (line 1). Hugo begins to interpret this (line 2) but then requires clarification of the information for himself. In order to request this, he must interrupt the doctor, and the entire clarification request is evidence that this poses a difficulty for him: "sorry can you go back (.) if: the condition: for you- sorry just (   ) for in- what you are saying is in order for you to find out" (lines 4, 5, 6). He is clearly attending to relational work through the use of mitigation by using strategies such as apologies ("sorry"), an indirect question ("can you"), and a softening device ("just"), as well as explaining what is needed ("go back"), along with at least three reformulations, which may also indicate an online processing issue. In this exchange the turn-initial "sorry" plays a crucial role, as it serves to interrupt the doctor while also serving as a mitigation and shift implicative device. This allows Hugo to create a turn and clarify, an act that he clearly—at least in this exchange—perceives as potentially face threatening to the doctor.

"So"-Prefaced Clarification Requests

The second multifunctional discourse device is the English marker "so," which occurred in 21 out of 105 clarification requests. In addition to marking inferential or causal connections in sequences of talk, "so" has also been shown to play an important role in maintaining discourse cohesion in English (Schiffrin, 1987). Based on a CA analysis of naturally occurring American English interaction, Bolden (2009) established that "so"-prefaced turns can be used to "implement incipient actions" (see also Bolden, 2006). That is, speakers can use this marker to indicate that an upcoming turn—which may appear to be sequentially irrelevant—is in fact related to previous talk or has been on the agenda for some time. Bolden (2006) refers to this function as marking "the current matter's emergence from incipiency" (p. 666).

Analysis of the English clarification requests revealed that interpreters frequently used "so" in a turn-initial position both to create a turn for themselves—particularly when interrupting the doctor—and to indicate the clarification request as emerging from incipiency. This seems to occur particularly in exchanges where the clarification request occurs after the doctor has already moved to a new line of talk (Excerpt 8). This exchange begins immediately after the doctor has explained the side effects as well as the benefits of two different types of pain relievers that she is going to prescribe.

EXCERPT 8. *"you're going to give me two tablets"*

D = Dr Bourke, P = patient (Phoebe), I = interpreter (Logan)

D:	that make sense?
P:	((nods head))
I:	((nods head))
D:	okay
D:	so what i- er
P:	<u>you're going to give me two tablets alright</u>
D:	when are you seeing the hosp-
I:	so you'll give me two different types of pills
D:	that's right
I:	<u>that's right</u>

EXCERPT 8. *Technical transcript (12:20-12:29)*

1	D	that make [sense?	
2	P	[((nods [head))]	
3	I	[((nods] head))	
4	D	okay	
5	D	so what i- er [when are you seeing [the hosp-	
6	P	[YOU GIVE-ME TWO [TABLETS ALRIGHT]	
7	I	[so you'll] give me=	
8	I	=two different types of pills	
9	D	that's [right]	
10	I	[((nods head))] RIGHT	

In line 1 Dr. Bourke asks Phoebe, "that make sense?" Phoebe nods her head in response, although in Auslan this does not necessarily mean "yes"; it can also be used as a form of minimal feedback (Johnston & Schembri, 2007). Additionally, Phoebe does so before an interpretation is provided, making it unlikely that this is a direct response to the question, although Dr. Bourke appears to interpret it as such. For some reason the interpreter does not convey the doctor's question but also nods his head, and Dr. Bourke's interpretation of this as an affirmative answer is evident in her response—"okay" (line 4)—and in the fact that she asks a new question (line 5). Phoebe, however, is still on the topic of the pain relievers and clarifies YOU GIVE-ME TWO TABLETS ALRIGHT. In lines 7 and 8 Logan conveys the patient-initiated clarification request at the earliest opportunity: "so you'll give me two different types of pills." The use of "so" signals both Logan's intention to speak and that a marked utterance is to follow: a clarification request that both interrupts the doctor and refers to a topic that she has moved on from. "So," in this case, is a turn-getting device, a "misplacement marker" (Bolden, 2009), and a cue that the clarification request emerges from and is related to the prior talk.

Excerpt 8 is by no means a unique example, with multifunctional turn-initial "so" (or "sorry so" or "okay so") appearing in ten clarification requests.[8] Interestingly, far less evidence of this type of cohesive work was found to be done by interpreters when clarifying or conveying clarification requests to the patient. It is not possible to know for certain why this might be the case, although it could be because the interpreters perceived the doctor to be higher in authority than the patient and/or because most of the interpreters were somewhat familiar with the patient in real life, but only one reported having previously met the doctor. In any case, this small analysis has shown that the use of "so" by interpreters performs cohesive and interpersonal functions that would be worthy of future research.

The Multifunctionality of Clarification Requests Themselves

The final findings from the role-play data concern a small group of clarification requests that are arguably multifunctional. In 11 cases interpreters were found to convey another's clarification request while also modifying or adding to it in a way that encouraged a particular response. That is, they sometimes used clarification requests to shape the flow of talk in pursuing what they believed to be the goals either of the immediate sequence or of the broader interaction. In Excerpt 9 Phoebe requests clarification of the word "density." Madeleine interprets the clarification request accurately but also expands on the original utterance based on her own assessment of what an ideal response from the doctor ought to be.

EXCERPT 9. *"could you explain that"*
D = Dr Bourke, P = patient (Phoebe), I = interpreter (Madeleine)

I:	. . .bone mineral denst- ity test that test
P:	what's the d word?
I:	what what do you mean by density sorry could you explain that
D:	how (.) how strong the bone is- so bone (.) mineral is like a salt (.)
	and density is the strength of it or how how . . .
I:	density means how strong your bones are . . .

1	D		[that test- that bone [mineral density test-	
2	I	BONE M-I-N-E-R-A-L D-E-N-S-T-[I-T-Y TEST	[THAT TEST	]=
3	P		[D WHAT?	]
4	D		[density means	]=
5	I	=((WELL)) *what what* do you mean by density sorry [could you explain that]		
6	D	how (.) [how strong the bone is- so bone (.) mineral is like a salt (.) and=		
7	I	[D:-E-N-S-I-T-Y MEANS HOW STRONG		
8	D	=density is the strength of it or how how] . . .		
9	I	=BONES ((nods head))] . . .		

In line 3 Phoebe asks for clarification: D WHAT ("what's the d word?")
In Madeleine's interpretation, she not only conveys Phoebe's request
for clarification, with added mitigation—"what do you mean by density sorry"—but also adds a subtle directive: "could you explain that?"
(line 5). Although one could argue that this information was implicit in
Phoebe's clarification request, the retrospective interview uncovered an
additional reason for this move, as Madeleine explained:

> I don't know if you ask me directly what bone density was if I could
> explain it properly. So maybe because [Phoebe] didn't know and I didn't
> also have like a bank of knowledge to feel confident if this doctor just
> gave me a one or two word response, I could patch it or fill it or put it
> out accurately. So maybe because we were both sitting there not really
> knowing . . . I let [the doctor] know that I wanted more information.

Madeleine therefore attributes the need for this additional directive to
her own lack of technical medical knowledge. Excerpt 10 also illustrates
an interpreter (Kate), who has 10 years of interpreting experience, adding
information to elicit the type of answer that she believes the doctor would
want from the patient. Her decision appears to relate to the local sequential context: prior to this exchange Dr. Bourke has been trying to find out
more information about the pain medication that Phoebe has been taking.

EXCERPT 10. *"you've had some tablets today?"*

D = Dr Bourke, P = patient (Phoebe), I = interpreter (Kate)

D:	okay so let me get this right you've had some tablets today:?
I:	alright so you've had tablets today? when was the first? you explain
P:	one hour ago i finished them ((nods head)) so that was all four of them yeah
I:	i- one hour ago i um took some tablets and they're finished all four of them have run out

EXCERPT 10. *Technical transcript (02:59-03:11)*

1	D	okay so let [me get this right you've had some tablets today:?]
2	I	[ALRIGHT SO FINISH TABLETS] TODAY?=
3	P	[ONE HOUR] AGO [FINISH (.)=
4	I	=FIRST WHEN? YOU-EXPLAIN [(YOU)] [i- one hour ago=
5	P	=((nods head)) SO ALL-FOUR ALL-FOUR ((nods head))]
6	I	=i um took some tablets and they're finished all four of them have run] out

In this excerpt Dr. Bourke's clarification request (line 1) is a yes/no question: "okay so let me get this right you've had some tablets today:?" The first part of Kate's interpretation (line 2) is a fairly close rendition, also keeping the yes/no question format. However, in line 4, Kate asks for further information about the medication: FIRST WHEN? ("when was the first?") and additionally gives a directive about the response required: YOU-EXPLAIN (YOU) ("you explain").

In the retrospective interview Kate was asked to reflect upon why she made that choice. Her reasoning is lengthy but is worth quoting in full here as it provides detailed insight into an interpreter's justification for an action that likely challenges perceptions of the "impartial" interpreter:

> [I was] probably just trying to draw out more information, to make it more specific. I don't know if it was very successful what I did. But I'm sure the intent was to make it a more specific question. I don't think the doctor wanted a yes or no. My opinion is she would want to know "have you had them and when did you have them." I'd have to say if I did that again, I'd probably say um "when, and how many"? Yeah. But I focused in on the "when." Yeah, it's interesting too because I don't know that deaf people- well, I wouldn't say categorically, but many deaf people that we work with, they don't give specific answers sometimes. The doctor wants a specific answer, not only a yes or no. So maybe that's from experience . . . I'm sure it was to get a little bit more than a yes or no.

Kate's explanation shows that she is drawing an inference about what kind of response the doctor wants and is using this additive strategy to elicit that response rather than the more restricted answer that is likely (on the basis of her experience) to result from a more literal interpretation of the doctor's original clarification request. While on the one hand this example reminds us of the power that interpreters can have over the trajectory and content of talk, it also highlights some of the contextual factors that interpreters take into account when making interpretation choices and the fact that these are largely based on their previous experiences.

Excerpts 9 and 10 are especially interesting in light of recent studies of ad hoc interpreters. Researchers have suggested that untrained interpreters can have a negative impact on communication between healthcare practitioners and patients by questioning patients themselves or answering rather than interpreting questions (Aranguri, Davidson, & Ramirez, 2006), having conversations with one party that are not translated to the other (Laws, Heckscher, Mayo, Li, & Wilson, 2004), and misinterpreting symptoms and prioritizing clinically relevant information (Elderkin-Thompson, Silver, & Waitzkin, 2001). Hale (2007) firmly believes that this kind of action should be viewed as "gatekeeping" and has the potential to perpetuate a "sense of powerlessness" for patients and therefore that interpreters should leave all decision making to healthcare practitioners and patients. It is interesting, then, to find trained and experienced interpreters using clarification requests to simultaneously achieve broader goals such as prioritizing clinically relevant information, directing responses, and subtly shaping the flow of information. According to the actors in this study, while some interpreters shone more than others, none performed inadequately; that is, there were no perceived negative consequences. It seems that in striving to achieve a successful interpretation, interpreters not only focus on sentence-level equivalence but also consider participants' implicit intentions and perceived immediate consequences of the chosen interpretation, as well as the overall goals of the interaction.

CONCLUSION

Clarification can be considered a key skill when it comes to mediating health talk with accuracy between patients and practitioners. The analyses presented in this chapter have shown that interpreters are indeed active agents when it comes to not only requesting clarification themselves but also conveying others' clarification requests. The professional Auslan/English interpreters in the study used discourse devices, body movement, and facial expressions to attend to the cohesiveness of talk and to do facework on behalf of themselves and others when requesting clarification. They were also found to purposefully influence the shape of talk by asking additional questions and adding subtle directives to others' clarification requests based on their understanding of likely participant expectations and a desire to achieve the best possible outcome for the patient. Overall, the study has highlighted the fact that clarification request forms and functions are highly context bound inasmuch as they are inextricably linked to the moment-by-moment judgments made by interpreters based on both interactional and interpersonal factors.

The findings of this chapter are based on role-play data rather than situated, naturally occurring data. To a certain degree, simulated interaction data are inherently artificial, and so it is possible that the participants did not behave in exactly the same way as they might have in a real-life setting. At the same time, however, there is much benefit in being able to systemically compare the clarification behavior of ten different professional interpreters within the same scenario, which would not have been possible with naturally occurring data. Further research is needed to shed light on clarification in other signed and spoken language pairs and in other interpreting contexts (e.g., education, law enforcement, immigration services) in order to provide a more solid research-based foundation for teaching this skill in interpreter education and professional development programs.

The study has shown that the exact forms of clarification requests cannot be meaningfully separated from the context in which they occur, which suggests that prescriptive teaching of this tool is unlikely to be useful. It would be ideal if interpreting students learned to clarify through exposure to and discussion of actual interpreted interaction. This could be achieved through observations in community settings as well as targeted classroom activities such as discourse analytical exercises based on naturally occurring interaction (Major, Napier, & Stubbe, 2012) and role-plays such as those described in this chapter (see also Metzger, 2000). Healthcare interpreting students could benefit from studying the different strategies used by the interpreters in this study in considering ways to create turns and mitigate perceived face threats. Such an exercise should not be aimed at rote learning of the exact same strategies but rather at a heightened awareness of the close links between interactional moves and context, as well as a greater understanding of the functions of discourse devices and nonlinguistic cues that experienced interpreters use.

Finally, I would like to stress—to interpreting students and working practitioners alike—that clarification does not always occur in response to problematic talk (or problematic interpreting). That is, even though the majority of clarification requests identified in this study could be said to represent "repair" in talk, as described by the CA literature, this was not always the case. Even if interpreters have native or nativelike bilingual fluency and are so experienced and/or confident that they feel no need to clarify, there is likely an expectation that a certain amount of clarification should take place nonetheless. Clarification is therefore an important tool for any healthcare interpreter: first and foremost in ensuring accuracy of information and mutual understanding between all of the parties but also in promoting trust in the interpreter's abilities.

ACKNOWLEDGMENTS

I would like to thank Dr. Linda Mann, Katrina Lancaster, and all of the interpreters who participated in this study. I would also like to acknowledge my PhD supervisors Prof. Jemina Napier and Dr. Maria Stubbe, as well as Dr. Agnes Terraschke and Dr. Jihong Wang for their assistance in the preparation of this manuscript.

NOTES

1. The study described in this chapter was conducted as part of a doctoral study on relational work in interpreted healthcare interaction (Major, 2013).
2. Interactional sociolinguistics traditionally relies on naturally occurring data (Gumperz, 2001, 2006); however, the current study was extracted from Major (2013), in which the role-play data were examined within an IS framework along with naturally occurring health interaction data.
3. Naturally, not all attempts at clarification and/or repair will be successful (Schegloff et al., 1977). Failed attempts at clarification, however, were not included in the analysis, and in any case, few were identified.
4. Note that not all interpreters who are native Auslan signers are untrained; this just happened to be the case in the current study.
5. This number includes the 15 interpreter-initiated English clarification requests (directed at the doctor) and the 45 patient-initiated clarification requests that were interpreted into English (see table 2).

"Sorry, Could You Explain That"? : 63

6. The total of 44 clarification requests includes the 26 interpreter-initiated ones in Auslan (directed at the patient) and the 18 doctor-initiated ones, all of which were interpreted into English (see table 2).

7. All three interpreters were relatively inexperienced at the time (at least in comparison to some of the other participants), with two, three, and four years of experience, respectively. However, it should be noted that both actors reported that they were very pleased with the interpreting styles of these three interpreters, and, as mentioned earlier, the doctor singled out Hugo as being her favorite interpreter to work with.

8. The patient also used SO (in Auslan) on three occasions, two of which appear to function as misplacement markers, as in Excerpt 8. One reason for this may be her fluency in English; that is, the actor may have borrowed an English discourse marker to indicate misplacement. Alternatively, this strategy may be used in the wider Auslan-signing community, although further research would be needed to confirm or disconfirm such a hypothesis.

REFERENCES

Angelelli, C. (2004). *Medical interpreting and cross-cultural communication.* Cambridge: Cambridge University Press.

Aranguri, C., Davidson, B., & Ramirez, R. (2006). Patterns of communication through interpreters: A detailed sociolinguistic analysis. *Journal of General Internal Medicine, 21,* 623–629.

Beach, W. A. (1993). Transitional regularities of "casual" "Okay" usages. *Journal of Pragmatics, 19,* 325–352.

Berk-Seligson, S. (1990). *The bilingual courtroom: Court interpreters in the judicial process.* Chicago: University of Chicago Press.

Bolden, G. (2006). Little words that matter: Discourse markers "so" and "oh" and the doing of other-attentiveness in social interaction. *Journal of Communication, 56,* 661–688.

Bolden, G. (2009). Implementing incipient actions: The discourse marker "so" in English conversation. *Journal of Pragmatics, 41,* 974–998.

Bot, H. (2005). *Dialogue interpreting in mental health.* Amsterdam: Rodopi.

Brown, S., & Attardo, S. (2000). *Understanding language structure, interaction, and variation: An introduction to applied linguistics and sociolinguistics for nonspecialists.* Ann Arbor: University of Michigan Press.

Coiera, E. W., Jayasuriya, R. A., Hardy, J., Bannan, A., & Thorpe, M. E. C. (2002). Communication loads on clinical staff in the emergency department. *Medical Journal of Australia, 176,* 415–418.

Davidson, B. (2000). The interpreter as institutional gate-keeper: The socio-linguistic role of interpreters in Spanish-English medical discourse. *Journal of Sociolinguistics, 4*(3), 379–405.

Elderkin-Thompson, V., Silver, R. C., & Waitzkin, H. (2001). When nurses double as interpreters: A study of Spanish-speaking patients in a US primary care setting. *Social Science & Medicine, 52,* 1343–1358.

Goffman, E. (1967). On face work. In E. Goffman (Ed.), *Interaction ritual: Essays on face to face behavior* (pp. 5–46). New York: Anchor.

Gumperz, J. (1982). *Discourse strategies.* Cambridge: Cambridge University Press.

Gumperz, J. (1999). On interactional sociolinguistic method. In S. Sarangi & C. Roberts (Eds.), *Talk, work and institutional order: Discourse in medical, mediation and management settings* (pp. 453–471). Berlin: Mouton de Gruyter.

Gumperz, J. (2001). Interactional sociolinguistics: A personal perspective. In D. Schiffrin, D. Tannen, & H. E. Hamilton (Eds.), *The handbook of discourse analysis* (pp. 215–229). Oxford: Blackwell.

Gumperz, J. (2006). Sociocultural knowledge in conversational inference. In A. Jaworski & N. Coupland (Eds.), *The discourse reader* (pp. 78–85). London: Routledge.

Hale, S. (2007). *Community interpreting.* New York: Palgrave Macmillan.

Harmer, L. M. (1999). Health care delivery and deaf people: Practice, problems, and recommendations for change. *Journal of Deaf Studies and Deaf Education, 4,* 73–110.

Heritage, J., & Clayman, S. (2010). *Talk in action: Interactions, identities, and institutions.* Malden, MA: Blackwell.

Hoza, J. (2007a). How interpreters convey social meaning: Implications for interpreted interaction. *Journal of Interpretation,* 39–68.

Hoza, J. (2007b). *It's not what you sign, it's how you sign it: Politeness in American Sign Language.* Washington, DC: Gallaudet University Press.

Hsieh, E. (this volume). Emerging trends and the corresponding challenges in bilingual health communication.

Jacobsen, B. (2008). Interactional pragmatics and court interpreting: An analysis of face. *Interpreting, 10,* 128–158.

Johnston, T. (2006). W(h)ither the Deaf community? Population, genetics, and the future of Australian Sign Language. *Sign Language Studies, 6,* 137–173.

Johnston, T., & Schembri, A. (2007). *Australian Sign Language: An introduction to sign language linguistics.* Cambridge: Cambridge University Press.

Laws, M. B., Heckscher, R., Mayo, S., Li, W., & Wilson, I. B. (2004). A new method for evaluating the quality of medical interpretation. *Medical Care, 42,* 71–80.

Leeson, L., Sheikh, A., Rozanes, I., Grehan, C., & Matthews, P. A. (this volume). Critical care required: Access to interpreted health care in Ireland.

Locher, M., & Watts, R. (2005). Politeness theory and relational work. *Journal of Politeness Research, 1,* 9–33.

Major, G. (2013). "Healthcare interpreting as relational practice." PhD diss., Macquarie University, Sydney.

Major, G., & Napier, J. (2012). Interpreting and knowledge mediation in the healthcare setting: What do we really mean by "accuracy"? *Linguistica Antverpiensia, 11,* 207–225.

Major, G., Napier, J., Ferrara, L., & Johnston, T. (2012). Exploring lexical gaps in Australian Sign Language for the purposes of health communication. *Communication and Medicine, 9*(1), 37–47.

Major, G., Napier, J., & Stubbe, M. (2012). "What happens truly, not text book!": Using authentic interactions in discourse training for healthcare interpreters. In K. Malcolm & L. Swabey (Eds.), *In our hands: Educating healthcare interpreters* (pp. 27–53). Washington, DC: Gallaudet University Press.

Merlini, R., & Favaron, R. (2005). Examining the "voice of interpreting" in speech pathology. *Interpreting, 7,* 263–302.

Metzger, M. (1999). *Sign language interpreting: Deconstructing the myth of neutrality.* Washington, DC: Gallaudet University Press.

Metzger, M. (2000). Interactive role-plays as a teaching strategy. In C. Roy (Ed.), *Innovative practices for teaching sign language interpreters* (pp. 83–107). Washington, DC: Gallaudet University Press.

Metzger, M. (2005). Interpreted discourse: Learning and recognizing what interpreters do in interaction. In C. B. Roy (Ed.), *Advances in teaching sign language interpreters* (pp. 100–122). Washington, DC: Gallaudet University Press.

Meyer, B., Apfelbaum, B., Pöchhacker, F., & Bischoff, A. (2003). Analysing interpreted doctor-patient communication from the perspectives of linguistics, interpreting studies and health sciences. In L. Brunette, G. Bastin, I. Hemlin, & H. Clarke (Eds.), *The critical link 3: Interpreters in the community* (pp. 67–79). Amsterdam: Benjamins.

Napier, J. (2004). Sign language interpreter training, testing, and accreditation: An international comparison. *American Annals of the Deaf, 149,* 350–359.

Napier, J. (2011, December). Interpreters and the law: Research on signed language interpreting in NSW courts. Paper presented at Applied Linguistics as a Meeting Place: 2nd combined conference of the Applied Linguistics Association of Australia and the Applied Linguistics Association of New Zealand. University of Canberra & Australian National University, Canberra, Australia.

Napier, J., Major, G., & Ferrara, L. (2011). Medical Signbank: A cure-all for the aches and pains of medical sign language interpreting? In L. Leeson,

M. Vermeerbergen, & S. Wurm (Eds.), *Signed language interpreting: Preparation, practice and performance* (pp. 110–137). Manchester: St. Jerome.

Napier, J., McKee, R., & Goswell, D. (2006). *Sign language interpreting: Theory and practice in Australia and New Zealand*. Sydney: Federation Press.

Pöchhacker, F., & Shlesinger, M. (2005). Introduction: Discourse-based research on healthcare interpreting. *Interpreting, 7*, 157–165.

Roberts, C. (2006). Continuities and discontinuities in doctor-patient consultations in a multilingual society. In M. Gotti & F. Salager-Meyer (Eds.), *Advances in medical discourse analysis: Oral and written contexts* (pp. 177–195). Bern: Lang.

Roberts, C., Wass, V., Jones, R., Sarangi, S., & Gillett, A. (2003). A discourse analysis study of "good" and "poor" communication in an OSCE: A proposed new framework for teaching students. *Medical Education, 37*, 192–201.

Roy, C. (1989). "A sociolinguistic analysis of the interpreter's role in the turn exchanges of an interpreted event." PhD diss., Georgetown University, Washington, DC.

Roy, C. (2000). *Interpreting as a discourse process*. Oxford: Oxford University Press.

Sanheim, L. (2003). Turn exchange in an interpreted medical encounter. In M. Metzger (Ed.), *From topic boundaries to omission: New research on interpretation* (pp. 27–54). Washington, DC: Gallaudet University Press.

Schegloff, E., Jefferson, G., & Sacks, H. (1977). The preference for self-correction in the organisation of repair in conversation. *Language, 53*, 361–382.

Schiffrin, D. (1987). *Discourse markers*. Cambridge: Cambridge University Press.

Smith, D. H., & C. L. Ramsey. (2004). Classroom discourse practices of a deaf teacher using American Sign Language. *Sign Language Studies, 5*(1), 39–62.

Tannen, D. (2000). Don't just sit there—interrupt! Pacing and pausing in conversational style. *American Speech, 75*(4), 393–395.

Ten Have, P. (1995). Medical ethnomethodology: An overview. *Human Studies, 18*, 245–261.

Ten Have, P. (1999). *Doing conversation analysis: A practical guide*. London: Sage.

Todd, A. D. (1983). A diagnosis of doctor-patient discourse in the prescription of contraception. In S. Fisher (Ed.), *The social organization of doctor-patient communication* (pp. 159–187). Washington, DC: Center for Applied Linguistics.

van den Bogaerde, B., & de Lange, R. (this volume). Healthcare accessibility and the role of SL interpreters.

Van Herreweghe, M. (2002). Turn-taking mechanisms and active participation in meetings with Deaf and hearing participants in Flanders. In C. Lucas (Ed.), *Turn-taking, fingerspelling, and contact in signed languages* (pp. 73–103). Washington, DC: Gallaudet University Press.

Vine, B., Johnson, G., O'Brien, J., & Robertson, S. (2002). *Wellington Archive of New Zealand English transcriber's manual.* Wellington, Victoria University of Wellington, Language in the Workplace Occasional Papers 5.

Wadensjö, C. (1998). *Interpreting as interaction.* London: Addison Wesley Longman.

Watts, R. (2003). *Politeness.* Cambridge: Cambridge University Press.

TRANSCRIPTION CONVENTIONS

The transcription conventions used in this study are largely based on Vine, Johnson, O'Brien, & Robertson (2002).

English Only	
lowercase text	English

Auslan Only	
SMALL CAPITALS in text FULL CAPITALS in technical transcripts	Auslan
HYPHENATED-WORDS	Represents one sign in Auslan
OKAY+	Sign is repeated once

Both English and Auslan	
((laughs)), ((obscured))	Nonlinguistic feature; depicting sign in Auslan; transcriber's comment
((laughs)) okay	Nonlinguistic feature that carries on over talk
((okay)) RIGHT *((RIGHT))* okay	Simultaneous speaking and signing
okay:	Word/sign is held
oka-	Word/sign is not completed
(.)	One second pause or less
(okay)	Best guess at an unclear utterance
( )	Unclear utterance that cannot be transcribed
A: [okay] B: [RIGHT]	Overlapping talk

A: [okay then we'll decide that later] B: [RIGHT OKAY NO PROBLEM] C: [OKAY]	Overlapping talk where C's overlapping contribution is minimal (for clarity, the exact place where C's contribution stops is not marked)
okay= =right	Indicates a continuous utterance even though it is on more than one line
gray text/ GRAY TEXT	Text that is not the focus of the excerpt

Clean Version Transcripts

black text	English
underlined text	Auslan, translated into English
gray text	English text that is not the focus of the excerpt
underlined gray text	Auslan text that is not the focus of the excerpt

Emerging Trends and the Corresponding Challenges in Bilingual Health Communication

Elaine Hsieh

ABSTRACT

The research on interpreter-mediated health care has advanced tre-mendously in both its theoretical scope and depth of analysis in recent years. I first identify the emerging trends in conceptualizing bilingual health communication by examining recent research find-ings. The four trends identified are: (a) recognizing interpreters as active participants in medical encounters, (b) examining medical interpreting as a coordinated accomplishment, (c) identifying the complexity of clinical demands, and (d) exploring contextual fac-tors in bilingual health care. Using the literature in bilingual health care and the data I've collected in the last 15 years, I explore these trends and provide insights into the current literature. I also identify future research directions based on these emerging trends.

Interpreters can be invaluable assets in helping minority patients nav-igate the healthcare system. In one of the largest studies of functional health literacy, 61% of Spanish-speaking patients in public hospitals had inadequate or marginal health literacy (Williams et al., 1995). Individuals with limited English proficiency (LEP) and low health literacy are at high risk for poor health, with LEP posing a greater health risk than low health literacy (Sentell & Braun, 2012). When compared to their English-speaking counterparts, LEP patients make fewer comments, and the ones they do make are more likely to be ignored by their providers (Rivadeneyra, Elderkin-Thompson, Silver, & Waitzkin, 2000). As a result, LEP patients are significantly disadvantaged when interacting with pro-viders (Ramirez, Engel, & Tang, 2008). Two major reviews have found that providing professional interpreter services improves patients' quality of care, treatment processes, health outcomes, satisfaction, and adherence

(Flores, 2005; Karliner, Jacobs, Chen, & Mutha, 2007). Some researchers even found that the quality of healthcare services and health outcomes of interpreted patients are equivalent to and, at times, better than those of English-speaking patients (Bernstein et al., 2002; Gany, Leng, et al., 2007; Hampers & McNulty, 2002). These findings suggest that interpreters can (a) facilitate patients' information-seeking and help-seeking skills with providers, (b) enhance patients' utilization of healthcare facilities, and (c) improve patients' health literacy and autonomy in their illness events.

Although researchers and practitioners generally agree on interpreters' positive influence in bilingual health care, little is known about the pathways and processes for accomplishing these positive outcomes. Somehow, the processes by which the interpreters shape the quality and process of care are simply taken for granted and yet remain a mystery. This is attributable to the traditional conceptualization of interpreters' roles and functions.

Moving beyond the Conduit Model of Interpreting

Several researchers have proposed communication guidelines (i.e., practice guidelines for providers to follow when working with interpreters) for the proper choice and effective use of various types of interpreters (e.g., Poss & Beeman, 1999; Tribe & Lane, 2009); however, until very recently, many of the guidelines have not been supported or examined by research (Flores, 2000). Because interpreters have significant influence over the process and the quality of bilingual health communication (Flores, Abreu, Schwartz, & Hill, 2000), it is essential that researchers do not take these guidelines for granted and begin to examine the influences and practices of interpreters in medical settings. By doing so, researchers may uncover the underlying factors that can facilitate and/or compromise the quality of bilingual health care.

Many researchers and practitioners have traditionally put great emphasis on the importance of and the necessity for interpreters to act as conduits (i.e., to transfer information neutrally without editorializing information; Simon, Zyzanski, Durand, Jimenez, & Kodish, 2006). Several physician researchers have continued to categorize any discrepancy between the original and interpreted texts as errors even today (e.g., omission, addition, substitution, and editorialization; Flores, Abreu, Barone, Bachur, & Lin, 2012; Gany, Kapelusznik, et al., 2007). When any deviation from an original text is marked as an error, interpreters are confined in a conduit role, as the only "correct" interpretation is the one that provides the direct word-for-word linguistic relay of the source-language texts. In other words, interpreters are conceptualized as (and expected to be) passive participants in the communicative process, relaying information from one language to another with minimal interference or personal judgment.

The ideology of the interpreter as a neutral, faithful, nonthinking, and passive participant in provider-patient interactions is also reflected in the codes of ethics and training for medical interpreters. Two reviews have concluded that many of the codes of ethics for medical interpreters emphasize an interpretation style that calls for an objective and neutral role (Dysart-Gale, 2005; Kaufert & Putsch, 1997). The prevalence of the conduit model is also reflected in the public's attitudes toward and expectations of interpreters, envisioning them as neutral translating machines (Brämberg & Sandman, 2013; Fatahi, Hellstrom, Skott, & Mattsson, 2008; Rosenberg, Leanza, & Seller, 2007), which is also embedded in interpreters' training and communicative styles (e.g., reduced nonverbal interactions with other speakers and minimized emotional expression; see also Hsieh, 2010). In short, the interpreter-as-conduit model minimizes the complexity of interpreting processes by minimizing, if not ignoring, the complexity of interpreters' roles and functions (Llewellyn-Jones & Lee, 2011).

The recent literature in bilingual health care, however, indicates several important and emerging trends in conceptualizing bilingual health communication. As researchers from a wide variety of disciplines have successfully challenged the preference for the interpreter-as-conduit model, a new world has been opened to researchers of medical interpreting. It is important to note that the identification of these emerging trends in this chapter is not a result of a quantitative analysis based on publication frequencies (cf. Brisset, Leanza, & Laforest, 2013). Rather, the trends highlighted here represent important shifts in conceptualizing bilingual health communication, shedding insights into research questions and directions that have been largely ignored in the past literature. Although these trends may be interconnected, each promises distinctive and exciting potentials for theorists and practitioners.

BACKGROUND

The chapter is formulated as a review that aims to provide a theoretical frame for bilingual health communication. By focusing on the phenomenon of interpreter-mediated medical encounters, I surveyed the literature in various disciplines, including medicine, communication, sociology, interpreting studies, and others. In addition, I supplement discussions with the data I collected for prior studies to support and/ or explore the theoretical and practical potential for each trend. Three datasets are included in this review. The first includes a one-year ethnographic study. I recruited 2 Mandarin Chinese interpreters, 4 patients, and 12 providers. I shadowed the interpreters in their daily routines and audio-recorded their interactions with the patients and the providers. In total, 12 medical encounters (each lasting 1–1.5 hours) were observed, audiotaped, and transcribed. The other two datasets are in-depth interviews and focus groups with healthcare providers and interpreters. I recruited 26 interpreters (from 17 languages) and conducted 14 individual and 6 dyadic interviews (each lasting 1–1.5 hours). Interpreters included in this study are all considered professional, on-site interpreters. The interviews focused on exploring interpreters' understanding and practice of their roles.

After the initial analysis of the interpreters' interview data, my research team recruited 39 healthcare providers from a major healthcare facility in the southern United States as a part of NIH-funded research to examine the providers' views of the roles of medical interpreters. We recruited 39 providers from five specialty areas: OB/GYN (n = 8), emergency medicine (n = 7), oncology (n = 11), mental health (n = 7), and nursing (n = 6). In total, the research team conducted 8 specialty-specific focus groups (each lasting 1–1.5 hours) and 14 individual interviews (each lasting 1–1.5 hours). Details of the interview questions for both providers and interpreters have been published in a previous study (Hsieh, 2010). Based on these datasets, I have examined interpreters' communicative strategies as demonstrated in their performances of specific roles (Hsieh, 2006a, 2007, 2008) and their corresponding challenges to provider-interpreter collaboration (Hsieh, 2010; Hsieh, Ju, & Kong, 2010). Although the narratives may have appeared in my prior work, they are included here as exemplars in supporting the themes I identified.

The transcription includes two primary types of notation. The texts are CAPITALIZED when they are the speakers' emphasis and *italicized* when they are my emphasis. Each participant is assigned a pseudonym, with a superscript I for interpreters and H for healthcare providers.

TREND 1: RECOGNIZING INTERPRETERS AS ACTIVE PARTICIPANTS

Recognizing interpreters as active participants is one of the earliest trends in shaping the recent paradigm shift in research in bilingual health communication. By recognizing interpreters' active roles, researchers can then begin to examine the complexity of interpreting as a communicative process. The following arguments and research findings successfully validate this trend: (a) interpreters' performance and self-perceived visibility, (b) the conduit role requires active judgment and intervention, and (c) nonliteral interpretation is necessary in healthcare settings.

Interpreters' Performance and Self-Perceived Visibility

Although the conduit model defines interpreters' appropriate performances through their invisibility, such a conceptualization has been challenged as impractical, if not unrealistic (Dysart-Gale, 2005; Hsieh, 2009). Interpreters also have questioned the conduit model (Hsieh, 2006a, 2008). For example, Silvia[1], a Spanish interpreter who has more than 10 years of experience, explained, "*Something is not right. I keep thinking about this interpreting.* This interpreting is very robotic. You know, you are a human being. You are a person. And you are not supposed to show emotions?"

Starting from the mid-1990s, researchers have noted that interpreters actively participate in the communicative process. Linell (1997, p. 55) explained, "Apart from being relayers (translators), interpreters must (and do) act as chairpersons and gatekeepers, monitoring the social and discursive situation" (see also Fenton, 1997; Wadensjö, 1998). Davidson (2000, 2001) and Angelelli (2002) also have found that interpreters function as covert co-diagnosticians and informational gatekeepers in medical encounters. In short, when observing interpreters' practices, researchers consistently found interpreters adopting nonconduit behaviors. In fact, Angelelli (2002, 2004) argued that interpreters perceived their role as visible in a variety of settings (e.g., courtrooms, conferences, and hospitals), a finding also supported by more recent studies (Hsieh, 2008; McDowell, Messias, & Estrada, 2011).

Many researchers have examined interpreters' construction of interactional frames to structure provider-patient interactions (Metzger, 1999; Pöchhacker & Shlesinger, 2005); however, very few studies examine interpreters' behaviors outside the medical encounter (i.e., beyond provider-patient interactions and/or outside the appointment). This research design blind spot is partially attributable to the traditional emphasis on the interpreter-as-conduit model, which implies that interpreters do not have tasks or roles to perform when the primary speakers are not in the same settings. However, an interpreter may actively denounce certain identities while claiming others when interacting with others to manage competing and/or conflicting goals (Hsieh, 2006a). For example, Christie[1] explained that she provided assistance to patients outside the medical encounter, because she was also a "volunteer for a charity organization" and did not perform those acts as an interpreter. An interpreter may also actively educate patients on the interactional norms and social sequences when providers are not present, expecting the patient to self-initiate the interactional sequences once the provider is present (for specific examples, see Hsieh, 2008, 2009). In short, interpreters have sophisticated understanding and management of their interactional frames, utilizing a wide variety of resources (e.g., discourse pragmatics, interpersonal relationships, and environmental contexts) both inside and outside a medical encounter to shape and influence others' communicative behaviors.

Conduit Role Requires Active Judgment and Intervention

Moving beyond the debate of interpreter (in)visibility, I have argued that interpreters' conduit role is *not* a passive role that simply relays the voices of others (see Hsieh, 2008). There are a couple of different ways in which an interpreter-as-conduit is actively involved in the process and content of provider-patient interactions. First, when discussing their conduit performances, interpreters talked about strategically adopting specific nonverbal behaviors to manipulate others' communicative behaviors and to reinforce the provider-patient relationship. For example, Sherry[1] explained, "What happens is when you stand here, the patient is going to look at you and you have to be doing this [looking down at the floor], 'I'm the voice, just look at each other.' So, if you stand behind the patient, then the patient can't [turning their head back], and they look at the physician, and then they are looking at each other." Second, interpreters often refrain from interpreting when one of the participants responded in the other speaker's language (e.g., they do not interpret if a patient answers "yes [in English]" to a provider's question), arguing that such behaviors reaffirm the primary relationship between the provider and the patient.

However, to do so, an interpreter must actively monitor the process of interaction, making real-time judgments about when and whether to interpret. In short, "interpreters' understanding of the conduit role is not a non-thinking, robotic way of interpreting but includes specific strategies to accomplish the communicative goal of reinforcing the provider-patient relationship" (Hsieh, 2008, p. 1381). In other words, interpreters-as-conduits are still active participants in the provider-patient interactions.

Nonliteral Interpretation as Necessity

The interpreter-as-conduit model assumes that: (a) all participants are competent speakers who can communicate effectively and appropriately, (b) it is desirable to maintain the existing structure of relationship and patterns of communication, and (c) there are minimal differences between speakers' cultural knowledge and social practices (for detailed discussion, see Hsieh, Pitaloka, & Johnson, 2013). However, due to the power, cultural, social, and/or educational differences in provider–LEP patient relationships, these assumptions are likely to be problematic. As a result, by adopting the conduit role, the interpreter is likely to reinforce the existing social/power imbalance in the provider–LEP patient relationship.

A recent review of 61 studies concluded that "non-literal translation appears to be a prerequisite for effective and accurate communication" in healthcare settings (Brisset et al., 2013, p. 131). Two recent studies have noted that interpreters' alterations to the original texts at times can lead to positive effects in clinical encounters (Butow, Goldstein, et al., 2011; Jackson, Nguyen, Hu, Harris, & Terasaki, 2011). Interpreters are active participants who systematically adopt purposeful strategies to improve a patient's health literacy, to protect institutional resources, to reduce the cultural gap between the provider and the patient, to reconcile provider-patient conflicts, and to ensure the quality of provider-patient interactions (Fatahi et al., 2008; Greenhalgh, Robb, & Scambler, 2006; Hsieh, 2007, 2009; Rosenberg, Seller, & Leanza, 2008). Metzger (1999) noted that interpreters' ability to identify, assume, and negotiate other speakers' goals is crucial in fulfilling others' satisfaction. As researchers noticed interpreters' active involvement in the communicative process, they have also questioned interpreters' ethics and raised concerns about how some of their communicative strategies may infringe on providers' authority or patients' autonomy (Hsieh, 2010; Hsieh et al., 2010). It is important not to romanticize interpreters' active role in interpreter-mediated medical encounters and examine their performance and communicative strategies critically.

Addressing Challenges within Trend I

Recognizing interpreters' active involvement in the communicative process is one of the most important trends in interpreting studies because such an approach highlights their agency, an issue that is largely ignored and undertheorized in the traditions of interpreting studies. Acknowledging interpreters' active roles in healthcare settings opens doors for researchers to critically examine (a) the specific process and ethical/clinical impact of interpreters' active involvement in the healthcare and delivery process and (b) other participants' understanding and evaluation of interpreters' active involvement.

For example, Brisset and colleagues (2013) questioned Karliner et al.'s (2007) finding, which concluded that when compared to ad hoc interpreters, professional interpreters make fewer errors (i.e., deviations from the original texts) and enhance provider satisfaction. By noting that interpreters' deviation from original texts may serve functional, meaningful purposes and that patients may have different criteria in evaluating the quality of interpreting, Brisset et al. argued that Karliner et al.'s understanding of the quality of interpreting and its corresponding impact oversimplifies the discursive process of medical interpreting and is biased toward providers' perspectives. In fact, a recent study found that even though 31% of interpreted utterances were altered, only 5% were clinically significant, with 1% having a positive effect and 4% having a negative effect on the clinical encounter (Jackson et al., 2011). A different study found that 70% of nonequivalent interpretations were inconsequential or positive, 10% could result in misunderstanding, 5% adopted a more authoritarian tone than the original speech, and 3% conveyed more certainty (Butow, Goldstein, et al., 2011). From this perspective, the key questions here should not be whether interpreters actively shape the process and content of interpreting but *why, how,* and *what happens when* they do so. What are the kinds of alterations that lead to positive outcomes versus negative ones? What kind of outcomes?

To move beyond the argument of interpreters' agency in healthcare settings, researchers need to question the effectiveness and appropriateness of interpreters' strategic behaviors and to consider how these behaviors impact other participants' identities, relationships, and agency as well as the overall communicative activity. It is time for researchers and practitioners to examine the reality and boundaries of interpreters' active involvement in healthcare settings.

TREND 2: EXAMINING MEDICAL INTERPRETING AS A COORDINATED ACCOMPLISHMENT

Whereas the first trend highlights interpreters' agency, the second trend in recent research presented here highlights the interdependence of the multiparty interactions in interpreter-mediated medical encounters. All participants (e.g., the provider, the interpreter, the patient, and even family members) in interpreter-mediated medical encounters can influence the process and quality of bilingual health communication (Fatahi et al., 2008; Greenhalgh et al., 2006). This trend is critical because it recognizes the impact of others in the interpreting process. Traditionally, an interpreter is viewed as the person who is solely responsible for the quality of interpreting. However, recent studies have challenged this presumption by noting: (a) the interdependence of participant performances, (b) participants' competition and coordination for control, and (c) medical interpreting as a goal-oriented activity.

The Interdependence of Participant Performances

Providers', patients', and interpreters' choices of a communicative style serve specific functions and are interdependent (Roy, 2000). The quality of interpretation by untrained interpreters can vary dramatically from one setting to another. For example, "A nurse [interpreter] could do an excellent job with one physician only to have difficulties with the next one. . . . Every physician . . . had an individual style for relating to the patient, and the nurse [interpreter] had to accommodate that style" (Elderkin-Thompson, Silver, & Waitzkin, 2001, p. 1355). Interpreters are more likely to misinterpret or to ignore a physician's questions when they are structurally more complicated (Harrison, Bhatt, Carey, & Ebden, 1988). These findings underline the importance of the physicians' role and communicative strategies in achieving successful bilingual health communication.

The interdependence of participants' communicative competence is not unique to bilingual healthcare. Patient communicative competence (e.g., the ability to seek and provide information) is positively correlated with the quality of provider information provision (Cegala & Post, 2009). When physicians interacted with high-participation patients, they provided more information overall, more information in response to questions, and volunteered more information than when they spoke with low-participation patients (Cegala, Street, & Clinch, 2007). The question here is whether interpreters (should) influence and/or enhance other speakers' communicative competence through their interpreting.

In bilingual healthcare, interpreters can play a significant role in this process by overtly and covertly enhancing the LEP patient's and/or provider's communicative competence. For example, to ensure effective and appropriate provider-interpreter interactions, interpreters may conceal the providers' problematic behaviors or ask questions on behalf of the patient (Hsieh, 2008). The following is a good example of an interpreter influencing participant communicative competence:

Extract 001

101	H:	One-third of a cup of rice is a serving.
102	I:	三分之一杯的煮熟的米飯就是, 一個分量。
103		(One-third of a cup of cooked rice is a serving.)
104	H:	Does she have measuring cups at home?
105	I:	家裡有沒有量杯?
106		(Do you have a measuring cup at home?)
107	P:	就是米飯的那個杯子。
108		(Just the cup for rice.)
109	I:	Is it the same measuring cup for rice?
110	H:	hmhm, yes.
111	P:	都是一樣的。
112		(It's the same.)
113	I:	Is it the same?
114	H:	The-
115	I:	Are they?

| 116 | H: | I don't know what she is referring to. I'll show her what I have. |

| 117 | I: | 她有一個。 |

| 118 | | (She has one) |

| 119 | | (H took out a glass measuring cup from the drawer.) |

| 120 | P: | 這麼大阿！ |

| 121 | | (That's big!) |

Claire[I] adopted several strategies here that are essential in improving participant communicative competence. For example, when the patient made statements (i.e., "just the cup for rice" [line 107] and "it's the same" [line 111]), Claire[I] changed it to a direct question to seek and clarify information ("Is it the same measuring cup for rice?" [line 109]). Similarly, when the patient acknowledged the provider's confirmation (line 110) by reinstating the implications ("It's the same" [line 111]), Claire[I] treated the patient's statement as an active information-seeking question, "Is it the same?" (line 113). In fact, Claire[I]'s persistence in seeking and verifying the information exposed a miscommunication that the provider would have originally ignored. Claire[I]'s direct question ("is it the same?" [line 113]) and its reinstatement ("Are they?" [line 115]) forced the provider to admit a potential misunderstanding ("I don't know what she's referring to" [line 116]) and to resolve the problem ("I'll show her what I have" [line 116]). The patient's comment on line 121 ("That's big!") showed that the measuring cups that the provider and the patient had in mind were very different in size; thus there could have been significant clinical consequences had Claire[I] not insisted on pursuing accurate information. From this perspective, Claire[I] enabled the patient to be much more engaged and competent in the provider-patient interaction that the patient actually was by herself.

Providers' and patients' identities and relationships can also be influenced by the interpreter, resulting in clinical impacts. One study found that, when interpreters are friendly and emotionally supportive, Latino patients are more receptive to providers' suggestions of amniocentesis (Preloran, Browner, & Lieber, 2005). A neutral/slightly cheerful interpreter can act as a buffer for the patient against the negative mood expressed by a despondent therapist (Brunson & Lawrence, 2002). In fact, interpreters actively provide emotional support by noting the needs to bridge cultural differences and to ensure quality care (Hsieh, 2006a, 2008; Hsieh & Hong, 2010; Leanza, 2008). On the other hand, interpreters' behaviors may compromise other speakers' communicative competence. For example, when interpreters focus on medical information and ignore providers' rapport-building talk, providers may appear emotionally detached (Aranguri, Davidson, & Ramirez, 2006).

In summary, all participants' communicative behaviors can shape the quality of interpreting. Interpreters can significantly shape others' communicative competence, identity, and relationships, all of which may carry significant clinical impacts. Alternatively, providers (and patients) can influence the quality of interpreters' performances through their ability to adapt, accommodate, and anticipate challenges in interpreter-mediated interactions.

Participants' Competition and Coordination for Control

Traditionally, interpreters are conceptualized as the only persons who have control over the content and quality of interpreting; as a result, both the research and practice communities have directed attention to restricting and controlling interpreters' power, such as requiring them to perform the conduit role to limit their influence in provider-patient interactions (Leanza, 2008). However, researchers have noted that other participants are not passive in the interpreting process. A recent review identified the trust-control-power triangle when working with interpreters as one of the three major themes in medical interpreting (Brisset et al., 2013). The trust-control-power triangle highlights the inherent tension in the provider-patient-interpreter relationship as each individual holds a unique perspective and potentially competing objectives concerning the patient's illness event.

Researchers have examined the collaboration and competition of participants in interpreter-mediated interactions from different perspectives. For example, different participants' competing agendas and/or expectations may influence their communicative processes. The latest findings suggest that family interpreters and professional interpreters may be good at different tasks due to differences in their (personal) agendas and communicative styles (Leanza, Boivin, & Rosenberg, 2010; Rosenberg et al., 2008). For example, professional interpreters may refrain from adopting cultural broker and advocate functions (as they are trained to be neutral conduits), whereas family interpreters may interject their personal perspectives in the medical discourse and be better during medical history taking sessions (Leanza et al., 2010). At the same time, researchers have found that a provider may also develop different expectations and adopt different communicative strategies when working with a family versus a professional interpreter (Hsieh et al., 2010; Rosenberg et al., 2007). For example, Cordell[H] said that she prefers a paid interpreter because "for right or wrong somebody who works for the [hospital] is going to translate what I said word for word, as opposed to family members who might tell their mother what they want to hear." From this perspective, a provider may have a stronger sense of trust and alliance with a professional interpreter than a family interpreter. A recent study also found that physicians are more likely to interrupt a professional interpreter (as opposed to a family interpreter) when the patient discloses contextualized everyday narratives (Leanza et al., 2010). Finally, whereas some studies suggest that patients may prefer family interpreters (Green, Free, Bhavnani, & Newman, 2005), others suggest that patients may prefer professional interpreters (MacFarlane et al., 2009). These findings suggest the individuals involved in bilingual healthcare may actively shape the communicative process based on their personal perspectives as well as their expectations for others' roles, functions, and performances.

The participants' perspectives, however, are not always compatible with each other. As a result, participants in bilingual healthcare often compete with each other to maintain and/or exert control over the communicative process. Earlier I noted that the conduit model is a way for the institution to control the interpreters' power and influence. However, providers also can exert control both inside and outside the medical encounter. For example, providers may question an interpreter if the interpreter fails to use the key term that the provider recognizes in the other language ("I did not hear you say *el glaucoma*") or if the interpreter's narrative is significantly shorter or longer than the patient's narrative (e.g., "You said more. What did you say?"). Providers may also monitor a patient's nonverbal communication to ensure that the interpreter conveyed the intended emotional tone (e.g., hopefulness) or repeat a particular portion of talk because they suspect the interpreter did not interpret faithfully. Many interpreters and providers in my study also reported incidents in which a provider filed a complaint or even requested that an interpreter be fired due to problematic interpreting. In short, although interpreters are the only bilingual persons in the medical encounter, providers do not simply accept their control over the provider-patient communication. Rather, providers actively monitor the discursive process and revise their communicative strategies, using both discursive strategies and institutional power to ensure that interpreters' performances are subject to their control.

Although the literature has traditionally focused on interpreters' management of the discursive process, no one has full control over medical encounters as each participant contributes to the dynamic, emergent communicative process through their competition for and resistance to control. As researchers examine how individuals incorporate their perspectives and agendas into the discursive process, it appears that participants' values and practices are shaped by forces beyond their individual perspectives.

Medical Interpreting as a Goal-Oriented Activity

Several researchers have suggested that organizational culture and environmental contexts are influential in shaping participants' evaluation of the quality of medical interpreting (Brisset et al., 2013), arguing that interpreters' performances are often shaped by system-level expectations and constraints (Bischoff & Hudelson, 2010b; Hsieh, 2006a). Interpreters often report frustration and conflicts when they feel that the conduit model has failed to ensure the quality of care (Brisset et al., 2013; Hsieh, 2006a, 2008). In addition, providers may also find interpreters' conduit performances to be disruptive to the communicative process. For example, Cara[H] commented, "Because the translator is a PERSON, for better or worse there, a person. And *for them to act like they are not. It just doesn't work*. I mean, it just doesn't work." When asked what he does when a patient tries to use broken English to communicate directly with a provider, Albert[I] said, "I let them to feel that they are not just a patient or a client or a patient begging somebody for the words to understand. He can express himself, how he feels, maybe." Some of the latest studies suggest that healthcare settings present unique contexts that set medical interpreting apart from other forms of interpreting. For example, compared to court interpreters, professional medical interpreters adopt different interpreting strategies, such as *suspended rendition* (e.g., delay interpretation for several turns but provide acknowledgment tokens that suggest attentive listening), to encourage the participation of medical dialogues, which also are favored by other participants (Gavioli & Baraldi, 2011). From this perspective, providers and interpreters seem to suggest that the criteria they use to evaluate the quality of their work is not based solely on the equivalences of the information conveyed in different languages.

Unlike other forms of interpreting (e.g., court interpreting and conference interpreting), medical interpreters are part of a larger healthcare team, in which the team is assembled with the purpose of improving patients' quality of care and health outcomes. In other words, the emphasis on neutrality and faithfulness upheld in the traditional interpreting literature can be ancillary to larger healthcare goals. Medical interpreting, thus, becomes a goal-oriented activity that is situated in the contexts of successful provider-patient communication.

Addressing Challenges within Trend 2

By recognizing medical interpreting as a coordinated communicative activity, researchers open up theoretical possibilities and intervention points in bilingual healthcare. This is a revolutionary step in the theoretical development of interpreting studies. By doing so, researchers can move beyond a generic claim of how other participants are also important in the interpreting process or a simple encouragement to other participants to familiarize themselves with interpreters' styles. Instead, this emerging trend seeks to understand both the process by which coordination occurs and the factors that shape such coordination.

For example, to achieve optimal bilingual healthcare, researchers need to understand how different individuals negotiate and coordinate their communicative needs, therapeutic objectives, and other concerns during dynamic, emergent provider-patient interactions. If interpreters are active participants, as suggested by Trend 1, do they have their personal goals and agenda in the medical encounter? How are those goals and agendas determined? How do they emerge during medical encounters? Are certain ways of negotiating these goals and agendas better than others? Researchers need to examine the theoretical, practical, clinical, and ethical consequences of the communicative strategies employed by the participants.

TREND 3: IDENTIFYING THE COMPLEXITY OF CLINICAL DEMANDS

The third trend in bilingual health communication emerges as researchers and practitioners acknowledge the unique characteristics of medical interpreting that set it apart from other forms of interpreting. Rather than focusing on the values embedded in traditional views of interpreting (e.g., accuracy, faithfulness, and neutrality), researchers seek to examine how healthcare services present distinctive demands and expectations that shape interpreting practices. By recognizing the complexity and reality of healthcare practices, researchers have begun to address two puzzles in bilingual healthcare, which I discuss shortly. Two themes support the development of this trend: (a) the reality of interpreter diversity and (b) providers' clinical decision making for interpreting.

The Reality of Interpreter Diversity

The first puzzle concerns the conflicting findings on the impact of medical interpreters (Hsieh, 2006b). Until the late 1990s, most studies have treated medical interpreters as a single category, with minimal discussion about the types of interpreters included in the studies. However, in recent years there has been an increasing trend toward identifying the specific types of interpreters and even comparing different types of interpreters (Brisset et al., 2013). Several studies have provided evidence of the benefits of providing interpreter services, arguing that when LEP patients have access to interpreters, their experiences with healthcare services and their health outcomes are often equivalent to, if not better than, those of English-speaking patients (Andrulis, Goodman, & Pryor, 2002; Bernstein et al., 2002). However, other studies have observed a negative impact, noting that interpreters often facilitated LEP patients' experiences of health disparities as these patients frequently have their comments ignored, are less likely to receive referrals, and are less satisfied with their care even in areas unrelated to language (Baker & Hayes, 1997; Baker, Parker, Williams, Coates, & Pitkin, 1996; Sarver & Baker, 2000). Hsieh (2006b) argued the conflicting findings were attributable to a failure to recognize the diversity of interpreters, noting that different types of interpreters have distinctive impacts on the dynamics and processes of communication.

In recent years, researchers and providers have shifted away from the argument that only professional interpreters should be used in healthcare settings as such an expectation is highly dependent on the patient's language and the service location and hours (Bischoff & Hudelson, 2010a). Rather, researchers and practitioners have argued that the ability of providers to work with different types of medical interpreters (e.g., family members, telephone interpreters, and on-site interpreters) is critical to the efficiency, quality, and informal economy of bilingual healthcare (Rosenberg et al., 2008). Although several reviews have noted the benefits of professional interpreters (Flores, 2005; Karliner et al., 2007), such observations do not equate to the conclusion that professional interpreters are universally better than nonprofessional interpreters. Evidence suggests that professional interpreters and nonprofessional interpreters, such as family interpreters, do behave differently in medical encounters (Butow, Goldstein, et al., 2011; Leanza et al., 2010). However, these studies also demonstrate that professional interpreters are not necessarily better. For example, although professional interpreters are less likely than family interpreters to produce nonequivalent interpretations, their nonequivalent interpretations have a higher proportion of negative consequences than those of family interpreters (26% vs. 21%; Butow, Lobb, et al., 2011). In fact, several studies suggest that family interpreters may be better in performing certain tasks (e.g., patient advocacy, cultural brokering, taking medical history, and gaining patients' trust) depending on contexts and circumstances (Angelelli, 2010; Butow, Goldstein, et al., 2011; Ho, 2008; Leanza et al., 2010).

By recognizing the variety of interpreters (e.g., on-site vs. telephone vs. family interpreters) available in healthcare settings, researchers can begin to explore the impacts of different types of interpreters on patient satisfaction, provider expectations, patient-interpreter relationships, institutional costs, and clinical consequences (MacFarlane et al., 2009; Messias, McDowell, & Estrada, 2009). As researchers begin to critically examine the types of interpreters and their corresponding impacts, researchers and practitioners can move beyond an ideological debate on and preference for professional interpreters and provide evidence-based findings on *how* different types of interpreters can facilitate and/or compromise the delivery of care. Because this is still an early trend, the literature on comparisons of various types of interpreters has often been limited to interview data. As a result, little is known about how different types of interpreters influence provider-patient interaction, providers' or patients' communicative competence, and the quality of care during actual medical encounters. Because researchers have noted that participants' impressions of their own and others' performances in medical encounters often differ from their behaviors (Cegala, Gade, Broz, & McClure, 2004), it is important for researchers to examine data on actual interactions.

Finally, the literature has developed some consensus but not universal agreement on how to best conceptualize and name different types of interpreters. In an earlier article I have presented a typology of interpreters that includes (a) chance interpreters, (b) untrained interpreters, (c) bilingual healthcare providers, (d) on-site interpreters, and (e) telephone interpreters (for detailed discussion about the strength and weakness of each type see Hsieh, 2006b). However, based on recent research, I believe that the classification needs some revision. In particular, the category of untrained interpreter originally included both family members and bilingual healthcare staff (e.g., bilingual nurses). Recent studies have demonstrated that family interpreters (i.e., patients' family members or friends who perform the interpreting task), due to their knowledge of and relationships with patients, have unique behavioral patterns and are perceived differently by providers (Leanza et al., 2010; Rosenberg et al., 2007; Rosenberg et al., 2008). On the other hand, providers may trust bilingual healthcare staff more than professional interpreters due to their medical knowledge and familiarity with the medical procedure within the clinic (Hsieh et al., 2010). As a result, I believe that sufficient evidence exists to warrant a separation of these two types of interpreters into distinct categories. As the technology of videoconferencing becomes more available (see Pöchhacker, this volume), future research should consider whether video-based interpreters should become a new category of interpreters or whether they share similar characteristics and impacts with other types of interpreters.

Providers' Clinical Decisions for Medical Interpreting

The second puzzle of bilingual health communication is the underuse of professional interpreters despite various federal and state legislations that have required healthcare facilities to provide interpreters to LEP patients since the late 1970s (Youdelman, 2008). Multiple studies have demonstrated that providers continue to underutilize professional interpreters, who consistently are used for less than 20% of LEP patients (Ginde, Sullivan, Corel, Caceres, & Camargo, 2010; Meischke, Chavez, Bradley, Rea, & Eisenberg, 2010; Schenker, Pérez-Stable, Nickleach, & Karliner, 2011). Instead, providers often rely on family interpreters, ad hoc interpreters, and bilingual staff. Although some researchers argue that providers are "getting by" with other forms of interpreters (Diamond, Schenker, Curry, Bradley, & Fernandez, 2009; Schenker et al., 2011), others argue that providers' choice of interpreters may involve multiple factors.

The literature has suggested time pressure and the lack of availability and/or accessibility were often cited as primary reasons for providers' underutilization of professional interpreters (Lee et al., 2006; Ramirez et al., 2008). However, in my own research I have identified other factors that shape providers' decision-making processes. For example, some providers expressed concerns for interpersonal contact and emotional support when disclosing bad news and commented that they would opt for a nonprofessional interpreter who is on-site rather than a professional telephone interpreter. Cara[H] commented, "It's a matter of eye contact, it's a matter of body habitus . . . sometimes the family NEEDS to be able to make eye contact and feel like they are having some human CONNECTION." Cecil[H] explained that when disclosing a poor prognosis, "I want somebody [who] stands in there WITH me. To look me in the face. . . . I just couldn't use a telephone [interpreter]." On the other hand, providers' concern over litigation and alliances may prompt them to choose professional interpreters. For example, Gram[H] noted, "I rely on the fact that the professional interpreter is supposed to be working for me, as a go-between with the patient; whereas the family member might be working for themselves or might be working for the patient or who knows what. They are not there for me."

In addition, providers may evaluate the urgency and complexity of clinical conditions as they choose the types of interpreters needed. For example, Natalie[H] stated, "I might use a six-year-old. Depending upon the immediacy of the need, like pain or something like that." Gloria[H] also commented, "If you are in a fairly urgent situation, where you have to make a decision doing an emergency C-section or something like that, you go with what the family member says and you don't think about it." Celia[H] explained, "We have some residents who are bilingual, and that can be very helpful sometimes, too. 'Cause they have a lot of medical knowledge." Nacia[H] also noted, "When I have little issues, my seventh-grade Spanish can get me through." Finally, providers' areas of expertise may also influence their preferences for a particular type of interpreter. For example, a provider in mental health care may prefer professional interpreters to family interpreters due to concerns about patient privacy and treatment efficacy; in contrast, an oncologist may feel that emotional support is more critical for the current tasks and decide that a family interpreter can serve multiple functions effectively (Hsieh et al., 2013). These findings demonstrate that providers' decisions with regard to the types of interpreters to use in medical encounters are the result of a calculated process.

Addressing Challenges within Trend 3

In summary, this emerging trend highlights the complexity of health-care practices and shifts attention away from interpreters' linguistic performances. Instead, researchers acknowledge the unique characteristics of healthcare settings that shape the processes and outcomes of medical interpreting. A crucial aspect of this perspective is researchers' willingness to challenge taken-for-granted ideology, critically examine the practices of bilingual healthcare, and develop meaningful and practical solutions.

For example, rather than assuming that professional interpreters are universally superior to other types of interpreters, researchers aim to provide evidence-based arguments for the distinctive impact that different types of interpreters make. In other words, this approach allows researchers and practitioners to develop meaningful practice guidelines for interpreters by investigating (a) the communicative strategies that may be used by different types of interpreters, (b) effective strategies to coordinate with different interpreters, and (c) the limitations and ethical boundaries of different types of interpreters.

Similarly, rather than simply attributing providers' underutilization of professional interpreters to providers' personal excuses, researchers continue to examine the interpersonal and organizational dynamics of bilingual medical encounters and to explore the various factors that are critical in shaping the communicative process of medical interpreting. Rather than presuming that certain types of interpreters or certain ways of interpreting are better than others, researchers who are influenced by this trend seek to generate evidence-based findings to back up their claim.

Finally, because the quality of interpreting is situated in healthcare contexts, researchers and practitioners can now consider various issues that may not be typically considered in other forms of interpreting. For example, even though family members are not typically considered to be primary participants in medical encounters, researchers have raised concerns that LEP patients' family members receive less emotional support from the clinicians even when an interpreter was provided (Thornton, Pham, Engelberg, Jackson, & Curtis, 2009). Imposing professional interpreters on patients who expressed a preference for a family interpreter may be problematic if not unethical due to the failure to respect patients' cultural and interpersonal considerations (Ho, 2008). In short, the third emerging trend, identifying the complexity of clinical demands, opens up innovative viewpoints to examine the quality and effectiveness of bilingual healthcare by highlighting the complexity and reality of health-care practices and proposes various (new) criteria that are essential to evaluate the outcomes of interpreter-mediated medical encounters.

TREND 4: EXPLORING CONTEXTUAL FACTORS IN BILINGUAL HEALTHCARE

Finally, contextual factors are critical to bilingual health communica-tion. Although contextual factors appear to comprise numerous issues, this emerging trend highlights researchers' attention to larger contexts, including cultural, socioeconomic, interpersonal, environmental, organi-zational/institutional, legal, policy, and ethical contexts. Although a wide variety of issues are involved in this trend, these considerations would be nonexistent in a world that assumes that the quality of interpreting is solely dependent on interpreters' ability to provide word-for-word interpretation. To recognize the role these factors play in shaping the content and process of interpreting is to acknowledge the diverse forces that shape the content and process of bilingual health communication. Although this line of research has been growing rapidly, the number of specific factors that have been identified and systematically investigated is still limited. Researchers have identified interpersonal trust (Brisset et al., 2013; Hsieh et al., 2010), organizational policies (Jacobs, Diamond, & Stevak, 2010), and modes of interpreting (Locatis et al., 2010; Price, Perez-Stable, Nickleach, Lopez, & Karliner, 2012) as contextual factors in interpreting practices. Rather than providing a comprehensive review of all of these contextual factors, I focus on two emerging ones that are likely to shape the future development of the field: (a) areas of medical specialty and, (b) interpersonal relationships.

Areas of Medical Specialty

Although medical interpreting is a fledgling subfield of the larger field of community interpreting, the literature has experienced exponential growth and challenged traditional thinking in interpreting studies since early 2000 (Brisset et al., 2013). The first contextual factor mentioned here, areas of medical specialty, is often implied but rarely systemati-cally examined in the literature on bilingual healthcare. Examination of this factor is possible only because of the influences of previous trends.

If interpreters were simply viewed as tools, as language machines, then interpreters' performances should not differ depending on the context (Hsieh & Kramer, 2012). After all, a hammer will always be used as a hammer in all contexts. To consider that the areas of medical specialty can or should influence an interpreter's performance is to argue that the "preferred" interpreting style/performances may differ depending on the clinical context.

As researchers have become more sensitive to the types of interpreters included in their studies, they have also become more aware of the clinical settings in which they conduct their studies. Many studies specifically identified these settings, which included pediatric, emergency, and palliative care (e.g., Cunningham, Cushman, Akuete-Penn, & Meyer, 2008; Flores et al., 2012; Grover, Deakyne, Bajaj, & Roosevelt, 2012; Kuo, O'Connor, Flores, & Minkovitz, 2007; Roat, Kinderman, & Fernandez, 2011). However, these studies did not explore how the specific characteristics and the provider-patient dynamics of pediatric and/or emergency medicine may exert special influences on or challenges to interpreter-mediated medical encounters. Nevertheless, by specifying the types of clinical contexts, they raised the question of whether and how the unique clinical contexts may influence participant expectations and performances in clinical encounters.

For example, providers of obstetrics-gynecology department often need to develop a long-term relationship with their patients, helping them through the months of pregnancy. Providers of the emergency department may be less concerned about developing long-term rapport with a patient and instead are under time constraints to make an accurate diagnosis. Providers of the oncology department often deal with issues that are highly emotional and cultural (e.g., death and dying) and may need to interact with the patient's family members regularly. For providers of mental health care, language is both a window to diagnose patients' symptoms and a tool for treatment. Finally, nurses often interact with patients more closely than physicians and thus, may have different communicative needs. The distinctive needs of the different specialties and their universal role as healthcare providers give researchers an opportunity to examine the commonalities and differences of providers.

For example, different specialties (e.g., mental health vs. oncology vs. nursing) would have specialty-specific needs and expectations for interpreters' role performances. Although an interpreter may feel that not engaging in some small talk might be perceived as being rude (Hsieh,

2006a), casual interactions with patients with mental illness (e.g., paranoia) may lead to serious clinical consequences (Hsieh et al., 2010). For example, Mira[H], a mental health provider, noted, "You don't want interpreters to interact with the patient so much that the patient begins to TRUST the interpreter more than the physician. . . . If the patient opens up so much to the interpreter that they become so emotional or have an emotional breakdown. That can interfere with the treatment process tremendously." In contrast, Curtis[H], an oncologist, mentioned a case in which both the mother and her child were diagnosed with cancer. He explained that the interpreter's emotional support was valuable and appreciated: "The translator has become very attached and would visit the patient before I go into the room and she'd visit them afterward. I've seen her visiting when I don't need her."

So far, in the field of bilingual health care, mental health care appears to be the only medical specialty in which researchers and practitioners have presented systematic discussions on how medical interpreting imposes unique challenges to and expectations for interpreters (d'Ardenne & Farmer, 2009; Jackson, Zatzick, Harris, & Gardiner, 2008; Tribe & Lane, 2009). This is likely because mental health providers are particularly sensitive to individuals' use of language as well as cultural influences in their diagnostic and treatment process. Several researchers have argued that interpreting in mental healthcare settings requires interpreters to adopt a much more active and aggressive role in assisting providers to understand patients' (culturally based) symptoms and provide culturally sensitive treatments (Tribe & Lane, 2009). Nevertheless, in a large survey, mental health providers placed less value on interpreters' ability to assist patients outside medical encounters than did providers in emergency medicine, OB/GYN, and nursing. They also placed less value on interpreters' ability to advocate for patients than did providers in emergency medicine and nursing (Hsieh et al., 2013). This reflects mental health providers' concerns about patient-interpreter bonding and its potential impact on patient-provider relationships and their therapeutic goals. By examining the specific contexts of mental health care and highlighting providers' potentially competing expectations, researchers are able to identify the specific behaviors that are essential to successful interpreter-mediated encounters and propose realistic expectations and guidelines to facilitate best practices in the field.

In addition, a topic that has recently emerged in the literature is interpreters' emotional work when they interpret for refugees or patients with traumatic experiences (Bontempo & Malcolm, 2012; Johnson, Thompson, & Downs, 2009; Splevins, Cohen, Joseph, Murray, & Bowley, 2010), highlighting the potential emotional distress (e.g., burnout and trauma) experienced by interpreters in these settings. I find this topic particularly exciting because it signals that the field of bilingual health care is maturing. Only when researchers and practitioners acknowledge interpreters' active roles and presence in medical encounters can we begin to recognize and discuss the impacts and consequences of such practices.

Finally, despite the attention to the unique needs, expectations, and conditions imposed by each medical specialty, there may still be universal needs and expectations with regard to bilingual health communication that apply to all healthcare providers. In particular, researchers continue to report that physicians still hold the general expectations that interpreters should assume a neutral conduit role (Abbe, Simon, Angiolillo, Ruccione, & Kodish, 2006; Fatahi et al., 2008). This finding is also supported by a recent survey in which providers from different specialties also appeared to expect interpreters to adopt a neutral, emotionally detached, and independent professional role (Hsieh et al., 2013). Although the literature has argued that the interpreter-as-conduit model is unrealistic and problematic, researchers need to explore if there are universal expectations held by all providers and how these expectations may influence bilingual health care.

In other words, I believe that areas of medical specialty is a growing theme as researchers begin to reflect critically on how differing clinical contexts impose different standards of "good" interpreting practices and expectations of appropriate interpreter performances. In addition, researchers can now reexamine how these different standards and expectations may influence interpreters' behaviors (and even health status). I expect that future research in this direction will need to further explore organizational and ethical guidelines for different medical specialties and to investigate to what extent interpreters can effectively respond to these unique standards and expectations.

Interpersonal Relationship

The *ongoing relationship* between the provider, the interpreter, and the patient (and the patients' family members) is another contextual factor that is essential to the quality of bilingual health care. Although it has been neglected in the literature, several recent studies have suggested that this is an important contextual factor in bilingual health care. In a recent review, Brisset and colleagues concluded (2013, p. 136), "Building *trust* and *respect* (recognition) is a prerequisite to establishing a collaboration that allows all protagonists to find their place in the relational dynamic. . . . Trust and control issues take place within the relation (and its dynamics) between patients, interpreters and practitioners."

Moving beyond an understanding of static relationship, recent literature highlights the dynamic, emergent, and changing nature of interpersonal relationships. For example, although a provider may have concerns about a family interpreter's lack of illness-related terminology and knowledge, the provider may eventually develop trust because the family interpreter has learned the relevant terms and knowledge by acting as a caregiver for the patient outside the medical encounter (Hsieh et al., 2010). Although the industry traditionally tries to avoid assigning the same interpreter to the same patient multiple times, both providers and interpreters have argued that an ongoing working relationship improves their collaboration. Candice[H] noted, "I know [some interpreters] personally. Often I've worked with them more than once or twice. So, I know their style and they know mine. They know the words I use and all that. I mean, it's just better to have someone you know and trust." Interpreters were observed to actively seek information about patients' medical history when working with new patients as an attempt to ensure the quality of later interpretation. Sandra[I] commented, "I also ask [the patients] what are the reasons they are there? Do they have any problems? Because I know that all these are going to come up when I get into the office and it is going to be easier for me when I say, 'Well, the patient is here for this reason.' . . . I think this is going to make it faster—the appointment." In other words, the lack of knowledge of the patients' medical history prompted Sandra to assume a co-diagnostician role to obtain information about the patient's medical history (see also Hsieh, 2007).

Professional interpreters' ability to develop trust with providers and patients over time is essential to their management of provider-patient interactions (Edwards, Temple, & Alexander, 2005; Robb & Greenhalgh, 2006). On the other hand, an on-site professional interpreter may not be trusted by the providers if they have been informed of the interpreter's alleged prior misconduct (Hsieh et al., 2010). Similarly, researchers have argued that despite providers' preference for professional interpreters, using family interpreters may be ethically necessary due to patients' long-term relationship and social obligations/responsibilities with the interpreter (Angelelli, 2010; Ho, 2008). Because the provider-patient-interpreter triad often works across many medical encounters, it is important to examine how such a relationship influences their coordination and collaboration in interpreter-mediated medical encounters over the course of an illness event.

Addressing Challenges within Trend 4

Researchers need to explore and identify the various contextual factors that influence interpreter-mediated medical encounters. Compared to other trends, this one is still in a very early stage. Few contextual factors have so far been systematically examined and theorized. However, recent studies have suggested great potential here. The literature in mental healthcare interpreting has provided good examples and directions for researchers to explore other clinical contexts. From this perspective, this trend views medical interpreting not simply as a generic form of interpreting but also as a communicative activity situated in multiple contexts. Researchers' abilities to identify and investigate specific contexts and their corresponding influences on interpreter-mediated encounters are essential to the theoretical development and practice implications of this trend.

CONCLUSION

In this chapter, I have examined four emerging trends in the literature of bilingual health communication, highlighting their potential for theory advancement and practice implications. These trends are interconnected. For example, without recognizing other participants' influences in interpreter-mediated encounters (Trend 2), one cannot truly understand and examine how providers' calculated use of interpreters might be dependent on specific clinical demands (Trend 3). Without seeing interpreters as active participants (i.e., individuals with agency influencing the process and content of medical encounters; Trend 1), there is little possibility of examining how the provider-interpreter, interpreter-patient, or provider-patient-interpreter relationship may shape the delivery of bilingual healthcare (Trend 4).

After all, if interpreters are passive tools such as computers, one would expect that any computer would function the same as any other regardless of context. In other words, the home computer should work the same way and produce the same output as other computers in a lab, office, or library. Anyone who uses a computer would expect identical processes and results across times and places. A computer can be broken, but otherwise they work the same. Similarly, an interpreter who fails to assume the conduit role has traditionally been regarded as a "bad" interpreter; otherwise, all interpreters are the same. All providers and patients should expect the same "good" interpreting from all "unbroken" interpreters. This has been the traditional thinking in interpreter performances. But this belief is not supported by the reality of interpreting.

These emerging trends, supported by evidence-based studies, provide strong counterarguments to the traditional thinking about interpreter-mediated interactions. In addition, they are opening up new perspectives to conceptualize interpreter-mediated medical encounters. By moving beyond the comparisons between source and target texts, researchers have demonstrated the value of viewing bilingual health communication as a goal-oriented, context-situated collaboration between multiple parties.

REFERENCES

Abbe, M., Simon, C., Angiolillo, A., Ruccione, K., & Kodish, E. D. (2006). A survey of language barriers from the perspective of pediatric oncologists, interpreters, and parents. *Pediatric Blood & Cancer, 47*, 819–824.

Andrulis, D., Goodman, N., & Pryor, C. (2002). What a difference an interpreter can make: Health care experiences of uninsured with limited English proficiency. Retrieved March 21, 2009, from http://www.accessproject.org/downloads/c_LEPreportENG.pdf

Angelelli, C. V. (2002). "Deconstructing the invisible interpreter: A critical study of the interpersonal role of the interpreter in a cross-cultural linguistic communicative event." PhD diss., University of Michigan, Ann Arbor.

Angelelli, C. V. (2004). *Revisiting the interpreters' roles: A study of conference, court, and medical interpreters in Canada, Mexico, and the United States.* Amsterdam: Benjamins.

Angelelli, C. V. (2010). A professional ideology in the making: Bilingual youngsters interpreting for their communities and the notion of (no) choice. *Translation and Interpretation Studies, 5*, 94–108.

Aranguri, C., Davidson, B., & Ramirez, R. (2006). Patterns of communication through interpreters: A detailed sociolinguistic analysis. *Journal of General Internal Medicine, 21*, 623–629.

Baker, D. W., & Hayes, R. (1997). The effect of communicating through an interpreter on satisfaction with interpersonal aspects of care. *Journal of General Internal Medicine, 12,* 117.

Baker, D. W., Parker, R. M., Williams, M. V., Coates, W. C., & Pitkin, K. M. (1996). Use and effectiveness of interpreters in an emergency department. *Journal of the American Medical Association, 275,* 783–788.

Bernstein, J., Bernstein, E., Dave, A., Hardt, E., James, T., Linden, J., . . . Safi, C. (2002). Trained medical interpreters in the emergency department: Effects on services, subsequent charges, and follow-up. *Journal of Immigrant Health, 4,* 171–176.

Bischoff, A., & Hudelson, P. (2010a). Access to healthcare interpreter services: Where are we and where do we need to go? *International Journal of Environmental Research & Public Health, 7,* 2838–2844.

Bischoff, A., & Hudelson, P. (2010b). Communicating with foreign language–speaking patients: Is access to professional interpreters enough? *Journal of Travel Medicine, 17,* 15–20.

Bontempo, K., & Malcolm, K. (2012). An ounce of prevention is worth a pound of care: Educating interpreters about the risk of vicarious trauma in healthcare settings. In L. Swabey & K. Malcolm (Eds.), *In our hands: Educating healthcare interpreters* (pp. 105–130). Washington, DC: Gallaudet University Press.

Brämberg, E. B., & Sandman, L. (2013). Communication through in-person interpreters: A qualitative study of home care providers' and social workers' views. *Journal of Clinical Nursing, 22,* 159–167.

Brisset, C., Leanza, Y., & Laforest, K. (2013). Working with interpreters in health care: A systematic review and meta-ethnography of qualitative studies. *Patient Education and Counseling, 91,* 131–140.

Brunson, J. G., & Lawrence, P. S. (2002). Impact of sign language interpreter and therapist moods on deaf recipient mood. *Professional Psychology: Research and Practice, 33,* 576–580.

Butow, P. N., Goldstein, D., Bell, M. L., Sze, M., Aldridge, L. J., Abdo, S., et al. (2011). Interpretation in consultations with immigrant patients with cancer: How accurate is it? *Journal of Clinical Oncology, 29,* 2801–2807.

Butow, P. N., Lobb, E., Jefford, M., Goldstein, D., Eisenbruch, M., Girgis, A., et al. (2011). A bridge between cultures: Interpreters' perspectives of consultations with migrant oncology patients. *Supportive Care in Cancer, 20,* 235–244.

Cegala, D. J., Gade, C., Broz, S. L., & McClure, L. (2004). Physicians' and patients' perceptions of patients' communication competence in a primary care medical interview. *Health Communication, 16,* 289–304.

Cegala, D. J., & Post, D. M. (2009). The impact of patients' participation on physicians' patient-centered communication. *Patient Education and Counseling, 77,* 202–208.

Cegala, D. J., Street, R. L., Jr., & Clinch, C. (2007). The impact of patient participation on physicians' information provision during a primary care medical interview. *Health Communication, 21,* 177–185.

Cunningham, H., Cushman, L. F., Akuete-Penn, C., & Meyer, D. D. (2008). Satisfaction with telephonic interpreters in pediatric care. *Journal of the National Medical Association, 100,* 429–434.

d'Ardenne, P., & Farmer, E. (2009). Using interpreters in trauma therapy. In N. Grey (Ed.), *A casebook of cognitive therapy for traumatic stress reactions* (pp. 283–300). New York: Routledge.

Davidson, B. (2000). The interpreter as institutional gatekeeper: The social-linguistic role of interpreters in Spanish-English medical discourse. *Journal of Sociolinguistics, 4,* 379–405.

Davidson, B. (2001). Questions in cross-linguistic medical encounters: The role of the hospital interpreter. *Anthropological Quarterly, 74,* 170–178.

Diamond, L. C., Schenker, Y., Curry, L., Bradley, E. H., & Fernandez, A. (2009). Getting by: Underuse of interpreters by resident physicians. *Journal of General Internal Medicine, 24,* 256–262.

Dysart-Gale, D. (2005). Communication models, professionalization, and the work of medical interpreters. *Health Communication, 17,* 91–103.

Edwards, R., Temple, B., & Alexander, C. (2005). Users' experiences of interpreters: The critical role of trust. *Interpreting, 7,* 77–95.

Elderkin-Thompson, V., Silver, R. C., & Waitzkin, H. (2001). When nurses double as interpreters: A study of Spanish-speaking patients in a US primary care setting. *Social Science & Medicine, 52,* 1343–1358.

Fatahi, N., Hellstrom, M., Skott, C., & Mattsson, B. (2008). General practitioners' views on consultations with interpreters: A triad situation with complex issues. *Scandinavian Journal of Primary Health Care, 26,* 40–45.

Fenton, S. (1997). The role of the interpreter in the adversarial courtroom. In S. E. Carr, R. P. Roberts, A. Dufour, & D. Steyn (Eds.), *The critical link: Interpreters in the community* (pp. 29–34). Amsterdam: Benjamins.

Flores, G. (2000). Culture and the patient-physician relationship: Achieving cultural competency in health care. *Journal of Pediatrics, 136,* 14–23.

Flores, G. (2005). The impact of medical interpreter services on the quality of health care: A systematic review. *Medical Care Research & Review, 62,* 255–299.

Flores, G., Abreu, M., Barone, C. P., Bachur, R., & Lin, H. (2012). Errors of medical interpretation and their potential clinical consequences: A comparison of professional versus ad hoc versus no interpreters. *Annals of Emergency Medicine, 60,* 545–553.

Flores, G., Abreu, M., Schwartz, I., & Hill, M. (2000). The importance of language and culture in pediatric care: Case studies from the Latino community. *Journal of Pediatrics, 137,* 842–848.

Gany, F., Kapelusznik, L., Prakash, K., Gonzalez, J., Orta, L. Y., Tseng, C.-H., & Changrani, J. (2007). The impact of medical interpretation method on time and errors. *Journal of General Internal Medicine, 22*(Suppl. 2), 319–323.

Gany, F., Leng, J., Shapiro, E., Abramson, D., Motola, I., Shield, D. C., & Changrani, J. (2007). Patient satisfaction with different interpreting methods: A randomized controlled trial. *Journal of General Internal Medicine, 22,* S312–318.

Gavioli, L., & Baraldi, C. (2011). Interpreter-mediated interaction in healthcare and legal settings: Talk organization, context, and the achievement of intercultural communication. *Interpreting, 13,* 205–233.

Ginde, A. A., Sullivan, A. F., Corel, B., Caceres, J. A., & Camargo, C. A., Jr. (2010). Reevaluation of the effect of mandatory interpreter legislation on use of professional interpreters for ED patients with language barriers. *Patient Education & Counseling, 81,* 204–206.

Green, J., Free, C., Bhavnani, V., & Newman, T. (2005). Translators and mediators: Bilingual young people's accounts of their interpreting work in health care. *Social Science & Medicine, 60,* 2097–2110.

Greenhalgh, T., Robb, N., & Scambler, G. (2006). Communicative and strategic action in interpreted consultations in primary health care: A Habermasian perspective. *Social Science & Medicine, 63,* 1170–1187.

Grover, A., Deakyne, S., Bajaj, L., & Roosevelt, G. E. (2012). Comparison of throughput times for limited English proficiency patient visits in the emergency department between different interpreter modalities. *Journal of Immigrant and Minority Health, 14,* 602–607.

Hampers, L. C., & McNulty, J. E. (2002). Professional interpreters and bilingual physicians in a pediatric emergency department: Effect on resource utilization. *Archives of Pediatrics and Adolescent Medicine, 156,* 1108–1113.

Harrison, B., Bhatt, A., Carey, J., & Ebden, P. (1988). The language of the bilingual medical consultation. In P. Grunwell (Ed.), *Applied Linguistics in Society: Papers from the Annual Meeting of the British Association for Applied Linguistics (20th, Nottingham, England, United Kingdom, September 1987)* (pp. 67–73). London: Centre for Information on Language Teaching and Research.

Ho, A. (2008). Using family members as interpreters in the clinical setting. *Journal of Clinical Ethics, 19,* 223–233.

Hsieh, E. (2006a). Conflicts in how interpreters manage their roles in provider-patient interactions. *Social Science & Medicine, 62,* 721–730.

Hsieh, E. (2006b). Understanding medical interpreters: Reconceptualizing bilingual health communication. *Health Communication, 20,* 177–186.

Hsieh, E. (2007). Interpreters as co-diagnosticians: Overlapping roles and services between providers and interpreters. *Social Science & Medicine, 64,* 924–937.

Hsieh, E. (2008). "I am not a robot!" Interpreters' views of their roles in health care settings. *Qualitative Health Research, 18,* 1367–1383.

Hsieh, E. (2009). Bilingual health communication: Medical interpreters' construction of a mediator role. In D. E. Brashers & D. J. Goldsmith (Eds.), *Communicating to manage health and illness* (pp. 121–146). New York: Routledge.

Hsieh, E. (2010). Provider-interpreter collaboration in bilingual health care: Competitions of control over interpreter-mediated interactions. *Patient Education and Counseling, 78*, 154–159.

Hsieh, E., & Hong, S. J. (2010). Not all are desired: Providers' views on interpreters' emotional support to patients. *Patient Education and Counseling, 81*, 192–197.

Hsieh, E., Ju, H., & Kong, H. (2010). Dimensions of trust: The tensions and challenges in provider-interpreter trust. *Qualitative Health Research, 20*, 170–181.

Hsieh, E., & Kramer, E. M. (2012). Medical interpreters as tools: Dangers and challenges in the utilitarian approach to interpreters' roles and functions. *Patient Education & Counseling, 89*, 158–162.

Hsieh, E., Pitaloka, D., & Johnson, A. J. (2013). Bilingual health communication: Distinctive needs of providers from five specialties. *Health Communication, 28*, 557–567.

Jackson, J. C., Nguyen, D., Hu, N., Harris, R., & Terasaki, G. S. (2011). Alterations in medical interpretation during routine primary care. *Journal of General Internal Medicine, 26*, 259–264.

Jackson, J. C., Zatzick, D., Harris, R., & Gardiner, L. (2008). Loss in translation: Considering the critical role of interpreters and language in the psychiatric evaluation of non-English-speaking patients. In S. Loue & M. Sajatovic (Eds.), *Diversity issues in the diagnosis, treatment, and research of mood disorders* (pp. 135–163). New York: Oxford University Press.

Jacobs, E. A., Diamond, L. C., & Stevak, L. (2010). The importance of teaching clinicians when and how to work with interpreters. *Patient Education and Counseling, 78*, 149–153.

Johnson, H., Thompson, A., & Downs, M. (2009). Non-Western interpreters' experiences of trauma: The protective role of culture following exposure to oppression. *Ethnicity & Health, 14*, 407–418.

Karliner, L. S., Jacobs, E. A., Chen, A. H., & Mutha, S. (2007). Do professional interpreters improve clinical care for patients with limited English proficiency? A systematic review of the literature. *Health Services Research, 42*, 727–754.

Kaufert, J. M., & Putsch, R. W. (1997). Communication through interpreters in healthcare: Ethical dilemmas arising from differences in class, culture, language, and power. *Journal of Clinical Ethics, 8*, 71–87.

Kuo, D. Z., O'Connor, K. G., Flores, G., & Minkovitz, C. S. (2007). Pediatricians' use of language services for families with limited English proficiency. *Pediatrics, 119*, e920–927.

Leanza, Y. (2008). Community interpreter's power: The hazards of a disturbing attribute. *Journal of Medical Anthropology, 31*, 211–220.

Leanza, Y., Boivin, I., & Rosenberg, E. (2010). Interruptions and resistance: A comparison of medical consultations with family and trained interpreters. *Social Science & Medicine, 70,* 1888–1895.

Lee, K. C., Winickoff, J. P., Kim, M. K., Campbell, E. G., Betancourt, J. R., Park, E. R., . . . Weissman, J. S. (2006). Resident physicians' use of professional and nonprofessional interpreters: A national survey. *Journal of the American Medical Association, 296,* 1050–1053.

Linell, P. (1997). Interpreting as communication. In Y. Gambier, D. Gile, & C. Taylor (Eds.), *Conference interpreting: Current trends in research; Proceedings of the International Conference on Interpreting: What Do We Know and How? (Turku, August 25–27, 1994)* (pp. 49–67). Amsterdam: Benjamins.

Llewellyn-Jones, P., & Lee, R. G. (2011). *Re-visiting "role": Arguing for a multidimensional analysis of interpreter behaviour.* Paper presented at the Suporting Deaf People 2011: An online conference from direct learn. http://www.online-conference.net/sdp2011/programme.htm#lee

Locatis, C., Williamson, D., Gould-Kabler, C., Zone-Smith, L., Detzler, I., Roberson, J., . . . Ackerman, M. (2010). Comparing in-person, video, and telephonic medical interpretation. *Journal of General Internal Medicine, 25,* 345–350.

MacFarlane, A., Dzebisova, Z., Karapish, D., Kovacevic, B., Ogbebor, F., & Okonkwo, E. (2009). Arranging and negotiating the use of informal interpreters in general practice consultations: Experiences of refugees and asylum seekers in the west of Ireland. *Social Science & Medicine, 69,* 210–214.

McDowell, L., Messias, D. K. H., & Estrada, R. D. (2011). The work of language interpretation in health care: Complex, challenging, exhausting, and often invisible. *Journal of Transcultural Nursing, 22,* 137–147.

Meischke, H., Chavez, D., Bradley, S., Rea, T., & Eisenberg, M. (2010). Emergency communications with limited-English-proficiency populations. *Prehospital Emergency Care, 14,* 265–271.

Messias, D. K. H., McDowell, L., & Estrada, R. D. (2009). Language interpreting as social justice work: Perspectives of formal and informal healthcare interpreters. *Advances in Nursing Science, 32,* 128–143.

Metzger, M. (1999). *Sign language interpreting: Deconstructing the myth of neutrality.* Washington, DC: Gallaudet University Press.

Pöchhacker, F., & Shlesinger, M. (2005). Introduction: Discourse-based research on healthcare interpreting. *Interpreting, 7,* 157–165.

Poss, J. E., & Beeman, T. (1999). Effective use of interpreters in health care: Guidelines for nurse managers and clinicians. *Seminars for Nurse Managers, 7,* 166–171.

Preloran, H. M., Browner, C. H., & Lieber, E. (2005). Impact of interpreters' approach on Latinas' use of amniocentesis. *Health Education & Behavior, 32,* 599–612.

Price, E. L., Perez-Stable, E. J., Nickleach, D., Lopez, M., & Karliner, L. S. (2012). Interpreter perspectives of in-person, telephonic, and videoconferencing medical interpretation in clinical encounters. *Patient Education & Counseling, 87,* 226–232.

Ramirez, D., Engel, K. G., & Tang, T. S. (2008). Language interpreter utilization in the emergency department setting: A clinical review. *Journal of Health Care for the Poor and Underserved, 19,* 352–362.

Rivadeneyra, R., Elderkin-Thompson, V., Silver, R. C., & Waitzkin, H. (2000). Patient centeredness in medical encounters requiring an interpreter. *American Journal of Medicine, 108,* 470–474.

Roat, C. E., Kinderman, A., & Fernandez, A. (2011). Interpreting in palliative care. Retrieved June 22, 2013, from http://www.chcf.org/publications/2011/11/interpreting-palliative-care-curriculum

Robb, N., & Greenhalgh, T. (2006). "You have to cover up the words of the doctor": The mediation of trust in interpreted consultations in primary care. *Journal of Health Organization & Management, 20,* 434–455.

Rosenberg, E., Leanza, Y., & Seller, R. (2007). Doctor-patient communication in primary care with an interpreter: Physician perceptions of professional and family interpreters. *Patient Education and Counseling, 67,* 286–292.

Rosenberg, E., Seller, R., & Leanza, Y. (2008). Through interpreters' eyes: Comparing roles of professional and family interpreters. *Patient Education and Counseling, 70,* 87–93.

Roy, C. B. (2000). *Interpreting as a discourse process.* New York: Oxford University Press.

Sarver, J., & Baker, D. W. (2000). Effect of language barriers on follow-up appointments after an emergency department visit. *Journal of General Internal Medicine, 15,* 256–264.

Schenker, Y., Pérez-Stable, E. J., Nickleach, D., & Karliner, L. S. (2011). Patterns of interpreter use for hospitalized patients with limited English proficiency. *Journal of General Internal Medicine, 26,* 712–717.

Sentell, T., & Braun, K. L. (2012). Low health literacy, limited English proficiency, and health status in Asians, Latinos, and other racial/ethnic groups in California. *Journal of Health Communication, 17,* 82–99.

Simon, C. M., Zyzanski, S. J., Durand, E., Jimenez, X., & Kodish, E. D. (2006). Interpreter accuracy and informed consent among Spanish-speaking families with cancer. *Journal of Health Communication, 11,* 509–522.

Splevins, K. A., Cohen, K., Joseph, S., Murray, C., & Bowley, J. (2010). Vicarious posttraumatic growth among interpreters. *Qualitative Health Research, 20,* 1705–1716.

Thornton, J. D., Pham, K., Engelberg, R. A., Jackson, J. C., & Curtis, J. R. (2009). Families with limited English proficiency receive less information and support in interpreted intensive care unit family conferences. *Critical Care Medicine, 37*, 89–95.

Tribe, R., & Lane, P. (2009). Working with interpreters across language and culture in mental health. *Journal of Mental Health, 18*, 233–241.

Wadensjö, C. (1998). *Interpreting as interaction.* London: Longman.

Williams, M. V., Parker, R. M., Baker, D. W., Parikh, N. S., Pitkin, K., Coates, W. C., & Nurss, J. R. (1995). Inadequate functional health literacy among patients at two public hospitals. *Journal of the American Medical Association, 274*, 1677–1682.

Youdelman, M. K. (2008). The medical tongue: U.S. laws and policies on language access. *Health Affairs, 27*, 424–433.

An Examination of Medical Interview Questions Rendered in American Sign Language by Deaf Physicians and Interpreters

Laurie Swabey, Brenda Nicodemus, and Christopher Moreland

ABSTRACT

In the healthcare system of the United States, signed language inter-preters frequently facilitate communication between deaf individuals who use American Sign Language (ASL) and their nonsigning physi-cians. A small but growing number of deaf individuals are pursuing medical training and becoming physicians, creating an opportunity for some deaf patients to communicate directly with their doctors in ASL. In addition to providing direct access for deaf patients, this also creates a situation in which it is possible to examine the linguis-tic features used by deaf bilingual physicians. We analyzed 18 ASL translations of three common medical interview questions as pro-duced by both deaf physicians (*n* = 3) and experienced ASL-English interpreters (*n* = 3). Results indicate that the physicians and the interpreters consistently utilized *contextualization, contrasting,* and *specification* in their translations but showed variability in the pro-duction of these discourse features. We provide an overview of the current state of ASL-English healthcare interpreting, examine chal-lenges in creating ASL translations of common medical interview questions, provide descriptions and samples of the ASL translations, and discuss patterns in the data. Our aim in this investigation is to better describe and understand how typical medical questions are translated into ASL as a step toward the ultimate goal of improving healthcare communication for deaf patients.

Medical interviews often entail a conventionalized protocol in which a physician or other healthcare professional poses a series of questions about the patient's health status, use of medications, and family medical history. The interview may be structured in a branching format, in which clusters of diagnoses can either be pursued or ruled out as information is gathered. In this manner, the physician begins the hypothesis-testing procedure immediately upon patient intake. Effective communication during the medical interview may facilitate the identification of patients' needs, perceptions, and expectations (Ha, Anat, & Longnecker, 2010). Patients who report good communication with their doctor are more likely to share relevant information, adhere to the prescribed treatment, and be satisfied with their care (Williams, Weinman, & Dale, 1998). It is not surprising that the medical interview is regarded as a critical component of both diagnosing illness and developing an effective treatment plan (Lichstein, 1990; Ong, de Haes, Hoos, & Lammes, 1995). In fact, clinicians have rated the information gathered during medical interviews as having greater diagnostic value than either the physical examination or laboratory results (Rich, Crowson, & Harris, 1987). Therefore, the medical interview has become an institutionalized practice in the U.S. healthcare system and may be regarded as a routine practice by both physicians and patients.

When a patient and a physician use different languages, the process of information exchange may be compromised (Angelelli, this volume). For deaf patients who use American Sign Language (ASL), communicating directly with a physician has rarely been an option since so few physicians know ASL. Historically, deaf people have attempted to exchange information with their physicians through a variety of means, including lipreading, writing notes, or enlisting the assistance of a family member, all of which result in less than effective communication (Steinberg, Wiggins, Barmada, & Sullivan, 2002; Steinberg, Barnett, Meador, Wiggins, & Zazove, 2006). Thus, although native speakers of English may experience medical interviews as routine, deaf patients have reported that communication in the healthcare setting is challenging and has the potential for serious misunderstandings (Barnett, 2002; McKee, Barnett, Block, & Pearson, 2011).

With passage of federal legislation, most recently the Americans with Disabilities Act of 1990, healthcare facilities became legally mandated to provide signed language interpretation for deaf patients. The intent of the federal mandates is to ensure communication access for deaf patients; however, the provision of interpreters has not fully resolved the communicative challenges that arise between deaf patients and English-speaking (nonsigning) healthcare providers. Numerous studies have documented deaf patients' health disparities in comparison to the general population. For example, deaf signing adults are less likely to see a physician (Barnett & Franks, 2002), report more frequent use of emergency departments than primary care offices (Harmer, 1999), and are more likely to be dissatisfied with physician-patient communication (Witte & Kuzel, 2000). Compounding the problem, many deaf adults also disproportionally have low health literacy (i.e., ability to seek, process, and use health-related information for decision making and health management), which may be the result of a lifetime of limited access to information that is readily accessed by people who can hear (Hedding & Kaufman, 2012; Pollard, 1998).

These challenges are exacerbated further by a lack of training for signed language interpreters who work in healthcare settings. Fueled by civil rights legislation passed in the 1960s and 1970s, the nascent interpreting profession was under pressure to create a critical mass of generalist practitioners who could meet the communication needs of deaf people across a wide range of settings (Swabey & Nicodemus, 2011). Interpreters with no specialized training or knowledge were called upon to work in almost every type of environment (e.g., legal, educational, vocational, and medical). The first certificate and degree program in ASL-English healthcare interpreting in the United States was established in 1983 at St. Catherine University,[1] and it was nearly 20 years before a second healthcare interpreting certificate program (at the National Technical Institute of the Deaf) was offered.

Since the establishment of the first generalist degree programs for interpreters in the late 1970s, more than 125 postsecondary interpreter education programs have become available. However, many of these degree programs offer only a single course in interpreting in "specialized settings" with a few weeks dedicated to healthcare interpreting. Thus, despite increased opportunities for education, specialization in healthcare interpreting has not been systematically instituted within the educational system (Witter-Merithew & Nicodemus, 2010). Further, a national credentialing system for ASL-English healthcare interpreters does not exist, although certification is in place for interpreters who specialize in legal and educational settings (Swabey & Nicodemus, 2011). In fact, it was only in 2012 that the Registry of Interpreters for the Deaf, the national organization of signed language interpreters in the United States, established a special members section on healthcare interpreting, whereas other such sections have been available for educational and legal interpreters for many years.

Another challenge is the dearth of research on signed language interpreting in healthcare settings. Swabey and Nicodemus (2011) note that linguistic examination of the work of ASL-English interpreters in healthcare settings is necessary to advance the current literature. However, this type of examination is not often seen in the literature. A small number of studies report the attitudes of deaf patients who use interpreters in healthcare settings (e.g., Harmer, 1999; MacKinney, Walters, Bird, & Nattinger, 1995); however, these studies focused on language attitudes of deaf patients rather than linguistic analyses of interpretation in healthcare settings. Given that effective communication influences patient compliance and lowers medical costs (Ha et al., 2010; Mitchell & Selmes, 2007; Williams et al., 1998), the absence of research in ASL-English interpretation in health care is surprising.[2]

Despite the lack of specialized education, credentialing, and research specific to signed language interpreting in medical settings, there have been encouraging developments in healthcare provision for deaf patients. Among the most positive changes is the small but growing number of deaf healthcare professionals who use ASL. The benefits of having deaf bilingual physicians are suggested by research findings on bilingual physicians who use spoken languages. For example, in studies of language-concordant provider-patient pairs, results indicate higher rates of patient satisfaction (Freeman et al., 2002; McKee et al., 2011), better overall well-being and functioning of patients (Perez-Stable, Napoles-Springer, & Miramontes, 1997), closer adherence to treatment (Manson, 1988), and better recall of communication during the patient visit (Seijo, Gomez, & Freidenburg, 1991). In a related study, physicians with greater Spanish-language proficiency received higher interpersonal care ratings from their Spanish-speaking patients (Fernandez et al., 2004).

In our study we examined the language production of three physicians who are deaf ASL-English bilinguals (hereafter identified as deaf bilingual physicians) and three nationally certified ASL-English interpreters recognized for their expertise in the healthcare setting. Each of the participants translated common medical questions and statements consecutively from English into ASL. We address the following question: What are the linguistic challenges and discourse features used by deaf bilingual physicians and interpreters when rendering medical questions from English into ASL?

We pursue this question through a descriptive analysis of the translations and note the variation and similarities that emerge in the data. Although it is tempting to attribute any variation between the two groups to their respective roles as either physicians or interpreters, the small sample size (three physicians and three interpreters) does not allow for such generalizations that can be derived from a larger numbers of participants. It is worth noting that the design of the study controls for many of the variables that occur in medical interviews, including that of patient variability; however, we acknowledge that these controls may also influence the authenticity of the data. That is, we recognize that the translations provided by the participants may have been different had we incorporated actual deaf patients or deaf actors. Large-scale studies and observational research are clearly needed. Our aim with this initial investigation is to better describe and understand how typical medical questions are translated into ASL as a step toward the ultimate goal of improving healthcare communication for deaf patients.

METHODOLOGY

Participants

Two groups participated in this study. The first group comprised three deaf bilingual physicians who had experience working with deaf signing patients. These physicians were all fluent users of American Sign Language and regarded ASL as one of their primary languages. Two of the physicians in the study were male. The second participant group comprised three ASL-English interpreters. The practitioners each had 22 or more years of professional interpreting experience and were recognized for their expertise in healthcare interpreting. All held national certification from the Registry of Interpreters for the Deaf and had completed bachelor's degrees (one held a master's degree). All three had learned ASL as adults and reported that English was their native language. All three were female.

Materials and Task

In a pilot study, a broad sampling of medical questions and statements was presented to a deaf bilingual physician who first created translations that followed the protocol designed for the study. The physician then made recommendations for the final subset of questions and statements to be used. The eight questions and statements selected as stimuli were identified as being frequently used in medical interviews involving both gender groups (table 1). Three of the statements relate to medication dosages

(2, 3, and 4), and these translations have been analyzed (Nicodemus & Swabey, 2014). The remaining five items consisted of medical questions. After analysis of the full dataset, we selected the translations of three questions (1, 5, and 8, in bold in table 1) to present in this chapter. These three questions were identified as occurring frequently in medical interviews and represented the linguistic features used in the full dataset.

The physicians and the interpreters had similar but not identical tasks to perform. The physicians were individually given instructions in ASL by one researcher, a deaf bilingual physician. The questions and statements were presented in written English on individual 8½ × 11 papers placed face down in front of the physician. Each physician was instructed to turn over a paper one at a time, review the question, and translate its meaning into ASL. The researchers and a professional videographer were present in the testing room during the study.

The three interpreters were also given the same eight questions and statements individually but in a slightly different format. On a laptop computer, they viewed a video-recorded simulation of a doctor, who asked each question or statement separately in English. The interpreters were instructed to interpret consecutively, that is, to provide an ASL translation after hearing the entire statement. The two hearing researchers for this study were in the room with the interpreters. One of the researchers provided instructions in English while the other video-recorded the translations.

The physicians and the interpreters were recruited by the researchers and were video-recorded at four separate locations in the North, Southwest, Midwest, and Eastern regions of the United States. Before beginning the

TABLE 1. *Medical Questions and Statements in the Order Presented to the Participants*

1. **Are you allergic to any medications?[3]**
2. Take this liquid medication four times a day—once after every meal and once before bedtime.
3. Take one tablet twice a day with food or as needed for pain.
4. Take one teaspoon three times a day for 10 days. You should finish this medicine even if your symptoms disappear.
5. **Are you sexually active?**
6. Do you have a history of glaucoma in your family?
7. On a scale of 1 to 10, how would you rate your pain right now?
8. **Do you take any over-the-counter medications?**

task, each participant was informed that the study was being conducted to examine ASL translations of typical medical interview questions, specifically to learn more about the linguistic features used in the translations. The participants were given an opportunity to ask questions at any point during the study. Prior to creating their translations, the participants were provided with an identical patient profile (i.e., an adult deaf patient with a high school education and who uses ASL). The participants were instructed to create their translations to match the needs of the patient profile. No time or length constraints were imposed for translating the questions.

Transcription and Analysis

The video data were transcribed by three individuals: a deaf native signer with more than 15 years of signed language research experience and two doctoral students in an interpreting program. The ASL was transcribed using standardized glossing techniques that included indexing, that is, pointing to a concept established in space (e.g., INDEX), fingerspelling (e.g., M-O-T-R-I-N), lexicalized fingerspelling (e.g., #PHMCY for "pharmacy"), and classifier constructions (e.g., CL: C indicating a classifier with a C handshape). By convention, ASL signs are glossed in small capital letters. The transcriptions were compiled in an Excel spreadsheet and reviewed for accuracy by the researchers. Both the transcription and the video-recorded translations were used in the analysis. The data were examined for patterns of linguistic features within and between the participant groups.

We first present each medical question in English and discuss potential challenges in creating an ASL translation. We then provide a linguistic analysis of the ASL translation, with attention to the participants' use of contextualization, contrasting, and specification. In total, we provide an analysis of 18 translations (three medical questions by six participants) and present two sample translations (one physician and one interpreter) for each question (Appendices A–C).

ANALYSIS OF MEDICAL QUESTIONS

"Do You Take Any Over-the-Counter Medications?"

Most native English speakers are familiar with the phrase "over-the-counter" and understand it to mean medications that do not require a prescription, such as minor pain remedies, sleep aids, cold medicines, vitamins, and herbal supplements. However, the phrase "over-the-counter" is not transparent in meaning, and nonnative English speakers may not understand it during a medical interview. Specifically, for deaf patients who use ASL, there is no standard sign or phrase that conveys "over-the-counter" (although some deaf people use the abbreviation o-t-c), thus the phrase may pose a challenge to translate from English into ASL.

Similarly, the English verb "take" has a broad semantic range and is used in a wide array of contexts (e.g., take a walk, take a test, take a drink, take medication). Furthermore, in English, the way in which medicine is "taken" (e.g., inhaler, injection, pill, salve) is not obligatory, although information may be added to the verb (e.g., take orally, take by mouth). Conversely, in ASL, verbs can express a high degree of specificity by the simultaneous use of multiple articulators (the hands, face, and body) to indicate specific information about where a medication is taken (e.g., INJECTION-in-arm, INJECTION-in-hip), the manner in which the medication is taken (e.g., INHALE-slowly, INHALE-quickly), and the amount of medication that is taken (e.g., TAKE-PILL-1-time, TAKE-PILL-2-times). A challenge with this question, then, is how to translate the unspecified English form of "take" to the specified form in ASL. In the following sections we examine the use of three linguistic devices—contextualization, contrasting, and specification—used in translating this question.

CONTEXTUALIZATION

Contextualization is an inherent part of the interpretation process that been linked to the intersubjectivity of the interpreter (Janzen & Shaffer, 2008). *Contextualization* is any linguistic feature that contributes to the signaling of certain presuppositions (Gumperz, 1982). Gumperz (ibid.) observed that contextualization may have a number of linguistic realizations "depending on the historically given linguistic repertoire of the participants" (p. 131). Further, linguistic expressions frequently underspecify meaning; thus a lexical item or construction may be understood only when it is linked to some specific context (Fox, 1994). Contextualization adds specificity in language, an aspect of communication that is critical in the healthcare setting. It is especially salient to this analysis because of the 18 ASL translations examined, 17 included some form of contextualization.

For the question "Do you take any over-the-counter medications?" half of the participants contextualized the phrase "over-the-counter medications" by providing examples in fingerspelling (e.g., A-S-P-I-R-

I-N, T-Y-L-E-N-O-L) or as a lexical item (VITAMIN). Of note is the variety of examples the participants used (T-Y-L-E-N-O-L was the only one expressed by more than one participant) (table 2). The use of contextualization by listing real-world examples is interesting in light of an ASL phonological process in which multiple signs are compounded to create a categorical referent. For example, in ASL, compounding the three signs RING, BRACELET, and NECKLACE is taken to mean "jewelry," and FORK, KNIFE, and SPOON is understood to mean "silverware." These instantiations occur through the compounding of individual lexical items that are selected as best examples, or prototypes, of the superordinate category (Klima & Bellugi, 1979).

A second instance of contextualization occurred in the description of the type of store in which medications can be purchased. Although the location is not overtly stated in the English version, all six participants framed the question using one or more examples (e.g., PHARMACY, STORE, C-V-S). Their translations included a variety of contextualizations from general (STORE) to specific (PHARMACY) to highly specific (C-V-S, W-A-L GREEN). Thus, all of the participants framed the phrase by adding information about the place of purchase, but a variety of examples were utilized across the participants (table 2).

TABLE 2. *Contextualization for Medication Types and Place of Purchase*

	Contextualization for Medication Types	Contextualization for Place of Purchase
DP1*	PAIN (medicine)	STORE
	VITAMINS	PHARMACY
	M-O-T-R-I-N	
	T-Y-L-E-N-O-L	
DP2	--	STORE
DP3[	--	DRUG-STORE
INT1	(not) PRESCRIPTION	PHARMACY
	A-D-V-I-L	
	T-Y-L-E-N-O-L	
INT2	--	C-V-S
		W-A-L GREEN
		DRUG-STORE
INT3	A-S-P-I-R-I-N	PHARMACY
	I-B-U-P-R-O-F-E-N	
	COUGH (medicine)	

*DP = Deaf physician, INT = interpreter

As mentioned earlier, the English term "over-the-counter" does not have a ready ASL correspondent. Although "over-the-counter" could be a candidate for compounding, these participants did not express medication names or types that fit into an overarching category, a condition necessary for creating a compound. Another means of mitigating the lack of a corresponding term in ASL for "over-the-counter" is seen in the participants' addition of information about the place of purchase, although this information was not present in the original question. The store names were not uniform, however; the examples varied across the participants (table 2).

CONTRASTING

A second linguistic feature the participants used was *contrasting*. Four of the six participants emphasized the difference between over-the-counter medications and prescription medications by describing and comparing the way in which each type of medication is obtained.

By creating contrast, participants bring focus to the topic (over-the-counter medications) and away from a related topic (prescription medications). It is interesting to note that when contrasting was absent, the duration of each translation was markedly shorter (table 3).

SPECIFICATION OF THE ENGLISH VERB "TAKE"

In ASL, *specification* is often used to express the type and manner of the action for the concept "take." Although ASL has a citation form of TAKE (figure 1), the form was not used by any of the participants as its semantic range does not include the taking of medication. Rather, the specified form for TAKE-PILL in ASL (figure 2) was used by all of the participants.

TABLE 3. *Contrasting (OTC and Prescription Medications) and Length of Translations*

	Contrasting OTC and Prescription Medications	Length of Translation (in seconds)
DP1*	Yes	40
DP2	No	6
DP3	No	5
INT1	Yes	27
INT2	Yes	40
INT3	Yes	41

*DP = Deaf physician, INT = interpreter

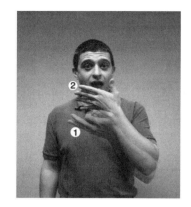

FIGURE 1. TAKE *(ASL)*.   FIGURE 2. TAKE-PILL *(ASL)*.

In addition to the lexical sign TAKE-PILL, two interpreters also specified another form of taking medicine. One interpreter included the lexical
item TAKE-LIQUID-from-cup. Another interpreter included the lexical item
TAKE-LIQUID-from-spoon. This is a common linguistic feature in ASL,
that is, providing the topic followed by signs or gestures that specify the
information.

Since ASL can indicate a high degree of specificity in place, manner,
and amount, the choice of TAKE-PILL by the majority of the participants
might suggest that this sign has undergone semantic broadening.

SUMMARY

We have described how contextualization, contrasting, and specification are used to translate the question "Are you taking any over-
the-counter medications" from English into ASL. Even though similar
approaches are taken, the physicians and interpreters demonstrated
variation in their productions, both in the specific lexical choices and
the amount of information they included. In Appendix A, we provide a
full transcription of one of the physician's (DP1) ASL translation of the
question (Example 1) and a full transcription of one of the interpreter's
(INT1) ASL translation of the question (Example 2). In Example 1,
contextualization of the type of medication is found in line 8 (M-O-T-
R-I-N, T-Y-L-E-N-O-L) and the location for purchasing the medication
in lines 1, 2, and 7 (STORE); contrasting is expressed in lines 1–6; and
specification of "take" is found in line 8 (TAKE-PILL). In Example 2,
contextualization of the type of medication is found in line 3 (A-D-V-I-L,

T-Y-L-E-N-O-L, ASPIRIN), and contextualization of location is present in line 2 in a lexicalized form of "pharmacy" (#PHMCY); specification of "take" is present in line 1 (TAKE-PILL, TAKE-LIQUID-from-cup) and line 4 (TAKE-PILL).

"Are You Allergic to Any Medications?"

"Are you allergic to any medications" is a critical question in the medical interview. If misconstrued or misunderstood, it could have life-threatening implications for a patient. In translating this question from English into ASL, a challenge arises with the word "allergic." In English, "allergic" is understood as a reaction to a number of possible triggers such as foods, pollen, animal dander, dust, as well as to certain medications. Thus the concept of "allergies" in English has a fairly broad semantic range. In ASL, ALLERGY may be perceived with a more limited semantic range than in English since its perception is driven by its production. That is, ALLERGY is constructed in a two-morpheme blend: first, indexing the nose, followed by a sign that could be glossed as OPPOSED-TO (figure 3). Thus the first morpheme in ALLERGY immediately implies nasal symptoms, which typically occur in response to airborne allergens.

In the next two sections we examine the contextualization of "allergic" and the specification of "take." Note that the concept of "take" is implied in this example, unlike in the earlier question discussed (i.e., "Do you take any over-the-counter medications?"), where "take" is overtly stated.

FIGURE 3. ALLERGY *(ASL)*.

As table 4 shows, the participants chose to contextualize "allergic" by incorporating a range of allergic reactions in their translations. One physician (DP1) contextualized "allergic" by incorporating two verbs (REACT, NOT-AGREE); another (DP3) provided examples of symptoms (NAUSEA, FLUSH, RASH); and one physician (DP2) chose not to contextualize the term in either manner. All three interpreters contextualized "allergic" by providing a variety of symptoms as examples.

Regarding specification, as in the earlier question ("Do you take any over-the-counter medications?"), all of the participants used TAKE-PILL as the generic equivalent of taking medication. This pattern occurs again with this question, as illustrated in table 4. Note that one physician (DP1) specified two examples in addition to TAKE-PILL (INJECTION-in-arm and INHALER).

It is notable that each interpreter included RASH as a symptom, as did the physician who provided a symptom example. This suggests that RASH may be regarded as the prototypical allergic reaction among the possible types. Further, in ASL it is common to add specificity, such as incorporating the location of the rash (e.g., RASH-on-arm, RASH-on-chest), as shown in table 4.

TABLE 4. *Contextualization for "Allergic Reactions" and Specification of "Take"*

	Contextualization for "Allergic Reactions"	Specification of "Take"
DP1*	REACT	TAKE-PILL
	NOT-AGREE	INJECTION-in-arm
		INHALER
DP2	–	TAKE-PILL
DP3	NAUSEA	TAKE-PILL
	FLUSH	
	RASH-on-arm	
	R-A-S-H	
INT1	RASH-on-chest	TAKE-PILL
	RASH-on-cheeks	
	THROAT-SWELL	
	CAN'T BREATHE	
INT2	MAKE SICK	TAKE-PILL
	RASH-on-arm	
INT3	THROAT-SWELL	TAKE-PILL
	RASH-on-face-and-body	

DP = Deaf physician, INT = interpreter

One option in translating this question into ASL is to contextualize "medications" by providing specific examples (e.g., penicillin, insulin, and sulfa drugs). However, in this question, no participant contextualized "medications." Because allergic reactions are highly variable and hold high-risk implications for patients' health, we speculate that this lack of contextualization reflects a judicious decision to avoid influencing the patients' response.

SUMMARY

In the ASL translations of "Are you allergic to any medications?" we identified instances of contextualization and specification. Appendix B provides two examples. In Examples 1 (DP2) and 2 (INT1), TAKE-PILL is specified. In Example 2, contextualization of allergic reaction appears in lines 2 and 3 (RED RASH-on-chest, RASH-on-face, THROAT-SWELL, CAN'T BREATHE).

"Are You Sexually Active?"

This question, only four words in length, raises linguistic challenges that may be further influenced by the interlocutors' social and cultural status. The question is commonly asked during medical interviews in which pregnancy, sexually transmitted diseases, or other conditions relating to the genitourinary system are discussed. This is a potentially sensitive question, particularly when the physician or interpreter and the patient are of the opposite sex. In English, the phrase "sexually active" is understood to include a variety of unspecified sexual activities. As previously described in the "over-the-counter" analysis, several examples representing a single category are frequently used in ASL to provide contextualization. With this question the main challenge is to determine how to select examples that will represent the meaning of "sexually active" while being sensitive to the social and cultural taboos that underlie the phrase.

CONTEXTUALIZATION

The ASL translations varied among the participants, although similarities were also evident. All of the participants expressed the overarching topic of "sex" with either the conventional signs INTERCOURSE or SLEEP-TOGETHER, followed by examples. However, the physicians and interpreters diverged in their use of specific examples of sexual activity.

All three physicians used the example of ORAL INTERCOURSE; in addition, one added the example of ANAL INTERCOURSE. By using continuers (e.g., ALL-LIST, AND-SO-ON), all three indicated that there might be a number of additional but unspecified behaviors. In contrast, the interpreters used what may be argued as more conservative, less explicit selections for their contextualization examples (see table 5).

This question also implies that the physician is asking about sexual activity with any partner. Although this implicit meaning may be understood in English, again, ASL users tend to provide specific examples. Three of the participants (one physician, two interpreters) included different types of partners, as illustrated by INT2's translation, which included HUSBAND, GIRLFRIEND, and ANYONE. In contrast, DP3's translation does not specify any information about partners but does provide two specific sexual activities as examples (see table 5). Overall, the interpreters provided more information about partners, while the doctors provided more information about sexual activity.

Once again we see different renderings of an English phrase that does not have an correspondent in ASL. Both the physicians and the interpreters

TABLE 5. *Contextualization for "Sexually Active" and "Partner"*

	Contextualization for "Sexually Active"	Contextualization of (Implied) "Partners"
DP1	INTERCOURSE, SLEEP, INTERCOURSE, SEX ANY KIND	MAN, WOMAN
DP2	INTERCOURSE, ORAL-INTERCOURSE, SEX ETCETERA	OTHER PERSON
DP3	SEX ACTIVE, INTERCOURSE, ANAL-INTERCOURSE, ORAL-INTERCOURSE, ACTIVE	–
INT1	SEX, INTERCOURSE, ANAL-INTERCOURSE, AND-SO-ON	–
INT2	SLEEP TOGETHER, SEX	PARTNER, HUSBAND, GIRL-FRIEND, ANYONE
INT3	INTERCOURSE, ACTIVE, MASTURBATION	PARTNER, MAN, WOMAN, OTHER PERSON

DP = Deaf physician; INT = interpreter

provide examples of sexual activity and partner types, but again the number and the type of examples vary.

In the ASL translations of the question "Are you sexually active?" we identified instances of contextualization. Full transcriptions of one of the physician's (DP3) translations and one of the interpreter's (INT2) translations are provided in Appendix C. In Example 1, two instances of contextualizing "sexual activity" are evident in lines 2 and 3. In Example 2, contextualization is evident for the concept of "partners" in line 2.

CONCLUSION

We have previously argued that healthcare interpreting between ASL and English needs to be recognized as a type of interpreting that requires specialized education and credentialing (Swabey & Nicodemus, 2011). Across age, gender, education, socioeconomic status, ethnicity, and health conditions, all deaf citizens need quality access to communication in healthcare settings. Further, education and professional development are critical for interpreters who work in health care as this type of work is often physically and cognitively demanding, which taxes the practitioner's linguistic, ethical, and emotional capacities. Without national standards, underqualified interpreters will continue to work in this setting, potentially compromising the health and well-being of deaf patients.

We pursued this study with the aim of informing and improving ASL-English interpretation in the healthcare setting and enhancing the dialogue between interpreters, deaf bilingual healthcare providers, and deaf patients who use ASL. To our knowledge, this is the first study that examines the translations of common medical questions as rendered by deaf bilingual physicians and nationally certified interpreters. The results of this study are based on a small sample size and, although a larger participant group would have led to more conclusive results, the number of deaf bilingual physicians is miniscule compared to the total physician population.

It is noteworthy that no standard translations were observed for these typical medical questions, especially given that each participant was working with the same patient profile. Although similar discourse features were used in these translations, particularly with contextualization, which occurred in 17 of the 18 translations, the translations exhibited considerable variation. One potential explanation for the variation is the lack of standard lexical correspondents in ASL for English phrases such as "over-the-counter" and "sexually active." Further, the contextualization of these terms may require the use of additional concepts that also do not have standard ASL equivalents, such as "pharmacy" and "prescription." Moreover, although ASL has standard lexical equivalents for the English terms "allergic" and "take," the semantic range of each term appears to be broader in English than in ASL, presenting additional challenges for an accurate translation. Again, we saw similar approaches (specification of the verb "take" and contextualization of "allergic") and some similar patterns (TAKE-PILL for "take"; R-A-S-H consistently used as one example of "allergic"). These factors may explain the variation in length and detail found in these translations.

This aim of this study was to identify and document linguistic features used by deaf bilingual physicians and expert healthcare interpreters when translating common medical questions. The main findings include the patterned use of contextualization, contrasting, and specification. The results also illustrate the lack of standard ASL lexical correspondents for common terms in the healthcare setting. Further research is needed on this topic to ensure quality communication for deaf patients. We suggest that such investigations be conducted using a community-based participatory research approach, that is, a collaborative process between researchers and community partners, both deaf and hearing (Starr & Graybill, 2012). Although communication that occurs "in the moment" will be based on a variety of linguistic, social, and cultural factors, the investigation of both direct and interpreted medical discourse in ASL is an idea whose time has come.

ACKNOWLEDGMENTS

This study was supported by a research grant from the Registry of Interpreters for the Deaf awarded to Laurie Swabey and Brenda Nicodemus. We extend our thanks to the following individuals for their assistance with this project: Doug Bowen-Bailey, Elaine Hsieh, Richard Laurion, Annette Miner, Dianne Oberg, Lucinda O'Grady, Derek Roff, Joseph Santini, Marty Taylor, and Leandra Williams. We are especially grateful to Roberto Santiago for his significant contributions to the transcription, translation, and photography necessary for this study. This study would not have been possible without the generous contribution of the physicians and interpreters who participated, and we extend our gratitude to them.

NOTES

1. Formerly St. Mary's campus of the College of St. Catherine.
2. Spoken language interpreters have followed a different trajectory. The need for qualified healthcare interpreters has been recognized and addressed through the establishment of dedicated organizations (e.g., National Council on Interpreting in Health Care, California Healthcare Interpreting Association, International Medical Interpreting Association) and certifying bodies (e.g., Certification Commission for Healthcare Interpreters, National Board of Certification for Medical Interpreters). Further, there is a growing body of literature on healthcare interpreting for spoken language interpreters (e.g., Angelelli, 2004, 2008; Brashers, Goldsmith, & Hsieh, 2002; Hsieh, 2006, 2007; Pöchhacker & Shlesinger, 2007).
3. Data from the questions in boldface type are discussed in this chapter.

REFERENCES

Angelelli, C. V. (2004). *Revisiting the interpreter's role: A study of conference, court, and medical interpreters in Canada, Mexico, and United States.* Amsterdam: Benjamins.

Angelelli, C. V. (2008). The role of the interpreter in the healthcare setting: A plea for a dialogue between research and practice. In C. Valero-Garcés & A. Martin (Eds.), *Building bridges: The controversial role of the community interpreter* (pp. 139–152). Amsterdam: Benjamins.

Barnett, S. L. (2002). Communication with deaf and hard-of-hearing people: A guide for medical education. *Academic Medicine, 77,* 694–700.

Barnett, S. L., & Franks, P. (2002). Healthcare utilization and adults who are deaf: Relationship with age at onset of deafness. *Health Services Research, 37,* 105–120.

Brashers, D. E., Goldsmith, D. J., & Hsieh, E. (2002). Information seeking and avoiding in health contexts. *Human Communication Research, 28*(2), 258–271.

Fernandez, A., Schillinger, D., Grumbach, K., Rosenthal, A., Stewart, A. L., Wang, F., & Perez-Stable, E. J. (2004). Physician language ability and cultural competence: An exploratory study of communication with Spanish-speaking patients. *Journal of General Internal Medicine, 19*(2), 167–174.

Fox, B. A. (1994). Contextualization, indexicality, and the distributed nature of grammar. *Language Sciences, 16*(1), 1–37.

Freeman, G. K., Rai, H., Walker, J. J., Howie, J. G. R., Heaney, D. J., & Maxwell, M. (2002). Non-English speakers consulting with the GP in their own language: A cross-sectional survey. *British Journal of General Practice, 52,* 36–38.

Gumperz, J. J. (1982). *Discourse strategies.* Cambridge: Cambridge University Press.

Ha, J. F., Anat, D. S., & Longnecker, N. (2010). Doctor-patient communication: A review. *Ochsner Journal, 10,* 38–43.

Harmer, L. M. (1999). Health care delivery and deaf people: Practice, problems, and recommendations for change. *Journal of Deaf Studies and Deaf Education, 4*(2), 73–110.

Hedding, T., & Kaufman, G. (2012). Health literacy and deafness: Implications for interpreter education. In L. Swabey & K. Malcolm (Eds.), *In our hands: Educating healthcare interpreters* (pp. 164–189). Washington, DC: Gallaudet University Press.

Hsieh, E. (2006). Conflicts in how interpreters manage their roles in provider-patient interactions. *Social Science and Medicine, 62*(3), 721–730.

Hsieh, E. (2007). Interpreters as co-diagnosticians: Overlapping roles and services between providers and interpreters. *Social Science and Medicine, 64*(4), 924–937.

Janzen, T., & Shaffer, B. (2008). Intersubjectivity in interpreted interactions. In J. Zlatev, T. Racine, C. Sinha, & E. Iktonen (Eds.), *The shared mind: Perspectives on intersubjectivity* (pp. 333–355). Amsterdam: Benjamins.

Klima, E. S., & Bellugi, U. (1979). *The signs of language.* Cambridge, MA: Harvard University Press.

Lichstein, P. R. (1990). The medical interview. In H. K. Walker, W. D. Hall, J. W. Hurst (Eds.), *Clinical methods: The history, physical, and laboratory examinations* (3rd ed.). Boston: Butterworth-Heinemann. Retrieved February 14, 2014, from http://www.ncbi.nlm.nih.gov/books/NBK349/

MacKinney, T. G., Walters, D., Bird, G. L., & Nattinger, A. B. (1995). Improvements in preventive care and communication for deaf patients: Results of a novel primary health care program. *Journal of General Internal Medicine, 10*(3), 133–137.

Manson, A. (1988). Language concordance as a determinant of patient compliance and emergency room use in patients with asthma. *Medical Care, 26*(12), 1119–1128.

McKee, M. M., Barnett, S. L., Block, R. C., & Pearson, A. P. (2011). Impact of communication on preventive services among deaf American Sign Language users. *American Journal of Preventive Medicine, 41*(1), 75–79.

Mitchell, A. J., & Selmes, T. (2007). Why don't patients take their medicine? Reasons and solutions in psychiatry. *Advances in Psychiatric Treatment, 13,* 336–346.

Nicodemus, B., & Swabey, L. (2014). Conveying medication prescriptions in American Sign Language: Use of emphasis in translations by interpreters and deaf physicians. *International Journal for Translation & Interpreting, 6*(1), 1–22.

Ong, L. M. L., de Haes, J. C. J. M., Hoos, A. M., & Lammes, F. B. (1995). Doctor-patient communication: A review of the literature. *Social Science and Medicine, 40*(7), 903–918.

Perez-Stable, E. J., Napoles-Springer, A., & Miramontes, J. A. (1997). The effects of ethnicity and language on medical outcomes of patients with hypertension or diabetes. *Medical Care, 35*(12), 1212–1219.

Pöchhacker, F., & Shlesinger, M. (Eds.). (2007). *Healthcare interpreting: Discourse and interaction*. Amsterdam: Benjamins.

Pollard, R. Q. (1998). Psychopathology. In M. Marschark & D. Clark (Eds.), *Psychological perspectives on deafness* (Vol. 2, pp. 171–197). Mahwah, NJ: Erlbaum.

Rich, E. C., Crowson, T. W., & Harris, I. B. (1987). The diagnostic value of the medical history: Perceptions of internal medicine physicians. *Archives of Internal Medicine, 147*, 1957–1960.

Seijo, R., Gomez, H., & Freidenburg, J. (1991). Language as a communication barrier in medical care for Hispanic patients. *Hispanic Journal of Behavioral Sciences, 13*, 363–376.

Starr, M., & Graybill, P. (2012). *Engaging the deaf community in research action*. Paper presented at Gallaudet University, Washington, DC, October 15.

Steinberg, A. G., Barnett, S., Meador, H. E., Wiggins, E., & Zazove, P. (2006). Health care system accessibility: Experiences and perceptions of deaf people. *Journal of General Internal Medicine, 21*(3), 260–266.

Steinberg, A. G., Wiggins, E. A., Barmada, C. H., & Sullivan, V. J. (2002). Deaf women: Experiences and perceptions of healthcare system access. *Journal of Women's Health, 11*(8), 729–741.

Swabey, L., & Nicodemus, B. (2011). Bimodal bilingual interpreting in the U.S. healthcare system: A critical linguistic activity in need of investigation. In B. Nicodemus & L. Swabey (Eds.), *Advances in interpreting research: Inquiry in action* (pp. 241–260). Amsterdam: Benjamins.

Williams, S., Weinman, J., & Dale, J. (1998). Doctor-patient communication and patient satisfaction: A review. *Family Practice, 15*, 480–492.

Witte, T. N., & Kuzel, A. J. (2000). Elderly deaf patients' health care experiences. *Journal of the American Board of Family Practice, 13*(1), 17–22.

Witter-Merithew, A., & Nicodemus, B. (2010). Intentional development of interpreter specialization: Assumptions and principles for interpreter educators. *International Journal of Interpreter Education, 2*, 135–147.

Appendix A

"Do You Take Any Over-the-Counter Medications?"

In Appendix A we offer a full transcription of one of the physician's (DP1) ASL translation of the question. In Example 1, contextualization of the type of medication is found in line 8 (M-O-T-R-I-N, T-Y-L-E-N-O-L), and the location for purchasing the medication in lines 1, 2, and 7 (STORE); contrasting is expressed in lines 1–6; and specification of "take" is found in line 8 (TAKE-PILL). In Example 2 we present a full transcription of one of the interpreter's (INT1) ASL translation of the question. Here, contextualization of the type of medication is found in line 3 (A-D-V-I-L, T-Y-L-E-N-O-L, ASPIRIN), and contextualization of location is present in line 2 (#PHMCY); specification of "take" is present in line 1 (TAKE-PILL, TAKE-LIQUID-from-cup) and line 4 (TAKE-PILL).

EXAMPLE I. *Deaf physician's (DP1) translation of "Do you take any over-the-counter medications?"*

1. YOU MEDICINE YOU GO-TO STORE INDEX-store?
   "Have you gone to a store to buy medicine?"
2. YOU HAVE MEDICINE FROM STORE INDEX-store YOU?
   "Do you have medicine that you got at a store?"
3. YOU BUY CL:C (right hand) CL:C (left hand) – "many bottles on shelves" ANY INDEX-bottles YOU?
   "Have you bought the kind of medicines you get off the shelf?"
4. FOR PAIN OR VITAMIN ALL-LIST?
   "such as pain remedies or vitamins or that type of thing?"
5. YOU (gesture –"no") MEDICINE DOCTOR WRITE GIVE-TO-YOU (head-shake and gesture –"no").
   "I'm not referring to prescription medications that you get from a doctor."
6. YOU GO-TO PHARMACY MUST GIVE PAPER FROM DOCTOR GIVE EXCHANGE-FOR MEDICINE (headshake and gesture –"no").
   "I don't mean the type of medications that you obtain from a pharmacist."

---

7. BUT YOU YOURSELF GO-TO STORE YOURSELF BUY WHATEVER YOU WANT INDEX-store YOU (headshake)?

"I'm talking about the nonprescription medicines that you buy at the store."

8. NONE TAKE-PILL YOU NOW UP-TO-NOW ONE-WEEK TWO-WEEKS UP-TO-NOW MONTH TAKE-PILL ANY INDEX-medicine? GIVE-NAME M-O-T-R-I-N ALL-LIST T-Y-N-E-O-L ALL-LIST GIVE-NAME + +(headshake) (nod)/

"Have you taken any of those over-the-counter medications, such as Motrin or Tylenol, recently or in the past?"

EXAMPLE 2. *Interpreter's (INT1) translation of "Do you take any over-the-counter medications?"*

1. WAVE-HAND-GET-ATTENTION YOU DOCTOR WANT KNOW YOU MEDI-CINE TAKE-PILL++ TAKE-LIQUID-from-cup.

"Your doctor wants to know if you are taking any medications."

2. SO YOU FOLLOW #RX MEDICINE GIVE-YOU GO #PHMCY BUY?

"Do you take prescription medication that you purchased at a pharmacy?"

3. HAND-WAVE-GET-ATTENTION OTHER KIND MEDICINE O-T-C MEANS DON'T NEED DOCTOR WRITE GIVE-YOU/SAME EVERYDAY A-D-V-I-L LIKE LIST T-Y-L-E-N-O-L, ASPIRIN, OTHER

"The doctor is asking about over-the-counter medications, such as Advil, Tylenol, or aspirin—other medications that don't require a doctor's prescription."

4. YOU TAKE-PILL OTHER QUESTION?

"Are you taking any of these other types of medications?"

Appendix B

"Are You Allergic to Any Medications?"

Examples 1 (DP2) and 2 (INT1) both illustrate specification: TAKE-PILL. In Example 2, contextualization of allergic reaction is found in lines 2 and 3 (RED RASH-on-chest, RASH-on-face, THROAT-SWELL, CAN'T BREATHE).

EXAMPLE 1. *Deaf physician's (DP2) translation of "Are you allergic to any medications?"*

1. MEDICINE TAKE-PILL, YOU ALLERGY ANY?
   "Do you take any medications that cause allergic reactions?"

EXAMPLE 2. *Interpreter's (INT1) translation of "Are you allergic to any medications?"*

1. DOCTOR ASK-YOU YOU ALLERGY MEDICINE
   "Your doctor is asking if you are allergic to medicine."

2. SAME-AS TAKE-PILL MEDICINE BEFORE RED RASH-on-chest, RASH-on-face?
   "For example, when you take a pill, does it result in a rash on your chest or face?"

3. #OR THROAT-SWELL CAN'T BREATHE?
   "Or does your throat swell and you can't breathe?"

4. ANY PROBLEM TAKE-PILL MEDICINE FROM-PAST-TO-NOW?
   "Have you had any problems with medications at any time in your life?"

Appendix C

"Are You Sexually Active?"

In the ASL translations of the question "Are you sexually active?" we identified instances of contextualization. We have provided full transcriptions of one of the physician's (DP3) translations and one of the interpreter's (INT2) translations. In Example 1, two instances of contextualizing "sexual activity" are evident in lines 2 and 3. In Example 2, contextualization is evident for the concept of "partners" in line 2.

EXAMPLE 1. *Deaf physician's (DP3) translation of "Are you sexually active?"*

1. YOU SEX ACTIVE?
   "Are you sexually active?"
2. MEAN INTERCOURSE, ANAL-INTERCOURSE
   "By that I mean vaginal or anal intercourse"
3. SECOND-EXAMPLE ORAL-INTERCOURSE?
   "or fellatio"
4. YOU ACTIVE QUESTION?
   "Are you sexually active?"

EXAMPLE 2. *Interpreter's (INT2) translation of "Are you sexually active?"*

1. YOU PARTNER SLEEP-TOGETHER #SEX YOU?
   "Do you have sex with your partner?"
2. WITH HUSBAND SEX GIRLFRIEND #OR ANY-ONE?
   "With a husband, a girlfriend, or anyone else?"

Diagnosing Healthcare Assignments: A Year of Medical Interpreting for Deaf People in Austria and Germany

Patricia Brueck, Juliane Rode, Jens Hessmann, Britta Meinicke, Daniela Unruh, and Anja Bergmann

ABSTRACT

This chapter presents the insights of five practicing signed language interpreters into the conditions and factors that characterize professional interpreting in the medical field in Austria and Germany. To this purpose, a total of 142 healthcare assignments, completed by the five interpreters in 2012, were documented and analyzed. After considering general challenges offered by the medical setting and outlining field-specific conditions in Austria and Germany, we discuss recurrent features of medical encounters between deaf patients and hearing doctors that involve a signed language interpreter. The data presented here suggest that, more often than not, interpreters will encounter conditions that are conducive to the satisfactory outcome of healthcare assignments. However, a number of risks and potential stumbling blocks require the reflective practitioner to practice circumspection.

Just like anyone else, deaf people need medical appointments, some of which may be of a routine nature, while others may involve severe health problems. Unlike most people, however, deaf people often rely on mediated communication in order to be able to access what may be very personal, sensitive consultations and treatments. In countries like Germany and Austria, this has given rise to social regulations that enable them to draw on the financial support necessary to employ the services of professional interpreters. Accompanying a deaf person to see a doctor is a standard feature in the wide range of public service interpreting assignments offered by most signed language interpreters in both countries.

Depending on the circumstances, being involved as a third party in encounters between deaf patients and hearing doctors may be experienced as particularly challenging and emotionally trying. Since healthcare interpreting assignments deal with matters of immediate personal concern, they often involve dimensions of closeness and trust that go beyond the demands of many other settings.

This chapter reflects the experiences of five full-time signed language interpreters working in the medical field. We, the interpreters, are all female and professionally active in the western and southern regions of Germany and in the Vienna area in Austria. For the purposes of the study presented here, we tracked all of our healthcare assignments in 2012. These assignments account for some 10–15% of our total assignments that year. All of the healthcare assignments that form the basis of this study are listed in the appendix; expressions like "A:006," for "assignment no. 6 in 2012" refer to this list.

The study continues efforts to enhance the research orientation of working professionals and encourage the evolution of a practice-oriented research community, as cultivated in the EUMASLI (European Master in Sign Language Interpreting) study program (Hessmann et al., 2011; cf. www.eumasli.eu). All five of us graduated from the EUMASLI program in 2011. For the purposes of this study, we continued our cooperation with one of the EUMASLI teachers in the collaborative spirit of the study program. We did not consider ourselves specialists in medical interpreting. Rather, as a routine part of a varied professional practice, the specific features of healthcare assignments may easily be overlooked, and accompanying a deaf person to the doctor becomes "just another job." Thus, this study started as an attempt to counter the lack of awareness and reflection that may develop with the routine handling of what more often than not is a sensitive kind of assignment. We decided to take stock: if success resides in the satisfaction of the participants and, more particularly, in enabling deaf patients to achieve the goals of obtaining medical advice and treatment, then what is it that contributes to the successful outcome of a medical assignment? Conversely, what are the aspects that are experienced as problematic and potentially detrimental to such success?

Here we try to answer these broad questions by looking at a year of collective experience in the medical field. With reference to the literature we first review relevant features that concern deaf people's access to the healthcare system and the special challenges that medical settings present to signed language interpreters. We then provide background on the healthcare system in Germany and Austria as relevant to deaf people and characterize general aspects of our data. After that we describe (in some detail and with reference to particular assignments) the stepping-stones and stumbling blocks encountered in this one year of professional interpreting work in the medical field. In conclusion, we consider a number of limitations of this study and point out consequences for research as well as professional practice.

SIGNED LANGUAGE INTERPRETING IN THE HEALTHCARE SYSTEM

Deaf People's Access to the Healthcare System

Signed language interpreters generally work in a wide range of settings. They offer their services in almost any situation where deaf people encounter the hearing world. Assignments in the healthcare system are a routine part of the professional life of most signed language interpreters. Ideally, deaf people might prefer the services of a doctor who is competent in sign language (McKee et al., 2011), but, as a rule, one must have access to the dominant language in order to benefit from the services of the healthcare system. Therefore, deaf people need signed language interpreters if they are to be able to communicate in their natural language, given that the proficient use of one's own language is necessary for identity and self-esteem (Wedam, 2009, p. 185). That patients must be enabled to make informed decisions is universally acknowledged as a basic right (Gonzalez-Nava, 2009, p. 74). Moreover, the difficulties that deaf people encounter within the healthcare system underlines the importance of signed language interpretation to bridge gaps in communication between deaf patients and hearing medical staff and enable deaf patients to get all the information they need: "Interpreters for deaf people in medical settings are not a luxury or nicety but rather a service mandated by law" (Frishberg, 1990, p. 118).

Physicians often report significantly greater difficulties communicating with deaf patients than with their patients in general (Ralston, Zazove, & Gorenflo, 1996). In fact, many healthcare providers have unrealistic expectations regarding the use of spoken and written language by deaf people:

[M]any health care workers expect deaf individuals to write notes in English that clearly express the thoughts or questions of the individual and to read lips perfectly. No other subset of Americans who use English as their second language are expected to do this, nor are they presumed to be retarded when they fail at these efforts. Deaf individuals, on the other hand, are expected to do both. (Harmer, 1999, p. 96, in reference to Lotke, 1995)

Similarly, in their study of observations by persons who are deaf or hard of hearing, Iezzoni et al. (2004) found that respondents perceive "that physicians do not fully recognize the implications of communication barriers and have fundamental misconceptions about effective communication modalities" (p. 360). Inquiring into the knowledge, beliefs, and practices of physicians, Ebert & Heckerling (1995) concluded that "although most physicians recognized the appropriateness of using sign language interpreters to communicate with deaf patients, only a minority used these interpreters in their practices" (p. 229). An analysis of the perceptions of 25 Brazilian signed language–using patients demonstrates "the existence of a scenario of incommunicability that discourages enlightened decision making by patients about their own health" (Pereira & Fortes, 2010, p. 36).

The ability to communicate accurately with a patient is "one of the most effective and least expensive tools in diagnosing and treating patients" (Swabey & Nicodemus, 2011, p. 243), considering that medical diagnoses are often based on a medical history recorded during a conversation between patient and doctor (Harmer, 1999, p. 75).

Byrne and Long (1976) identified six phases of a medical consultation:

- establishing the doctor-patient relationship
- finding out the reason for the patient's attendance
- a verbal or physical examination
- consideration of the patient's condition
- explanation of treatment or further investigation
- termination

All of these phases depend on two-way communication and on information passing between the two parties involved. "Communication is often the most important feature of a successful relationship between a health care provider and . . . patient" (Shipman, 2010, p. 434; cf. van Dulmen, 2011). It is therefore crucial to use interpreting services for an accurate and meaningful diagnosis and treatment of deaf patients.

However, "the magnitude of the problems posed by speaking through an interpreter" (Aranguri, Davidson, & Ramirez, 2006, p. 627) needs to be recognized.

Special Challenges of Medical Settings

One of the problems facing signed language interpreters in medical settings is the huge variety of situations such as initial medical consultations, medical interviews, physical checkups, diagnoses, medical examinations, emergency room visits, in- and outpatient services, operations, healthcare education, explanations of treatments and prescriptions, and descriptions of discharge and follow-up care. Humphrey and Alcorn (1995) discuss settings in which interpreters are contracted for medical appointments that may take place in a neighborhood clinic or at a doctor's office. They may also be called to interpret in a variety of laboratory or hospital procedures, which can range "from emergency room procedures to routine tests and surgical/post-surgical events" (ibid., p. 308). Clearly, medical interpreting is nothing short of "diverse and unpredictable" (Napier, Locker McKee, & Goswell, 2006, p. 111).

Because of the huge variety of situations, the importance of accurate interpretation, the technical knowledge needed, and the emotional challenge involved, interpreting in healthcare settings is especially demanding (Tomassini, 2012). Interpreters in these settings should have a general knowledge of common illnesses, medical tests, treatments, procedures, and equipment. They also need to be familiar with human anatomy and the roles of various medical professionals (Napier, Locker McKee, & Goswell, 2006, p. 112; Humphrey and Alcorn, 1995, p. 311; Frishberg, 1990, p. 119). However, currently few interpreters have any specific medical training or background, and most of them have to rely solely on their everyday experience and general knowledge, which may give rise to serious communication problems in a field characterized by specialized expertise and terminology (Gorjanc, 2009, p. 85; Napier, Locker McKee, & Goswell, 2010, p. 118f.).

In medical settings, doctors are often regarded as authority figures who have their own ways of interacting with the client. However, the degree of participation of the patient may well have an impact on physicians' patient-centered communication (Cegala & Post, 2009). One relevant aspect of interpreted interaction is the positioning of the participants in relation to each other, which can significantly influence the communicative setting not just in terms of physical proximity but also because the seating arrangement may imply a hierarchy among the parties involved (Felgner, 2009, p. 58). The "interpreter will need to tactfully negotiate where to position themselves in the doctor's space" (Napier, Locker McKee, & Goswell, 2010, p. 119). Still, it is virtually impossible to find an ideal placement that can be kept for the whole assignment (Humphrey & Alcorn, 1995, p. 309). Initially, the interpreter needs to be flexible and adjust her position, based on the type of examination, the size of the room, the visual needs of the patient, and the medical equipment. The interpreter must also be ready to reposition herself to stay in visual contact with the patient without being in the doctor's way (cf. Felgner, 2009, p. 59; Frishberg, 1990, p. 121).

For obvious reasons, healthcare assignments can be embarrassing for patient and interpreter alike (e.g., if the patient has to undress or expose private body parts), and interpreters must take care to respect the patient's privacy (Humphrey and Alcorn, 1995, p. 309; Frishberg, 1990, pp. 119–120). "[T]he trick is knowing how to maintain sightlines with the deaf client, without embarrassing them" (Napier, Locker McKee, & Goswell, 2010, p. 119). If the patient has to get undressed, interpreters should give instructions beforehand as clearly as possible and then avert their eyes for the undressing. If an interpreter is necessary for the examination itself, the interpreter should make sure that she sees the deaf client's face, while facing away from any sensitive body parts (ibid.).

Interpreters often report that service providers and patients may have conflicting expectations as to the outcome of the consultation (Gonzalez-Nava, 2009, p. 72) as well as to the structure of the communication itself (Paulini, 2008, p. 95). While doctors generally expect short and pertinent answers to their questions, people from different cultural backgrounds, like Spanish or deaf people, tend to answer in a narrative style by telling a personal story (Angelelli, 2004, p. 19). When patients' and doctors' cultural beliefs and values differ, establishing a cooperative partnership is impeded (Lee, 2002, cited in Angelelli, 2004, p. 19). Disparities in cultural background leave ample room for "interlinguistic and intercultural mediation" (Pignataro, 2012). Mindess (1999) mentions substantial differences between hearing and deaf cultures and suggests techniques for cultural adjustment to compensate, such as skillful handling of the situation and elimination of misunderstandings to allow patients to control the interaction themselves (p. 188). As Metzger's seminal work (1999) has made clear, interpreters cannot afford to stay neutral but must be actively involved in the interaction if healthcare interpreting, or any other assignment, for that matter, is to succeed.

The Interpreter's Role in Healthcare Settings

Shortcomings of traditional models that propagate an ideal of "invisibility" and see interpreters as "conduits" or "machines" have long been recognized. Although "neutrality" is still a key term in many professional codes of ethics, medical interpreters' associations generally take into account that interpreting is just as much about cultural mediation and advocacy. The International Medical Interpreters Association (IMIA) states the following in its Code of Ethics:

> 7. Interpreters will engage in patient advocacy and in the intercultural mediation role of explaining cultural differences/practices to health care providers and patients only when appropriate and necessary for communication purposes, using professional judgment.

> 8. Interpreters will use skillful unobtrusive interventions so as not to interfere with the flow of communication in a triadic medical setting. (http://www.imiaweb.org/code/)

A study by Angelelli (2003) and a survey by Tate and Turner (1997) found that interpreters' self-perceptions follow these lines, whereas other studies show that, when questioned, interpreters answered in the spirit of the conduit model, as implied by their professional codes, but acted differently in their daily work (Dysart-Gale, 2005; Hsieh, 2009). Interestingly, studies from Switzerland found that most of the doctors viewed interpreters as "translation machines" (Leanza, 2005; Singy & Guex, 2005). Similarly, in a Canadian study, Rosenberg, Leanza, and Seller (2007) found that professional interpreters tended to be regarded as conduits or "cultural brokers," while family members were seen in a care-giving role.

Wadensjö studied medical interviews interpreted into spoken languages. She categorized interpreters' performances as "relaying" and "coordinating." The first category refers to interpreting in a narrow sense, that is, conveying what the participating parties intended to say, whereas the second category includes activities such as asking for clarification, prompting a response or turn at talk, and offering explanations (Wadensjö, 1992, pp. 18f.).

With reference to signed language interpreting, the best-known discussion of the interpreter's role is found in Metzger (1999). In her study on healthcare interpreting, Metzger analyzes two types of discourse mediated by interpreters. One dataset came from role-plays in which students interpreted simulated medical interviews; the other set was taken from real medical interviews. Metzger found that interpreters actively participated in the communication and influenced the discourse in accordance with the participants' goals. More recently, Major (2013) stresses that healthcare interpreting is "relational practice": professional interpreters can be shown to get actively involved in the flow of interaction in order to maintain good relationships between all participants (see also Major, this volume).

Angelelli (2004) observed and interviewed experienced spoken language interpreters working at the California Hope Hospital. She found that interpreters do not see themselves as invisible but get involved as "co-constructors to the interaction" (Angelelli, 2004, p. 7). She proposed a continuum of visibility with a corresponding impact on the medical information involved. Interpreters in her study used a wide range of metaphors to describe their roles (ibid., pp. 130f.). In his study of Spanish-English medical discourse with immigrants to the United States, Davidson (2000) found that interpreters were officially required to act as an "instrument," "saying all and only what has been said" (p. 400). In practice, however, interpreters are encouraged "to keep the interview short, and to keep patients 'on track'" (p. 401). In a note of criticism Davidson notes that the interpreters in his study in effect "work as an extra gatekeeping layer through which patients must pass in order to receive medical care" (ibid.).

More recent attempts at modeling actual interpreting behavior and decision making recognize that interpreters cannot always act by the book but must respond flexibly to the demands of specific situations. Based on interaction research on monolingual dialogues, where the dimensions of cooperation, enactment of roles, alignment, and accommodation figure prominently, Lee and Llewellyn-Jones (2011) postulate that "interpreters should make use of many of the same behaviors that the other participants make use of in an interaction, rather than calling upon some special interpreter-specific behaviors that might come across as strange and alien to the interlocutors" (p. 2).

Starting from this premise, Lee and Llewellyn-Jones's role space model identifies presentation of self, interaction management, and alignment to deaf or hearing participants as the three dimensions that work together in the creation of actual interpreting behavior. One might predict that, in healthcare assignments, relatively little self-presentation of the interpreter would coincide with high interaction management and a high level of alignment to deaf patients.

In another attempt at going beyond considerations of "right or wrong" and providing a realistic account of interpreting behavior, Rozanes (2013) suggests that interpreters tend to be protective about their goals and try to stay as much as possible in their "comfort zone." Healthcare assignments may well pose challenges that put the dynamic equilibrium of the comfort zone at risk, but, as Rozanes asserts, it is challenges such as these that allow interpreters to grow as professionals.

Healthcare Interpreting Research in Austria and Germany

Only a few articles have been published dealing with signed language interpretation in healthcare settings in German-speaking countries. Those publications include two studies, one from 2001 and the other from 2012, both of which focus on the situation in Austria.

The older of the two studies (based on a questionnaire) analyzes the conversation practices of deaf patients in medical appointments. Deaf people from the Vienna area were asked about their experiences, their communication practices with doctors, and any problems they encountered when using interpreting services. The questionnaire was interpreted into signed language (Seeber, 2001). The more recent Austrian work is a qualitative interview study. Interviews were conducted with three deaf patients, one interpreter, and one doctor. They were asked about their experiences and communication strategies in medical assignments. The study also analyzes the extent of interpreter use and the challenges deaf people face when using an interpreter (Winkler, 2011).

As for Germany, we know of only a single study done in 1996 (Paulini, 2008). For this qualitative field study, 50 people with a hearing impairment were asked about their experiences in the healthcare field. These interviews took place in the course of two different workshops and via a communication forum. On the basis of the results of these interviews, Paulini formulated nine hypotheses that were tested in a follow-up questionnaire.

These studies are helpful in outlining basic aspects of how deaf people in Austria and Germany access the healthcare system. Our own study adds to this as yet small body of research and knowledge by presenting the views and experiences of interpreters who are professionally active in the healthcare field.

ONE YEAR OF SIGNED LANGUAGE INTERPRETING FOR DEAF PEOPLE IN THE GERMAN AND AUSTRIAN HEALTHCARE SYSTEM

This section describes the general situation of healthcare interpreting for deaf people in Germany and Austria and summarizes general aspects of the data that form the basis of our study.

General Situation

In Germany, deaf people are legally entitled to use signed language in medical appointments. The wording of the relevant Code of Social Law is as follows:

> Hearing-impaired people have the right to use signed language in the execution of social services, particularly in medical examinations and treatments. The social service providers in charge are obliged to cover the costs incurred by the use of signed language and other communication aids. (German Code of Social Law [*Sozialgesetzbuch*], Book 1, §17)

This regulation, which went into effect in 2001, provides a basis for the reimbursement of signed language interpreting costs by the statutory health insurance programs. As a consequence, medical practitioners themselves are generally not directly involved in the provision and financing of signed language interpreters.

General regulations notwithstanding, some health insurance providers may refuse to cover the costs for interpreters at certain special appointments like preoperative discussions. In such cases deaf people must file a complaint and fight for their rights. Such appeals may well be successful and may eventually compel health insurance companies to cover interpreting costs. However, regulations do not apply in the same way in cases involving hospitalization because medical clinics must cover the costs for interpreting services from the case-based daily allowance that is provided by the deaf person's health insurance company. Private clinics are exempt from these regulations and decide for themselves whether to cover these costs, but even publically funded hospitals may try to minimize interpreting services in order to economize.

The situation in Austria is similar to that in Germany. A federal law passed in 2006 (*Bundesbehindertengleichstellungsgesetz*) requires all public services, including services by associations or private companies funded with public money, to be accessible to people with disabilities. Apart from Carinthia,[1] all federal states cover the cost of interpreters at doctors' offices up to a maximum of €2,400 per year per client (including interpreting costs for other matters in their private lives, such as parent-teacher conferences).

Public hospitals and clinics are required to cover the costs of interpreting services out of their budgets, following the provisions of the 2006 law. Private clinics, exempt from the law, make their own determination whether to pay; some of them occasionally pay for some assignments, whereas others refuse payment altogether. In such cases, interpreting costs must be covered by the federal government, up to the aforementioned annual limit of €2,400 per individual deaf person.

In addition, Austria has four publicly funded deaf clinics, in Graz, Linz, Salzburg, and Vienna. These clinics were established as a part of public hospitals run by the Roman Catholic Order of the Brothers Hospitallers. They provide medical, psychological, and social services by professionals in Austrian Sign Language (http://www.barmherzige-brueder.at).

General patterns of making use of interpreters are similar in both Austria and Germany. If deaf people need to see a doctor, they must first make an appointment. Often the deaf person will contact the medical interpreter first and ask her to make the appointment by telephone. Since the availability of interpreters is often a problem (cf. Parisé 1999, p. 67), many deaf clients will ask their regular interpreter to arrange an appointment according to the interpreter's availability. Alternatively, interpreters may be contacted through agencies, listings on the Internet, and so on (see the section titled "Procurement"). If deaf clients want to consult a medical specialist or a specialist clinic, their general practitioner will need to make a specialist referral.

Usually the deaf client and the interpreter will meet at the doctor's office or the clinic at the appointed time. They will register at the front desk, then wait in the waiting room until being brought in to see the doctor or other medical staff for consultation, examination, or treatment. If a follow-up appointment is necessary, this is arranged at the front desk after the consultation.

Overall, increasing numbers of deaf people in both countries are taking advantage of their legal right and book a signed language interpreter when they have scheduled a medical appointment. However, as this study confirms, the use of interpreters is often limited to meetings with medical specialists, whereas general practitioners are frequently consulted without an interpreter. This may be due to a number of reasons, including already established long-term, trusting relationships between general practitioners and deaf patients; the use of family members, friends, or healthcare staff members as interpreters; or, in some cases, a general practitioner who is skilled in signed language. Another reason may be that a deaf person who sees a medical specialist rather than a general practitioner has a more complicated problem that needs detailed clarification and more specialized language. In such cases, deaf patients may prefer to bring in an interpreter to make sure they understand all of the details and are able to ask questions.

Assignments and Clients

In this section we outline the general characteristics of the assignments and the deaf clients involved in the 142 instances of medical interpreting in 2012 that form the basis of this study. A complete list of these assignments and more specific, relevant details appear in appendix 1.

HEALTHCARE ASSIGNMENTS

The whole dataset consists of 142 assignments for 60 patients that cover general practitioners (3%), public medical officers (1%), and 16 special medical areas (96%) (see figure 1).

The fact that 96% of all assignments are with medical specialists is striking. As mentioned earlier, this may be due to a number of reasons, including the fact that deaf patients may prefer to use an interpreter when seeing a specialist to avoid miscommunication but use other ways of communicating with their general practitioners (see the later section on procurement).

The most frequented specialties were the following:

–   internal medicine (18%, including vascular medicine, cardiology, diabetology, gastrology, nephrology, and colorectal surgery)
–   ophthalmologists (15%)
–   gynecologists and orthopedists (11% each)

The high percentage of visits to ophthalmologists may be related to the fact that deaf people crucially rely on their eyes. Therefore, they may be particularly sensitive to problems connected with sight. Of special note is that three assignments consisted of repeated otolaryngological examinations of

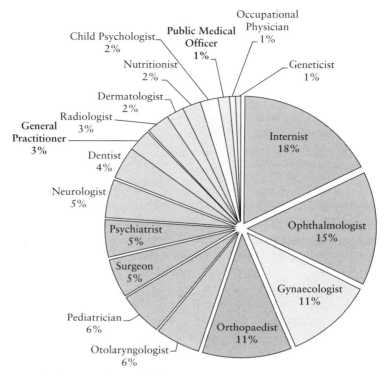

FIGURE I. *Assignments by medical area.*

a young deaf woman suffering from persistent headaches after cochlear implantation (A:050, A:090, A:095).

Ninety-one (64%) of the assignments were considered to be of moderate or "normal" urgency, 18% were classified as particularly urgent (25), and 18% were of low urgency (26). Urgent cases included a case of epilepsy (A:028), cataract surgery (A:029), and suspected rubella during pregnancy (A:055). Cases of low urgency involved routine checkups, follow-up visits, and so on (e.g. A:010, A:039, A:047). Most of the assignments were planned and arranged beforehand and not spontaneous. As far as we know from our daily work, generally only a few interpreting assignments are emergency cases in a narrow sense because, first, both countries have a shortage of signed language interpreters, and, second, hospitals and doctors may not even try to find an interpreter if immediate medical action is called for. Worse, hospitals and doctors may not even be aware of the possibility of contracting an interpreter or, if they do, may not know how to do so. Some hospitals may draw on various deaf staff

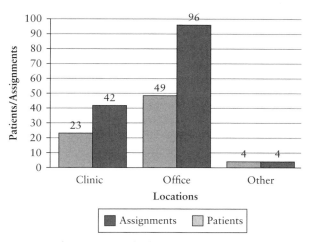

FIGURE 2. *Patients and assignments by location.*

members, who might be cleaning personnel or part of facility management, because they are deaf rather than because they have any medical interpreting competence (cf. Meyer, 2009, p. 144).

As figure 2 shows, 96, or 67.6%, of all assignments took place at doctors' offices, and only 42, or 29.6%, were at clinics. The remaining 4, or 2.8%, took place at offices where doctors examined the health status of the clients or their children in relation to decisions concerning school entry, retirement, disability allowances, and so on (see, for instance, A:027, A:100, A:129). The relationship between the number of patients and the number of assignments is very similar for both major types of location (1:1.8 for clinics, 1:2.0 for offices).[2]

DEAF PATIENTS

The patients were classified into six age groups. Figure 3 illustrates the numbers by patients and by assignments.

Figure 3 gives some indication of the distribution of patients to interpreters. Whereas in the age groups 30–39 and over 50, each deaf patient had, on average, two medical interpreting appointments; in the age groups 20–29 and 40–49, only a small number of deaf patients account for all of the assignments. Overall, the distribution of age groups seems to confirm the generalist approach practiced by most signed language interpreters: none of the interpreters in this sample reported a preference for any particular age group. Rather, assignments are accepted and carried out as they come in.

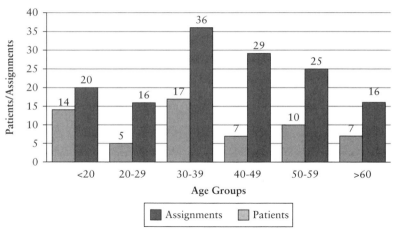

FIGURE 3. *Patients and assignments per age group.*

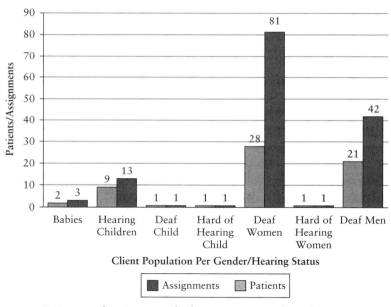

FIGURE 4. *Patients and assignments by hearing status and gender.*

Patients were further categorized by their gender and hearing status. Figure 4 compares the number of patients and assignments in seven categories: babies, hearing children, deaf children, hard of hearing children, deaf women, hard of hearing women, and deaf men.

Fifty-one clients, or 81%, were deaf or hard of hearing persons; 12, or 19%, were deaf family members of hearing children or babies whose hearing status was not recorded. In about 12% of all cases, the deaf client was the parent of a hearing, deaf, or hard of hearing child who was the subject of the medical consultation. Assignments that involved female deaf patients account for 57% of all assignments, compared to 30% that involved deaf men. This difference is partly accounted for by the fact that deaf women have more assignments with the same interpreter than do men (2.7 vs. 2.1 assignments per person). It is perhaps the case that deaf women are more aware of their health and may therefore see doctors more regularly, but gender distribution in the profession of signed language interpreting may also be a factor to consider: Deaf men may prefer to consult doctors on their own rather than rely on the services of a female interpreter.

Assignments were coded for two further broad factors that tend to complicate the work of interpreting. Nine of the 60 patients (23 assignments) displayed some kind of motoric, perceptual, or cognitive impairment. For example, spasms made the signing of one deaf patient difficult to understand (A:048), deaf patients' Usher syndrome needed particular attention (e.g., A:004, A:019, A:030), and one patient's mild dementia prompted frequent interventions by his deaf wife (A:092). Finally, a further 9 deaf patients (16 assignments) had a migrant background and had learned the national signed language as a foreign signed language with varying success (A:060, A:091, A:138).

All in all, even though coincidental to five interpreters' work in 2012, the assignments and deaf clients represented in our dataset seem to reflect quite adequately the range of tasks and challenges any signed language interpreter in Germany or Austria (and perhaps elsewhere) may expect.

STEPPING-STONES AND STUMBLING BLOCKS: 142 MEDICAL ASSIGNMENTS

The main goal of this study was to enable the participating practitioners to reflect on the experiences of professional signed language interpreting in the healthcare system and identify conditions that they consider supportive as opposed to factors that make their task difficult or stressful. In line with this broad intention of taking stock of interpreting experiences in the medical field, all of the 2012 assignments were recorded in a diary fashion: after each assignment the interpreter concerned noted down the basic facts of the assignment, gave a rough sketch of "how it went," and commented on aspects that were perceived as "positive" or "negative." This rather loose format had it drawbacks since the level of detail that was recorded varied from interpreter to interpreter, and in some instances it proved difficult to verify particular aspects of the assignment from memory at a later date. We use extracts, translated from the original interpreters' notes, to illustrate particular cases.

For the purposes of analysis, all of our notes were entered into a database and evaluated with regard to a number of recurring features that we considered as distinctive components of medical interpreting assignments. Although the triad of patient, doctor, and interpreter is at the center of medical consultations, additional components contribute to the overall progression and success of an assignment. These components demonstrate the complexity of interpreting in healthcare environments, and their analysis is at the heart of our chapter:

- **Procurement**: Someone has to arrange for an interpreter. Given the way interpreters are generally procured in Austria and Germany (see the following section), this is often related to the degree of familiarity and the type of personal relationship that exists between deaf clients and interpreters.
- **Medical staff**: Besides doctors, other medical staff are generally also involved in an assignment, often as receptionists but also in conducting examinations and administering treatments.
- **Waiting room interaction**: More often than not, even with an appointment, patients have to wait before they can see the doctor. Interestingly, this time is rarely idly spent but rather may allow for crucial interaction between deaf patients and interpreters.
- **Visually accessible environment**: Care must often be taken during an appointment when arranging adequate lines of sight and negotiating seating arrangements.
- **Doctors**: All of the doctors in this study were hearing. Obviously their attitudes and behaviors crucially contribute to the success of the interpreted interaction.
- **Patients**: Patients in this study were deaf (including a small number of patients who might be considered hard of hearing in audiological terms). In a number of cases, deaf clients accompanied their deaf or hearing children. Again, attitudes and behaviors of deaf patients contribute to the outcome of the consultation in obvious ways.

- **Interpreters:** The situation may prompt interpreters to react or get involved in different ways. Generally, more is involved than simply rendering messages.
- **Escorts:** Quite commonly, deaf patients were accompanied to the appointment by other people. While a deaf mother may simply take a child to the doctor's office, more typically, accompanying people are related to the patient in a caregiving or supervisory role and may get involved in the interaction.
- **Medical examinations:** When they occur as part of the consultation, physical examinations, often involving the use of medical equipment, may pose particular challenges for the interpreter.
- **Debriefing:** Assignments may not end with the consultation but will often involve some kind of debriefing situation that allows for direct communication between deaf clients and interpreters.

In the following section we review each of the previously mentioned components of medical assignments with reference to our data in search of stepping-stones and stumbling blocks, that is, factors that contribute, on the one hand, to the success of the interpreted interaction and the satisfaction of the participants and, on the other, factors that complicate or impede this particular form of encounter between deaf people and the hearing world.

Procurement

As discussed earlier, healthcare assignments imply increased responsibility for the interpreter and a great deal of trust on the part of the deaf patient. A study about trust in interpreted primary-care consultations in the UK found that "trust was a prominent theme in almost all the narratives" of service users, interpreters, doctors, nurses, and receptionists (Robb & Greenhalgh, 2006, p. 434). Following Ian Greener's (2003) categories, Robb and Greenhalgh distinguish three types of trust. "Voluntary" trust has to be built up and comes into play when deaf people choose their interpreters; "coercive" trust may also be relevant if the deaf person did not have a choice of interpreter. Third, "hegemonic" trust is established by the system and induces people to trust without knowing that they have any alternative (e.g., general trust in doctors).

A study of immigrants to the UK who needed spoken language interpreters for healthcare consultations consisted of 50 interviews in which participants asked interviewees to give their opinion of interpreters in medical consultations (Edwards, Temple, & Alexander, 2005). The results showed that "trust emerged as a key feature in people's understandings and experiences of the process and ideals in needing and using interpreters" (ibid., p. 90).

Procurement patterns confirm the relevance of personal relationships between deaf clients and their interpreters. A 2013 study highlights the importance of choice: enabling deaf consumers to choose their interpreters creates the rapport and trust necessary for a successful interpreting assignment (Major, 2013, p. 269). Clearly, this is at work in our data as well, where in 88% of all cases (125) clients had known their interpreters before the assignment, and in 80% of the assignments (114) it was the deaf person who directly contacted the interpreter.

When asked for the reasons for taking the same interpreter to all of her medical appointments, a deaf woman answered that it was organizationally advantageous because of the notorious scarcity of interpreters since the interpreter she is familiar with will prioritize her assignments or find a replacement when necessary. She added that she knew the interpreter well, trusted her, and was satisfied with her performance (for similar responses by other deaf women see Steinberg et al., 2005). She stressed that the interpreter's knowledge of her health situation and her special needs was a huge advantage (A:064). This is how the interpreter in question described arrangements for an appointment at a gynecologist's office:

> I had already known the deaf person for some time and had interpreted for her occasionally. We had not been in contact for some months, when she contacted me via e-mail, asking me if I was available to interpret an assignment at the gynecologist for her. She gave me the name and contact details of the specialist and asked me to call his office to make an appointment at a time that would suit me, as she was much more flexible with her time than me. (A:064)

The interpreter emphasized that her background knowledge of the deaf patient's health situation and special needs was greatly beneficial (on the problem of familiarity with the interpreter, cf. Parisé, 1999, p. 71ff). In addition, the rapport between doctor and patient is of the utmost importance for the success of a medical communication (Major, 2013, p. 52f.). Clearly, good rapport between patient and interpreter is no less important.

Very few assignments were organized by hearing doctors (5, or 3.5%), while 14.8% (21) were organized by others, such as family members, caregivers, social workers, or other signed language interpreters. Only 12% of the 142 assignments (17) were new encounters, in which the interpreter and the patient met for the first time, and most of these had been arranged by a third party or an agency. In very few exceptional cases, deaf clients contacted a previously unknown interpreter themselves, for instance, by sending an email to a list of interpreters. More generally, contact between deaf clients and interpreters was established directly by sending brief informal emails or text messages or using messaging services like WhatsApp. A total of 60 deaf people, more than half of whom had two or more assignments with the same interpreter, were involved in the 142 assignments. Some interpreters had regular clients with up to nine medical assignments in 2012.

The procurement system in Austria and Germany can be criticized for imposing much of the burden of organizing interpreting services on the deaf client. However, given a choice, deaf persons will understandably follow a preference for choosing a familiar and trusted interpreter for a sensitive setting such as health care.

Communication with Medical Staff

In most cases, the initial contact at a clinic or a doctor's office is with a receptionist, whose attitude may have a considerable impact on the doctor's manner and on the climate and tone of the consultation. Without regard to assignments in which deaf patients had no relevant contact with receptionists or other medical staff (51, or 36%) and in which receptionists were considered as neutral or matter of fact (21, or 15%), most receptionists (52, or 37%) were perceived as friendly, polite, and helpful, as in the following instance:

> I [the interpreter] arrive at the dentist some time before the assignment to be able to get to know the client, as I have not met the deaf person before. On my arrival, I am warmly welcomed by the dentist's assistant, who seems to be relieved to see me. The assistant informs me that the deaf patient has already arrived. She explains that this is the first deaf patient they have had and that basic communication seems to work, but that she did not understand some details. She shows me to the waiting room, where I present myself to the patient. The patient is very excited

and immediately starts to tell her life story and explain the reasons she has come to see the dentist. After a short wait, the assistant returns to tell the patient that it is her turn. During the whole assignment, the medical staff is very respectful and friendly with the deaf patient and me. (A:006)

In some cases (4, or 3%), the medical staff interacts directly with the deaf patient:

I [the interpreter] asked the assistant to explain the X-ray procedure to the patient by demonstrating it to her before starting the actual examination. The assistant follows my advice and has the patient go through the procedure without really switching on the X-ray machine. In this way, the patient is well informed and feels more at ease with the procedure. (A:018)

In 8 cases (6%), rather than addressing the deaf person, the medical staff tried to interact with the interpreter by discussing aspects of her work or signed language in general. This might have been prompted by what the staff member perceived as a parallel in status and function. Thus, the receptionist in the following example may have considered the interpreter to be in a supportive role similar to her own:

A patient who is under guardianship sees her ophthalmologist regularly. The receptionist knows me [the interpreter] and her because we have been there many times. The receptionist considers me to be her hard-working colleague and prefers to bond with me and not with the patient, who is obviously mentally deficient. Every time the patient and I see the doctor, the receptionist treats me with a lot of consideration and asks how my day was, if I had problems in my profession and so on. I always feel burdened by her attention, but the patient does not seem to be bothered, and the receptionist's attitude seems to have some advantages: we do not have to wait long before we see the doctor, [and] there is no problem with changing appointments when necessary. (A:030)

In only 7% of the assignments (10) were the medical personnel unable to deal with the situation, which had a negative impact on the assignment. Some of them did not understand the need for a signed language interpreter (cf. Frishberg, 1990, p. 119):

When I [the interpreter] arrive, the patient is already registering. I present myself to the registration staff. The receptionist presents the deaf patient with a form that needs to be filled in. She starts to explain the form to the patient and asks me not to interpret. Because the patient does not understand the receptionist's explanations, she makes eye contact with me, which angers the receptionist, who wants the patient to communicate with her and seems to feel disturbed by my presence. I intervene and explain to the receptionist the lack of eye contact (in order to follow the instructions the patient must look at the form and cannot maintain eye contact with the receptionist), but the receptionist is not really convinced. The medical assistant in the examination room has no experience with interpreting, either, and mocks the patient about being two people with the same name ("Oh, I have two Ms. Millers here, do I?"). (A:102)

In two cases the medical staff had a negative and arrogant attitude:

The assignment is at a group practice where several doctors work. The waiting room is huge and very crowded. There are several examination rooms, and the patients are called in by the doctors themselves. When registering, the patient and I [her interpreter] are treated with little respect. The staff seems to be stressed and to have little patience for the deaf patient. They do not care about her difficulties with sitting for a long time (she has recently had surgery) and tell her that there is no way to affect the order in which patients see the doctors. (A:089)

The influence of the surrounding medical staff on the tone of a medical consultation should not be underestimated, but all in all, the personnel encountered during our study seemed to be able to deal quite well with deaf patients and their interpreters. Where possible, most of them were welcoming and tried to give good service to the deaf patient. A few, however, were unfriendly; some, even hostile. It is possible that these staff members felt challenged by the presence of an interpreter, but a lack of kindness may, of course, be caused by many things, some of which may be explained by the demands of daily work in a medical institution.

Waiting Room

As we have emphasized, the successful completion of healthcare interpreting assignments crucially depends on the relationship between the interpreter and the deaf client. "[E]xperienced interpreters engage in and actively facilitate relational work to such a degree that it should be considered an integral part of the healthcare interpreter's role" (Major, 2013, p. xiii). Clearly, relational work must start before the actual contact with the doctor. In fact, our data show that most of the relational work is done in the waiting room before the consultation, if not during preceding assignments. In 49% of the healthcare assignments (69), the interpreter and the deaf patient use the time in the waiting room to reestablish their relationship and prepare for the upcoming consultation:

> When I [the interpreter] arrive at the hospital, the client and her husband have already passed registration and are waiting for admission. I have known her for a long time and have already interpreted for her several times. She uses the waiting time to brief me about her reason to be there. We reestablish our relationship by chatting because we have not had contact for some time. (A:012)

In 6% (9) of the cases, the interpreter can be regarded as a support person who has become a confidante by having regularly interpreted for the client. The interpreter may have known the deaf person as a friend before the assignment:

> I [the interpreter] and the patient have had private contact and are well known to each other. While we are waiting for admission, the patient tells me her life story and expands on her current problems. I switch into "friend mode" and try to give her advice. Before admission, the patient tells me that she needs to ask the doctor for a prescription for a certain medicine. At the end of the consultation, I remind the patient of the prescription. She signs to me that she doesn't dare ask the doctor. Hence, I "interpret" the request to the doctor. (A:046)

In this case, the interpreter takes the initiative and reminds the deaf person of what she has planned to do. In another case (A:103) the interpreter finds herself acting as a confidante because of the lack of family or friends to support the deaf client, who is undergoing an operation. She takes the patient home afterward.

If there is a briefing for the interpreter (67%, or 95 cases), as a rule, it is given by the deaf client (58.5%, 83 cases, of which 13 are new encounters). Occasionally it is the person escorting the deaf patient who briefs the interpreter (5%, 7 cases). In only 3.5% of the cases (5) is the interpreter briefed by the doctor or an assistant because the deaf patient has not yet arrived or is late:

> The patient arrives late because he had trouble finding the clinic in the huge hospital. In the meantime, I [the interpreter] make use of

the waiting time to ask the doctor for a short briefing and to explain the SLI [sign language interpreter] process to him. After the patient's arrival, I also get a briefing by him. He gives me detailed information about his illness and the prognosis that has been given to him. (A:085)

Only 12% (17) of the 142 assignments were new encounters between the interpreter and the client. Generally, waiting time was used for getting to know each other and briefing the interpreter about the upcoming assignment. This may be a vital procedure:

In the waiting room I [the interpreter] realize that the deaf person does not use fingerspelling correctly when she tries to explain the symptoms that made her come to see the doctor . . . Finally, we agree on a sign for the term the patient needs to use to explain her symptoms to the doctor to enable fluent communication between me and her. (A:051)

As in this case, getting to know each other and establishing a common base of communication with the deaf client may be essential for the success of the triangular communication in a stressful situation.

Waiting time in clinics or doctor's offices may, of course, be excessive (this was reported for 22, or 15%, of the assignments in both settings). However, more generally, time that may appear to be idly spent is in fact used to procure vital information and develop rapport between deaf clients and interpreters, which is crucial for handling the subsequent encounter between patients and doctors.

Creating a Visually Accessible Environment

In his discussion of the influence of nonverbal and paraverbal factors on the quality of interpreter-mediated interactions in medical settings, Felgner (2009, pp. 58–65) stresses the importance of creating a visually accessible environment because the interpreter's position in the room may have a considerable impact on the interpreted communication. The situation is even more complicated for signed languages: deaf patients and interpreters need to have eye contact, they need to be able to observe the doctor, who may give visual information, and the deaf patient should be able to make eye contact with the doctor as much as possible to help establish good doctor-patient rapport. The deaf patient's visual needs require interpreters to be flexible, adapt to the situation, and change position if necessary, especially during physical examinations and the use of special equipment. Occasionally, it may be necessary to adopt unusual positions, such as sitting on desks or bending down to make eye contact with a patient who is lying on an examination table.

In medical settings, patients and their escorts tend to sit down before the start of the consultation. Therefore, the spatial arrangement is likely to be fixed for all of the participants throughout most of the event. In most cases, the doctor and the patient will be sitting in chairs. A chair is often provided for the interpreter and may be next to the doctor, beside the doctor's desk, or next to the patient. In most cases, the interpreter will try to choose her own position. Usually deaf clients intervene only if they cannot see the interpreter well. Our data reveal only one case in which the interpreter and the patient discuss and agree upon the interpreter's position before the start of the consultation (A:010). In 36% of the assignments (51 cases) the interpreters reported having chosen their position themselves, either by asking the doctor whether it was okay to move a chair next to the doctor or next to the doctor's desk or simply by sitting down or standing where they thought it best:[3] "When called in, the patient enters the examination room first, I follow . . . She introduces herself. I introduce myself and ask for a place next to the doctor. He agrees without hesitation, and the communication goes on smoothly" (A:012).

Generally, proceeding like this meets with the doctor's tacit approval, though two doctors in this study rejected the interpreter's request for a position next to the doctor. In the preferred constellation, the interpreter takes a seat beside the doctor's desk, while the deaf patient is seated facing the doctor's desk. This "triangle" is also best for spoken language interpreting because all three parties have equal eye contact with each other, and no one is excluded (Haenel, 2001, p. 315).

Occasionally, clear-sighted doctors who are familiar with the interpreting environment will have provided a chair next to themselves for the interpreter before the start of the consultation (8, or 5.6% of the assignments). Some doctors will tell the interpreter where to get a chair or where to sit (3 cases reported). In a single case, the position assigned to the interpreter by an accompanying social worker caused a problem:

> At one medical assignment I was the last person who entered the consultation room. The doctor was friendly, but the social worker who accompanied the deaf client decided who was to sit where. I came to sit next to the social worker, and the deaf client sat next to the doctor. I asked the patient whether she wanted to change seats, but

she declined. Maybe I was not clear enough with my reasons. The deaf client was sitting on a swivel chair so she could change eye contact between the doctor and me. She decided to lip-read from the doctor, leaving me to interpret mostly consecutively. (A:017)

Most doctors seems to be familiar with or to adapt well to the interpreting environment. Only a minority (3 cases, or 2.1%) felt disturbed by the presence of the interpreter and the interpreter's movements. One such case occurred at a dentist's office: "[H]e treats two teeth and is obviously irritated by my presence. He seems to be disturbed by my 'dancing' to stay in the view of the patient" (A:105).

Special positioning may be needed when the deaf patient undergoes an examination (cf. Frishberg, 1990, pp. 120–121). This was recorded in three cases, at a dentist's (A:105), a gynecologist's (A:135), and a radiologist's office (A:079), where patients needed to follow instructions meticulously while at the same time adopting positions that impeded visual communication. Further visual conditions such as glaring light or an insufficiently lit room need to be taken into account, especially if the patients have a visual impairment. Thirteen, or 9.2%, of the assignments involved patients with sight disorders (e.g., related to Usher's syndrome), which meant that options for the interpreter's position were even more limited.

Occasionally (two cases), the consultation room itself may have a negative impact. It may simply be too small to allow for optimal positioning and adequate lines of sight:

> The problematic spatial arrangement is due to the fact that the doctor sits behind his desk, which is covered by stacks of papers to his right and left. Because of these barriers I have to sit next to the patient in front of the desk, opposite the doctor. I cannot sit next to the doctor or in one corner of a triangle. It does not feel professional and is a clear disadvantage for my interpreting. (A:124)

To summarize, although establishing clear lines of sight is crucial for signed communication, difficulty with this is rarely an insurmountable problem. A certain measure of clarification or negotiation may indeed be necessary, but, with few exceptions, hearing parties seem to understand and accept that the spatial arrangement must allow visual communication. Generally, interpreters can choose their spatial position comfortably and establish a suitable place in the triangular relation between the three main participants.

Hearing Doctors

In their reports, interpreters rated the doctors' overall behavior as "positive," "negative," or "unremarkable" to allow for an analysis of person-related factors that were perceived as either beneficial or detrimental to the interpreting situation. Of all of the assignments, 78 cases (55%) were rated as positive, and only 22 (15%) as negative.[4]

Initially, we suspected that a doctor's lack of experience with and knowledge of interpreted interaction with deaf people might prompt negative perceptions. There seems to be some truth in this since in just over half of the negatively evaluated cases (13) the doctor and deaf patient were meeting for the first time. However, not having met before does not, in and of itself, determine the outcome of the interaction. Rather, it seems that doctors' attitudes need to be considered: in 15 of the 22 negatively rated assignments, interpreters commented on what they perceived as condescending behavior by the doctor, lack of respect for the patient, or disregard for the deaf person as an interlocutor regardless of whether the doctors and patients had known each other before. In a few extreme cases, the deaf patients were not taken seriously or were even treated as if they were objects:

> The receptionist comes to take the patient to an eye test. To me [the interpreter]: "We do not need interpreting service. So far it's always gone pretty well. The patient knows what to do." Then she stops speaking and starts to use only gestures to communicate with the deaf patient. The deaf patient reads numbers in the eye test aloud, and the receptionists talks to her like to a child. The ophthalmologist shows up and starts talking to me. "She has always come alone. She can lip-read perfectly. Are you family?" "No. I'm the interpreter." Then he draws close to the patient's face and speaks in telegraphic style. The patient does not understand at all and looks at me. I interpret. The ophthalmologist looks at me, copies me, and seems to be proud. He stops speaking and uses only gestures to communicate with the patient. After the examination, the doctor wants to say good-bye, but first, the deaf patient mentions blurred vision and headaches while reading. The doctor answers that it is ophthalmic migraine, turns around, and is about to leave the room. He turns his back on an obviously terrified patient. She asks for clarification; I do the voice-over, which is ignored by the doctor, and the doctor turns around and waves good-bye to us. (A:059)

In four cases, it was the doctor's moody, willful, or authoritarian behavior that was perceived as negative and impeding communication between doctor and patient (A:032, A:051, A:059, A:105). Lack of empathy may be a further reason that interpreters experienced a situation as negative. In extreme cases, lack of empathy made the doctor misuse the interpreter as a bearer of bad news and the caregiver of a patient in despair:

> The physician tells me [the interpreter], "So good that you are here today!" It turns out that a tumor has been diagnosed, and the physician needs to tell the patient. For obvious reasons, the patient is very upset. The doctor is not responsive at all, ignores her psychological condition, and refers her to a colorectal surgeon. The woman struggles to keep back her tears. The doctor remarks that the tumor was tiny and that he was glad to have discovered it at such an early stage. The patient's questions are answered only minimally. He hands over the letter of referral for the hospital and asks her to take a copy of the pathology findings for the hospital's information . . . I am left with the feeling that the doctor is glad he did not have to deliver the diagnosis on his own. Apparently, he attributes to me (as a woman? as confidante?) the role of empathetic company. When we leave the office, he thanks me for having been there. (A:073)

Lack of time, as well as the pressure that institutional structures exert on doctors, are both detrimental to the success of medical consultations (Angelelli, 2004; Felgner, 2009, p. 59). In 18 (12.7%) of the assignments, the interpreters reported time pressure as a negative influence. The doctors could not really concentrate and seemed primarily interested in getting rid of the patients. In one case, a dentist did not even finish his explanations and abruptly left the room without even saying good-bye:

> The client asks some informed questions, which are not all answered by the doctor, who is distracted. The doctor performs the treatment in a casual way. When the patient asks a more complicated question, the doctor answers, but he disappears into the next room before he has finished his answer, leaving the patient and me entirely perplexed. He does not even return to say good-bye to the patient. (A:078)

Interestingly, none of the interpreters was under the impression that negative experiences were caused by a lack of confidence in their abilities, as Hsieh, Ju, & Kong (2010) found in their study of in-house interpreters and doctors working within hierarchically structured hospitals. One reason for this difference may be that freelance interpreters in Austria or Germany are not perceived as belonging to the doctor's team, so that neither competition nor hierarchical relations are involved.

In positively rated assignments, doctors were often familiar with the overall situation and knew either the deaf patient (49 cases) or both the deaf patient and the interpreter (34 cases). However, as might be expected, positive behavior does not depend on familiarity: 27 cases of a first encounter between a doctor, a deaf patient, and the patient's interpreter were also rated positively. Again, attitudes appear to be crucial. Thus, consultations were regarded positively when doctors treated the patient with respect, took time to fully answer the patients' questions, or adjusted to the patients' communicative needs by either using visual materials to illustrate their explanations (e.g., A:034) or attempting to communicate as directly as possible with the patient (e.g., A:016).

The following example illustrates a situation in which the doctors treated the deaf mother of a newborn patient with respect. They understood her concerns and showed interest in her by asking questions about signed language:

> The doctors are empathetic. They first look at all the data in their chart, then examine the baby. They ask the deaf mother how well she had made it through the previous night and then explain to her in detail why oxygen is so important for the newborn. They make sure that the mother knows what to do at home. After all the medical issues are settled, they start to show their interest in signed language and ask the deaf mother some questions. (A:033)

In some instances a doctor's efforts to communicate directly with the deaf patient can be evaluated as another way of showing respect:

> The neurologist speaks slowly and clearly in order to give the deaf patient the opportunity to lip-read. The patient is lip-reading, but as soon as she starts having trouble doing so, she looks at me [the interpreter]. For general small talk ("How are you? Are you tired?") direct communication is sufficient; for detailed medical information, interpretation is used. (A:016)

If direct communication is either impossible or limited, doctors may use models, pictures, radiographs, CT images, paintings, and so on to illustrate their explanations or to explain medical treatments. Often such strategies have a positive effect:

> The Deaf patient goes to an orthodontist because her dental prosthesis fits so badly that she cannot eat without severe problems. When describing her painful situation, the patient starts to cry and tears run down her cheeks. The doctor gives her the time she needs to regain her composure, answers her questions, and then suggests and discusses different options for a replacement. While doing so, the orthodontist shows different catalogues and models to make her explanations as visual and clear as possible. (A:017)

In a few cases, prescient doctors used email to inform their deaf patients in advance of the consultation about what they might expect and how they might prepare for their visit to the office.

All in all, even though unpleasant encounters with disrespectful, intimidating, or overly stressed doctors did occur, positive impressions prevailed. Familiarity with the particular needs of deaf people as well as with the interpreting situation clearly helps but is not necessary. If doctors are cognizant and respectful of the needs of deaf patients, their efforts go a long way toward creating an atmosphere that feels supportive and helpful to both the interpreters and, as one might suspect, the deaf patients.

Deaf Patients

Now we take a closer look at a number of cases that interpreters found noteworthy: in 13, or 9.2%, of all of the assignments, deaf patients expressed their dissatisfaction with the medical communication; in 35, or 24.6%, of all of the assignments, patients' behavior was regarded as "proactive"; and in 15, or 10.6%, of the cases interpreters labeled the patient as "difficult."

The data support three main reasons for deaf clients' dissatisfaction with a medical appointment. They may feel that they have received inadequate explanation or that a diagnosis is given without sufficient clarification (5 cases; for instance, see A:059, quoted earlier; cf. Paulini, 2008, p. 94). A situation in which there was confusion about the flow of communication and the roles of the people present was also perceived as unsatisfactory:

> The doctor comes to call us into his office and is surprised: "Oh, three people? Why's that?" The patient explains: "I am deaf and need an

interpreter to interpret for me. This is the interpreter with her trainee." The interpretation of this utterance is accompanied by pointing at the respective people, so it should be clear who is who. But the doctor still has problems understanding. Doctor: "So, who is hearing? You are deaf, aren't you?" Deaf patient: "No, this is my interpreter. She is hearing, I am deaf." The doctor still cannot figure out who is who. His irritation doesn't seem to subside . . . In the middle of the examination it starts again. The doctor asks again who is who and why we are there. The deaf patient starts to be annoyed. (A:027)

However, in a few cases, dissatisfaction may also reflect on the patient, who may suffer from misguided expectations, which gives rises to disappointment when the doctor does not prescribe the preferred medicine (e.g., A:099). In a rather special case, an older doctor gave reason for dissatisfaction when he made salacious comments about his young female patient (A:080).

Clients were labeled as "proactive" when they took the initiative and tried to control the communication at certain points. Twenty-four, or 40%, of the clients were considered proactive in 24.6% of the assignments (35). However, this included quite ordinary behavior, such as introducing themselves and their interpreters (12 cases, or 8.5%), asking questions (13, or 9.2%), or trying to influence the communication (8 instances, or 5.6%). For the interpreters, such behavior appeared to be "proactive" against a background of what they perceived as the often unassertive or even diffident behavior of deaf patients. In contrast, interpreters experienced it as helpful if a deaf client took control of the communication and acted autonomously, as was the case with a deaf mother who was interacting with a pediatrician who was inexperienced in dealing with deaf people and an interpreter (A:047). In one case (A:079), the doctor, fascinated by the interpreting process, which was new to him, engaged the interpreter in conversation. Quite rightly, the deaf patient insisted on knowing everything that passed between the two hearing people. Even proactive deaf patients were not always successful in their attempts to get what they wanted, and sometimes it took great assertiveness to worm answers out of a doctor:

The mother [of a deaf child] uses the opportunity to repeat some questions she had already asked during the previous visit because there had been no interpreter present then. The doctor explains in a very cursory way and keeps referring to the leaflet he had given them at the last visit. The mother explains that it is important for her to get the information directly from him due to her difficulties in fully understanding written information . . . In the end, the doctor gives in and gives the necessary information to the parents. (A:087)

Interpreters considered patients to be difficult mainly when the patients demonstrated an obvious mismatch of communication cultures or a lack of knowledge about communication rules in the hearing world (12 cases, or 8.5%). Some deaf patients repeatedly interrupted the doctor (A:067) or would not stop talking even after the doctor had clearly brought the consultation to a close (A:117). Some patients complained and made demands without acknowledging that the doctor had already made an effort to accommodate their wishes (A:104). Communication culture could also have been an issue when escorts were present, for instance, when husband and wife disagreed and argued in front of the doctor (A:130) or when the hearing mother and her deaf adult daughter spoke at the same time (A:104). Another difficult situation arose when a deaf patient refused to cooperate with the doctor, came unprepared, questioned the usefulness of the procedure, and did not accept the doctor's advice (A:040). Occasionally the lack of signing skills or the unskilled use of fingerspelling can also cause problems (3 cases):

> She spells the word using the finger alphabet. I [the interpreter] do not understand. She repeats herself and is irritated when I still do not get it. She writes the word on a piece of paper. I visualize the letters she had spelled and realize why I had not understood her. She mixed up the letters of the finger alphabet. We agree on a sign for the word. I keep in mind that the finger alphabet is useless because she mixes up the letters. (A:051)

To summarize, deaf patients were dissatisfied for good reason with some of their doctors' behavior, they tended to lack assertiveness, and the interpreters perceived active participation as helpful. However, on occasion, difficulties arose when deaf patients disregarded the communication rules of the hearing world.

Interpreters

Next we consider a number of cases in which interpreters described their own behavior as "proactive." Because our data do not allow for any detailed discourse analysis, this assessment has to be taken with a grain of salt. There is no simple opposition here between "staying neutral" and "getting involved" (see earlier section titled "The interpreter's role in healthcare settings"). Rather, a classification as proactive implied a degree of involvement that the interpreter considered as particularly pronounced and exceeding the demands of more commonly experienced situations. This was the case in 28, or 19.7%, of all the assignments.

In about one-third of these cases of pronounced activity, the interpreter's intervention was prompted by the need to create suitable conditions for the interpreting tasks. For instance, the interpreter might have asked for a change in the position of a chair (A:062), intervened to shorten the waiting time (A:103, A:109), or instructed medical staff about how to proceed during an examination (A:018, A:079):

> X-ray of the neck. Beforehand, the doctor explains what is going to happen. The X-ray technician asks me [the interpreter] for help and explains how to stand and how to wait for the X-ray. . . . I interpret her instructions concerning the posture to be adopted by the patient. The X-ray technician is not yet perfectly satisfied and repeats several times the posture the patient should adopt. I suggest to the X-ray technician: "You can guide her gently into the right position. I am sure it is ok for her." (A:113)

In five cases the interpreter intervened when faced with ignorance on the part of a doctor or staff member concerning deaf patients or the interpreting process (see, for instance, A:102, quoted earlier). In four situations, the interpreter tried to stop patronizing or dominating behavior by the hearing doctor or staff member, as in the following case:

> I [the interpreter] am at the doctor's office before the patient arrives. I inform the receptionist that I am the interpreter for patient xyz. The receptionist replies that I can stay in the waiting room and that they would call me when I am needed. I respond that the deaf person should decide if she wants me to be with her. When the deaf person arrives, I inform her about the conversation I had with the receptionist. I ask her to decide if I should accompany her or not. She answers, "You come with me!" (A:123)

In four assignments the interpreter became an advocate because of the diffidence or insecurity of the deaf person in interacting with hearing people or the doctor (see A:046, quoted earlier). In one case, the interpreter intervened to make sure that the patient understood the doctor's instructions. Realizing that the client had not fully under-stood, she decided to repeat the doctor's instructions after the end of the consultation:

> The doctor explains to the patient how to use the medicine, then says good-bye and asks the receptionist for a follow-up appointment for the next examination. Now the patient and I are leaving the doctor's office. I ask her if she has understood the doctor's explanations—she says no. Therefore, I repeat the explanations and instructions the doctor had given. In the end, she tells me that she has finally under-stood. (A:061)

Finally, in a specialized field such as medicine it is not surprising to find that an inconsiderate use of jargon may prompt the interpreter to intervene:

> The deaf couple and I [the interpreter] meet in the waiting room. The husband explains the reason for the appointment. It is the first time the doctor has had deaf patients, and I am the first interpreter he has had to deal with. The doctor only uses the technical language of his profession. It is too much of a challenge for me. At one point, I have to interrupt the doctor and ask for clarification. (A:034)

All in all, the interpreters felt convinced that the interventions described here were necessary and contributed to successful and satisfying appoint-ments by helping to clarify the message or support the deaf clients in asserting their rights to complete information.

Medical Examinations

Not every medical consultation involves a distinct physical exami-nation, and those that do may not necessarily involve much commu-nication. Of all of the recorded assignments, 37, or 26%, included an examination that was considered to be of interest in terms of interpreta-tion, though often the main question was whether to interpret. Thus, in 20 instances the medical examination took place without the interpreter being present. Most of these were routine procedures that required no explanations: "He [the doctor] shows her [the patient] to the changing room. She already knows the procedure. I take a seat in the hallway and hear phrases like 'Does it hurt?' 'Ouch!' and 'Already done!' Back to the changing room, all of this has been routine for both of them" (A:127).

In a number of such cases, instructions were given and interpreted first, and then the interpreter left the room for the examination to take place, either because the examination was particularly intimate or because no visual contact with the patient was possible:

> The deaf patient undergoes an MRI. He is lying on his back. His head is fixed because he needs to stay immobile for the whole procedure. I ask the medical staff to give important information beforehand because communication will become difficult as soon as the patient is immobilized. The medical staff adapts easily to my request and gives all the information needed before the procedure starts. (A:079)

Where intimate examinations require the interpreter's presence, her discretion is called for: "When the patient is undressing and dressing, I avoid looking . . . The doctor examines her breasts. I look into the patient's eyes, avoiding looking at her breasts. Turning away was not an option for me because of the necessity to communicate" (A:043).

When interpreters are present in medical examinations, they often have to change their position during the procedure. In a few cases, interpreters reported that medical equipment obstructed their view. Adapting positions may occasionally irritate a doctor or, in one case, even the patient:

> The vision test is tricky: the hearing daughter is sitting on the deaf mother's lap. I position myself in the mother's field of view so that she can see me, and the daughter can see the eye chart. The daughter answers the ophthalmologist's questions in spoken German, while I interpret into signed language. Unfortunately, the daughter can see me, which irritates her. I try to change my position but find no better place because of the size of the room and the equipment. (A:015)

As reported here, medical examinations pose a challenge to the interpreter's flexibility and discretion. Spatial conditions may be such as to cause problems, and the physical examination itself may give reason for discomfort. Still, although irritations cannot always be avoided, more generally this seems an aspect of healthcare interpreting that most interpreters can deal with quite confidently.

Escorts

Quite frequently, in 39, or 27.5%, of the assignments, deaf patients were accompanied by a third person who might get involved in or otherwise influence the situation. On occasion, such a presence can be beneficial. For instance, when an elderly deaf man who displayed early symptoms of Alzheimer's was not able to recount his medical history, the accompanying deaf wife took over the task of informing the doctor (A:092). In another case, the patient knew very little German Sign Language, and his partner, who had lived in Germany for a number of years, acted as a relay interpreter. She also seemed to know her partner's medical history better than the patient himself. Having an additional person in the interpreting chain required detailed monitoring by the interpreter, but the escort's assistance was appreciated by both the interpreter and the doctor:

> The doctor is young, businesslike, and in a rush and asks about the patient's symptoms and previous illnesses. The patient barely understands me. His partner acts as a relay or simply answers the questions herself. She explains everything to him using her own signs. Managing the conversation is difficult. The doctor talks to me, the deaf woman answers, signs with the patient. I abandon the attempt to tell the doctor to talk to him directly. I interpret, sometimes signing two to three times until I am sure that both have understood. I check what the deaf woman signs to her partner, to be sure what she signs is correct . . . I am glad that the deaf woman is present, she can explain the symptoms better than the patient himself. (A:118)

Generally, more problematic were situations that involved the presence of hearing relatives. Doctors tended to choose the "easy option" and talk to the hearing person, neglecting the deaf patient. Hearing relatives may be too accustomed to interfering in the lives of their deaf children or siblings to notice:

> In the waiting room and during the consultation the grandmother is very dominant. She cares very much for the child and is apparently in charge of her often while the parents are working. The psychologist is very friendly. At the beginning, she includes the parents, but in the course of the conversation she drifts more in the direction of the grandmother. The parents more or less become spectators and just follow the conversation. (A:056)

A patient and an escort may quarrel, interrupt each other, or talk all at once, creating a challenge to make sense of the conversation for doctor and interpreter alike: "At the doctor's office, mother and daughter often talk at the same time, also to each other. I steer a lot, signing what the mother says, doing voiceovers when she uses home signs with the daughter" (A:104).

The presence of a social worker, caregiver, or custodian may deflect the doctor's attention from the deaf patient, but some such third parties differed in their degree of involvement in the situation. In some instances, a caregiver would "take over" (e.g., A:028, A:076, A:133), whereas others displayed a professional behavior, staying in the background and providing useful information (e.g., A:025, A:133).

Accompanied by the escort, a part of the deaf patient's life enters the interpreting situation. The effect may be helpful at times, but more often than not it complicates the interaction or creates an imbalance in the relationship between the hearing and deaf parties and thus poses a real challenge to the interpreter and the deaf patient, who is the focus of the interpreter's attention.

Debriefing

Healthcare assignments may effectively be concluded when the consultation ends. In fact, in 81, or 57%, of all cases, the reporting interpreters did not consider what happened after the consultation worth documenting, and even when something was reported, it was often considered unremarkable (26 cases). In most of the remaining 35 cases, the deaf client and the interpreter used the time following the appointment to exchange their opinions of the consultation. Thus, if a doctor had not administered the expected treatment or had behaved in an unexpected, negative way, this became a topic of discussion:

> Outside the office, the deaf patient tells me that she is surprised by the way the doctor had talked to her and even more that her GP recommended this doctor to her. She has experienced his way of talking as rude and asks me for my impression. I tell her that I had the same feeling. We discuss alternatives. Finally, she decides to wait for the results and consult a different cardiologist next time, if necessary. (A:071)

In another case, the exchange was initiated by the deaf patient, who wanted to express her satisfaction: "After the consultation, the patient is very happy and satisfied. She feels she has been taken seriously and treated with respect by the doctor. She wants to know if I share her opinion and asks for my feedback" (A:124).

In 6 cases, the situation was used for clarification. The initiative may be taken by the interpreter, who feels responsible for the complete delivery of the message (as in A:061, quoted earlier), or by the deaf patient:

> After the appointment the deaf patient asks me for clarification. There was a detail he didn't understand. I have more time now than in the situation itself. I sign as visually and clearly as I can to explain why the sternum needs to be cut open. He got a lot of paperwork he has to deal with, so I offer some help, if needed. He declines and tells me that his daughter will do that. (A:116)

In another 6 cases, the interpreter made phone calls for the deaf patient to arrange follow-up assignments with other doctors or specialists: "She asks me to call another specialist. I wonder if she wants to hire her usual interpreter. No, she wants me to interpret the assignment because it is easier for her. I call the specialist and make an appointment (no interpretation)" (A:043).

Occasionally (4 cases) the interpreter accompanied the patient to a drugstore nearby or, in a case involving surgery, back home:

> All the nurses know the patient well because he already had his other hand operated on. One of the nurses asks me to see the patient home after the operation. I agree. After the surgery, I do so. I'm glad that everything went well. I had a double role which contradicts any code of conduct: jumping back and forth from interpreter to escort and back again. (A:103)

In only two cases, a debriefing in the narrow sense of the word took place. Here the interpreter's strategies were discussed, and decisions were made concerning modifications for follow-up assignments:

> In the street I have a short discussion with the couple, who want to know why I interrupted the doctor. They expect me just to interpret. I try to explain that I needed to ask for clarification to be able to translate. The patient isn't satisfied. For the next time, we agree that I will ask if I do not understand but will simultaneously use signed German so that the deaf clients can follow the conversation. (A:034)

When significant interaction between deaf clients and interpreters takes place after the consultation, it may be to clarify something or to undertake some small service for the deaf person. That the interpreting process itself is not more often the subject of discussion may be unexpected. However, it is hardly surprising that the medical experience the deaf client and the interpreter have just been through together is a natural focus of their exchange.

Summary

We have reviewed the medical interpreting that took place as part of the daily professional practice of five signed language interpreters in Germany and Austria in 2012. Clearly, any of the various aspects of healthcare assignments that we have considered may turn out to be problematic and present a challenge to the interpreter. Healthcare assignments may concern medical problems of a critical nature, which put an emotional burden on the interpreter. Deaf patients and interpreters may encounter unfriendly or even hostile medical staff. They may be rushed through a series of consultations and treatments, or their patience may be tried by spending long hours in the waiting room. It may be hard to create adequate spatial arrangements either because of physical conditions that make visual communication difficult or because of a lack of understanding or empathy on the part of the doctor. Doctors may lack the time, patience, or the will to treat deaf patients with the respect they, like any other patient, deserve. Deaf patients may have unrealistic expectations or may not be aware of problems created by communication styles that alienate hearing interlocutors. In addition, they may be accompanied by relatives or caregivers whose well-intentioned interventions may be misplaced. Interpreters may feel they need to take action in order to bring messages across or support deaf clients in asserting their rights to complete information. After the consultation, interpreters may face dissatisfied, irritated, or helpless patients in need of clarification and assistance.

All of these complicating factors did occur in our data, and interpreters will do well to anticipate the possibility of such problems. However, the overall picture that we have painted is more balanced and, all in all, more positive. Encounters between deaf clients and interpreters in the waiting room often provide welcome opportunities to exchange information and establish the kind of personal relationship that is crucial for successful cooperation. In many cases, medical staff members are supportive and may go out of their way to offer good service to deaf patients. More often than not, the triangular spatial arrangements that are conducive to visual communication can be established as a matter of course. Even when doctors have no previous experience with deaf patients or interpreted consultations, many of them invest time and patience and treat their deaf patients with due attention and respect. In such situations deaf patients may confidently assert their rights and cooperate with circumspection and understanding. At times, an accompanying third person may turn out to contribute vital information during the consultation. Medical examinations may be negotiated tactfully and carried out adequately even when interpreted communication is not feasible. Debriefing situations often serve to resolve uncertainties and allow deaf patients and interpreters to reach a common understanding of the preceding medical encounter.

Healthcare interpreting takes place in situations that vary according to general interactive patterns that occur between layperson and specialist, consulter and consultant, deaf and hearing people. On the basis of the experiences that we have reported here, it would seem that interpreters have reason to be confident that, generally, they will encounter circumstances that are conducive to the satisfactory outcome of medical assignments. However, enough risks and stumbling blocks remain to prompt the reflective practitioner to practice circumspection and prudence.

CONCLUSION

As we pointed out at the beginning of this chapter, creating a space for reflection was a major aim of this study, which has served to heighten our awareness of aspects of our work that are often blurred by the routine handling of day-to-day assignments. The resulting picture is informative and rich in descriptive detail though not rigorous in its attention to structural conditions and overall patterns.

One aspect that emerges clearly is the particular role that close relationships between deaf clients and interpreters play in healthcare assignments. This partly reflects general conditions of the medical setting, where immediate personal concerns are of prime importance. The particular circumstances in which healthcare assignments take place in Germany and Austria seem to be conducive to the development of trusted relationships, too: in the great majority of cases, it is the deaf clients or their representative who contract the interpreter. Most deaf clients know their interpreters before the assignment and can draw on established relationships. As a rule, it is the deaf patients who brief the interpreter and explain their views and goals.

From the point of view of hearing doctors, this close relationship between deaf patients and interpreters is often taken for granted, and the interpreter is seen as an aide or assistant to the deaf patient. At times, such a view may cause imbalances and interactive problems, but it seems to reflect something real: while, as most recent commentators have stressed, the interpreter is involved as an active participant in a "triadic" conversation of three parties, the interactive triangle is not equilateral. Rather, the interpreter will give precedence to achieving the deaf clients' goals. We, as the interpreters involved in this study, were not overtly concerned about following the rules and regulations of a professional code of conduct. Rather, we attempted to follow a course of action that, in any particular situation, seemed humanely appropriate and in the best interest of the deaf clients. Any more specific application is beyond the scope of this chapter, but, generally speaking, such an approach to the professional task seems to be in line with more recent attempts to account for interpreting behavior and decision making in interactive models that transcend earlier conceptions of "interpreting roles" (see earlier, the section titled "The Interpreter's Role in Healthcare Settings," and, in particular, the discussion of Lee and Llewellyn-Jones's [2011] role space model or Rozanes's [2013] notion of a comfort zoning process).

Although the data of this study are revealing in certain respects, they lack some of the detail that would allow for more finely tuned analyses. As a first attempt at taking stock of relevant interpreting experiences, analytical criteria established at the outset of this study were left deliberately vague and open. All of the assignments were recorded rather loosely in the form of minutes written from memory. Not all of these minutes covered the same kind and the same level of detail. In some cases it proved difficult or impossible to reconstruct critical elements of a particular assignment at a later date. More detailed inquiries into any of the aspects of the overall picture that we have painted here with rather bold brushstrokes will do well to be selective in their analytical focus and work on the basis of preestablished sets of observational criteria. More generally, our views need to be complemented by the perspectives and experiences of other participants in medical settings. In particular, it needs to be determined whether deaf patients share the largely rather positive views outlined here and confirm our impression that interpreting enables deaf patients to take an active role as major participants in medical encounters. The results of such inquiries will inform the training of signed language interpreters and provide a basis for developing awareness-raising strategies directed at medical staff as well as deaf patients.

Acknowledging the limitations of this study does not preclude us from reaching a preliminary diagnosis of healthcare interpreting for deaf people, as currently practiced in Austria and Germany. It is a challenging, often rewarding, professional task that brings interpreters into close personal contact with their deaf clients. Insight and experience will help interpreters avoid some of the most obvious stumbling blocks and, in the interest of deaf people, make good use of all the available stepping-stones.

NOTES

1. As the federal government of Carinthia has a very tight budget, it refuses to cover interpreting costs for doctors' consultations. The interpreters' association has found alternative funding with the regional health insurance companies who pay better rates than government authorities in other federal countries. There are no personal budgets, deaf clients in Carinthia get all interpreting they may need for their health care.

2. Patient numbers do not add up to 60, as some patients had several appointments in different locations.

3. Often the particulars of the seating arrangement were not recorded in the interpreters' notes. From subsequent discussions, we deduce that what we are describing here is a general practice.

4. Twenty-five cases were considered unremarkable. The remaining assignments include a handful of cases in which either no relevant doctor-patient interaction was involved (e.g., A:005, A:023, A:039) or the doctor's behavior was of special interest but was not classified as either positive or negative (e.g., A:010: the doctor started using the patient's native spoken language, which was unknown to the interpreter; A:093: the doctor tried to communicate in signed German; A:079: the doctor was thrilled by the interpreting and kept asking the interpreter interested questions).

REFERENCES

Angelelli, C. (2003). The interpersonal role of the interpreter in cross-cultural communication: A survey of conference, court and medical interpreters in the US, Canada, and Mexico. In L. Brunette, G. Bastin, I. Hemlin, & H. Clarke (Eds.), *The critical link 3: Interpreters in the community* (pp. 15–26). Amsterdam: Benjamins.

Angelelli, C. (2004). *Medical interpreting and cross-cultural communication.* Cambridge: Cambridge University Press.

Aranguri, C., Davidson, B., & Ramirez, R. (2006). Patterns of communication through interpreters: A detailed sociolinguistic analysis. *Journal of General Internal Medicine, 21,* 623–629.

Byrne, P. S., & Long, B. E. L. (1976). *Doctors talking to patients: A study of the verbal behaviours of doctors in the consultation.* London: Her Majesty's Stationery Office.

Cegala, D. J., & Post, D. M. (2009). The impact of patients' participation on physicians' patient-centered communication. *Patient Education and Counseling, 77*(2), 202–208.

Davidson, G. (2000). The interpreter as institutional gatekeeper: The sociallinguistic role of interpreters in Spanish-English medical discourse. *Journal of Sociolinguistics, 4*(3), 379–405.

Dysart-Gale, D. (2005). Communication models, professionalization, and the work of medical interpreters. *Health Communication, 17*(1), 91–103.

Ebert, D. A., & Heckerling, P. S. (1995). Communication with deaf patients: Knowledge, beliefs, and practices of physicians. *Journal of the American Medical Association, 273*(3), 227–229.

Edwards, R., Temple, B., & Alexander, C. (2005). Users' experiences of interpreters: The critical role of trust. *Interpreting, 7*(1), 77–95.

Felgner, L. (2009). Zur Bedeutung der nonverbalen Kommunikation im gedolmetschten medizinischen Gespräch. In D. Andres & S. Pöllabauer (Eds.), *Spürst Du, wie der Bauch rauf-runter? Fachdolmetschen im Gesundheitsbereich* [Is everything all topsy turvy in your tummy? Healthcare interpreting] (pp. 45–70). Munich: Meidenbauer.

Frishberg, N. (1990). *Interpreting: An introduction.* Silver Spring, MD: Registry of Interpreters for the Deaf.

Gonzalez-Nava, S. (2009). Das Gespräch als Qualitätsfaktor der Behandlung. In D. Andres & S. Pöllabauer (Eds.), *Spürst Du, wie der Bauch rauf-runter? Fachdolmetschen im Gesundheitsbereich* [Is everything all topsy turvy in your tummy? Healthcare interpreting] (pp. 71–84). Munich: Meidenbauer.

Gorjanc, V. (2009). Terminology resources and terminological data management for medical interpreters. In D. Andres & S. Pöllabauer (eds.), *Spürst Du, wie der Bauch rauf-runter? Fachdolmetschen im Gesundheitsbereich* [Is everything all topsy turvy in your tummy? Healthcare interpreting] (pp. 85–95). Munich: Meidenbauer.

Greener, I. (2003). Patient choice in the NHS: The view from economic sociology. *Social Theory and Health, 1,* 72–89.

Haenel, F. (2001). Ausgewählte Aspekte und Probleme in der Psychotherapie mit Folteropfern unter Beteiligung von Dolmetschern. In M. Verwey (Ed.), *Trauma und Ressourcen* (pp. 307–315). Berlin: Verlag für Wissenschaft und Bildung.

Harmer, L. (1999). Health care delivery and deaf people: Practice, problems and recommendations for change. *Journal of Deaf Studies and Deaf Education, 4*(2), 73–110.

Hessmann, J., Salmi, E., Turner, G. H., & Wurm, S. (2011). Developing and transmitting a shared interpreting research ethos: EUMASLI, a case study. In B. Nicodemus & L. Swabey (Eds.), *Advances in interpreting research: Inquiry in action* (pp. 177–198). Amsterdam: Benjamins.

Hsieh, E. (2009). Bilingual health communication: Medical interpreters' construction of a mediator role. In D. E. Brashers & D. J. Goldsmith (Eds.), *Communicating to manage health and illness* (pp. 135–160). New York: Routledge.

Hsieh, E., Ju, H., & Kong, H. (2010). Dimensions of trust: The tensions and challenges in provider-interpreter trust. *Qualitative Health Research, 20*(2), 170–181.

Humphrey, J. H., & Alcorn, B. J. (1995). *So you want to be an interpreter? An introduction to sign language interpreting.* Amarillo, TX: H & H Publishers.

Iezzoni, L. I., O'Day, B. L., Killen, M., & Harker, H. (2004). Communicating about health care: Observations from persons who are deaf or hard of hearing. *Annals of Internal Medicine, 140*(5), 356–363.

Leanza, Y. (2005). Roles of community interpreters in pediatrics as seen by interpreters, physicians and researchers. *Interpreting, 7*(2), 167–192.

Lee, R. G., & Llewellyn-Jones, P. (2011). *Re-visiting role: Arguing for a multidimensional analysis of interpreter behavior.* Supporting Deaf People Online Conference.

Major, G. C. (2013). Healthcare interpreting as relational practice. PhD diss., Department of Linguistics, Macquarie University, Sydney.

McKee, M. M., Barnett, S. L., Block, R. C., & Pearson, T. A. (2011). Impact of communication on preventive services among deaf American Sign Language users. *Journal of Preventative Medicine, 41*(1), 75–79.

Metzger, M. (1999). *Sign language interpreting: Deconstructing the myth of neutrality.* Washington, DC: Gallaudet University Press.

Meyer, B. (2009). Deutschkenntnisse von Migrant/innen und ihre Konsequenzen für das Dolmetschen im Krankenhaus. In D. Andres & S. Pöllabauer (Eds.), *Spürst Du, wie der Bauch rauf-runter? Fachdolmetschen im Gesundheitsbereich* [Is everything all topsy turvy in your tummy? Healthcare interpreting] (pp. 139–157). Munich: Meidenbauer.

Mindess, A. (1999). *Reading between the signs: Intercultural communication for sign language interpreters.* Yarmouth, ME: Intercultural Press.

Napier, J., Locker McKee, R., & Goswell, D. (2006). *Sign language interpreting: Theory and practice in Australia and New Zealand.* Sydney: Federations Press.

Napier, J., Locker McKee, R., & Goswell, D. (2010). *Sign language interpreting: Theory and practice in Australia and New Zealand* (2nd ed.). Sidney: Federations Press.

Parisé, N. (1999). Breaking cultural barriers to health care: The voice of the deaf. Master's thesis, McGill University, Montreal.

Paulini, A. (2008). Hörgeschädigte Patienten: Ärztliche Behandlungszufriedenheit gehörloser, schwerhöriger und ertaubter Patienten. PhD diss., University of Hamburg.

Pereira, P. C., & Fortes, P. A. (2010). Communication and information barriers to health assistance for deaf patients. *American Annals of the Deaf, 155*(1), 31–37.

Pignataro, C. (2012). Interlinguistic and intercultural mediation in healthcare settings. *Interpreters' Newsletter, 17,* 71–82.

Ralston, E., Zazove, P., & Gorenflo, D. W. (1996). Physicians' attitudes and beliefs about deaf patients. *Journal of the American Board of Family Practice, 9*(3), 167–173.

Robb, N., & Greenhalgh, T. (2006). "You have to cover up the words of the doctor": The mediation of trust in interpreted consultations in primary care. *Journal of Health Organization & Management, 20*(5), 434–455.

Rosenberg, E., Leanza, Y., & Seller, R. (2007). Doctor-patient communication in primary care with an interpreter: Physician perceptions of professional and family interpreters. *Patient Education and Counseling, 67,* 286–292.

Rozanes, I. (2013). Comfort zoning: A grounded theory of medical interpreters. Unpublished slides used at MEDISIGNS: Interpreting in Healthcare Conference, Trinity College, Dublin, Ireland, March 1–2, 2013.

Shipman, B. (2010). The role of communication in the patient-physician relationship. *Journal of Legal Medicine, 31,* 433–442.

Seeber, K. (2001). Das Dolmetschen im medizinischen Bereich: Exzerpt aus der Diplomarbeit zur Erlangung des Grades Magister der Philosophie an der geisteswissenschaftlichen Fakultät der Universität Wien. *VUGS Informationsheft 37,* 98–115, 256–275. Zurich: Verein zur Unterstützung der Gebärdensprache der Gehörlosen.

Singy, P., & Guex, P. (2005). The interpreter's role with immigrant patients: Contrasted points of view. *Communication and Medicine, 2*(1), 45–51.

Steinberg, A., Wiggins, E., Barmada, C., & Sullivan, V. (2005). Deaf women: Experiences and perceptions of healthcare system access. *Journal of Women's Health, 11*(8), 729–741.

Swabey, L., & Nicodemus, B. (2011). Bimodal bilingual interpreting in the US healthcare system: A critical linguistic activity in need of investigation. In B. Nicodemus & L. Swabey (Eds.), *Advances in interpreting research: Inquiry in action* (pp. 241–259). Amsterdam: Benjamins.

Tate, G., & Turner, G. H. (1997). The code and the culture: Sign language interpreting—in search of the new breed's ethics. *Deaf Worlds: International Journal of Deaf Studies, 13*(3), 27–34.

Tomassini, E. (2012). Healthcare interpreting in Italy: Current needs and proposals to promote collaboration between universities and healthcare services. *Interpreters' Newsletter, 17,* 39–54.

van Dulmen, S. 2011. The value of tailored communication for person-centred outcomes. *Journal of Evaluation in Clinical Practice, 17*(2), 381–383.

Wadensjö, C. (1992). "Interpreting as interaction: On dialogue-interpreting in immigration hearings and medical encounters." PhD diss., Lindköping University.

Wedam, U. (2009). Sprachkultur: Plädoyer für das Dolmetschen im therapeutischen Kontext. In D. Andres & S. Pöllabauer (Eds.), *Spürst Du, wie der Bauch rauf-runter? Fachdolmetschen im Gesundheitsbereich* [Is everything all topsy turvy in your tummy? Healthcare interpreting], (pp. 181–194). Munich: Meidenbauer.

Winkler, I. C. (2011). "Sprechende Hände in der Medizin: Gebärdensprachdolmetschen im Gesundheitswesen." MA thesis, University of Vienna, Institute of Translation Studies.

Appendix

Medical Assignments in 2012

The following table lists the 142 medical assignments that form the core of this study. Each assignment is numbered and dated for the purpose of reference (all of the dates refer to the year 2012). To ensure anonymity, no geographical information is given: the assignments, however, took place in the western and southern regions of Germany and the Vienna area of Austria. The column "medical field" indicates the area of medical advice or treatment involved. The column "location" indicates the type of medical facility; in most cases this was either a smaller doctor's office or practice or a larger clinic or hospital. The "patient" column indicates the person who was the subject of the doctor's advice or treatment; generally, this was a single deaf woman or man, but it was occasionally a deaf person's child, as indicated. The patient's age is broadly characterized (e.g., "20 + " indicates an age between 20 and 29, "30 + " an age between 30 and 39). Patients were sometimes accompanied by family members, caregivers, social workers, and so on, as indicated. When the patient was a child, the accompanying deaf parent was often the interpreter's client. The last column indicates the medical reason that prompted the appointment.

No.	Date	Medical Field	Location	Patient	Accompanied By	Reason for Consultation
001	January 4	pediatrician	clinic	hearing child	deaf mother (client)	child's unspecific stomach ache
002	January 5	neurologist	office	female/40+		regular checkup because of depression medication
003	January 9	ophthalmologist	clinic	female/40+		examination following cataract surgery
004	January 10	ophthalmologist	office	male/50+		regular checkup of intraocular pressure in a patient with Usher syndrome
005	January 12	neurologist	office	female/40+		advice on numb arm and fingers
006	January 12	dentist	office	female/60+		advice on dental prosthesis or crowns
007	January 25	ophthalmologist	office	female/40+		prescription for new glasses after cataract surgery
008	January 26	ophthalmologist	clinic	male/20+		advice on restricted field of vision
009	January 30	pediatric psychiatrist	clinic	hearing child	deaf mother (client)	assessing special educational needs
010	January 30	gynecologist	office	female/30+		routine checkup during pregnancy
011	January 30	gynecologist	office	female/30+	deaf husband	advice on involuntary childlessness
012	February 1	orthopedist	clinic	female/50+	deaf husband	acute back pain (slipped disk)
013	February 2	ophthalmologist	clinic	female/40+		examination following cataract surgery
014	February 2	pediatrician	office	hearing infant	deaf mother (client)	routine checkup and vaccination
015	February 6	ophthalmologist	office	hearing child	deaf mother (client)	orthoptic practice
016	February 15	neurologist	office	female/40+		regular checkup because of depression medication
017	February 16	orthodontist	clinic	female/50+	hearing social worker	consultation because of problems with badly fitting dental prosthesis
018	February 16	radiologist	office	female/50+	hearing social worker	X-ray of jawbones

No.	Date	Medical Field	Location	Patient	Accompanied By	Reason for Consultation
019	February 24	public medical officer	police depart-ment	male/50+		medical exam after an accident
020	February 28	gynecologist	office	female/40+		consultation in preparation for upcoming surgery
021	March 15	internist	clinic	female/20+	child (son)	regular checkup because of diabetes
022	March 20	orthopedist	clinic	female/40+		consultation because of severe pain after an operation
023	March 21	radiologist	clinic	female/40+		examination because of severe pain after an operation
024	March 26	neurologist	office	female/40+		regular checkup because of depression medication
025	March 27	psychiatrist	office	female/< 20	caregiver	consultation because of aggravation of psychological condition
026	March 27	pediatrician	office	infant	deaf mother (client)	scheduled medical examination of the child
027	March 29	health authority	health office	preschool child with hearing impairment	deaf mother (client)	school aptitude examination
028	April 2	psychiatrist	office	female/50+	legal custodian	change of medication in a treatment for epilepsy
029	April 2	ophthalmologist	clinic	male/50+		hospitalization because of cataract operation

No.	Date	Medical Field	Location	Patient	Accompanied By	Reason for Consultation
030	April 5	ophthalmologist	office	female/40+		regular checkup of intraocular pressure in a patient with Usher's syndrome
031	April 11	ophthalmologist	office	male/20+		prescription for new contact lenses
032	April 11	pediatrician	clinic	infant	deaf mother (client)	emergency consultation because of unclear symptoms
033	April 12	pediatrician	clinic	infant	deaf mother (client)	ward rounds and discharge examination
034	April 12	geneticist	genetic center	deaf couple/30+		genetic counseling
035	April 18	internist	clinic	female/30+	child (son)	regular checkup because of diabetes
036	April 24	neurologist	office	deaf woman		regular checkup because of depression medication
037	May 2	orthopedist	clinic	female/50+		follow-up consultation after a hospital stay
038	May 2	otolaryngologist	office	male/40+		regular checkup because of asthma
039	May 3	dentist	office	male/30+		routine checkup
040	May 8	nutritionist	office	female/30+		consultation because of blood in stool
041	May 9	ophthalmologist	office	male/20+		prescription for new glasses
042	May 9	orthopedist	office	male/20+		general checkup
043	May 10	surgeon	clinic	female/60+	deaf partner	examination because of changes in the breast after an operation in the past
044	May 11	orthopedist	office	male/50+		checkup after an operation
045	May 21	dentist	office	female/60+		dental treatment
046	May 21	vascular specialist	office	female/60+		regular checkup because of varices

No.	Date	Medical Field	Location	Patient	Accompanied By	Reason for Consultation
047	May 22	pediatrician	office	infant	deaf mother (client)	scheduled medical examination
048	May 23	surgeon	clinic	male/30+	caregiver with hearing impairment	medical advice after work-related accident
049	May 30	orthopedist	office	male/50+		checkup after an operation
050	May 31	otolaryngologist	office	female/20+		persistent headache after cochlear implantation
051	May 31	dermatologist	office	female/60+		rash
052	June 4	psychiatrist	office	male/30+	caregiver	medical advice in a case of trauma
053	June 6	pediatrician	clinic	hearing boy	deaf parents (clients), social worker	first consultation because of behavioral syndrome
054	June 6	internist	clinic	female	child (son)	regular checkup because of diabetes
055	June 13	gynecologist	office	female/30+		suspected case of rubella during pregnancy
056	June 14	child psychologist	clinic	infant	deaf parents (clients), hearing grandmother	developmental delays
057	June 18	gastroenterologist	office	male/30+		gastroscopy
058	June 20	ophthalmologist	office	male/50+		regular checkup of intraocular pressure in a patient with Usher's syndrome
059	June 22	ophthalmologist	office	female/60+		eye exam, ophthalmic migraine
060	June 22	nephrologist	office	male/50+		examination of kidneys in a case of sarcoidosis
061	June 25	general practitioner	office	female/40+		suspected hemorrhoids
062	June 26	nutritionist	clinic	female/30+		consultation because of blood in stool

No.	Date	Medical Field	Location	Patient	Accompanied By	Reason for Consultation
063	June 28	orthopedist	office	female/40+		consultation because of aching legs
064	June 29	gynecologist	office	female/30+	deaf husband	pregnancy test
065	July 3	ophthalmologist	office	female/40+		regular checkup of intraocular pressure in a patient with Usher's syndrome
066	July 3	pediatrician	clinic	hearing boy	deaf parents (clients), social worker	follow-up consultation because of behavioral syndrome
067	July 5	gastroenterologist	office	male/30+		gastroscopy
068	July 9	orthopedist	office	female/40+		discussion of examination findings related to aching legs
069	July 10	nephrologist	office	male/50+		discussion of analysis of patient's urine
070	July 24	diabetologist	office	female/30+		suspected gestational diabetes
071	July 26	cardiologist	office	female/40+		consultation because of chronic fatigue
072	July 30	radiologist	office	male/50+	caregiver	examination because of back pain
073	July 30	gynecologist	office	female/50+		consultation after biopsy and tumor diagnosis
074	July 30	neurologist	office	female/40+		regular checkup because of depression medication
075	July 31	colorectal surgeon	clinic	female/50+		preoperative interview and examination
076	July 31	ophthalmologist	office	male/30+	caregiver	prescription for new glasses after cataract surgery
077	August 7	gynecologist	office	female/30+	hearing parents, hearing child	3D ultrasound of unborn baby
078	August 8	dentist	office	male/20+		annual checkup at a new dentist

No.	Date	Medical Field	Location	Patient	Accompanied By	Reason for Consultation
079	August 8	radiologist	office	male/30+		tomography after operation for brain tumor
080	August 9	cardiologist	office	female/40+		discussion of examination findings related to chronic fatigue
081	August 9	ophthalmologist	office	hearing child	deaf mother (client)	consultation regarding light strabismus
082	August 10	gynecologist	office	female/30+	deaf husband	scheduled consultation during pregnancy
083	August 13	otolaryngologist	clinic	female/20+		follow-up consultation because of persistent headache after cochlear implantation
084	August 14	orthopedist	clinic	female/40+		consultation because of severe pain after hip operation
085	August 16	cardiologist	clinic	male/60+		consultation to discuss the pros and cons of heart surgery
086	August 17	diabetologist	office	female/30+	hearing child	consultation because of suspected gestational diabetes
087	August 20	orthopedist	office	infant	deaf parents (clients)	consultation because of positional deformity of baby's foot
088	August 21	gynecologist	office	female/30+		routine checkup during pregnancy
089	August 21	dermatologist	office	female/40+		consultation because of rash and itching
090	August 22	otolaryngologist	clinic	female/20+		follow-up consultation because of persistent headache after cochlear implantation

No.	Date	Medical Field	Location	Patient	Accompanied By	Reason for Consultation
091	August 22	otolaryngologist	office	female/30+	hearing brother and mother	intended removal of cochlear implant
092	August 27	surgeon	clinic	male/60+	deaf wife, deaf daughter	preoperative interview for an operation
093	August 28	ophthalmologist	office	female/60+		first consultation because of vision problems
094	August 29	surgeon	clinic	male/60+	deaf wife, deaf daughter	consultation after operation
095	August 29	otolaryngologist, neurologist, psychologist, pain clinic	clinic	female/20+		examinations because of persistent headache after cochlear implantation
096	August 30	colorectal surgeon	clinic	female/50+		checkup after an operation
097	Sept. 5	otolaryngologist	clinic	female/50+		checkup after hospital treatment for constant dizziness
098	Sept. 7	gynecologist	office	female/30+		routine checkup during pregnancy
099	Sept. 11	nutritionist	clinic	female/30+		consultation because of blood in stool
100	Sept. 12	occupational physician	social security office	male/30+	deaf wife	medical exam for an application for disability benefits
101	Sept. 18	general practitioner	office	female/40+		consultation because of kidney pain
102	Sept. 19	dentist	office	female/40+		obtaining a detailed cost estimate for dental work

No.	Date	Medical Field	Location	Patient	Accompanied By	Reason for Consultation
103	Sept. 19	orthopedist	clinic	male/50+		preoperative discussion
104	Sept. 24	occupational physician	office	female/40+	hearing mother	consultation because of knee pain
105	Sept. 24	dentist	office	male/20+		dental treatment
106	Sept. 24	orthopedist	office	male/50+		follow-up consultation after operation
107	Sept. 24	orthopedist	office	infant	deaf mother (client)	examination of clubfoot
108	Sept. 25	internist	office	male/60+		enlarged thyroid; referral to hospital for an operation
109	Sept. 25	orthopedist	clinic	female/40+		consultation because of severe pains after a hip operation
110	Sept. 25	ophthalmologist	office	female/40+		prescription for new glasses after cataract surgery
111	Sept. 28	internist	office	female/20+	infant	scheduled medical exam for a driver's license extension for a patient with diabetes
112	Oct. 1	nephrologist	clinic	male/50+	hearing mother	biopsy of kidney
113	Oct. 8	orthopedist	office	female/30+	caregiver	radiological examination because of pain in back and arms
114	Oct. 8	pediatrician	office	infant	deaf mother (client)	scheduled medical exam
115	Oct. 8	ophthalmologist	office	female/60+	deaf husband	preoperative discussion for cataract surgery
116	Oct. 9	surgeon	clinic	male/60+		preoperative discussion for thyroid surgery

No.	Date	Medical Field	Location	Patient	Accompanied By	Reason for Consultation
117	Oct. 9	pediatrician	office	preschool child	deaf mother, deaf partner, deaf acquaintance	vaccination consultation
118	Oct. 10	internist	clinic	male/20+	deaf partner	detailed examination because of abdominal pain
119	Oct. 11	internist	clinic	female/20+	child	regular checkup because of diabetes
120	Oct. 16	ophthalmologist	office	female/40+		regular checkup of intraocular pressure in a patient with Usher's syndrome
121	Oct. 17	otolaryngologist	office	male/40+		regular checkup because of asthma
122	Oct. 18	neurologist	office	male/30+		treatment after operation for a brain tumor
123	Oct. 22	gynecologist	office	female/30+		ultrasound during pregnancy
124	Oct. 25	gynecologist	office	female/30+		consultation because of pregnancy
125	Oct. 29	gynecologist	office	female/30+	deaf husband	scheduled consultation because of pregnancy
126	Oct. 29	otolaryngologist	office	deaf mother and two deaf children		removal of cerumen (daughter) and prescription for hearing aid (mother)
127	Oct. 31	colorectal surgeon	clinic	female/50+		examination because of discomfort after an operation
128	Nov. 8	ophthalmologist	office	female/30+		routine eye exam because of diabetes
129	Nov. 8	general practitioner	welfare office	female/20+	infant	medical exam for the evaluation of disability by the authority for people with disabilities

No.	Date	Medical Field	Location	Patient	Accompanied By	Reason for Consultation
130	Nov. 9	nephrologist	office	male/50+	deaf wife	discussion of results of examinations and further treatment
131	Nov. 15	gynecologist	office	female/30+		consultation because of pregnancy
132	Nov. 26	internist	clinic	male/60+	deaf wife	preoperative discussion for intestinal surgery
133	Nov. 28	psychiatrist	office	male/< 20	guardian	scheduled consultation for medication
134	Dec. 3	orthopedist	office	female/30+	caregiver	consultation because of pain in neck and arms
135	Dec. 4	gynecologist	office	female/30+	deaf husband	scheduled consultation because of pregnancy
136	Dec. 6	psychiatrist	office	female/30+	caregiver	routine checkup and prescription for medicine
137	Dec. 10	surgeon	clinic	male/60+	deaf wife	checkup after intestinal surgery
138	Dec. 10	dermatologist	office	male/20+	deaf partner	examination because of severe acne
139	Dec. 13	ophthalmologist	office	male/50+		regular checkup of intraocular pressure in a patient with Usher's syndrome
140	Dec. 13	internist	office	male/60+		checkup after thyroid surgery
141	Dec. 17	gynecologist	office	female/30+		consultation because of pregnancy
142	Dec. 20	colorectal surgeon	office	female/50+		examination because of discomfort after an operation

Critical Care Required: Access to Interpreted Health Care in Ireland

Lorraine Leeson, Asim A. Sheikh, Ilana Rozanes, Carmel Grehan, and Patrick A. Matthews

ABSTRACT

In this chapter we contextualize interpreter healthcare provision in Ireland, focusing specifically on data collected from Irish Sign Language/English interpreters in the Republic of Ireland, data from Deaf community members, and feedback from agencies providing ISL/English interpreting services.

Ireland has a population of approximately 6,500 Deaf Irish Sign Language users (Leeson & Saeed, 2012) and while there are some 100 trained interpreters in the country, only an estimated 70 to 75 of these are currently practicing as interpreters. Given that interpreter training is a relatively new phenomenon in Ireland, there has traditionally been very limited access to continuous professional training, especially regarding medical/mental health settings (Phelan, 2009; Turner et al., 2012). At the same time, for one national interpreting agency, some 25% of all assignments in 2011 were in the medical/mental health domain (Sign Language Interpreting Service, personal communication). From discussions with interpreter agencies/referral services in Ireland and Deaf community organizations, key problems that are inhibiting better service provision are:

- Lack of policy at national level (Health Service Executive) despite the existence of best practice guidelines (2009)
- No obligation on general practitioners to allow interpreters into their surgeries
- Lack of a statutory register of interpreters (spoken or signed)
- Lack of awareness on the part of Deaf community members as to routes to complain about inadequate services
- Lack of specialist training for interpreters

- Lack of training for medical professionals regarding the work of interpreters and the risks associated with use of untrained personnel
- Need for input to Deaf community members regarding the nature of interpreting (particularly regarding cognitive/interactive models
  of interpreting, and the functionality of consecutive versus simultaneous modes of interpreting [e.g., Shaffer & Wilcox, 2005; Russell, 2005; Metzger, 1999]).

We compare and contrast findings from a survey and focus group meetings with interpreters with those from Deaf community focus groups, noting critical concerns that arise. These include issues of attitude: the attitudes of hospitals to Deaf sign language users is cited as a critically important issue—what Deaf people experience as poor/negative attitudes may be a lack of awareness of cultural norms in Deaf communities. In GP clinics, there is a need for clarification about who provides (and pays for) interpreters. Further, the actual provision of interpreters is problematic and often ad hoc, causing stress to vulnerable, ill patients. Doctors often assume that a deaf patient should/will lipread or write notes and this is problematic for many reasons. Assumptions are often made regarding who will "help" by interpreting: doctors sometimes assume that a deaf friend/partner or family member or child should/will interpret. This is highly problematic, not least because there is no guarantee of accuracy and it is not appropriate if they are personally involved. This is especially true in maternity care settings (see also Steinberg, 2006). Further, there is the critically important issue of facilitating informed consent: Deaf people must be provided with appropriately qualified interpreters.

We look at these and other factors and consider best practice approaches to facilitating change that assists the development of interpreter competency, enhances awareness of medical service providers, and engages in Deaf community partnership as the primary basis for pushing forward an agenda for quality, accessible health care.

Our work on healthcare interpreting stems from our participation in a European Commission–funded project called Medisigns[1] (2010–2012).

Medisigns is an award-winning project[2] that represents a groundbreaking initiative focused on providing a better understanding of the impact of interpreted interaction in medical contexts within the framework of a blended learning program for deaf people, interpreters, and medical professionals. The European Union's 27 member states (INRA [Europe] European Coordination Office S.A., 2001) are home to some 900,000 sign language users,[3] but access to interpreting services in health care is varied and could be described as 'hit and miss' despite the existence of EU equality legislation such as the European Charter of Fundamental Rights (Parliament, 2000).

At the same time, there is very little empirical evidence benchmarking the current situation regarding access to interpreted health care (de Wit, Salami, & Hema, 2012; Pöchhacker, this volume); as a result, no research has led to training programs to promote change in the European Union. Very few studies have focused on the experiences—interpreted or not—of deaf people in healthcare settings in Europe (Turner, Nilsson, Sheikh, & Dean, 2012; de Wit et al., 2012; Smeijers & Pfau, 2009). Though several chapters in this volume increase our empirical knowledge significantly (e.g., van den Bogaerde & de Lange; Brück et al.; Smeijers et al.). Thus, a key aim of the Irish team was to benchmark aspects of the Irish experience vis-à-vis our European project partners.

It is against this backdrop that the Medisigns project was funded, and the Centre for Deaf Studies at Trinity College Dublin was a partner, along with Scotland (Heriot-Watt University), Sweden (Stockholm University), Cyprus (University of Nicosia), and Poland (FRP), all of which were led and promoted by Interesource Group (Ireland) Limited.[4]

In benchmarking the current context experienced by Irish Deaf community members and interpreters, we carried out focus group meetings with both communities in 2011 and 2012 in conjunction with a survey of interpreters in Ireland. The engagement with interpreters is particularly significant as it represents the first empirical snapshot of the settings in which healthcare interpreters work in Ireland today. Our data informed the development of the training content, which ultimately became the Medisigns Project suite of online, open-access materials to support healthcare professionals, interpreters, and deaf patients.

As we will see, although some things have changed in Ireland since the first Irish study on deaf women's access to maternity care was carried out (Doyle, Buckley, & McCaul, 1986), the key systemic barriers remain. The most significant positive changes include the availability of professional interpreters and the increasing awareness at the national level of the existence of a community of Irish Sign Language (ISL) users. With some 100 interpreters trained (as of 2013), access is improving, but without top-down requirements for the provision and monitoring of interpreters, access retains an ad hoc dimension for Deaf community members; much remains to be done to ensure and monitor quality performance. Another critical change is the increased sense among Irish deaf people that their linguistic heritage is their cultural capital and that this needs to be recognized and responded to by both the Government and healthcare providers via the provision of accessible services. Such services entail the supplying of interpreters and online content in ISL.

From a stakeholder's perspective, the most critical issue raised by all of the participants (interpreters and members of the Deaf community alike) is the attitude of medical staff: respondents reported that negative attitudes lead to the lack of interpreters and seem to underpin the assumption that any "signer" will do even if that signer happens to be a patient's 8-year-old child. In one case reported to us, the "interpreter" was a hospitalized hearing child who was called on to interpret for the deaf parents. Other assumptions that remain include some doctors' beliefs that gesturing suffices as linguistic input and that deaf patients will be able to read, write, and lipread. Doctors seem to be unaware of the levels of stress that deaf patients experience as a result of these assumptions.

Irish Sign Language interpreters, both in focus groups and in an online survey also expressed grave concerns about healthcare providers' lack of knowledge and understanding. Although no formal research has been carried out on how healthcare staff approach deaf patients, anecdotal evidence suggests that interaction with both deaf and hard of hearing patients is seen as challenging, and there is openness to embedding guidelines for best practice into the education of doctors and nurses.

The goal of the Medisigns Project was the creation of research-led, criteria-driven, open-access continuing professional development (CPD) materials for interpreters, healthcare staff, and deaf people. The research process facilitated the identification of critical issues, which were then embedded (often as case studies) in the teaching materials. Medisigns teaching and learning multimedia data are available as open-access content that supports CPD requirements for interpreters throughout Europe and potentially farther afield (though we anticipate that localization may be necessary).

The Irish project team also filmed interviews with Irish deaf people, interpreters, interpreter providers, healthcare professionals, and legal experts as documentary evidence of the key issues emerging. These interviews are available at www.medisignsproject.eu.

INFORMED CONSENT

As discussed in several chapters in this volume, access to health care is considered a basic human right in developed countries. Despite this, there is no pan-European legislation that mandates entitlement to either a spoken or a signed language interpreter in medical settings, although Directive 2010/64/EU of the European Parliament and the Council of October 20, 2010, spells out the rights to interpretation and translation in criminal proceedings (de Wit et al., 2012). We suggest that this directive offers a model on which further healthcare-specific legislation could be developed. A central pillar of such access is the concept of "informed consent," which underpins modern patient care. This is more than rhetoric about best practice: it has a legal basis in Irish law and a solid foundation in international medical and ethical best practice. The reason for this, in theory, is quite simple: one's autonomy is best served when one is well informed about one's health care. Armed with this information, one is in a position to make decisions regarding that health care. A patient may wish to ask questions about a medical procedure that is of concern; a patient may wish to think further about a suggested treatment; or a patient may decide not to go ahead with the treatment. Properly informed consent in theory, therefore, implies that a patient has sufficient information to make well-considered healthcare decisions. According to this rationale, "the objective of risk disclosure is preservation of the patient's interest in intelligent self-choice on proposed treatment, a matter that the patient is free to decide for any reason that appeals to him. When, prior to commencement of therapy, the patient is sufficiently informed on risks and he exercises his choice, it may truly be said that he did exactly what he wanted to do" (Judge Kearns, 2000, p. 552).

Reflecting this thinking and endorsing the concept of patient autonomy, the latest edition of the Irish Medical Council guidelines (Medical Council, 2009) advises medical practitioners to "ensure that informed consent has been given by a patient before any medical treatment is carried out. The ethical and legal rationale behind this is to respect the patient's autonomy and their right to control their own life. The basic idea of personal autonomy is that everyone's actions and decisions are their own. Therefore, the patient has the right to decide what happens to their own body" (2009, p. 34).

The right to autonomy has been long understood and established in deaf-related healthcare research. Moreover, the aforementioned norms state that:

> If autonomy is offered in a healthcare relationship, the liberty of each individual is respected. To exercise their right of autonomy, patients must be able to provide truly informed consent. To do this, patients must understand all of the pertinent information about the health condition, available treatments, and the probable risks and benefits of each treatment option. If a patient is so informed, he or she can make a decision based on his or her own values and beliefs, free of coercive influences from any source. (Harmer, 1999, p. 102)

Despite the fact that communication is central to informed consent, the issue of access to health care and, more critically, the quality of access to health care for Deaf communities is significantly under documented. In the United States, research suggests that doctor–deaf patient communication is an issue of serious concern. "[P]ersons who are deaf or hard of hearing (D&HH) have altered healthcare utilization patterns and significant communication difficulties with physicians, often experiencing misunderstandings about their disease or treatment recommendations. They are a 'silent' group to many physicians" (Meador & Zazove, 2005, p. 218).

More serious issues of access to health care due to communication problems have also been reported. For example, a deaf patient was left isolated and unable to communicate for 12 days in Ninewells Hospital because she was not provided with access to a sign language interpreter (Urquhart, 2013). A complaint was referred to the Scottish Public Services Ombudsman (SPSO), who investigated the matter and upheld the complaint on March 27, 2013. Moreover, although the patient had signed a consent form, since no interpreter had been provided to the patient, it was "impossible to say for sure if informed consent was given on the operation carried out" (SPSO, 2013, p. 9). The first recommendation made was that the hospital board's policy be changed to "highlight the legal duties staff have and to explain that using families, lipreading and pen and paper is not likely to be an adequate or reasonable response to the needs of a BSL [British Sign Language] user. This should make clear that BSL is a registered language and not simply signed English" (ibid.).

Having touched on the importance of patient autonomy in the doctor-patient relationship, we wish to mention that a patient exercises this autonomy in law and as a patient through the giving or withholding of consent. Therefore, legally, except in rare circumstances, medical treatment may not be provided to an adult person of full capacity unless the person's consent is secured. Judge Denham (now the Chief Justice of Ireland), speaking in the Supreme Court, pointed out that there are few exceptions to this general rule. Outlining the full rule, its exceptions, and the legal consequences of not obtaining consent, she stated the following:

> Medical treatment may not be given to an adult person of full capacity without his or her consent. There are a few rare exceptions to this e.g., in regard to contagious diseases or in a medical emergency where the patient is unable to communicate. This right arises out of civil, criminal and constitutional law. If medical treatment is given without consent it may be trespass against the person in civil law, a battery in criminal law, and a breach of the individual's constitutional rights. The consent which is given by an adult of full capacity is a matter of choice. It is not necessarily a decision based on medical considerations. Thus, medical treatment may be refused for other than medical reasons . . . the person of full age and capacity may make the decision for their own reasons. (Judge Denham, 1996, p. 156)

Thus, the concept of consent and informed consent is well established and not contemporary. Sheikh (2006) observes that:

> Consent is therefore the means in law and medicine by which we translate (i) that we wish to have something done to our body and (ii) what we wish to have done to our body. The Supreme Court has stated that, "The requirement of consent to medical treatment is an aspect of a person's right to bodily integrity under Article 40, s. 3 of the Constitution" and the Court of Appeal has stated that "Every human being's right to life carries with it, as an intrinsic part of it, rights of bodily integrity and autonomy—the right to have one's own body whole and intact and (on reaching an age of understanding) to take decisions about one's own body." Thus, the respect for someone's bodily integrity in the realms of medical treatment occurs when one allows that someone to decide what he/she wants done with their own body. It is this rationale that underpins the concept of self-determination and in medical law, it existed prior to what are regarded as the modern tenets of medical ethics as stated by the Nuremburg Code (1947) and the Declaration of Helsinki (1964–2004) and thus, in the oft-quoted case of *Schloendorff v. Society*

of New York Hospital, Cardozo J. stated that, "Every person being of adult years and sound mind has a right to determine what shall be done with his own body." (ibid., p. 54)

It is therefore no surprise that the Health Service Executive's (HSE) drive toward a national consent policy takes the issue seriously. The HSE notes that, "Seeking consent is not merely getting a consent form signed; the consent form is just one means of documenting that a process of communication has occurred" (HSE, 2013, p. 23). Furthermore, the HSE points out that for consent to be valid, a service user must be competent to make the particular decision. It also states that the service user must not be acting under duress and must have received sufficient information in a comprehensible manner about the nature, purpose, benefits, and risks of an intervention, service, or research project. For the HSE, receiving information in a comprehensible manner entails, "their [patient's] ability to understand the information provided/language used" (ibid., p. 24). The document advocates the use of professional interpreters, warning against family, friends, and children functioning as interpreters, and includes a section on appropriate provisions for deaf and hard of hearing patients: "[D]eaf and hard of hearing service users should be asked how they would like information to be provided. Some individuals with impaired hearing can lip read, some use hearing aids and others may require signed language interpreters. If required, a signed language interpreter should be obtained. In relation to the use of children, family and friends as interpreters see paragraph above" (ibid., p. 19).

This mirrors issues raised in the HSE's good practice guidelines, (HSE, 2009) which state the following:

> Informed consent is a legal requirement within the HSE. Patients must clearly understand what procedures are going to take place and the consequences of these procedures. (ibid., at p. 8)

Crucially, they go on to note that:

> In any consultation, if you believe that the patient has not understood what you have said it is safer to stop the consultation and seek further help, than to risk either undertaking a treatment without informed consent or sending the patient away with incorrect or incomplete information about their condition or treatment. (ibid., p. 8)

These guidelines outline the HSE's view on what constitutes best practice in facilitating non-English speakers in healthcare settings. These align with goals associated with the HSE's Transformation Program, which has six stated priorities: (1) simplified patient journeys, (2) easier access to primary care, (3) easier access to high-quality hospitals, (4) increased range of chronic illness programs, (5) more transparent and measurable standards, and (6) greater staff involvement in transformation (ibid., p. 5).

For our purposes, the key points of the document that relate to suggested practices surrounding the right to interpretation and the provision of interpreted services include the following:

- Staff should let patients know that they have the right to an interpreter to assist in communication. It should be made clear that there is no cost to the patient and that staff will arrange for the interpreter (the patient does not have to do this). The patient can use or refuse the assigned interpreter. (p. 10)
- Once you have confirmed that an interpreter is required it is important to record this in the patient's case notes. (p. 10)
- A consultation involving use of an interpreter will take longer than a routine appointment. Additional time should be allocated for this when appointments are made. (p. 10)
- Staff within the confines of their own profession, who feel they can communicate effectively in another language, may directly converse with their own patients who have limited English proficiency and/or who are deaf, for general conversation such as greetings, informing patients of any delays, explaining any administrative problems relating to their appointment, gaining information in an emergency situation. However, staff should not be asked to interpret in clinical situations. (p. 10)

Although policy documents suggest how effective communication should take place in healthcare settings, and even though a legal basis ensures that informed consent is obtained, in Ireland there is unfortunately no legal right to the provision of interpreters, and there is no requirement that healthcare services provide interpreters (Phelan, 2009).

Without a legal basis and a systemic approach to the implementation and monitoring of best practice in this regard, patients' experiences fall far short of what is desired. The bottom line is not a lack of policy—it is lack of implementation.

Before delving deeper into the details of our study, we first present a snapshot of the Irish Deaf community.

Ireland has a population of approximately 6,500 Irish Sign Language users (Leeson & Saeed, 2012), and although there are close to 100 trained ISL/English interpreters, approximately 75 of these are currently practicing as interpreters. Given that interpreter training is a relatively new phenomenon in Ireland, with the first cohort trained in 1992, access to continuous professional training has traditionally been very limited (Leeson & Lynch, 2009), especially regarding medical/mental health settings. At the same time, we know that the demand for medical interpreting is increasing as awareness levels rise. For example, for one national interpreting referral center, some 25% of all assignments in 2011 were in the medical/mental health domain, and demand for video relay interpreting is growing (Sign Language Interpreting Service, personal communication). From discussions with key stakeholders, the main problems that are inhibiting better service provision have been identified. These include the lack of policy implementation at the national level by the Health Service Executive, as outlined earlier. As a result, two localized services in Munster (the province in the south of Ireland comprising counties Cork, Kerry, Limerick, Clare, Tipperary, and Waterford) have pushed for local responses (e.g., the Kerry Deaf Resource Centre (KDRC); Sign Language Interpreters Munster (SLIM) in partnership with the Cork Association of the Deaf [CAD]).

Other factors include the lack of obligation for frontline healthcare providers, general practitioners (GPs), to allow interpreters into their offices. The lack of a statutory register of interpreters (spoken or signed) means that anyone can self-identify as an "interpreter," and there are no regulations governing who can be hired in such a role despite the introduction of tendering arrangements for the provision of interpreting services in all publically funded services (e.g., hospitals, police departments, courtrooms, schools) in recent years. For European deaf sign language users, full access to medical services would entail access to interpreting services as well as to general healthcare information translated into sign language (Turner et al., 2012).

Each of the Medisigns partner countries, with perhaps the enviable exception of Sweden, currently has an insufficient number of professional sign language interpreters; furthermore, most countries have a very limited number of sign language interpreters—if any—who have specialized training in health care or in interpreting in a medical setting. What is more, the exact number of sign language interpreters with specialist medical and healthcare knowledge in Europe is unknown (ibid.). Another key point is the fact that, in accessing appropriate health care, an additional issue to consider is the fact that "average" deaf sign language users may have less knowledge about which services they need, as well as where to find this information, due to a lower level of educational attainment, not to mention the extremely limited information from official sources in a signed language online. This is closely linked to the fact that, in many countries, the general level of literacy of the deaf population is lower than that of the overall population, thus putting the group at a serious disadvantage (Conroy, 2006). According to the Council of Europe (Leeson, 2006), general trends internationally suggest that the average reading age for deaf people of average intelligence in the European Union is 8.5 to 9 years. A critical point is this: "it is important to note that the provision of qualified sign language interpreters, and especially those trained in healthcare aspects, is not viewed as a luxury but as a fundamental human right to the access and provision of appropriate healthcare" (Turner et al., 2012, p. 6).

Linked to this, we know problems also exist in accessibility. But both healthcare providers in Ireland and certain segments of the Irish Deaf community are unclear about what constitutes appropriate interpreting provision. For the Deaf community, this is compounded by a lack of clarity regarding how one should complain about inadequate service provision on the part of healthcare providers. Although the Health Service Executive advertises a complaints procedure, "Your Service, Your Say,"[5] currently no information is available in Irish Sign Language (although, as a result of the Medisigns project, this is in development and due for release in 2014). Furthermore, even though a number of interpreting agencies and interpreting referral services are working in conjunction with individual hospitals or medical practices, the current lack of a statutory register[6] means that there is no centralized complaints procedure if a problem arises with interpreting services that are provided.

In addition, medical professionals typically receive no information about the work of interpreters (i.e., working with spoken or signed languages) and the risks associated with the use of untrained personnel.[7]

PREVIOUS IRISH STUDIES

Surprisingly little empirical work has focused on the experiences of Deaf communities in healthcare settings in Europe (Turner et al., 2012), and reference to Irish deaf people's experiences in healthcare contexts generally tends to be documented along with other experiences in more broad-based studies. The earliest Irish study that we know of, one that focused on Dublin-based deaf women's access to maternity services, dates to 1986. In the next section we report on the key findings of this study and other Dublin-based research before turning to additional sources that reference aspects of the Irish Deaf community's access to healthcare services.

Dublin-Based Studies

In 1986 the Adult Education Service for deaf people in Dublin reported on responses to a questionnaire (n = 30). In the Dublin area Doyle, Buckley, and McCaul (1986) undertook to clarify and identify needs in maternity services on the basis of the experience of deaf mothers. They also intended to secure improvements in service provision. However, this report was poorly disseminated and remained widely unknown until Steinberg (2006) located one of three remaining hard copies of the document during her research on maternity services. Given this, she rightly points out the importance of dissemination if researchers hope to facilitate community-level activism on important issues emerging from their work.

Doyle et al. (1986) found that medical personnel did not keep their patients informed about their condition and that mothers experienced patronizing attitudes from and poor communication with medical staff before, during, and after delivery. They concluded with a list of recommendations, the majority of which are related to communication. Steinberg (2006, p. 253) notes that even though interpretation was not discussed by the respondents at the time, the survey team recommended that *"every pregnant deaf mother should have access to the services of a well qualified interpreter"* (Doyle et al., 1986, p. 16, emphasis in original). At the time, this was clearly ambitious since interpreter training was not available in Ireland until 1992, and sadly, the goal of ensuring the appropriate provision of interpreters has still not been achieved in maternity settings or in healthcare settings more generally.

Reporting on access to maternity care, with a particular focus on Dublin-based mothers, Steinberg (2006) interviewed 11 deaf mothers. The mothers had collectively experienced 32 births, 27 of which took place in Dublin. Professional interpreters were present at just 4 of the births and, in only 1 case, for antenatal services despite the availability of a small pool of professional, trained interpreters since 1994. The majority of births took place in two key Dublin-based maternity hospitals—Holles

Street and the Rotunda—with hospital choice influenced by the experiences of friends and family members.

Steinberg (ibid.), citing Doyle et al. (1986) notes that little systemic change had occurred in the 20-year period that separates the two studies. She reports that the most significant issue affecting deaf mothers in accessing care still related to communication. Difficulties included negotiating the actual language barrier between ISL and English (either written or spoken English) and overcoming institutional-level barriers, which included accessing information about hospital policy and protocol, particularly with respect to treatment practices for deaf mothers and their babies. Steinberg (2006) notes that problems also arose with respect to accessing educational and health-related-information environments like antenatal classes and throughout the postnatal period, which is supported by nurses in the ward and by public health nurses either at the mother's own home or in local clinics. She suggests that communication barriers can be traced back to attitudinal barriers, preconceptions, and misconceptions of medical practitioners and sees this as emanating from the medical concept of deafness, which predisposes medical practitioners (and, we might add, other healthcare providers) to focus primarily on the deaf mother's audiological status. This situation has led to the inappropriate labeling of deaf women as "deaf and dumb." For example, Steinberg (ibid.) presents evidence of hospital staff disrespecting or disregarding mothers, in some instances as a direct response to a woman's deafness. Respondents reported a direct correlation between the treatment they received and the healthcare providers' attitudes toward deafness. Most worryingly, Steinberg reports the narratives of several respondents who told of complications experienced during pregnancy that were disregarded by medical staff until their situation had escalated and become quite severe.

The mothers reported using four main methods of communicating with healthcare staff. These were pen and paper, lipreading, a family member to interpret, or, in a very few cases, a professional interpreter. In some instances, strategies (e.g., writing notes and lipreading) that had proved successful in certain contexts became impractical in the delivery setting. Further, for the deaf patient, literacy in English may actually impede access and potentially add stress to the encounter. Indeed, one of Steinberg's respondents explained why she would prefer not to write: "English is my second language, so I'd go to write something down and then stop. Struggle to think how to say it, describe the details. I'm not great at English, I'm not. I can write, I can, but details, how to say something that specific,

I wouldn't know. With [my husband] there, that bit was easier, because he could translate . . . But writing, sometimes I felt it was not worth the bother" (Steinberg, 2006, p. 262).

Steinberg herself says the following:

> Writing reproduces the power dynamics of English over ISL, privileging the medical persona with the authority of the dominant language and rendering the deaf mothers' own language invisible and, because the doctors do not understand it, useless. It also introduces a reason for doctors to judge the mothers, as their struggle with English is often interpreted as a sign of being unintelligent. Mothers often feel uncomfortable challenging this perception. (ibid., p. 262–263)

The general lack of sign language interpreters, in combination with the fact that the group of deaf sign language users and interpreters is small, makes privacy an issue, and this was frequently mentioned also in our own focus groups with deaf sign language users. Steinberg (ibid.) argues that when regulations and policies are constructed, it is essential to take these concerns into account.

Many mothers in Steinberg's study reported that they did not regularly attend antenatal classes because they were not accessible to them. Steinberg also reports that many mothers did not see their GP as a source of information and, as a result, never asked questions when visiting the GP. In terms of postnatal issues, the practice of testing newborn infants was raised. At the time of Steinberg's study, universal neonatal screening for deafness was not conducted in Ireland; as a result, healthcare providers would select certain infants for screening on the basis of potential for deafness. The mothers in Steinberg's study expressed indignation at this practice, noting that it is carried out only on babies with deaf mothers, indicating that they are not being treated as equal to hearing mothers. Another area of concern for the respondents was the lack of information about and support for breastfeeding. Thus, we can say that Irish deaf women have been reporting difficulty in terms of information access, communication, and respect for personal agency for close to thirty years.

In addition, even though Dublin is the best-served population in terms of interpreter provision, the use of professional interpreters by Deaf community members is still very limited, in great part because of their lack of experience in working with interpreters, a perfect "Catch 22" situation. This is confounded by concerns for privacy: Deaf people understandably do not want interpreters to know their private business. Noting that signers are most likely to experience interpreting in education, Leeson (2012) reports that, in Ireland, unlike in many other countries such as Canada and Belgium (Heyerick & Vermeerbergen, 2012), deaf and hard of hearing students do not have interpreters provided to them in secondary school. Moreover, one of the issues facing deaf sign language users in higher education is knowing when they need an interpreter and how to work effectively with one. Indeed, fewer than half of Irish deaf and hard of hearing students in higher education access their courses via interpretation (Leeson, 2012). When we factor in that deaf people are ten times less likely than their hearing peers to have a college or university degree, it becomes clear that only a very few well-educated deaf people have the most established frameworks for working with interpreters: for the broader Deaf community, this is not necessarily so. Coupled with the fact that healthcare providers seem unaware of their responsibilities in fulfilling the communicative-access needs of their deaf patients, we have the potential for a perfect storm: insufficient communication leading to insufficient information about one's own health, compromised decision-making pathways, and compromised patient compliance.

Another study that touches on the Irish Deaf community's access to health care included a pilot survey of the Dublin[8] Deaf community ($n = 35$; 20 female, 15 male) regarding the provision of interpreters to deaf people at that time (Matthews, 1996). Within the wider context of exploring issues associated with the Irish Deaf community, the participants were asked about interpreter provision in healthcare settings. The healthcare domains that deaf patients most often frequented were their local GP, the hospital, and social welfare services.

The responses of participants who stated that they worked with interpreters in healthcare settings are shown in figure 1. Further data provided responses that showed that deaf people called on a wide range of people,

	YES	Sometimes	NO	Never happened
Family doctor	5 (14.3%)	7 (20%)	21 (60%)	2 (5.7%)
Hospital	3 (8.6%)	5 (14.3%)	15 (42.8%)	12 (34.3%)
Social services/welfare	3 (8.6%)	4 (11.4%)	12 (34.3%)	16 (45.7%)

FIGURE 1. *Working with interpreters in medical and social service settings (Matthews, 1996).*

other than trained interpreters, when needed. When responding about visiting a GP, seven deaf participants said they asked a relative to interpret. Other respondents said that they asked a social worker, a deaf friend, a hearing friend, or a teacher of deaf students to interpret for them in such settings.

When it came to hospital visits, five participants (14%) responded that a relative interprets for them. One reported using a social worker, and two people (5.7%) responded that they use a hearing friend. When dealing with social services five people (14%) responded that they use a relative as their "interpreter."

The participants were then asked what kind of signing the person who interpreted for them used on visits to their local family doctor. One person said that the interpreter used ISL; two said sign-supported English; one mentioned Total Communication; five said oral communication; one deaf-blind person used specialist techniques; and one said that the interpreter fingerspelled everything. Of Matthews's (1996) respondents, 86% believed that the government should provide interpreting services, while 3% reported that they paid for the interpreters themselves.

The Mid-West Region

In 2006 Conama (2008) reviewed community responses to the short-term provision of an Irish Sign Language interpreter in the Mid-West Region (i.e., counties Limerick, Tipperary North, and Clare) under the auspices of the Signing Information Mid-West Project. This was the first time that a professionally trained interpreter was available in the region: prior to this, no trained/qualified interpreter was obtainable within a 100-km radius of Limerick City (ibid., p. 6).[9] The study explored the uptake of interpreting services and the viability of provision.

For our purposes, what is particularly interesting is the inclusion of several questions relating to domains in which interpreters were used. Of 20 respondents (10 male, 9 female, 1 unspecified) aged 18–65+ years, only 3 (17%) said that they had availed themselves of interpreter services in medical settings during the Signing Information Mid-West Project (2006–2007), but 23% said that if they had an opportunity to do so, they would. Prior to 2006, only 2 of the 20 respondents say they had had an interpreter in a medical setting. Just like Matthews's (1996) respondents, most reported that when dealing with service providers (in medical, educational, and other public service settings), they relied on family members, neighbors, colleagues, or friends to facilitate communication.

The most frequently called-on communicator was a mother or sister (39%). As one respondent put it, "I live by myself and have no access to any social contact with other deaf people. I had to spend three days in hospital last year and had no help with communicating with nurses and doctors" (Conama, 2008, p. 34).

The provision of a locally based professional interpreter helped to ameliorate this kind of experience, but the community reported that one interpreter was not sufficient to meet their needs and pointed out that written and electronic information remain inaccessible.[10] They further noted that full access to information would not be achieved via the provision of interpreters alone, suggesting that service providers could move to make information on websites available in ISL as one means of improving access more generally.

Another key concern for people in the region was privacy. Conama (2008, p. 42) reports that while focus group participants emphasized that they trusted the interpreter in their area and commended her ethical practice, they were concerned that the one interpreter in their region was "privvy to a significant amount of personal information about Deaf people, which understandably, is a significant issue for the community." Conama goes on to note that until more interpreters become available, this one interpreter's access to the local community's personal affairs (i.e., those that are mediated via interpretation) will remain unchecked. This fact causes some deaf people to reconsider whether they will use an interpreter in every situation in which they would like one. Thus, the sense that one's privacy is protected is affected by whether one has a choice of interpreters. As we will see, the issues of privacy and choice of interpreter are recurrent themes.

National Perspectives

Conama and Grehan (2002) find that the majority of Irish deaf people live in relative poverty. With respect to accessing health care, they report that "dealing with medical professionals and health issues can be a disastrous and traumatic experience for deaf people" (ibid, p. 5). The main reason reported for such difficulties is the existence of a language barrier.

The studies we have mentioned thus far focus on the experience of members of the Irish Deaf community. Very little has been documented regarding the provision of interpreting services or the experiences of interpreters in healthcare settings. From documents pertaining to the provision of interpreters, we know that, following an assessment of interpreters' skills in 1996, recommendations for continuous professional development for interpreters included reference to developing language for specific purposes in a range of domains, including medical (Accreditation Board, 1997). A subsequent review of the provision of sign language interpreting in Ireland (Prospectus, 2006) reports frequent requests for interpreting for maternity classes, healthcare education, and clinic appointments. In 2004 Irish Sign Link (a now defunct, government-funded interpreting provider) had a total of 81 clients in the healthcare domain, but no figures are available to illustrate how many requests for an interpreter were made or could not be accommodated. This is one of the major difficulties in challenging the provision of interpreting services in Ireland: no centralized data exist, and no mechanism is available for evaluating the number of interpreting requests that are turned down (either at the frontline level or because of the unavailability of interpreters). Prospectus also reports that its respondents ($n = 81$) noted many gaps in public service provision, including the lack of clarity regarding the routine provision of interpreting support for a deaf person attending a private medical consultation or in counseling situations. It also notes that access to interpreting for emergency services, such as emergency responders and ambulance services, is a particularly urgent need that should be met at all times but is not. Another key issue reported is the mismatch between supply and demand: the combination of increasing demand for and the limited supply of interpreters, coupled with the fact that the majority of interpreters are freelancers and that the geographic spread of interpreters is disproportionate, affects the reality of access for Irish deaf people.

THIS STUDY

Research ethics approval was sought from and granted by the School of Linguistics, Speech, and Communication Sciences at Trinity College Dublin. The data collection included three key phases: an online, anonymous survey of interpreters; focus group meetings with Deaf community members; and focus group meetings with interpreters. The research phase ran from December 2011 to December 2012.

We hypothesized that despite the existence of a national Health Service Executive (HSE) best practice document on the provision for interpreting in medical contexts (2009), few stakeholders would be aware of it and that experience would run counter to the best practice guidelines discussed earlier in this chapter. From individual stories reported in the media (e.g., Hands On, the Radio Telefís Éireann [RTÉ][11] program for the Irish Deaf community), we knew that cases of misdiagnosis and other problems have occurred in medical encounters in which untrained or no interpreters were provided, but little had been done prior to this to study the scope of the problems or to cross-reference the Deaf community's experiences and those of interpreters. There was also no Irish study that reported on the experiences of interpreters in healthcare settings, in great part because interpreting is a relatively new profession in Ireland (Leeson and Lynch, 2009).

Our aim was to capture a clear snapshot of the context as experienced by deaf people and reported by interpreters. Results facilitated the development of a research-led, blended-learning training course for deaf people, interpreters, and medical staff as a key deliverable of the Medisigns project. A second stage (for future development) is to triangulate these initial findings with Irish hospital and medical practitioner experiences and to identify major barriers to successful interpreter-mediated medical interactions from their perspective.

In terms of research design, we took an emancipatory and participatory approach to our research for Medisigns, one that enables positive user involvement and empowerment (Chambers, 2004; O'Reilly-de Brún & de Brún, 2010). We also wished to follow international and national policy practice, which advocates user involvement in primary care (World Health Organization, 1978; Health Service Executive, 2008). We adopted peer researcher approaches insofar as two members of the Medisigns research team are deaf and experienced researchers in the field of deaf studies (Grehan and Matthews). A third research team member is an experienced interpreter and interpreter educator (Leeson). The fourth member of our team is a doctoral student working on interpreting issues in healthcare settings (Rozanes), while Sheikh is a barrister (attorney) and an expert in medicolegal issues. Peer research approaches facilitated the maintenance of rapport directly with our target communities.

The Deaf community has been described as an oppressed minority (e.g., Ladd, 2003), and our objective was to work with the community, collaborate with its members on a research topic of vital interest to them, and provide feedback to them over the life of the project. Our approach included inviting Deaf community members to participate in focus groups to talk about issues of concern in healthcare settings and reporting through established avenues like the *Irish Deaf Journal* and the Kerry Deaf Resource Center.

The goal of this approach was to better position our team to identify the range of problem areas in contemporary healthcare settings, as reported by Deaf community members. It also facilitated our work with these people by prioritizing the issues they felt needed urgent attention. Another key goal was to ensure that the issues they raised were addressed in the development of the training program to be offered to interpreters and healthcare staff as a Medisigns project output.

With interpreters, we began with an anonymous questionnaire run on SurveyMonkey. We included a note informing the interpreters that they could opt in to further engagement with the project by contacting the primary investigators (Leeson, Grehan, and Matthews) or simply turning up at the Dublin/Limerick–based focus group meetings for interpreters.

We then convened a focus group in Dublin (Center for Deaf Studies), on the east coast of Ireland, and in Limerick (Deaf Community Centre), on the west coast to further tease out relevant issues. This geographical spread mirrored previous studies of Deaf communities, allowing for a preliminary diachronic examination of the situation from their perspective. Critically, we emphasized that we would not be naming participants at any stage of reporting and assured participants that confidentiality would be upheld. We also used a "snowball" approach to invite participation through channels that facilitated a "purposeful sample" of participants (Patton, 2002).

Focus group meetings lasted between 1.5 and 2 hours. In order to respect the anonymity of the participants, we did not video-record the sessions. Instead, a rapporteur for the focus groups kept detailed, anonymized notes. Data were then shared with participants via email, and they had a 7-day period in which to review and amend the record. After this, a final version of the notes of the meeting was circulated to all of the participants of each focus group.

The Survey

A total of 25 interpreters completed the survey. Of those, 80% reported that they had interpreted in healthcare settings. In addition, 73% had more than 3 years of experience, and 26% had 5–10 years of experience, which is in line with the relatively recent development of interpreting as a profession in Ireland. Furthermore, 43% of respondents were 30–39 years of age, and 91% had completed formal interpreter training. The majority (84%) were female. In terms of geographic distribution, the majority (74%) were Leinster-based interpreters (comprising eastern and midlands counties Dublin, Meath, Laois, Offaly, Wexford, and Carlow). A further 22% were based in Munster, and 4% were Connaught based (northwestern counties Leitrim, Sligo, Galway, Mayo, and Roscommon). No one self-reported as being based in the northern province, Ulster, although we estimate that about 1,500 ISL users live in the north of Ireland (Leeson and Saeed, 2012). Of the group, 4% reported ISL as their first language, while 78% had English as their mother tongue. Also, 17% reported that they grew up in a bilingual ISL/English household.

Just 30% reported that they interpret in medical settings more than ten times a year, suggesting that this is an area where interpreters remain quite inexperienced in absolute terms. Some 70% noted that they had not received specific training to work in these contexts. The interpreters reported that the highest level of demand is in mental health settings: 81% had worked in this domain. Figure 2 illustrates the range of domains where respondents have worked.

Of the interpreters who reported having completed some specific healthcare-related training, 47% stated that this consisted of a general first-aid course. Also, 78% of the interpreters have experienced difficulties in interpreting in medical settings, and 77% reported having had difficulty conveying information about specific medical terms to a deaf patient. A further 37% reported having trouble with the accents of medical front-line staff. All of the respondents said they would like to avail themselves

	Response Percent	Response Count
GP visit	66.7%	14
Accident and Emergency	47.6%	10
Meeting with a consultant	71.4%	15
Pre/ante natal care	38.1%	8
Dentist visit	23.8%	5
Procedure with a nurse	66.7%	14
Surgical procedure	52.4%	11
Delivery of a Baby	19.0%	4
Medical Testing Procedures	57.1%	12
Mental health settings	81.0%	17
Other (please specify)		3
answered question		21
skipped question		4

FIGURE 2. *ISL interpreters experience in healthcare settings.*

of continuous professional training in healthcare interpreting, and 90% identified training in medical terminology and in conveying medical terminology in ISL as key factors that would improve their practice.

The most significant concern was the attitudes of healthcare professionals, especially in mental health settings. When asked to indicate the factors they believed affected their interaction with a doctor and a patient, 86% mentioned the doctor's willingness to slow down the interaction and make information clear by drawing diagrams or explaining terms. In addition, 77% of interpreters rated the doctor's attitude toward interpreters as significant, while 73% reported that the doctor's attitude to deafness was important. As we will see, this turned out to be the major issue raised by both interpreters and Deaf community members in the focus groups.

The doctor's attitude toward a deaf patient was reported by 27% of interpreters as influencing how they feel about interpreting personal or intimate questions. This contrasts with just 9% who stated that the gender of the deaf person might affect them when interpreting delicate material.

The attitude of healthcare staff (including administrators and frontline reception personnel) was the issue that Deaf community members and interpreters in the focus groups spent the most time discussing, too, and, as we have seen, this has been a persistent topic, first reported in Doyle et al.'s (1986) study. Of the interpreters in our survey, 85% identified training for frontline healthcare staff as a crucial factor that could affect support for their work in healthcare settings. For example, one respondent wrote that "One deaf person said 'I need an interpreter' and the doctor said 'what is an interpreter?' " Another interpreter reported that in at least two appointments the doctor started gesturing and was very surprised when the deaf person did not understand his gesticulations. It seems that in some cases the starting point required for developing a discourse around the goals of the HSE's best practice guidelines is extremely basic indeed. Of the respondents, 75% reported that the provision of universal access supports (e.g., electronic display systems) in accident and emergency services would assist their work, which parallels comments made by deaf informants. Interestingly, only 35% believed that remote interpreting-service development holds promise for improving practice in healthcare settings in Ireland, whereas deaf informants were rather enthusiastic about this.

As mentioned earlier, the most significant practical concern reported by interpreters in the survey was a doctor's willingness to slow down the interaction and make information clear (e.g., by drawing or explaining terms) (86%). This is critical to the ideal of all parties assuming responsibility for their part in making triadic healthcare exchanges successful (Turner et al., 2012). Interpreters also reported struggling to deal with "information overload"; for example, they reported that they struggled to understand and deal with medical terminology in context. It seems that they coped with this by managing the mode of interpreting they utilized: 90% stated that they use a mix of simultaneous and consecutive interpreting when working in healthcare settings, with only 4.5% reporting that they use only consecutive mode in these domains despite the fact that consecutive interpreting has been demonstrated to support higher levels of accuracy in meaning transfer (Russell, 2005). One interpreter noted, "I have asked doctors to draw diagrams or access charts/images in the environment or on their new software systems but have not had much success with it. They don't seem to understand the significance, and either refuse or don't use it effectively or just ignore the request." However, other interpreters have had some measure of success with requests: "I find that doctors are generally very good at explaining terminology if the interpreter clarifies. Sometimes I ask them to draw what something looks like. I find the medical setting very accessible as there is always room to clarify."

Figure 3 shows the strategies interpreters used when interpreting in healthcare settings:

		Response Percent	Response Count
I get the doctor to draw diagrams		59.1%	13
I get the doctor to use charts/ images in the environment		54.5%	12
I get the patient to draw diagrams		18.2%	4
I work with a Deaf interpreter		27.3%	6
I fingerspell a lot of terms		45.5%	10
I simplify a lot of terms		40.9%	9
Other (please specify)		13.6%	3
	Other (please specify)		8
	answered question		22
	skipped question		3

FIGURE 3. *Strategies used by ISL/English interpreters when working in healthcare settings.*

Other issues that concern interpreters in healthcare settings include the patient's state of mind (55%) and having access to background information about the case (68%). Regarding state-of-mind issues, interpreters wrote that these sometimes arose when, for example, someone was being treated for addiction or had been the victim of an assault that led to subsequent depression. Interpreters expressed concerns about what a patient might do in the absence of adequate support (e.g., advocacy, intervention) and/or how a patient's state of mind might affect the interpretation: what would happen if the patient were disengaged, distressed, or psychotic or in a state of arousal? What would it mean for them when they were attempting to make sense of the source language in an interactive setting? Crucially, the interpreters reported that they often feel that they are the only ones in the room who read some of these cues. One interpreter reported having interpreted in a psychiatric setting with a deaf patient who sat with his head in his hands throughout the appointment, clearly disengaged, but the psychiatrist seemed oblivious to this.

Access to preparation, even on a very rudimentary level, was also raised as an issue. Interpreters asked for some detailed information to be provided to their booking agency while maintaining patient confidentiality. They pointed out that knowledge of an individual's symptoms and the target setting (e.g., physical health, mental health) is important when considering whether to accept or reject a booking. Other basic information such as the patient's age and gender can be vital for the interpreter, not least because, in Ireland, gender and generation are associated with highly divergent sign variants (LeMaster, 1990; Leeson & Grehan, 2004; Leeson & Saeed, 2012).

Interpreters were also concerned that they were not being treated as professionals by many of the healthcare providers they encountered. One interpreter said that if all of the parties were aware of how best to work with an interpreter in a medical setting, this would ameliorate many of the challenges. For this interpreter, this entails several things: being booked directly by the hospital and not by the deaf person or a family member, being treated as a professional and not an inconvenience, and not being left waiting while doctors are doing their rounds without any communication regarding when the patient (inpatient) will be seen.

Interpreters submitted their views on what helps make healthcare interpreting successful:

- Knowing the person. As we said earlier, gender and age significantly influence ISL usage, and this information can be invaluable when identifying the interpreter best suited for a particular task.
- Working with a deaf interpreter. However, no clear-cut guidelines pertaining to this have yet been established for healthcare settings in Ireland.
- Knowing the deaf person personally (but not too well). Having worked with the deaf person before in nonmedical circumstances may help in making decisions regarding the preferred target language style, reducing the interpreter's stress and facilitating the deaf patient more effectively.

Interpreters also commented on interpreting in difficult circumstances. When giving bad news, interpreters experience a tension between professional disassociation and reaching out to a deaf patient: "In one instance when the professional had left, the deaf client then looked at me for support as a friend until their own support had arrived."

Another interpreter wrote of how the highly emotive response of a family to bad news can be "traumatic." In dealing with the particular challenges of healthcare interpreting, interpreters say that it really helps to be able to talk about things with other interpreters; at the same time, however, they note that they are selective about which other interpreters they would wish to talk to. They also note that trying to determine the boundaries of their scope of practice is difficult in some circumstances.

Another issue that one interpreter flagged relates to the interpreter's own safety in some healthcare settings:

> I had an issue one time with the physical setting/interaction [that had] nothing to do with the interpreting process but after we had finished the deaf client left the room and while I was picking up my coat and the doctor's back was turned the deaf client came back through the door and grabbed me and began dry humping my leg. It was such a tight space I had no where to go to get away. Granted this was a mental health setting and the conversation had consisted of information of a sexual nature, which I can only assume in turn aroused the patient, who acted on their feelings albeit in an inappropriate manner which left me shaking.

This brings up issues of institutional responsibility for the health and safety of contracted practitioners working in healthcare settings and the need for other professionals working in such domains to ensure that interpreter providers and interpreters themselves are briefed regarding particular protocols for engaging with patients in a specific setting: fundamentally, freelance interpreters should not be put in potentially precarious positions that employees of the healthcare setting are explicitly guided to avoid. Another issue that deserves attention but which we cannot explore here is that of vicarious trauma for interpreters working in such situations (Dublin Rape Crisis Centre, 2009; Hethrington, 2011). This is clearly an area requiring further analysis and continuous professional development interventions. We suggest that support services should be made known to interpreters (e.g., Rape Crisis Helpline) and that the impact that vicarious trauma can have on an individual should be something that interpreters, interpreter providers, and healthcare providers are aware of and respond to (for example, see Dublin Rape Crisis Centre, 2009).

Focus Groups with Deaf Participants

As mentioned earlier, two focus groups were convened with members of the Deaf community: one in Limerick and one in Dublin. Both were facilitated by a deaf researcher while a notetaker, fluent in ISL, took notes that were circulated to the members of each meeting for modification. The meetings were not video-recorded.

At the beginning of each session, participants were provided with information about the research in English and were asked to sign a consent form. The facilitators of each group ensured that the content of the participant information leaflet and the consent form was translated into ISL for clarity. Time was also available for clarifications of the process and the project goals.

The participants were 20 deaf men and women from across Ireland (11 in Limerick, 9 in Dublin) who felt strongly about the current state of access to health care.

The focus groups were unstructured in the sense that the facilitator/interviewer followed the direction taken by the participants. The opening question in both groups was, "What is it like for you when you go to see your doctor or to a hospital or other healthcare provider?" In both meetings the participants responded with examples of their experiences, focusing on the negative attitudes they perceived in these settings, underpinned by what seem to be highly medicalized constructions of deafness on the part of healthcare providers. For example, one person reported that, after a hearing test, the doctor said that the patient had an issue with certain frequencies. The doctor then sent the deaf person a letter of referral to the cochlear implant unit in Beaumont Hospital in Dublin, but the deaf person did not want a cochlear implant. This story was told with humor and prompted a lot of laughter from the group, suggesting that this experience of being medicalized, that is, of being constructed from a hearing view of "normalcy," is commonplace. This was also mentioned by interpreters in our focus groups: one interpreter reported that, in her experience, "Medical professionals see deaf people as abnormal, deficient, something that needs to be cured. Deaf people are viewed negatively. Sometimes the medical professionals bring up deafness even when it has nothing to do with the case."

The impact of this is far reaching. Not only does this approach circumvent the authenticity of Deaf cultural ways of being in the world, but it also characterizes members of the Deaf community not so much as "other" but as "lesser versions" of "normal" hearing people. This sets the scene for assuming that the "hearing" way of communicating is the way that communication should occur, with the result that Deaf community members report experiencing high levels of stress when they need to engage with healthcare providers, especially in hospitals: "I can speak a little, not 100%, but in the hospital they told me that I have very good speech and wouldn't write things down for me. I was left feeling very frustrated." This overlooks the fact that there are differences in how languages are used. Leeson (2012) discusses the difference between competence in basic interpersonal communication skills (BICS) and cognitive academic language proficiency (CALP) with regard to interpreting in educational settings, and we hold that this is equally true for interpreting in healthcare settings. Another deaf person expanded on this theme:

> Lipreading is hard for us. Sometimes you forget what was said very quickly and it takes so much concentration to try and figure out what is said in the first place. It can be extremely stressful in a medical situation. Add to this the fact that you might be tired/medicated . . . Medical people need to be aware of this and remember that deaf people want to have some kind of record of what was said. Often we depend on what is written down for us in situations like this.

Despite this, participants reported on the reluctance of healthcare providers to give them information in writing: "In the 10 years that I've been a patient at a particular GP practice, I've only met one doctor who was willing to communicate with me via email."

Other deaf people in both focus groups reported that they had experienced the same problem and had to rely on children or parents to call the GP for them. Other deaf people who were present noted that they can text their GP, but the GP never replies via text, creating an asymmetrical relationship that holds in a range of communicative interactions: the deaf person's communicative preferences come second to those of the healthcare providers even though the deaf person is in a better position to judge the potential success or failure of the communicative strategy proposed (or imposed) by the hearing healthcare provider.

This demonstrates the asymmetrical power relation that holds between healthcare provider and deaf patient, which is experienced as patronizing and disempowering by deaf people, leading to stress, uncertainty, and ultimately a lack of access. The seemingly institutionalized lack of awareness of the requirement to ensure that deaf patients are able to access critical information about their health, which underpins the legal requirements for informed consent, is a damning indictment of current healthcare providers.

One informant (Lynch) in a follow-up interview (available online) reported that a nurse had slapped her husband's hand when he began to sign to her because the nurse expected that she would lipread. Another interviewee (Grehan) reported that she was not aware that she had had her wisdom teeth extracted under general anesthetic as a young adult because no one had explained to her why she was brought to the hospital or what would happen. It was only years later when she requested her medical records from her boarding school under the Freedom of Information Acts 1997 and 2003[12] that she discovered what had happened. A third interviewee (Redmond) reported that he had been prepped for heart-bypass surgery in error when what he needed was surgery on a finger. In each of these situations, interpretation was not provided, and the question of whether informed consent was obtained and, if so, how, as well as why the relevant healthcare professionals assumed that they had discharged their duty appropriately, remains a mystery. Indeed, deaf participants in both focus groups reported on the common experience of asking a hospital to provide an interpreter but having their request ignored. One deaf participant brought the issue back to the legality of the situation by noting that informed consent is a requirement of the law.

The participant asked, "How legal is that to ask us for our consent for surgery when the hospital has not provided information in a wholly or partially accessible way to us? They *must* provide interpreters."

The provision of interpreters is also fraught with difficulty as deaf informants reported that their requests for interpreters are often denied, leading them to depend on other modes of communication instead (e.g., lipreading, writing, bringing a relative or friend to interpret). There was some discussion about what participants would do in an emergency. Given the discrepancies between service provision in Dublin and other parts of the country, some participants from more rural parts of Ireland said that they would rather drive to Dublin (some 3–5 hours away) to ensure better potential access via interpretation than wait locally. However, when an interpreter is provided, the experience can be good: "I had an interpreter in the hospital and had one who was really easy to work with. Very relaxed experience. I don't want someone who is going to sign really fast. I like smooth communication and want to make sure that the event goes well. So I was lucky."

Many expressed concern about working with an interpreter they don't feel comfortable with. Discussion about governmental tendering arrangements for the provision of interpreters in public hospitals and the possibility of requesting a preferred interpreter through the booking system was new information to some participants. Significantly, there was also a very real lack of awareness of the complaints about healthcare and/or the quality of interpreting provided.

Another important issue was the fact that a deaf person is not always the patient in a healthcare setting but instead may be the primary caregiver. In such instances, the willingness of healthcare providers to take the time to explain the circumstances of a loved one's condition can make all the difference: "The family members of a patient should be aware of what is happening. It isn't only when the patient is deaf that there is an issue with communication. For example, I was concerned about whether my mother had Alzheimer's and it wasn't clear from the report that we had received whether she did or did not. But when a nurse was willing to talk it through with me, we had a clearer picture on things."

The biggest concern when working with interpreters was confidentiality: "One interpreter who is a CODA and has a deaf partner told their partner that I was in hospital. They breached confidentiality. I will never use that interpreter again." The key issue is trust. It is the same for meetings with doctors. Trust is essential:

> One of my main fears about using an interpreter at a hospital is the quality of the interpreter and if they are appropriate in medical domains. Some hospitals have fixed lists and they include interpreters that I would not have faith in the quality of their work. I tend to fight tooth and nail to have my say in the process of booking an interpreter. Most of the time I'm satisfied with the interpreter during the appointment but stressed out unnecessarily in making sure this happens. I would prefer no interpreter than someone who I cannot trust to understand me.

One suggestion made was that, out of a desire to ensure best practice, interpreting agencies should clearly ask for feedback on the interpreters they provide. As one informant put it, "We must have guidelines to protect interpreters."

The limited number of interpreters, particularly outside Dublin, was also a matter of concern. In parallel with findings in Conama's (2008) study of interpreter provision in the Midwest, the limited pool of interpreters in some regions restricts the use of the same interpreter for very private settings due to worries about privacy. Associated with this, participants from rural areas noted that sometimes deaf people deliberately choose not to request an interpreter because they believe that an issue is too personal, and they report feeling inhibited when a third party is present (e.g., in a counseling session).

The issue of language transfer was also a subject of concern. There was discussion about the complexity of working between two languages in healthcare settings and acknowledgment of the existence of lexical gaps. One comment on the subject mentioned the need for interpreters to be creative in their language use but sensitive to the deaf client's particular linguistic style: "deaf people create signs when they are talking about different issues . . . Interpreters have to be creative but they have to think . . . and to modify their language to match the deaf person."

In wrapping up the Deaf community focus groups, we asked the participants to list the key issues that could improve deaf people's experiences in healthcare settings. Their list is highly congruent with the topics raised separately by interpreters both on the questionnaire and in the focus groups. They reported that the attitudes they experience in hospitals is an issue and ascribe this to healthcare workers' lack of knowledge about the Deaf community and sign languages. They suggested that specific training in working with Deaf community members and interpreters should be a part of every medical student's university education. This training should emphasize the necessity of making pertinent information maximally accessible to patients, for example, by teaching the healthcare provider to be flexible in the range of strategies (e.g., using images) used to communicate with deaf patients. Deaf participants suggested that the HSE, the Irish Council of General Practitioners, and the Royal College of Surgeons in Ireland, among others, have a responsibility to educate doctors about the needs of the Deaf community. This entails recommending that hospitals and GPs remember that a deaf patient may need extra time for a consultation. This recommendation stemmed from one participant's experience of bringing an interpreter to a consultation (not something that the patient normally did). Taking advantage of the interpreter's presence, the deaf patient asked a number of questions in order to learn more about his health condition from the GP. Because the consultation ran beyond the normal 20-minute slot, the GP imposed a surcharge of almost 50%. The recommendation on this matter is that doctors need to be more flexible.

In practical terms, the deaf participants argued that if an interpreter is required, the deaf person's request should be honored. Deaf people believe that it is inappropriate for a hospital to decide that no interpreter will be provided when a deaf patient believes that this is a reasonable accommodation. Equally, they argue that it is not appropriate for doctors to assume a deaf person will lip-read or write notes, especially when the person is ill, as this places the deaf patient under additional stress. Participants noted that although some deaf people will use their voice to speak, they still require interpreting from English to ISL to ensure that they understand the English source message. They emphasized that hospitals should not assume that because they can speak, they can cope by lipreading or writing.

Deaf participants strongly believe that it is not appropriate for doctors to assume that a deaf friend, partner, family member, or child should interpret for a deaf patient or caregiver. Such circumstances do not guarantee accuracy, and it is simply not appropriate if the ad hoc interpreter (or language broker) is personally involved. This, deaf participants argue, is especially true in maternity care settings. They noted the risk of using untrained interpreters, and they believe that children in particular should not be used as interpreters. They were very clear that interpreters must be provided for the purpose of informed consent. However, there was a high degree of uncertainty regarding what constitutes appropriate provision in some settings: questions arose regarding who is responsible for providing an interpreter in a GP practice or an emergency setting. Due to the lack of appropriate provision in certain places, some deaf people shrugged and said that having someone who can sign, even badly, was better than having no one at all. This prompted quite a lively exchange, and the group at large wanted to emphasize that this was not best practice in their eyes: for them, provision of appropriately trained interpreters was vital. With this in mind, they suggested that a list of interpreters who specialize in working in medical settings should be made available to hospitals to increase awareness within these institutions. They also suggested that video relay interpreting may be an option worth exploring for last-minute appointments, meetings with GPs, and emergency calls. This is something that is new to Ireland, with a government-funded pilot service that began in October 2013 (Irish Remote Interpreting Service [IRIS]).[13] This, as we have seen, contrasts with the higher degree of hesitancy expressed by interpreters in our survey and focus groups.

Focus Groups with Interpreters

We ran two focus groups with interpreters in two Irish cities in order to facilitate a diversity of responses. A total of 16 interpreters participated: 15 in focus groups and 1 in a face-to-face interview as one interpreter could not attend any of the group sessions. Their professional experience ranged from 3 to 20 years, with an average of 9.25 years. As a whole, the participating interpreters have worked in various domains: religious, theatrical, legal, educational, conference, and medical (including mental health). Of the 16 interpreters, 11 have worked in the medical domain (including mental health). The inclusion of 5 interpreters with no experience in the medical domain helped us further understand the uniqueness of medical interpreting.

These focus groups lasted approximately 1.5 hours each, while the face-to-face interview lasted approximately 45 minutes. Both the focus groups and the one-on-one interview were unstructured in the sense that the facilitator/interviewer followed the direction taken by the participants. The first question was the same in all cases: What is it like being a medical interpreter? Such an open question was chosen to avoid directing the participants' attention to any specific issue. Our goal was to hear the interpreters' thoughts and concerns about interpreting in Ireland on their own terms.

The same facilitator and two notetakers worked in both of the interpreter focus groups. Contributions from the floor were anonymized to minimize the risk of identifying the participants and to eliminate even oblique references to the people they were referring to. At the end of each focus group, the notes were merged and sent to the participants, encouraging comments, additions, and/or corrections. In the case of the one-on-one interview, the focus group facilitator served as the interviewer and the notetaker. The notes were then sent to the interviewee, who sent back comments and corrections.

The notes from the sessions were coded into themes that were organized into three major areas: the hearing medical staff; the deaf clients and their relatives; and the interpreters. Of course, these areas are not meant to indicate that it is not possible to have deaf medical staff working with hearing clients, but there were none in our study.

As with the responses to the questionnaire and the contributions of the deaf focus groups, lack of awareness on the part of hearing healthcare providers working with deaf clients and interpreters was the major theme. In some cases, interpreters seem to base their conclusions about the degree of awareness on the questions and comments from staff members. In addition, it seems that awareness, as perceived by the interpreters in our study, is intertwined with attitudes and behaviors. That is, a staff member may act in a way or have an attitude that makes the interpreter believe that the person has a certain degree of awareness. An external observer might argue that it is possible for a staff member to have a high degree of awareness about working with deaf clients and interpreters but also have behaviors and attitudes that the interpreters perceive as incongruent with someone who truly understands these topics.

Although the question of awareness versus actions that are actually taken is an interesting avenue for future studies, the scope of this section covers the perspectives of the participating interpreters with regard to the situation in Ireland.

Two dimensions of awareness emerged from the data: degree and dispersion. Degree of awareness refers to how much awareness a person has. According to the interpreters, awareness on the part of hearing staff members is very low or completely lacking. As one interpreter put it, "[the] main issue tends to be hearing staff and their lack of awareness."

The second dimension of awareness identified, dispersion, refers to the spread of awareness. In this sense, dispersion on two levels was discussed: individual (each staff member's awareness) and systemic (overall awareness in the healthcare system). At the systemic level, according to both the interpreters and the Deaf community members in our study, the degree of awareness is very low to nonexistent. At an individual level, the degree of awareness is high in exceptional cases: "a hospital will have maybe one staff member considering ISL interpreters important" (interpreter). That is, as we discuss further in the next sections, participating interpreters believe that the current situation in Ireland can be described as exhibiting a very low (to nonexistent) awareness at the systemic level, with exceptional cases of a high degree of awareness at the individual level.

Individual awareness, it seems, can be enhanced in at least three general ways: (1) by a staff member's own experience (personal or professional); (2) by building relationships; and (3) through training. A staff member's experience can be personal or professional and can make a real difference: "There is a particular maternity hospital in Munster where traditionally no interpreters were used, but then outpatients in maternity started to book interpreters. It turned out that a social worker with a deaf family member was working there, and they insisted that if a deaf person was coming in that interpreters be provided. So one person and their good attitude makes a big difference."

Deaf people commented on this, too: "When I make an appointment to see a GP, I always ask which doctor is available. The relationship with the GPs varies a lot depending on the doctor."

And as we have already seen, the relationship with the healthcare provider also depends in large part on the interpreter. Further, a good experience working with an interpreter may result in a hearing staff member's increased willingness to request an interpreter in the future. Such satisfactory experiences are the result not only of the interpreter's work but also of the relationship that forms between the interpreter and the staff member on the one hand and the interpreter and the deaf patient on the other. Relationship building is facilitated when there are multiple appointments involving the same staff member. It seems that the relationship that forms between the staff member and the patient is also crucial. In this case, such a relationship feeds into the staff member's experience, which, as we have seen, may increase awareness. It also facilitates a better experience for the deaf patient: "I'm aware that there is a high staff turnover in hospitals but I find that I really depend on the staff with whom I'm familiar! Usually when I go for a follow-up appointment or for a checkup I always hope there will be some familiar faces on duty. Otherwise my blood pressure will give a false reading!" (deaf participant).

However, such relationships are not always easy. For example, in the emergency department, with its fast-paced consultations, relationships between staff members and patients may be temporary at best, and under such conditions a more durable relationship that could raise awareness levels is hard to form. The absence of longer-lasting relationships may, at least in part, explain the lack of awareness in the following case, not to mention the hospital's seeming lack of concern about securing informed consent: "But A&E [Accident and Emergency; in Munster] never calls, and we know of deaf people who have been in A&E and had no communication with staff, and the deaf person has no lipreading skills, no gestures were used with them, just nothing and then invasive processes were carried out and you know that the deaf person did not know what was going to be done to them" (interpreter).

When interpreters are not called, it goes without saying that a professional relationship between interpreters and staff members cannot develop. In the same hospital described earlier, it seems to be possible to create a longer-term relationship between patient and staff member in other departments. In those departments, the degree of awareness seems to be greater, interpreters have been called, and the formation of a professional relationship between the staff member and the interpreter is facilitated: "Again it comes back to certain people being good and developing contacts in certain sections of the hospital, say accounts, physio, etc., and then you get an interpreter provided and you hope the contact person in the hospital won't be promoted or go on holidays, etc." (interpreter).

The problem of fleeting relationships is challenging: once an individual relationship is forged in a department, there is no assurance that the staff member will stay, and indeed, in some instances, medical staff are routinely rotated every six months, confounding all possibilities for relationship building. Therefore, although individual relationships with a specific staff member can help in raising awareness, the effect is as fleeting as the relationship itself. But rotating staff members are not the only issue. Because a high degree of awareness is not systemic, willingness to act according to awareness training seems to be dependent on individual staff members' attitudes. As interpreters noted:

> A deaf advocate in Munster went into a hospital and gave them information, and the hospital lost the data. [The deaf advocate] went in again. Typically, you make contact with one staff member and so much depends on them; they either have a great attitude or a bad attitude (if they think that you cost too much). This impacts significantly. (interpreter)

> Sometimes the information that we provide [and the] advice that is given to hospitals [by deaf organizations, advocates, and interpreters] fall on deaf ears. You can feel that we are getting nowhere. (interpreter)

Finally, as with deaf participants, interpreters mentioned training as a mechanism for increasing awareness. Nevertheless, awareness training does not currently reach all staff members: "In Munster, some DAT [deaf awareness training] is provided. Physios, admin, OT came. No nurses or doctors. Since training, we see that physios will book interpreters but the question is how to get to other staff in the hospital to ensure that there will be a shift in attitude and behavior" (interpreter).

Like deaf participants, interpreters believe that future medical professionals do not now receive adequate training while they are still pursuing their degrees:

> One thing that hasn't happened to date and hopefully will happen is that DAT training is made available for medical people in training. Doctors, nurses, social workers, OT, physiotherapists, etc. (social work in Munster is very good). [Training] has to be a top-down thing about money. Attitude is a big issue.

> That's a hard battle. I know right now there is some training going on with nurses here [in Ireland], which is great. But it would also be good to see this type of training at med schools.

In the end, however, increasing awareness at the individual level (regardless of the way in which it happens) does not have a great impact on attitudes and behaviors overall. In any case, and as discussed, awareness at this level is fleeting, as staff members change positions and locations. As one interpreter puts it, "Sometimes issues are passed back to KDRC [Kerry Deaf Resource Center] or SLIS [Sign Language Interpreting Service]. Sometimes they have to deal with it. The problem is that the issue is raised but not dealt with systemically and then the problem persists."

The interpreters in our study identified various areas in which an increase in awareness is especially important. In terms of working with deaf clients (including Deaf culture and Irish Sign Language), interpreters mentioned the following: understanding what sign language is (and is not), understanding what it means to be deaf and clarifying assumptions of what a deaf person can and cannot do, and seeing the whole individual (beyond deafness). With regard to working with interpreters, awareness topics include understanding what an interpreter is, understanding the need to work with interpreters and how to do so, and responding to cost-, time-, and confidentiality-related assumptions and attitudes.

Interpreters expressed concern at healthcare professionals' (even highly specialized ones') lack of awareness of the interpreters' role. For example, one neurosurgeon told an interpreter that the last deaf person who had been in for a consultation had brought his 8- or 9-year-old child, who did a "great" job. The lack of insight into the myriad issues arising from this are mind boggling: the question of the child's relationship to the patient, the child's understanding of the information, the child's emotional response to being placed in the position of interpreter, and the power relations that hold between child and parent, on the one hand, and between the child and the surgeon on the other. Then there are issues having to do with the patient: did the patient ask for an interpreter? Had he gone through all preliminary healthcare channels without being offered an interpreter? What kind of understanding did the patient have of his condition? What kind of understanding did the neurosurgeon have of the patient's condition? Did they share the key concepts? Or did the neurosurgeon, as was reported in the Netherlands, believe that the patient understood more than was actually the case (Smeijers & Pfau, 2009; van den Bogaerde & de Lange, this volume)? We will never know.

The issue of payment for interpreting seems to underpin some reluctance to approve this service in certain hospitals, and several informants reported instances of hospitals asking children to interpret seemingly because they believed that the services of a professional were too costly. Yet, as one interpreter suggested, "When you interpret for free, they don't seem to question your presence at all." Another interpreter framed the issue in terms of compliance. This person reported interpreting at meetings where the healthcare team discussed the noncompliance of a deaf patient (e.g., in terms of following instructions for medications) when the deaf person had simply not understood because the directions were not provided in an accessible manner (i.e., no interpreter was present). Again, we raise concerns about what healthcare staff understand as ensuring "their [patient's] ability to understand the information provided/language used," as suggested in the HSE's best practice guidelines (2009, p. 24).

The interpreters also mentioned various types of consequences that a low awareness of the need for interpreters can have for the health and even the life of deaf clients. First, it can result in misunderstandings when the hearing staff communicate directly with the deaf patients. These misunderstandings can then cause the deaf clients to behave in ways that the hearing staff wrongly see as intentional noncompliance: "There is one deaf person who has glaucoma and didn't realize they should have taken drops. On their chart, the medical team recorded that s/he was noncompliant. The deaf person is now practically blind" (interpreter).

In cases such as this, the negative consequence is not only the misconception that the deaf patient was noncompliant but also, and more critically, the associated health outcome (e.g., the patient became almost blind), potentially including death:

> There is a well-documented case about a deaf man in Galway—a man [was] walking home to Clifton and got hit by a car; [the man was] about 60. [He was] working on a part-time scheme and fell off a chair and broke his arm. The school [where the man was working] called the hospital. An HSE taxi brought him to hospital [where they] patched up his arm. [The hospital staff] didn't look for any supports from deaf services, etc., and [they] asked the deaf man (I'm not sure how) if he was ok to get home. He had no mobile phone. He was in a tracksuit and a t-shirt, so you'd think they would have thought this through. But the man wandered around the hospital for an hour and set off to walk home, which was about 50 miles away. He was hit by a car and killed. The inquest showed some problems, too, because the reports show that the taxi driver should have been more responsible and the taxi driver had nothing to do with it. [But there was] no mention of the hospital's responsibility. (interpreter)

Two salient themes related to patients and their relatives emerged from the data: establishing relationships and setting expectations. With regard to relationships, interpreters explained that creating a connection with a client, who comes to trust the interpreter's skills and ethics, is crucial for achieving good results for everyone. However, managing the extent and quality of the relationship is also important, as being too friendly can also be problematic and cause the patient to feel uncomfortable.

Sometimes relatives and/or friends of the deaf patient are also present, and associations with them also need to be managed. On one hand, this can be positive for the interaction, as relative and friends are eager to support the deaf patient as much as possible. On the other hand, interpreters are mindful of issues of partiality that can arise when relatives help in the communication process: "If the relative takes over and doesn't allow the deaf person to talk for themselves, that is problematic. It is very hard to be neutral when you are interpreting for a family member/partner" (interpreter).

In addition, interpreters also believe that it is important to provide relatives with the space to just be relatives (rather than interpreters):

There also needs to be space for a family member to be a family member. In many families, there are CODAs who don't engage in the Deaf community, but they take care of their family's communication needs; they see it as their role within the family—to communicate, just as someone else might do the washing up or the cooking. I don't think they know that they can avail [themselves] of [interpreting] services and free themselves up to be the family member. It would be good if training/information was available for them to know about what is possible. (interpreter)

In this case, the relatives of the deaf patient may not be aware of interpreting options. Sometimes, however, as we have seen, interpreting for a relative is the only option in Ireland. That is, in private or alternative healthcare settings, interpreting costs must be covered by the patient, who cannot always afford them: "I know it is not the ideal situation, and it would be better to have someone impartial go in with him [the deaf patient]. But who will pay for this? In private healthcare settings or in alternative healthcare settings like visits to osteopaths/GP appointments, who is going to cover the costs?" (interpreter).

Nonetheless, even when the costs are covered, as we have seen in our discussion of the deaf focus groups, deaf patients may still choose to have their relatives or friends serve as the interpreter because of privacy concerns or lack of trust in an interpreter's skills: "Some deaf people prefer to have a family member interpret to keep an issue within the family" (interpreter).

The interpreters in our study talked about various topics that have been mentioned elsewhere in interpreting literature: roles (advocate vs. interpreter), alignment issues, and management of the expectations of the hearing staff and deaf clients. For all of these, it was said that different interpreters may have divergent views about how best to deal with these aspects of their work. In part, this may reflect the emergence of a profession without strong public recognition and, as yet, without a strong professional body representing their interests. As a result, these interpreters struggle to do their best in an imperfect climate. For example, they mentioned regional differences and characteristics of the health system overall that require them to take on responsibilities that may be considered outside their remit. For instance, with regard to regional differences, interpreters have to act and react according to the location: "The needs in Dublin and in other parts of the country are different, and we have to respond to them locally." In part, such differences may account for a number of disagreements within the Irish interpreting community as to what interpreters should or should not do or what issues interpreters should refer to other professionals, such as advocates: "Some counties in Ireland are not as well resourced as others. Some have Deaf centers and advocates, but many do not. So sometimes you [the interpreter] are the expert on Deaf culture, and I think it would be remiss of us to not tell what we know in such settings. In this way, we are having to do work that a different professional would do in other places" (interpreter).

Interpreters do not necessarily take on the responsibilities of an advocate by choice but because of the demands of a particular situation: "Sometimes the ISL interpreters are left with dealing with the advocacy of getting interpreters for deaf patients." The interpreters reported sometimes having to cover different facets of the advocate's role: acting as educator and coordinator of access or providing impromptu awareness training to staff members, deaf clients, and their relatives when such training is nonexistent. One interpreter even mentioned sending literature in advance of a medical appointment in the hope of making a difference, "even with something small, like the doctor uses direct speech rather than 'ask her, tell her' and looks at the deaf person."

Such responsibilities have arisen from the fact that in a number of areas the provision of interpreters is not the norm (at least not in practice). Therefore, some interpreters are working with the community to ensure improved access to interpreting services:

> If deaf [patients] have asked for an interpreter and have been told they can't have an interpreter, what do they do next? Also because of lack of awareness with staff and movement of staff, what do we do?

We went back to the Deaf community—[we] have a letter drafted by a barrister (really to scare the hospital!) to ensure that the community is empowered so they know what their rights are and encouraging them to do it. (interpreter)

For interpreters in other areas (or perhaps even in other countries) where provision is ensured by alternative means, such direct work with the community and the sending of cards and letters may be seen as outside the realm of what interpreters "normally" do. But in Ireland, some interpreters have assumed this responsibility since they have not seen top-down initiatives (or any other initiatives for that matter) being implemented. So, depending on local circumstances, interpreters—sometimes as a team—may on occasion decide to work as access coordinators.

Interpreter availability and the problems of mapping onto service providers' schedules are two other issues of concern when planning in this resource-limited context. Hospitals are said to be lacking in flexibility with regard to consultation times. At the same time, however, they need to secure informed consent from a deaf person before an operation. According to one of the interpreters, one hospital said,

"This is too much trouble, we will be fine. Her sister can do this [interpret for the deaf person]" [They were trying to get the interpreter at 1:30 a.m. on a Monday]. There were no local interpreters available at short notice, and the hospital didn't want to pay for an interpreter to come from another region . . . To get around the issue, local interpreters had to arrange a change in interpreting arrangements for three deaf people [in three different regions] to facilitate covering this job. As it happens, the interpreter met the sister of the patient in question, and she herself said that she couldn't sign properly (and she couldn't!). So, if there hadn't been an interpreter present, what kind of informed consent could possibly have been achieved? (interpreter)

The focus group also discussed the training of interpreters. Recognizing the on-the-job difficulties, including matters that are especially salient in Ireland, we asked how interpreters could be better prepared to cope with such challenges. For one thing, it is important that interpreters-to-be feel that, as part of their degree program, they are receiving adequate training and feedback. But what happens to working, professional interpreters who may need to update their knowledge and obtain feedback or support? Interpreters believe that, in Ireland, continuing education programs need improvement and that these could help professionals in other domains take the plunge and decide to work in the medical field:

> I'm only recently involved in legal/medical interpreting and it is hard to make the leap. You hear so many horror stories. You do know that you are privy to serious information. If you make an error, it can impact on someone's life. You need some coaxing to start, but then you have to take the plunge and be careful about what kinds of work you take on. When you go into a medical setting, if you know it is more routine or a first appointment, then you might feel better equipped to do it; try and select the jobs that you have the skill set to do at that point in time. But it is scary.

> I think that [shadowing] is needed. At the moment people just jump in and try for the best, but there needs to be something transitional.

Thus we believe that training solutions for working interpreters must take into account their location and availability and explore ways to deliver asynchronous, atemporal training effectively across geographic boundaries. We also would like to see an HSE-run system supporting internships for interpreters in hospitals in a manner akin to that provided for professionals in various healthcare settings.

DISCUSSION

We have explored three areas with salient themes that were brought out in the data: (1) hearing healthcare providers' lack of awareness of how to work with interpreters; (2) relationships with and expectations of deaf clients (and their relatives) with respect to the interpreter's work; and (3) interpreters' strategies for adapting to local needs. It is important to note here that the first item is the issue most discussed by both Deaf community members and interpreters in our study and the area they identified as requiring the most improvement. For all three items, training seems to be an important step in addressing some of these challenges. Critically, we emphasize the potential legal consequences for healthcare providers who do not recognize the important implications of these issues, and the human element of ensuring that they and their patients (and, as relevant, their patients' caregivers) are well informed.

When providing awareness training to hearing healthcare staff, it is important to address the lack of awareness on a systemic level. That is, it seems that bottom-up training (i.e., from deaf advocacy groups and interpreters), as has been occurring, is not enough. A top-down training program may ensure a more consistent implementation of policy at all levels. This will require alliances with those who can enforce such efforts and ensure monitoring and evaluation of provision over time; in Ireland, these stakeholders would necessarily include the HSE, university medical schools, and the Medical Council, among others. At this level, inroads may be made by tackling cost concerns. To do this, it will be necessary to establish the economic cost of providing reasonable accommodation and to weigh it against the cost and the consequences of non-provision. This will entail a bottom-up approach, with input from the Deaf community and advocacy groups. Some headway has already been made via recommendations to the HSE made by a group of stakeholders comprising deaf organizations, interpreting agencies, and representative bodies, and we are hopeful that moves to appoint access officers to each HSE-managed hospital throughout Ireland will create an opportunity for positive change.

Whether efforts tackle individual or systemic awareness, the awareness of staff or of clients, the ongoing question for interpreters will be what role they should play in this effort. In practice, it seems that, at least for a number of interpreters in Ireland, the answer is to provide some awareness information when remaining silent conflicts with what interpreters feel is their duty of care, a denial of their understanding of the "interpreter as ally" model. To suggest otherwise is to place interpreters in uncomfortable or even unbearable situations in the life-critical domain of healthcare and to leave them feeling that they are complicit with the system in deviating from the core goal of the healthcare professional's mandate, "do no harm."

Besides talking about the training needs of hearing staff and deaf clients, both deaf participants and interpreters discussed interpreters' training needs. These discussions focused on the lack of both training and support for working, professional interpreters. As solutions to this situation are considered, it is crucial to remember that working interpreters have limited time and resources, and geographic considerations must also be factored in. Blended or online training and support solutions could assist in providing on-time, asynchronous training and support in these cases—something that the Medisigns project has accomplished as an initial step in the development of online open-source materials.

Finally, our study clearly demonstrates that the Deaf community has training needs, too. Information about how to request and book an interpreter, what constitutes the scope of an interpreter's practice, and, as consumers of healthcare services in Ireland, how to give feedback on an interpreter's performance all require attention and will be revisited in the future. One of the most salient issues for deaf patients attempting to access health care is a lack of information, and yet, for many deaf individuals, information is conspicuous by its absence when it comes to accessing health care in contemporary Ireland.

SUMMARY

Despite a long-standing and legally binding requirement to ensure that patients' informed consent is secured, our study demonstrates that the provision of information to the Irish Deaf community in a healthcare setting seems problematic. This, therefore, raises questions about the reliability of the consent obtained. It seems that healthcare providers supply a professional interpreter relatively rarely despite best-practice guidelines advocating this, which, according to our deaf informants, affects their stress levels. It is also clear that members of the Deaf community and interpreters alike believe that members of the healthcare profession are not well informed as to the potential consequences of working without trained interpreters in many settings. One of the major roadblocks in evaluating the current levels of provision is the lack of centralized data on the provision of interpreting service in Ireland. However, from the perspective of Irish interpreters and Deaf community members, much needs to be done to alter the situation. This entails a systemic appreciation of the need to provide interpreters, the establishment of a system that allows the deaf patient to request a preferred interpreter, and the facilitation of feedback to the HSE regarding deaf patients' experiences. With regard to interpreter training, we believe that the HSE should support the development of a mentoring program for interpreters within hospital settings akin to those available to healthcare professionals, as well as programs of continuing education for interpreters and healthcare providers working with Deaf community members.

ACKNOWLEDGMENT

The Medisigns Project is cofunded by the European Commission under the auspices of the Leonardo da Vinci program. The information about and results of the project are presented here with the permission of Interesource Group (Ireland) Limited. We would like to thank the Deaf community members and interpreters who gave their time and shared their insights over the life of the Medisigns Project.

NOTES

1. See http://www.medisignsproject.eu/_(LLP/LdV/TOI/2010/IRL-511) (accessed July 16, 2013).
2. Medisigns is one of four projects awarded the prestigious European Language Label in 2013 (http://ec.europa.eu/languages/european-language-label/index_en.htm) (accessed July 16, 2013).
3. See also http://ec.europa.eu/languages/languages-of-europe/sign-languages_en.htm (accessed 16 July 2013).
4. http://interesourcegroup.eu/.
5. Http://www.hse.ie/eng/services/Publications/Your_Service,_Your_Say_Consumer_Affairs/.
6. In 2013 the Council for Irish Sign Language Interpreters (CISLI) began working on this matter with key stakeholders.
7. There have been some changes over the life of the Medisigns project in this regard and we discuss these further in the paper.
8. Dublin is the capital of Ireland.
9. Today there are three interpreters living and working in this area.
10. Unfortunately, no regional statistics are available for the period 2006–present, and despite the success of the Signing Information project, funding was not available for the continuation of the provision. Despite this, since 2006 the availability of interpreters in the region has increased. Currently there are 3 trained interpreters based in the city of Limerick, servicing the Mid-West region.
11. Radio Telefís Éireann (RTÉ) is Ireland's national public broadcaster.
12. Http://foi.gov.ie/freedom-of-information-act-1997/ (accessed December 1, 2013).
13. See http://www.citizensinformationboard.ie/news/news20131007.html (accessed December 1, 2013).

REFERENCES

Accreditation Board. (1997). *Register of Irish Signed Language/English interpreters*. Recommendations Report. Dublin: National Rehabilitation Board.
Chambers, I. (2004). *Migrancy, culture, identity*. London: Routledge.

Conama, J. B. (2008). *Evaluation of signing information Mid-West*. Limerick: Paul Partnership.

Conama, J. B., & Grehan, C. (2002). *Is there poverty in the Deaf community?* Dublin: Irish Deaf Society and Combat Poverty Agency.

Conroy, P. (2006). *Signing in and signing out: The education and employment experiences of Deaf people in Ireland. A study of inequality and deaf people in Ireland*. Dublin: Irish Deaf Society.

de Wit, M., Salami, M., & Hema, Z. (2012). Educating signed language interpreters in healthcare settings: A European perspective. In L. Swabey & K. Malcolm (Eds.), *In our hands: Educating healthcare interpreters* (pp. 229–260.). Washington, DC: Gallaudet University Press.

Denham, J. (currently the Chief Justice of the Irish Supreme Court), (1996) *In re a Ward of Court* (withholding medical treatment) (No. 2), 2 I.R. 79.

Doyle, Rev. G., Buckley, M., & McCaul, E. (1986). *A report on prenatal and maternity services as experienced by a group of deaf mothers*. Dublin: Irish Deaf Society.

Dublin Rape Crisis Centre. (2009). *Interpreting in situations of sexual violence and other trauma*. Dublin: Dublin Rape Crisis Centre.

European Parliament. (2000). *Charter of fundamental rights of the European Union*. Brussels: Official Journal of the European Communities.

Harmer, L. (1999). Healthcare delivery and deaf people: Practice, problems, and recommendations for change. *Journal of Deaf Studies and Deaf Education, 4*(2), 73–110.

Health Service Executive (HSE) (2008). *National strategy for service user involvement in the Irish Health Service 2008–2013*. Dublin: Department of Health and Children.

Health Service Executive (HSE) (Social Inclusion Unit and the Health-Promoting Hospitals Network). (2009). *On speaking terms: Good practice guidelines for HSE staff in the provision of interpreting services*. Dublin: HSE Social Inclusion Unit and the Health Promoting Hospitals Network.

Health Service Executive (HSE) (2013). HSE National Consent Policy. Dublin: Health Service Executive.

Hethrington, A. (2011). A magical profession? Causes and management of occupational stress in the signed language interpreting profession. In L. Leeson, S. Wurm, & M. Vermeerbergen (Eds.), *The signed language translator and interpreter: Preparation, practice and performance,* (pp.138–159). Manchester: St. Jerome.

Heyerick, I., & Vermeerbergen, M. (2012). Signed language interpreting in educational settings in Flanders, Belgium. In L. Leeson & M. Vermeerbergen (Eds.), *Interpreting with the Deaf community: Mental health, education and interpreting,* (N.p.). Dublin: Interesource Group.

INRA (Europe) European Coordination Office S. A. (2001). *Special Europeans and languages*. Brussels: European Commission's Education and Culture Directorate-General Unit.

Kearns, J. (now President of the Irish High Court) (2000). *Geoghegan v. Harris*, 3 I.R. 536.

Ladd, P. (2003). *Understanding Deaf culture : In search of deafhood*. Clevedon: Multilingual Matters.

Leeson, L. (2006). *Signed languages in education in Europe: A preliminary exploration*. Preliminary study: Languages of education. Strasbourg: Council of Europe, Language Policy Division.

Leeson, L. (2012). Interpreters in tertiary education. In L. Leeson & M. Vermeerbergen (Eds.), *Working with the Deaf community: Mental health, education and interpreting*, (N.p.) Dublin: Interesource Group.

Leeson, L., & Grehan, C. (2004). To the lexicon and beyond: The effect of gender on variation in Irish Sign Language. In M. Van Herreweghe & M. Vermeerbergen (Eds.), *To the lexicon and beyond: Sociolinguistics in European Deaf communities* (pp. 39–73). Washington, DC: Gallaudet University Press.

Leeson, L., & Lynch, T. (2009). Three leaps of faith and four giant steps: Developing interpreter training in Ireland. In J. Napier (Ed.), *Signed language interpreter education and training: A world survey* (pp. 35–56). Washington, DC: Gallaudet University Press.

Leeson, L., & Saeed, J. I. (2012). *Irish Sign Language*. Edinburgh: Edinburgh University Press.

LeMaster, B. (1990). "The maintenance and loss of female and male signs in the Dublin Deaf community." PhD diss., University of California–Los Angeles.

Matthews, P. A. (1996). *The Irish Deaf community*. Dublin: Institiúid Teangeolaíochta Éireann.

Meador, H. E., & Zazove, P. (2005). Healthcare interactions with Deaf culture. *Journal of the American Board of Family Medicine, 18*(3), 218–222.

Medical Council. (2009). *Guide to professional conduct and ethics for registered medical practitioners*, 7th ed. Dublin: Medical Council.

O'Reilly-de Brún, M., & de Brún, T. (2010). The use of participatory learning & action (PLA) research in intercultural health: Some examples and some questions. *Translocations: Migration and Social Change, 6*(1), http://www.dcu.ie/imrstr/volume_6_issue_1/Centre%20for%20Participatory%20Strategies.pdf

Patton, M. Q. (2002). *Qualitative research & evaluation methods*, 3rd ed. Thousand Oaks, CA: Sage.

Phelan, M. (2009). Interpreter provision in healthcare in Ireland. *MLJI, 15*(2), 93–104.

Prospectus. (2006). *Review of signed language interpretation services and service requirements in Ireland*. Dublin: Comhairle.

Russell, D. (2005). Consecutive and simultaneous interpreting. In T. Janzen (Ed.), *Topics in signed language interpreting* (pp. 135–164). Amsterdam: Benjamins.

Sheikh, A. A. (2006). Medico-legal issues and patient autonomy: Here yesterday gone tomorrow? (editorial). *Medico-Legal Journal of Ireland,* 12 (2), 54–55.

Smeijers, A. S., & Pfau, R. (2009). Towards a treatment for treatment: On the communication between general practitioners and their deaf patients. *Signed Language Translator and Interpreter,* 3(1), 1–14.

Scottish Public Services Ombudsman (SPSO) (2013), *Investigation Report: Tayside NHS Board*, Report Date: 27 March 2013, Report Number: 201104213, Retrieved March 26, 2014 from http://www.spso.org.uk/investigation-reports/2013/march/tayside-nhs-board-0

Steinberg, E. J. (2006). Pushing for equality: Deaf Irish mothers and maternity care. In B. K. Eldredge, D. Stringham, and M. M. Wilding-Diaz (Eds.), *Deaf studies today!: Simply complex: 2006 conference proceedings,* vol. 2, 249–291. Orem: Utah Valley State College.

Turner, G. H., Nilsson, A. L., Sheikh, H., & Dean, R. (2012). *Report on healthcare provision for deaf sign language users.* Dublin: Interesource Group.

Urquhart, F. (2013). Deaf patient denied interpreter by Dundee Hospital. *The Scotsman Newspaper*, March 28, 2013. Retrieved February 4, 2014, from http://www.scotsman.com/news/health/deaf-patient-denied-interpreter-by-dundee-hospital-1-2862772

World Health Organization. (1978). *Declaration of Alma-Ata.* International Conference on Primary Healthcare (Ed.). Alma-Ata: World Health Organization.

Direct, Interpreter-Mediated or Translated? A Qualitative Study of Access to Preventive and Ongoing Healthcare Information for Australian Deaf People

Jemina Napier and Joseph Sabolcec, with Josie Hodgetts, Stephanie Linder, Gavin Mundy, Marijana Turcinov, and Linda Warby

ABSTRACT

The chapter will give an overview of a qualitative study conducted in Australia, which sought to gain an in-depth picture of the preventive and on-going needs of deaf people that use Auslan in terms of access to healthcare information. Using a purposeful sampling approach, this study surveyed the Deaf community throughout Australia about their perceived health information and communication access needs through face-to-face interviews and focus groups conducted in Auslan by deaf peers. Each filmed interview was thematically analyzed for key issues in relation to access to healthcare information, and whether deaf people receive information directly in Auslan, via an interpreter, or through translated materials. The investigation of healthcare needs of different generations of deaf people in Australia directly informs the policy and provision of on-going and preventive healthcare information to deaf people in Auslan (via interpreters or other translated texts). In the long-term, federal and state governments will be able to predict and plan for healthcare support needs of the Deaf community.

Research has shown that even between patients and healthcare practitioners who share a common language background, misunderstandings and miscommunications may arise because patients may not (fully) understand the terms used by their healthcare practitioners (e.g., Thompson & Pledger, 1993). Unfortunately, at least in the United States, research shows that this is more often the case for Deaf people, as they typically belong to a low-English-proficiency group who have limited access to public health information (Pollard & Barnett, 2009). This means that the average Deaf person generally experiences a "lower level of English literacy, a smaller fund of healthcare knowledge, and fewer health education opportunities than his average hearing counterparts" (Harmer, 1999, p. 80).

Understanding and using health terms has been shown to relate directly to experience and educational background (Cerny, 2008; Hadlow & Pitts, 1991; Thompson & Pledger, 1993). With Deaf patients an additional challenge relates to the healthcare provider's level of Deaf awareness (Smeijers & Pfau, 2009). Recent studies in various countries have found that Deaf people report concerns with the lack of Deaf awareness on the part of healthcare practitioners (Iezzoni et al., 2004; Leeson, Sheikh, Rozanes, Grehan, & Matthews, this volume; Major, Napier, Ferrara, & Johnston, 2012; Middleton et al., 2010; van de Boegaerde & de Lange, this volume). It can be expected then that Deaf patients who use Australian Sign Language (Auslan) as their first or preferred language may encounter barriers in accessing healthcare information.

THE AUSTRALIAN HEALTH CONTEXT

The National Health Priority Areas initiative, which began in 1996, focuses its efforts at the national level (Australian Institute of Health and Welfare, 2011). Priority areas include arthritis and musculoskeletal conditions; asthma; cancer control; cardiovascular health; diabetes; injury prevention and control; mental health; and obesity. The Australian National Preventive Health Agency (2011) has also been tasked with conducting educational, promotional, and community awareness programs relating to preventive health, including the promotion of a healthy lifestyle and good nutrition; reduction of tobacco use; minimization of alcohol consumption; prevention of substance abuse; and reduction of obesity.

Jordan, Briggs, Brand, and Osborne (2008) cite studies that estimate that 77% of Australians have at least one long-term health condition, defined as a condition that has lasted or is expected to last 6 months or more. Socially disadvantaged groups, especially indigenous Australians, are at greater risk of chronic disease (Harris, 2008).

In Australia, signed language interpreters are provided in various medical and mental health contexts through different booking agencies depending on the type of appointment and the services available.

Generally, interpreters are provided in public healthcare settings via individual state government–funded healthcare interpreting services, and private medical consultations are provided through the federally funded National Auslan Interpreter Booking and Payment Service (NABS).

NABS provides interpreters for private medical appointments only; thus Deaf people cannot request an interpreter to access preventive healthcare information (e.g., through drop-in clinics, antenatal classes). Deaf Auslan users also cannot currently obtain ongoing healthcare information via health information workshops (e.g., at Diabetes Australia) or other such sources since there are no provisions for interpreters as translation of information into Auslan is minimal.[1] Currently, the costs of interpreting services provided by NABS for access to critical health care when patients become sick are increasing exponentially each year (Keri Gilbert, NABS, personal communication, June 2011).

This is a major gap in the provision of access to health care for Deaf people. General access to preventive healthcare information is crucial in preventing longer-term critical health care as patients take better care of their health if they are informed (Jordan et al., 2008). Access to such information may also prevent the misuse of consultations with family physicians (general practitioners, or GPs) when Deaf people seek information about their ongoing health issues (e.g., diet, exercise, diabetes, pregnancy, asthma), which other hearing people can learn about elsewhere. Giving access to preventive health care would reduce the number of appointments with GPs, emergency issues, and appointments with specialists.

Although other discussions of signed language interpreting access in healthcare contexts pertain to Australia (Johnston & Napier, 2010; Major, Napier, Ferrara, & Johnston, 2012; Napier, Major, & Ferrara, 2011), until the study reported in this chapter was carried out, no research had ever been conducted in Australia to investigate Deaf Auslan users' access to general preventive and ongoing healthcare information.

This study[2] therefore sought to form an in-depth picture of the preventive and ongoing healthcare information needs of Deaf people that use Auslan. The aim was to make recommendations for preventive and ongoing healthcare information and communicative requirements of Deaf Auslan users, building on the known importance of the quality of communication between health practitioners and patients, with a view to both informing policy and enhancing the provision of and access to healthcare services for Deaf people in Australia. This chapter contextualizes the study initially with an overview of relevant literature before reporting on findings from the study and concluding with suggestions for further research.

WHAT WE KNOW ABOUT SIGNED LANGUAGE USERS' ACCESS TO HEALTHCARE INFORMATION

Numerous studies have documented low literacy levels in the Deaf community, often suggesting adult reading levels commensurate with those of an 8-year-old (Furlonger & Rickards, 2011). Despite the universality of this issue, healthcare practitioners generally appear to be unaware of the resulting communication barriers created by low literacy (Bostock & Steptoe, 2012; Denman, 2007; MacKinney, Walters, Bird, & Nattinger, 1995; Ubido, Huntington, & Warburton, 2002). Moreover, numerous studies demonstrate that written materials used by the health sector are inappropriate because they are too complex and densely written for many Deaf people to comprehend (Briffa, 1999; Feinauer & Lesch, 2011; Harmer, 1999; Zazove, Meador, Reed, Sen, & Gorenflo, 2008).

It has been recommended that health information should be available in signed languages with subtitles (Alexander, Ladd, & Powell, 2012; Ubido et al., 2002) and in plain English (Middleton, 2010). Such an arrangement would have obvious benefits for Deaf signed language users, who could then access healthcare information in their first or preferred language, especially given that the notion of "health literacy" is already an issue for the broader population, let alone the Deaf community.

Low literacy contributes to what Pollard (1998) has termed "fund-of-information deficit"—a distinct limitation in one's factual knowledge base in comparison to the general population despite normal IQ and educational achievement. More recently, the concept of "health literacy" has also emerged and been defined as "the degree to which individuals have the capacity to obtain, process, and understand basic health information and services needed to make basic health decisions" (Bostock & Steptoe, 2012, p. 1). Although educational accomplishment is typically stable after early adulthood, an individual's health literacy may increase (for example, through interaction with peers or medical professionals) or decrease as part of a general decline in cognitive capabilities with age (Bostock & Steptoe, 2012). Thus, if the general population experiences barriers to health literacy, how does this affect the Deaf community?

For Deaf people, low English literacy and limited access to information via the mass media conspire to further increase the risk of fund-of-information deficit. Among the many topics to which such a deficit may pertain are health issues (Pollard & Barnett, 2009). Studies have found that many Deaf people may lack the requisite background information necessary to understand and evaluate the information presented in a captioned TV program (Harmer, 1999).

In a study examining Deaf health literacy, Pollard and Barnett (2009) found that nearly one-third of adult participants earned scores that were "below ninth-grade" level, which they considered indicative of low health literacy. This was despite the fact that the small sample they used was deemed to be "highly educated." Other studies have found inadequate knowledge of specific health issues such as cardiovascular disease, diabetes, sexually transmitted diseases, cancer screening, and oral hygiene in the Deaf community (Alexander et al., 2012; Deafax, 2012; Jin & Daly, 2010; Margellos-Anast, Estarziau, & Kaufman, 2006; Orsi, Margellos-Anast, Perlman, Giloth, & Whitman, 2007).

Simply providing an interpreter may not be sufficient to address low health literacy, which results in healthcare consumers who are not aware they are able to or are even expected to play an active role in their own health management. This has ramifications when doctors expect some level of self-diagnosis and treatment at home and a timely appointment when the matter requires it (Harmer, 1999).

In a longitudinal cohort study of the general British population, Bostock and Steptoe (2012) found that low health literacy had a measurable impact on life expectancy; adults who were deemed to have low health literacy were more than twice as likely to die within five years than were adults with no health literacy limitations. They cite similar findings from the United States, suggesting that a lack of knowledge and skills may lead to less effective information seeking.

Doctor-patient communication when both interaction participants are speaking the same language is challenging enough, primarily because of doctors' general lack of communication skills (Skelton, 2005). Thus, if monolingual doctor-patient communication is already challenging, multilingual doctor-patient interaction (not always facilitated by an interpreter) may be an even more vexed issue regardless of whether the patients use a spoken or a signed language (Allotey & Reidpath, 1999; Feinauer & Lesch, 2011; Ferguson & Candib, 2002; Frank, 2000; Rivadeneyra, Elderkin-Thompson, Silver, & Waitzkin, 2000).

We know that Deaf people encounter barriers to primary health care (Alexander et al., 2012; Middleton et al., 2010; Bramwell, Harrington,

& Harris, 2002). Although this is generally perceived to be the result of healthcare workers' poor awareness of the needs of Deaf patients, the communication choices made by Deaf patients themselves may also compound the situation; some patients are reluctant to use interpreters in healthcare settings because of issues of confidentiality and independence (Earis & Reynolds, 2009). Deaf people may not be aware of the limitations this reluctance imposes. Busy healthcare practitioners are unlikely to write notes with the level of detail that would be provided by speech (Harmer, 1999). Deaf people may also not understand these notes fully, especially if healthcare terminology is used.

It has been observed that Deaf people avoid healthcare appointments due to communication problems and as a result experience significant gaps in their understanding of treatments. For example, 35% of Deaf and hard of hearing people in the UK are unclear about their condition, and 33% of British Sign Language (BSL) users are unsure about instructions for their medications (Royal National Institute for Deaf People, 2004).

In terms of preventive healthcare, most risk assessment occurs opportunistically during GP appointments (Harris, 2008). Thus, this has implications for Deaf patients if they do not have adequate access to their preferred mode of communication (Barnett & Franks, 2002). For this reason the healthcare records of deaf people could be flagged with their preferred communication methods, and longer appointments than usual could be scheduled (Middleton, 2010; Alexander et al., 2012). Moreover, deaf people visit a doctor more often than the general population (Harmer, 1999), a fact confirmed by NABS in the Australian context (K. Gilbert, personal communication, June 2011). A number of reasons are put forward for this situation, including poor communication, which results in return appointments to clarify what was not understood in a prior visit.

Several interacting factors appear to influence the sources of information Deaf people may turn to for health information. Studies generally report that doctors are a preferred source of such information (Folkins et al., 2005; Kaskowitz, Nakaji, Clark, Gunsauls, & Sadler, 2006; Roberts & Mulgavin, 2007), followed by interpersonal sources rather than printed materials. Increasingly the general community is turning to the Internet for a "second opinion" on health matters, similar to using a reference manual, yet not as a replacement for a physician, although the credibility of the information found on the Internet is an issue (Quintana, Feightner, Wathen, Sangster, & Marshall, 2001). This is being found to be the case in the Deaf community as well (Kaskowitz et al., 2006; Roberts & Mulgavin, 2007).

Barriers to obtaining preventive health information are most commonly cited as difficulty in communicating with doctors (40%), lack of education (which is assumed to refer to literacy: 31.3%), and insufficient access to interpreters (26.1%) (Kaskowitz et al., 2006). Thus these obstacles have implications for the general health of the Deaf community.

MacKinney (1995) found that Deaf ASL users who attended a primary-care practice with full-time interpreter services were more likely to report receiving preventive services (such as pap smears, mammograms, and rectal examinations) than a comparison group of Deaf ASL users who sought care elsewhere.

Although many authors mention the need for patient information leaflets and government health advice to be available in a signed language with subtitles (e.g., Alexander et al., 2012), others point to the need to consider the cultural context: who presents the information (are they known to the Deaf community? do they have a good reputation?), the information-giving environment (e.g., a Deaf club), the need to address gaps in knowledge in an appropriate way and to present information in a "Deaf friendly," "graphically enriched" format (Fellinger et al., 2005a; Jones, Renger, & Firestone, 2005; Margellos-Anast et al., 2006; Pollard, Dean, O'Hearn, & Haynes, 2009; Roberts & Mugavin, 2007; Shabaik et al., 2010). In fact, any adaptation of materials for Deaf audiences requires careful consideration, and information presented in the form of a dialogue is the preferred format (Pollard et al., 2009).

This review of the literature reveals that Deaf people encounter challenges in accessing health care and also in understanding healthcare information due to the lack of healthcare literacy and to communication barriers. Even when signed language interpreting services are provided, they may still experience challenges in understanding healthcare information if they do not have access to other forms of follow-up materials in the form of translated leaflets, and so on, presented in a signed language on video. The goal of this study was, therefore, to focus on the Australian context and examine the nature of Deaf Auslan users' access to preventive and ongoing healthcare information in particular.

RESEARCH QUESTIONS

The study addressed the following research questions:

1. How and where do Deaf people access preventive and ongoing healthcare information?

2. What are the experiences of Deaf Auslan users in accessing information about their own health?
3. What are the major themes in Deaf people's perceptions of their own access to healthcare information?
4. How much awareness do Deaf Australians have about health issues generally?

METHOD

A qualitative, inductive approach was adopted in order to enable an in-depth, phenomenological exploration of the experiences of Deaf Auslan users, allowing participants to discuss issues from their own perspective. Qualitative studies are an effective way to explore healthcare questions as long as the research is well designed and is of high quality (Daly, Kellehear, & Gliksman, 1997; Kitto, Chesters, & Grbich, 2008).

A Note about Other Methodologies

According to Harmer's (1999) review, many studies of Deaf people's access to health care do not differentiate between pre- and postlingually deafened individuals and subjects who identify themselves as being Deaf, deafened, or hard of hearing; they have used nonrandomized and small sample sizes, inappropriate methodologies, or testing instruments and rely on convenience samples (such as Deaf clubs).

Barnett and Franks (2002) provide a case in point. When the age of onset of deafness and the participants' preferred communication mode were controlled, they found that healthcare utilization by deaf and hard of hearing people in the United States was markedly different: prelingually deafened adults reported lower health status and fewer visits to physicians.

A key issue is the small number of studies conducted in the signed language of the Deaf community under investigation (Barnett, McKee, Smith, & Pearson, 2011; Fellinger et al., 2005b). This is evident in recent work. For instance, Tamaskar et al. (2009) base their assessment of attitudes toward preventive health activities on an English self-administered instrument, while a survey to assess health and healthcare utilization (Woodcock & Pole, 2007) was conducted by telephone. One notable exception is the study conducted by Margellos-Anast et al. (2006), which involved data collection via ASL interviews. Authors have generally agreed that collecting data from the Deaf community is best done in a signed language by trained data collectors who are fluent in the relevant language.

Any data collected in a text-based form are immediately problematic, given what we know about the English literacy levels and subsequent health literacy levels of Deaf people. Thus, we wanted to ensure that our study design circumvented the limitations of previous studies by enabling the Deaf participants to talk to Deaf people in their own signed language and ensuring that the study conformed to ethical guidelines for conducting deafness research (Harris, Holmes, & Mertens, 2009; Pollard, 1992; Singleton, Jones, & Hanumantha, 2012).

Methodological Framework for This Study

This was a one-year study that utilized participatory research (Cornwall & Jewkes, 1995) to conduct in-depth, semistructured interviews with Deaf Auslan users. Drawing on principles from grounded theory (Glaser & Strauss, 1977), the findings were data driven in that we analyzed the interview data using thematic analysis (Silverman, 2006) to identify patterns (themes) that emerged. Community-based participatory research is an established and effective methodology for health-related research (Minkler & Wallerstein, 2011) and has been used, for example, in the exploration of healthcare needs of migrant communities in Ireland (Macfarlane et al., 2009).

Participatory research enables both positive user involvement and marginalized, "hidden" voices to be heard. Through purposeful sampling (Patton, 2002), "information rich" stakeholder groups who have a certain depth of experience to share contribute to the research process. Our participatory approach included forming an advisory group and working with a team of Deaf Auslan users to conduct in-depth qualitative interviews.

Advisory Group

An advisory group with representatives from stakeholder groups was established. It met several times with members of the project team and also had intermittent email contact between meetings. With a view to ensuring the qualitative outcomes of the study, the group was to collaboratively guide the research team on methodology, data collection, consideration of results, and recommendations.

Research Team Recruitment and Training

An important element of community-based participatory research is the level of trust between participants and researchers (Christopher, Watts, McCormick, & Young, 2008). Therefore, at the commencement of the project, Deaf Auslan users were recruited to the research team from five different cities to conduct interviews in Auslan with Deaf participants throughout Australia.

During a training weekend for the whole research team, the project's objectives were discussed, and the team worked collaboratively to revise the draft interview questions; to agree on criteria for and identify potential participants in their home states; and to concur on a procedure for recruiting participants. The team also participated in simulated interviews that were video-recorded and discussed in terms of efficacy in order to refine the interview procedure.

Part of the weekend workshop also focused on the analysis of data using ELAN software, which is a computer program that allows transcription and detailed annotation to be precisely aligned with video data (Johnston & Schembri, 2005). The team decided on a technique for annotating the video-recorded interviews, which would be used as a basis for data analysis. The team training enabled consistent approaches to data collection and analysis across all interviews.

Risk Assessment and Ethics Approval

Development of the methodology and interview protocols included a risk assessment to consider the potential risks to both the research team and the participants in discussing health issues. An advice sheet was developed so that the interviewers could tell the participants where they could get follow-up support locally if they were distressed by the content of the interview discussion. Once the methodology had been finalized with the research team and the advisory group, ethics approval was received from the Macquarie University Human Research Ethics Committee.[3]

Participant Recruitment

Potential participants were identified by the Deaf research team members and recruited through network and purposeful, nonprobabilistic sampling. The criteria for recruitment had been agreed on during the training weekend, when the potential participants in each state were grouped according to the size of the local Deaf population and what we felt were realistic targets.

A protocol was developed for approaching these target individuals, which all of us followed, so each person was approached only once in order to avoid creating any feelings of pressure or coercion. When an individual agreed to consider participating, the person was given information about the project and a link to an Auslan version of the consent and information form to watch before attending the interview.

The time and venue for the interviews were mutually arranged, and participants were informed they could attend individually or with a friend or family member. In some states, when we could not identify sufficient numbers of participants through networks, a generic flyer was also circulated in the Deaf community seeking expressions of interest for participation in the study.

Interview Procedure

All of the interviews were conducted in Auslan and filmed so as to free the interviewer from having to take notes. All of the participants signed a consent form to permit the use of the video data for analysis. Although an interview protocol was developed for all of us to use, they were free to explore any additional areas of interest within the original objectives of the study.

The interview procedure involved the collection of demographic information, then a series of questions to prompt discussion about how the participants would describe their own health; their most recent health appointments; their sources of health information; and their access to general preventive health information.

To act as a prompt for discussion about preventive health and potential sources of information during the interviews, participants were also asked to rate their awareness of various health issues. The terminology was simplified slightly to allow for English literacy issues. Participants were free to complete the questionnaire themselves or to have us sign and explain any unclear terms.

The majority of interviews were conducted with individuals on a one-to-one basis, although focus groups of five or six people were also conducted in some states as a way of facilitating the involvement of older participants and indigenous Deaf community members.

Interviews lasted on average between 30 and 60 minutes, and at the end of each interview, all of us followed a postinterview checklist to ensure that we had all of the required information and had saved and backed up the data.

The research coordinator moderated the interview process by reviewing the initial interviews and giving general feedback to the whole research team. This process ensured a consistent (reliable and valid) approach to interviewing for the entire team.

Data Analysis

A grounded-theory approach was used to extract themes from the data for analysis (Glaser & Strauss, 1977), meaning that we did not approach the data with preconceived ideas of what we would discover and instead allowed our findings to be entirely data driven.

The interview video data were imported into ELAN, translated into English, and analyzed by a six-stage process of thematic analysis: (1) becoming familiar with the data, (2) generating initial codes, (3) searching for themes among the codes, (4) reviewing themes, (5) defining and naming themes, and (6) producing the final report (Braun & Clarke, 2006). In order to ensure anonymity, each participant was allocated a unique code, which was then used for all subsequent identification. References to specific individuals or organizations in the interviews were also removed during the translation process.

Guide translations and preliminary thematic analyses were completed by the Deaf researchers and then forwarded to the research coordinator for finalization of the English translation and further comparative thematic analysis.

RESULTS AND DISCUSSION

The results are provided here in two sections. First, we present an overview of participant characteristics, based on the demographic survey conducted at the beginning of the interviews. Second, we provide a detailed discussion of the principle themes identified in the interview data.

Participant Characteristics

A total of 72 participants from six states and one territory were interviewed (figure 1). In some states, data were collected in multiple locations.

In the identification of potential participants, the research team aimed to recruit individuals who demonstrated a demographic spread in terms of gender and age. Of the 72 interviewees, 45 (62.5%) were female and 27 (37.5%) were male. In terms of age, participants were grouped into five categories: young, middle, senior, elderly, and not known; 15 (20.5%) were between 18 and 35 years of age (young); 18 (25.5%) were between 36 and 50 years of age (middle); 14 (19.5%) were between 51 and 65 years of age (senior); 19 (26%) were elderly (over 65); and 6 (8.5%) did not disclose their age (not known). Furthermore, the participants were recruited to represent other subgroups of the Deaf community (figure 2).

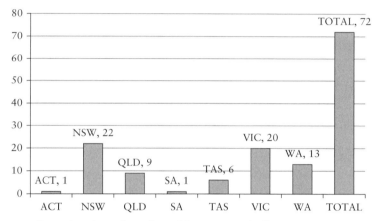

FIGURE 1. *Spread and number of participants recruited*[4].

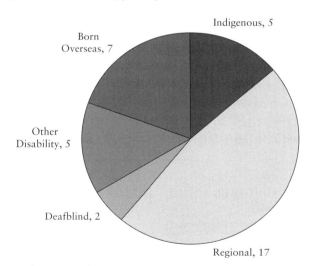

FIGURE 2. *Numbers according to other participant variables.*

Given that the Deaf community population of Auslan users is estimated at 6,500 (Johnston, 2003), the sample of interviewees in the study is just over 1% of the population. Since this is a qualitative study, the number of participants is not intended to be a representative sample of the Deaf community population but rather a snapshot of Deaf people with legitimate experience of healthcare issues.

Thematic Discussion

Eleven themes emerged from the interviews, which have been collapsed into seven overall themes. Sample quotes have been extracted from the participants' comments in order to provide insight into their perceptions of their access to preventive and ongoing healthcare information. The quotes provided in this section are translations from Auslan into written English; thus they are not a representation of the participants' English literacy levels. There are necessary limitations to presenting extracts of signed language data for publication in a translated written form (Stone & West, 2012). Therefore, some subtle aspects of the original Auslan discourse may not have been captured in written English.

English Literacy

All of the participants reported their level of English literacy at the start of the interview, although in the case of the larger focus groups, time constraints precluded collecting this information. See table 1 for an overview of the self-reported English literacy levels of the participants.

Table 1: Self-Reported English Literacy

Category	Number
1 (poor)	1
2	17
3 (good)	26
4	9
5 (excellent)	8
Not available	11
TOTAL	72

Nine participants expressed confidence in their English literacy skills or gave examples that could be interpreted as a functional level of English literacy. Here is one such example:

I am fine with reading the newspaper and also the Internet . . . In the old days I used to fax organizations for information. I used the TTY relay service as well. I remember my boy had head lice and I contacted the local community nurse by TTY. The information was free, they told me what to do and it was useful information. They faxed me some information with pictures, telling me the right product to buy, so rather than making an appointment and visiting the doctor, I had all the information I needed.

Eleven participants qualified their English literacy skills by saying they could follow what they read, but they preferred text that was presented in bullet points or had accompanying images. They also said they could read but needed to check information in the dictionary.

Almost half of the participants (n = 31) expressed greater difficulties with English and in some cases said they relied on a friend or family member to help them understand written information:[5]

P: I got some letters . . . from school and I had to get a friend to explain them to me. I also checked with a Deaf friend who works as a support worker to make sure I understood everything.

I: So most things you receive in writing, you request someone to sign them to you?

P: Yes, most.

We usually don't understand what is written [in brochures] but we do see the pictures. If we want to understand what is written, we ask someone to explain it. That's what most Deaf people do.

Although many people may develop strategies for coping with low English literacy, these techniques also expose them to potentially inaccurate information and the associated consequences (Harmer, 1999; Jones et al., 2005). In addition, for deaf-blind people, web-based information is not easily accessed, a further challenge:

I have some difficulty trying to access the Internet. Braille is not very convenient for the Internet. Sometimes I ask people but I need to be wary of that because I am given some different information by different people. I get confused and tend to worry more because I don't know what's true. It is a bit of a catch-22 because my English is limited and I ask people to help but [once] it went very wrong. There were misconceptions . . . I worried and became stressed so as a result my health deteriorated.

In two cases, limited English literacy was due to migration to Australia from a non-English-speaking country:

I was given a paper explaining how shingles happens and how to resolve it. But I found it hard to read because of the language and the amount of information on the page. I went home and went on the Internet and found some information in Japanese. I read that and I understood it.

These findings are consistent with the literature, demonstrating that English literacy is a key barrier to Deaf people in attempting to access information before, during, and after a healthcare appointment (Bostock & Steptoe, 2012; Denman, 2007; MacKinney et al., 1995; Ubido et al., 2002). Understandably, many participants commented on a preference for information in Auslan:

Sometimes when I read information I don't quite understand it until it is being signed to me. I tend to understand and remember information if it was signed to me . . . I do read books, yes, but there are no examples. There are no explanations and I need it to be signed so I understand and remember it more easily.

This type of quote supports the need for materials that are already translated into community languages to also be translated into Auslan, so that this information is available to the Deaf community. Translations could then be disseminated either online via a central website or on DVD. Simply translating existing material into Auslan may not fully address other barriers, however, particularly the level of health literacy in the Deaf community.

Attitudes toward Preventive or Ongoing Health Care

Although the participants were not asked to disclose their specific medical conditions or treatments, many of them did mention that their healthcare practitioner was monitoring them with regard to regular (unspecified) blood tests, cardiovascular issues, diabetes, cancer, musculoskeletal difficulties, weight management, and sight problems (e.g., glaucoma).

Many of the participants expressed the desire to improve their health, to manage an existing medical condition more effectively, or to be more active in their health care:

> I would like to know more about issues I may have in my family history—to prepare for them. I have a family history of diabetes for example. And if I was borderline, I would need to know how to prepare by eliminating certain foods, for example. So in terms of the future, who knows? But I would like to know more, definitely.

> [Heart disease] runs in my family . . . my grandfather had a heart attack. I watched my father change his diet. I didn't like the way my father had to start the morning with a big bowl of medication . . . I didn't want the same . . . I would prefer to prevent this from happening and so I do yoga for example.

> I like to read so that I can ask questions when I see the doctor or to be familiar with some of the medical terms.

Given the purposeful sample design that targeted people who had experienced a medical condition, one-third of the interviewees ($n = 23$) expressed their health objectives in terms of varying degrees of frustration or inability to access the desired information:

> There are barriers. Before my treatment, I was given a video. I asked if there were captions but there were none. I had to have the treatment but I didn't have any access to the information. I only knew about the treatment from a pamphlet. The treatment was very serious and I needed full information . . . I am not sure if I would have taken the treatment if I had known the side effects . . . I would never want to go through that experience again. Really it shows the hospital did not realize that they had a duty to Deaf people. Deaf people have the right to access full information.

> My doctor explained things but later when I went home, I was a bit confused. I wanted to know more. The doctor wrote some things down and the interpreter interpreted everything well but . . . it was later that I realized I had forgotten or that I wanted to know more. The interpreter signed everything and that was it. But because of limited time,

what did it mean? I went home and read something on the Internet and that clarified things a bit more.

If you're sick and you get medication with instructions, it is always hard to work out how to take the medication. Take in the morning, after or before eating . . . I need to go and ask the pharmacist to clarify what it says . . . It can be so confusing . . . People get very frustrated with the information on medication. I always have to clarify that with the pharmacist because they're experienced and know what it should be.

People who are deaf-blind are at even more of a disadvantage in this regard:

Tactile signing and fingerspelling take more time. And deaf-blind people get behind with information. There are lots of gaps in access to information so we may need more time to understand new information. That is different from Deaf people, who are able to access everyday information. We are behind with terms and English skills as we have a poor education. We need more time.

Although we used the previous 12 months as a general reference point for the discussion of health issues, in several instances the participants mentioned medical situations that had occurred many years ago, demonstrating the potentially long-lasting impact of such events:

I had three cesareans. With the first two, I really didn't know why I needed them. For my third I finally had an interpreter so I could ask all the questions I needed to, throughout. You really must have an interpreter. When you're having a baby, you want to know what's happening. That's very important . . . [my partner would] ask me why I needed an operation and I felt like I'd failed. It felt like a criticism because he wasn't aware of the reasons. There's a bit of competition with men—"my wife had a natural birth," that sort of thing. And if it's not, it's embarrassing. It may not be correct, but that's why they need information. It would help them to be proud of a healthy child, doesn't matter how it was born.

Although health literacy was not assessed directly, the preceding examples clearly demonstrate significant areas of concern that participants were not able to address and which exacerbate rather than alleviate the "fund-of-information deficit" reported in the literature (Pollard & Barnett, 2009).

Only a few participants gave examples of accessible preventive or ongoing healthcare services:

> When I was pregnant I went to the birthing classes. I really enjoyed them because there was Auslan in the class. Having an Auslan interpreter meant I learned very quickly and was interested in it. I was confident and was able to ask questions in the group of hearing people. I learned from seeing their questions. It is better than one-on-one with the GP, as I don't get much out of it. Just reading is not enough, having discussion in a group I found more interesting. I loved it.

This situation may partly be due to the purposeful sample utilized for this study. More often, participants gave instances of services that were not accessible to them because of a lack of funded interpreting, for example, for weight-management programs:

> I've always liked going [to the weight-management specialist], but I would only be weighed, then that was it. I missed out on the discussion and I didn't have motivation to achieve goals. For example if I put on weight, I didn't have to explain because there wasn't an interpreter. If I had been able to participate in group sessions, listened to others . . . it might have made a difference.

> My partner had a friend who lost a lot of weight [through stomach banding]. He wanted me to do the same. I was a bit unsure, and then I decided to go ahead. There was a support group, but I didn't get involved. I did go to an exercise group. The instructor spoke and I explained I was Deaf. They apologized and tried to show the exercises, but it was frustrating and I gave up after two classes. There was no interpreter. I called NABS but because it was a group, they couldn't provide an interpreter.

Barriers in relation to cancer counseling and support were also mentioned:

> I went to the free cancer support group provided by [hospital name] public hospital . . . It was a hearing group with about 12 members . . . I was really upset that an interpreter was not provided for me to access the group . . . They asked me to go to the class every

month but I couldn't without an interpreter . . . We wrote notes, but it was all brief. So I didn't really know what was going on in the group. It was hard to know what was being discussed. I talked to the staff at the [state Deaf society]. But they said there wasn't anything they could do because interpreters can only be provided for medical appointments with doctors and hospitals and that was all. But not for counseling groups. I think they should be included . . . I was really disappointed.

Three participants referred to drug or alcohol services for which an interpreter could also not be provided:

[The drug and alcohol service] has a special "steps" program but they wouldn't provide interpreters. We tried to use the written materials they gave us but it was hard because there was no information in Auslan that might have been motivating, only writing with pen and paper, which wasn't motivating and we gave up.

My husband had depression. It was severe. I called [the mental health provider] and they sent us a form for registering. When we handed in the form, we asked them to book an interpreter. They told us that they don't have any funding for interpreting. I could not believe it, after all the paperwork, referral, visiting the doctor and everything I did . . . There was no funding for an interpreter! My husband received no information on how to reduce [his] depression or how to get support. When he got worse, I tried to support him as much as I could.

Moreover, although barriers to access for some of the preceding participants may not have had significant health implications, access to support services relating to chronic conditions such as diabetes and multiple sclerosis (MS) would limit the degree to which individuals are able to manage their condition:

I couldn't go to the clinic because there was no interpreter. I got emails regularly, inviting me to join a [diabetes] group or go to a workshop to talk about shopping and food but I couldn't go because there was no interpreter. They'd regularly email me to join in and I wanted to go, but couldn't, because no interpreter was provided. That means I have never attended one of their workshops or groups . . . I would like to join a group to talk to others, understand their situation. I would like a group, but I've never gone.

Another time there was a guest speaker organized [by the MS support group]. Some speakers would talk about the future, medication . . . or about what exercises to do, what modifications to make in the home. So there was a lot of information . . . [Other members of the group] were all angry because they had paid for the interpreter! I thought it wasn't fair to me—I was Deaf—I wanted to know what was going on. None of them wrote notes with me, ever. The guest speaker said that we should ask the head office to pay for an interpreter. The others didn't seem happy with that. And I didn't bother going back again . . . It would have been impossible to concentrate on who was speaking and what they were saying. And the interpreter struggled with that as well. There would have been about ten people in the group . . . Money was the issue though.

Being excluded from participating in self-management programs for chronic illness like those shown here has clear implications for the individual as well as the Deaf community in general, which becomes further marginalized by not being actively engaged (Jordan et al., 2008).

Access to Interpreters for Primary Health Care

Although access to primary health care was not the initial objective of the study, as already noted, primary healthcare providers play a significant role in preventive health, ongoing health maintenance, and referrals to other services and sources of information (Harris, 2008), none of which can be successfully achieved without clear doctor-patient communication. In some cases ($n = 11$) participants were satisfied with interpreting provision in primary health care and gave examples demonstrating effective communication:

[In the past] we wrote notes. I understood a little bit. Then when I moved here and had the specialist appointments, the specialist booked an interpreter and that was much better. The doctor explained things and I understood more . . . It was much better with an interpreter, definitely. Time is the problem, when you're writing notes . . . You only have 15 minutes so writing notes means it has to be brief. Having an interpreter means you have time to ask the reason for things and get a full response. And it helps you to understand things clearly . . . [The doctor's] writing can be really sloppy as well. So you have to ask them to repeat things and that can take a lot of time.

Participants also gave examples of healthcare providers who were aware of the importance of interpreting:

> If an emergency happened and an interpreter couldn't be booked, I'd have to wait. My doctor knows my English is poor and so to communicate properly, we need an interpreter. So when an interpreter does arrive, we can talk freely and quickly. We never use notes to communicate. Never. And my doctor won't accept a hearing friend to interpret. We must have a [qualified] interpreter.

> The doctor saw that I understood his explanations better [with an interpreter] . . . We Deaf people are not that good with English. We can understand some words but for more complex things we need interpreters so that we understand everything thoroughly.

Despite funding for the provision of Auslan interpreters, participants ($n = 21$) gave examples of instances in which they had been unable to access Auslan interpreters for primary healthcare appointments, especially when an appointment was made on short notice or in a nonmetropolitan region:

> In the last 12 months, we have had problems with getting interpreters for appointments. We went to the doctor without an interpreter. It was a new doctor. We wanted a refill for a prescription. We went home and my son, who was concerned that [my wife] had new tablets and there was no interpreter, called his daughter, who was a nurse, and they told us that my wife should not be taking one of the five tablets she had been given. If that hadn't happened, she would have just continued taking five tablets a day!

> I always book an interpreter but if there isn't enough notice [to do so], we write notes. You need to book in advance. If you need an interpreter *now*, it's hard.

> The problem with children is that illness can come up on really short notice. So you have to call and make an appointment with the doctor in the morning and then call NABS and ask for an interpreter urgently. But that's really difficult. So it usually means we have to use pen and paper. But then I have problems understanding what was written. I think I've had to use notes about 80% of the time. If it's something like having a blood test, booking an interpreter is fine. One day they [the children] all got sick. They were all vomiting and had a rash. I called and got them in but getting an interpreter was hard. It was very stressful.

Three participants also raised concerns about their elderly parents' ability to communicate with healthcare providers and the degree to which they would be able to participate in decision making relating to their health care:

> My mother is in her 80s. I look after her. I am worrying about having to go to the hospital—what happen if there is no interpreter? what happens to my mum or to me when I don't understand something? I can speak, yes, the doctor says to me that I can speak. But I can't understand what the doctor says because they talk too fast and I don't understand their medical language.

Participants (*n* = 12) also provided examples of primary healthcare providers who were not aware of Deaf patients' needs or the importance of interpreting as a way of improving communication:

> When I went to the doctor, the doctor was taken aback because I was Deaf. They asked me stupid questions—was I Deaf from birth? did I have Deaf family? if I wore hearing aids? and so on. They asked me about communication and if I could use my voice. I felt angry—it wasn't relevant to why I was there.

> In the intensive care unit, the nurses were more concerned with the expense of interpreters when we requested a full-time interpreter. We decided to go against them and hired interpreters on a full-time basis ourselves . . . As I couldn't always be there and the nurses did not know how to communicate with [partner] . . . a full-time interpreter should be booked—no question about that. I know maybe there will be some times where the interpreter will be doing nothing but they need to be there right when the Deaf patient wakes up.

> There was another time, I went to see a GP about my pension . . . [The doctor] kept talking at me. When I said I didn't understand a thing, she said that was nonsense because I can speak alright, not fluently though, but I can speak so she didn't believe me when I said I didn't understand her. I said I am legally blind but she didn't believe that either. I could only see her through tunnel vision, just her. She didn't have any knowledge of hidden disabilities, like my limited sight or lack of hearing. I didn't wear a hearing aid so I looked fine, your average "guy next door." But I am not just Deaf or blind, I am both. It is so frustrating.

Private healthcare providers appear to be an ongoing issue ($n = 3$):

> My father went to a private hospital and they refused to pay for an interpreter. But when it came to chemo and doctors, NABS provided interpreters. But not at the hospital. When we did have an interpreter for an appointment, I would ask questions about other things as much as I could but the hospital never offered anything to me.

Although most healthcare professionals may have little contact with Deaf patients, guidelines for professionals working with Deaf patients have been developed.[6] A recommendation arising from the literature is that Deaf patients' healthcare records note the communication requirements of the Deaf client and the adjustments required (Middleton, 2010).

COMMUNICATION PREFERENCES

Fifteen participants expressed a preference for speech, lipreading, or writing in order to communicate with their healthcare provider in some contexts despite the obvious limitations of these options (given the self-ratings of English literacy reported earlier in this chapter):

> I try my best, by myself and we use speech, lipreading, and writing and it goes well.

> I never use an interpreter. I talk but it is a bit hard to lip-read so we write. He [the doctor] comes from Jordan.

> I have no problem understanding [my doctor]. I have seen him for many years and he knows my health background . . . We write to each other . . . but at the hospital an interpreter was presented. Hospital is important so an interpreter was necessary . . .

In some cases this is qualified by the importance placed on the appointment by the participant and by privacy concerns:

> Depends on the issue. If I feel it is serious then I will [book an interpreter]. If it is small, like when kids get sick or any small health problems, then I will go myself . . . It is great with interpreters but I wish I could do it on my own. I value my privacy. Why can't I talk directly to the doctor? Sometimes you need to accept the fact that you do need an interpreter . . . For example if I have a pap smear I will not ask for an interpreter.

> I could lip-read him and I didn't need an interpreter . . . it was in regard to sexual health. I didn't want to advertise it. Well actually it was

embarrassing. I like to try to see if I can lip-read or understand what is being said. [The doctor] was just perfect so I was happy with him.

A minority of participants (n = 8) expressed a preference for non-professional interpreters who are known to them, particularly during a healthcare consultation, which is also noted in the literature on migrant communities (e.g., Macfarlane et al., 2009):

My partner is hearing and we go to medical appointments together. My partner interprets but not too fast, at an easy pace, so I can understand.

I want a little information about why I am sick or how to resolve the illness.

I don't want too much detail.

I: Do you understand the information your doctor gives you?

P: A little, but not fully . . . If there are big words I have to ask my daughter what that means. She helps me. So I understand a bit, but not fully.

My mom interpreted. I don't go on my own. I feel like sometimes I forget the questions. I feel more comfortable if my mom is with me, that I'm not alone.

A similar need for support during medical appointments was expressed by two other participants:

When I visit the specialist with an interpreter and I'm told something once, I feel some of the information goes over my head. But when I visit the GP, we usually write and I take these notes home to read over again. Therefore I understand more of the information. Sometimes I have my husband with me so he remembers what was said and he reminds me at home.

Maybe there could be someone else in the room for example an advocate to make sure that a deaf-blind person understands what is being said. A long time ago, I was shy and I didn't know much about health. There was an advocate present in the room. S/he made sure that I understood—s/he would see that I didn't really understand so s/he would stop and explain it to me. The interpreter couldn't say anything so it was useful. I started to understand.

Two participants stated that Deaf interpreters provide a level of support they require:

My preference would be for an interpreter and a relay interpreter. That would help. I know how to sign but I get stressed with an interpreter.

Deaf interpreters are sometimes easier to understand than hearing interpreters. Yes, hearing interpreters are good but Deaf interpreters are cleverer with the use of Auslan, to make it easier to understand. They could translate it into Auslan very well and hearing interpreters sometimes could not do that. They follow what doctors say . . . follow English structure. Sometimes deaf-blind people do not understand it. The interpreters need to change it more into Auslan structure. The interpreters need to say hold on and change the structure more to make it easier for deaf-blind [patients] to understand. Some interpreters do not care if deaf-blind people do not understand and follow what doctors said.

ACCESS TO GENERAL HEALTHCARE INFORMATION

Not surprisingly, when discussing access to information, most of the participants expressed a strong preference for information in Auslan via an interpreter. This was mentioned throughout the interviews in relation to GPs, pharmacists, and other service providers:

I: If an interpreter was not available, what would you do?

P: Most of the time I would postpone the appointment. Unless it was something really serious, I would postpone the appointment.

I must have an interpreter. If an interpreter isn't available I won't go to the doctor . . . But if an interpreter is available, I can express myself, ask questions in depth. Without an interpreter, it's much harder.

The quality and appropriateness of interpreting are issues for many, however:

The interpreter is not always an appropriate interpreter. For example, I made an appointment two weeks in advance. An interpreter was booked. Just before the appointment I was told that the interpreter had to be replaced with a less experienced interpreter. That was frustrating because it meant we didn't communicate well. I know it happens, but the interpreter didn't understand me.

In Australia the number of interpreters is smaller, so if I want to make a doctor appointment I refuse to have interpreters I know. I'd rather that they not know my health problem.

I: Have you asked the hospital for your preferred interpreter?

P: Yes, but the hospital refused. I went to the Deaf Society and told them the problem I had with the interpreter. But still the same interpreter is used. From the birth of my son onward, it's been the same person.

I: So basically the hospital ignores your request and uses their interpreter?

P: Yes.

Six participants also mentioned the potential to provide information in Auslan on the Internet:

In England they have information about diabetes in signed language, which looked really good. It would be great to have something like that for dieting—showing the food pyramid and what was important.

Having information in Auslan on the Internet would be good. One of the problems of workshops is that everyone is a bit conscious of who is around. But if I'm looking at the Internet, and I don't understand something, I would need to get someone to sign it to me. It's a bit more private, so you can do your own research. In a workshop, people may be a bit hesitant in opening up fully. That's why I would prefer the Internet and having information in Auslan.

It would be great if organizations like the Deaf Society had translated information with videos in Auslan. That would be fantastic and I would like to see more . . . I can read and absorb information but information presented in signed language is better for me.

Sources of General Healthcare Information
Participants were asked about the sources of information they used and their preferences for general information about preventive health or the maintenance of ongoing conditions. Table 2 summarizes the sources of information they mentioned.

TABLE 2. *Information Sources*

Information source mentioned by participants	Number
TV	40
GP	32
Internet	26
Magazines/newspaper	18
Family	18
Deaf/signing family and friends only	17
Books	15
Friends	14
Brochures	13
Workshops	9
Deaf/signing work colleagues	7
Other health organizations	6
Deaf Society/Deaf club	5
Chemist	4
Community health centers	4
Work colleagues	3

The greatest number of participants cited television as an information source, and health-related programs such as "Embarrassing Bodies" were specifically mentioned by several. Dramas such as "Home and Away" were also named as a source of information when their characters experienced health concerns. This finding contradicts the earlier conclusions of Folkins et al. (2005) in the United States, which reported television as a rare source of health information for Deaf people.

The participants acknowledged, however, that, in relation to literacy and captioning, television has obvious limitations as a source of information:

[Captioning on TV] is good but it can be a bit hard to understand some of the words.

There are a lot of advertisements about smoking, cancer, obesity and so on [on TV]. And a lot of this information is very visual, but, I don't know how you would do it, but if Auslan could be included. Or if all advertisements could be subtitled for Deaf people. Because there is a lot of medical information on the TV, so we can get that information in at least one way.

If there was something medical on TV I would be interested in watching but it doesn't always have captions. So sometimes my partner tells me what is being said, but briefly.

As a *preferred* source of information, many participants (*n* = 32) mentioned their GP, who in some cases was their most immediate or only source of health-related information:

> I've never thought of anywhere else. I always go straight to the doctor.

I: Do you go to the doctor if you're unsure, or do you look on the Internet?

P: No, never. I go straight to the doctor. Always.

I: So if a few things were explained to you and later you forgot something, what would you do?

P: I'd go back and ask them to repeat it and write it down.

I: So any other options? Like a computer?

P: There's never been any problems with talking to the doctor. I don't know. I can't think of anything different.

The reasons for this reliance on GPs include the provision of an interpreter to assist communication, as well as general satisfaction with the GPs' services:

> I go to the doctor regularly and communication is clear. And there's been a problem I've had for a while that my doctor is aware of. So communication has been good because of that.

> I've known my doctor for a long time and they're excellent and very open about everything so I can ask anything, from A to Z. So I feel free to ask any questions about anything. Yes, in fact I usually get more than I expect to get. So I get information about what to do, how to prevent something. It's really quite in-depth information.

However, many participants reported having limited access to their GP, especially in relation to the time available, which limits the potential preventive role the GP is able to provide:

> They are busy and sometimes you feel they want to rush you out the door and limit questions . . . Doctors will often just treat what I came in for. They won't ask if there are any other issues to talk about. I sometimes say I want my blood pressure checked but I'm not asked about anything else.

P: Sometimes [satisfied] but most of the times I leave the GP feeling unsatisfied.

I: What in particular were you unsatisfied about?

P: Limited, inadequate information . . . mainly because of the time limit and especially when you are Deaf you need more time to communicate. Most doctors do not like to spend lots of time with one patient. Sometimes I book the doctor for a double session to have more time with the doctor.

As already mentioned, many participants also experienced difficulties in requesting an interpreter due to limited Deafness awareness by healthcare staff. Such basic barriers are an impediment not only to general healthcare but also to more specialized healthcare needs, such as mental health given the role of the GP in diagnosis and referral (Fellinger, Holzinger, & Pollard, 2012). When asked whether they would approach their GP for general healthcare information, some of the participants felt this would not be appropriate:

The doctor would say "go away!"

If I actually had diabetes I would have to see a doctor but because I don't, I wouldn't ask them for information. You need to make an appointment, book the interpreter and so on. And yes they could give you information but you should get the information through the health line.

The Internet was also mentioned by the participants (n = 26) as a source of information, often a highly preferred one:

I always go to the Internet. If I think I have something then I do research thoroughly, overdoing it probably. If I felt that I have something then I go to the doctor. The doctor keeps telling me over [and over] again to stop researching on the Internet.

Often after a diagnosis from the doctor, I look [it] up on the Internet to see if the information matches then I accept it.

With the growth of health-related websites, many participants are clearly beginning to appreciate the value of information in English supplemented with video clips and graphics:

I prefer Auslan yes, but with the English text next to it. That way I can see what an English term means by looking at the Auslan. That means if the term comes up later, I'll know what it means. I think that's important. I think having pictures is also important. Examples. And maybe some Deaf people, sharing their experience. If people are courageous enough to do that. Maybe their faces could be covered, though that would create problems for facial expressions. Or if they were courageous enough . . . if I had a heart attack, I would share my experience. I would want to share my story so that others could learn from it.

It would be good if everything was in one [online] place, including visual information, to help Deaf people understand things better. It would be good too if a website had a human body with arrows pointing to the part of the body that is being talked about.

I wish there were video clips in sign language. A medical website with English you could read and Auslan clips. If it had information, I would go to it all the time. It would be good to have more information about how to live.

Many people also acknowledged the limitations associated with the Internet (e.g., their ability to understand the text, the difficulty posed by the many options, and the trustworthiness of the information). These interviewees shared their suggestions:

I always have a look at other organizations on the Internet to understand more. I always want to make sure they give the same information I've been given. It's not always completely clear. There are times that I look at the text and really don't understand it. So yes, more pictures and plain English.

P: It's easy to get confused with links all over the place.

I: So if there was one place that you could go to that had most of the information you wanted, that would be good?

P: That would be perfect!

I look on the Internet for the best way to look after myself. I know one problem is the amount of information available on the Internet. Pages and pages of words . . . it is not great for Deaf access. It really needs to be improved.

Where video clips are included [on a website], they often don't have captions, which is really frustrating.

Moreover, not everyone has acquired the Internet skills or sufficient English literacy required to adequately utilize these resources:

> I would go to [the State Deaf Society] first because I couldn't research which organization/service to go to. I didn't have the skills to do that. Sometimes they would say go and see the website. I couldn't access it . . . There are graphics so I couldn't access it. It needs to be in plain text. I am not the only one. Blind people have the same issues.

Although mentioned by many participants, print media (including books, magazines, and brochures) were generally not favored due to their limited English literacy:

> Even if I read about something, I would still not fully understand it.

> There are some brochures that are fantastic, for example, there's one about breast cancer for aboriginal women—it is very visual with diagrams and pictures. There was another one about grief . . . it had a more profound impact on me because it was visual.

> I do pick up brochures at the GP or the hospital. It can take me a while to fully understand them. I have to read them several times usually, to fully understand them. That's why I think we need something specific for Deaf people. Carefully worded, not quite so difficult. Plain English, with pictures.

> It would depend on what was on the front and how complex the information looked. And what it was for example, skin cancer, prevention . . . pictures of what to look for so I know what it looks like.

Not surprisingly, face-to-face communication with friends, family, or service providers who can sign, particularly the opportunity to interact with those persons directly, was most participants' general preference:

> I: Would you talk with hearing friends about health issues?

> P: Not really. Maybe something brief. I'd be able to communicate in more depth with Deaf friends. Communication with Deaf people is more open.

> I find it hard communicating with hearing people. Everything is brief. So how would someone explain things to you? With Deaf people it's more complete. So, I'd ask Deaf people basically.

Before about ten years ago, the Deaf Society organized a yoga class with interpreters. It was good and I liked it . . . going through interpreters is okay but I'd rather have a Deaf person leading the group and getting information directly from that person; being able to respond directly to them, not through an interpreter. I don't feel I am getting exactly the same information through an interpreter.

Few participants were aware of or could give examples of any other health-related services available to them:

I would like more information but I don't know where I would go. I want to know what will happen with diabetes when I get older. So I do need information but where? . . . I've never gone to any [organization]. I just go straight to my doctor.

I suppose it would depend on the type of information. If it was sexual health, for example, I know I can go to [name of center]. If it was blood, I could go to the Red Cross. So I know of them, but I've never had to use them as I've gone to my doctor.

No, I hadn't thought about [other organizations]. I hadn't thought about how to access other organizations. I just assumed I had to be referred by my GP. I just assumed you couldn't access other services directly, even though I would prefer that.

Similarly, very few participants commented on mass media campaigns such as posters on public transport. Where participants were aware of other service providers, they often commented on actual or perceived barriers to access:

[We] went to a pregnancy center to try and get support about the decision whether to keep the baby or not, to understand how it all works and so on. But there were no interpreters provided so it was very difficult as we had to communicate with pen and paper. They were nice people and they tried to help but the quality of access was not satisfactory.

I've been trying to access yoga classes but I am finding that they are not aware of interpreters and the need to provide access. They asked me to pay for the interpreter. So I am trying another provider . . . a private college. Again, they asked me to pay for the interpreters. There are so many access issues for Deaf people trying to look after themselves. It is not easy.

I: If you had depression, would you go to Beyond Blue, for example, to get information?

P: Yes I would but it is not Deaf friendly . . . There is nothing for Deaf people. They do not meet the needs of Deaf people so I am not interested . . . I wrote about my experience in the health system through a [Deaf] organization and they said I was the first [Deaf person] to share my experience. So it shows that the stories on their website are from hearing people.

I: So you could relate to a story if it was written by a Deaf person?

P: Yes. So that you don't feel alone. One of the main symptoms of depression is that you feel alone . . . I feel that my experience is a bit different from [that of hearing] people. I would feel better talking to someone who is also Deaf.

This raises serious questions about the extent to which mainstream services have attempted to raise awareness of their services within the Deaf community. The concerns raised in relation to the cost of Auslan interpreting would also be pertinent in this context.

Workshops were mentioned by several participants as a valued source of information. This clearly demonstrates not only the strong preference for information in Auslan but also the importance of sharing information within the community and the opportunity to interact:

There are already workshops for hearing people, but I would rather a Deaf-specific workshop because I believe mental health issues are a bit different.

I would prefer things to be signed, or for a workshop to go to because I would learn more . . . [The workshop] was valuable because there was a speaker and an interpreter so people could ask questions. And some of the questions asked were things I would never have thought to ask. So I gathered a lot of information from the Deaf people there as well as the presenter.

Workshops for parents, from the beginning, are important. So they know what to expect . . . I think it's not only the mother but also the father who needs information [about parenting]. The doctor and my mother would explain things to me but my partner would only get things in summary. He missed a lot, and I think he needed information as well.

LIMITATIONS OF THE STUDY

Before detailing our conclusions, we would like to mention some noteworthy limitations of the research design:

- Through our existing networks we recruited the participants in their home states. In most cases we prioritized those who were known to have experienced a medical condition themselves or have been responsible for providing immediate care to a family member and might therefore have experienced difficulties in doing so. This methodological approach may have limited the number of potential participants.
- We believe that approaching participants directly was generally effective; however, we did not interview all of the contacts due to difficulties in finding a convenient time.
- A few participants reported that they did not want to be interviewed on film despite assurances that the data would be viewed only by the research team. This feedback was particularly noticeable in South Australia and in the Australian Capital Territory. Using video analysis is recognized as a challenge in conducting qualitative research (Luff & Heath, 2012).
- Some of the potential participants believed they had already been involved in the study. This issue highlights the view that the Deaf community is to some extent an overresearched group in Australia, given the small size of the population and the numerous studies that ask members of the community to give their time.
- Our recommendations are based on in-depth qualitative interviews; thus, the healthcare information access situation for Deaf people as reported here may not be representative of all Deaf Auslan users throughout Australia.

CONCLUSIONS AND SUGGESTIONS FOR FURTHER RESEARCH

In conclusion, we have shown that the Deaf Auslan users who participated in this study experience significant barriers in accessing preventive and ongoing healthcare information, supporting the general findings of Steinberg, Barnett, Meador, Wiggins, & Zazove (2006) in the

United States and other countries as reported in this volume. In revisiting the research questions, we can state the following:

1. Deaf people access preventive and ongoing healthcare information through a variety of means, in English and Auslan, and rely heavily on their GPs, television, family, and friends in order to do so.

2. Deaf Auslan users' experiences in accessing information about their health are generally problematic in that they often feel they have insufficient information, find it difficult to obtain, or do not fully understand it.

3. In discussing their healthcare information access, Deaf people perceive that they are at a disadvantage compared to the general Australian population and that they need more Deaf-specific *(direct)* services, more support through the provision of *interpreter-mediated* services, and more access to sources of information in their preferred language, Auslan *(translated)*.

4. In relation to health issues generally, it was apparent from the interviews that many Deaf Australians have limited awareness of the national priorities as outlined by the Australian government, why they are priorities, and what they need to do in preventive terms to ensure the maintenance of their own health.

In sum, we find that access barriers can be attributed to four central issues: limited confidence in English literacy, inadequate provision of healthcare interpreting services, inaccessible healthcare services, and inaccessible electronic resources. Thus, in effect, Deaf Auslan users require more access to direct, interpreter-mediated and translated preventive and ongoing healthcare information.[7]

Suggestions for Further Research

- The participatory research methodology used in this study is known to also be effective when working with Aboriginal communities in the assessment of health (e.g., Dickson & Green, 2001). Thus we suggest that this study be replicated with a focus on indigenous deaf Australians, as it was apparent from the few indigenous participants in this study that their healthcare access issues may be even more complicated.

- Consideration could also be given to replicating this study with other subgroups in the Deaf community according to age, sexuality, mental health issues, and so on, in order to acquire an even clearer picture of their healthcare information access needs.
- Studies of authentic interpreter-mediated healthcare interactions between Deaf Auslan users and healthcare providers could provide further insight into how Deaf people access healthcare information and where the true information barriers lie.
- A tracking study of a few Deaf people with different healthcare needs could be conducted over a period of 2 to 3 years in order to ascertain their exact information needs and access barriers. This methodology would replicate existing tracking studies of healthcare communication between English speakers (e.g., Dew et al., 2008) and would add to the limited literature on Deaf healthcare communication.

ACKNOWLEDGMENTS

This study would not have been possible without funding from the National Auslan Interpreter Booking & Payments Service (NABS) and support from various Deaf societies throughout Australia who allowed us to use their venues to conduct interviews. In particular we would like to thank the 72 Deaf Auslan users who participated in the interviews for their willingness to share their stories.

NOTES

1. At present, a wealth of preventive healthcare information is translated into various languages by organizations such as the NSW Multicultural Health Communication Service. Virtually none of this information has been translated into Auslan, however.
2. This study was commissioned by NABS in 2011 with a view to informing its plans for providing access to health care.
3. Final ethics approval was received on September 30, 2011 (ref. no. 5201100732).
4. ACT: Australian Capital Territory (Canberra); NSW: New South Wales (Sydney): QLD: Queensland (Brisbane): SA: South Australia (Adelaide); TAS: Tasmania (Hobart); VIC: Victoria (Melbourne); WA: Western Australian (Perth).

5. Legend: P = participant, I = interviewer.
6. For example, the Royal Australasian College for General Practitioners has guidelines for healthcare professionals on best practices for consulting with Deaf signed language users.
7. Twenty-seven recommendations were provided in the final report to NABS, and an Auslan version of the executive summary can be viewed at http://www .youtube.com/watch?v = LqjOnsOzxoA, http://www.youtube.com/watch?v = Ab9nutAHgBw, and http://www.youtube.com/watch?v = a1JKOiqAICc (retrieved February 12, 2014).

REFERENCES

Alexander, A., Ladd, P., & Powell, S. (2012). Deafness might damage your health. *Lancet, 379,* 979–981.

Allotey, P. A., & Reidpath, D. D. (1999). Multicultural issues in general practice. *Current Therapeutics, 40*(12), 35–37.

Australian Institute of Health and Welfare. (2011). *National Health Priority Areas.* Retrieved January 19, 2011, from http://www.aihw.gov.au/health-priority -areas/

Australian National Preventive Health Agency. (2011). Retrieved January 19, 2011, from http://www.anpha.gov.au/internet/anpha/publishing.nsf/Content/ faqs

Barnett, S., & Franks, P. (2002). Healthcare utilization and adults who are deaf: Relationship with age at onset of deafness. *Health Services Research, 37*(1), 103–118.

Barnett, S., McKee, M., Smith, S. R., & Pearson, T. A. (2011). Deaf sign language users, health inequities, and public health: Opportunity for social justice. *Preventing Chronic Disease, 8*(2). Retrieved from http://www.cdc.gov/ pcd/issues/2011/mar/10_0065.htm

Bostock, S., & Steptoe, A. (2012). Association between low functional health literacy and mortality in older adults: Longitudinal cohort study. *British Medical Journal, Open Access,* doi: 10.1136/bmj.e1602.

Bramwell, R., Harrington, F., & Harris, J. (2002). Deaf women: Informed choice, policy, and legislation. In F. Harrington and G. H. Turner (Eds.), *Interpreting: Studies and reflections on sign language interpreting* (pp. 103–110). Gloucestershire: McLean.

Braun, V., & Clarke, V. (2006). Using thematic analysis in psychology. *Qualitative Research in Psychology, 3,* 77–101.

Briffa, D. (1999). Deaf and mentally ill: Are their needs being met? *Australasian Psychiatry, 7*(1), 7–10.

Cerny, M. (2008). Some observations on the use of medical terminology in doctor-patient communication. *SKASE Journal of Translation and Interpretation, 3*(1), 39–53.

Christopher, S., Watts, V., McCormick, A., & Young, S. (2008). Building and maintaining trust in a community-based participatory research partnership. *American Journal of Public Health, 98,* 1398–1406.

Cohen, S., Moran-Ellis, J., & Smaje, C. (1999). Children as informal interpreters in GP consultations: Pragmatics and ideology. *Sociology of Health and Illness, 21*(2), 163–186.

Cornes, A., Rohan, M. J., Napier, J., & Rey, J. M. (2006). Reading the signs: Impact of signed versus written questionnaires on the prevalence of psychopathology among Deaf adolescents. *Australian and New Zealand Journal of Psychiatry, 40*(8), 665–673.

Cornwall, A., & Jewkes, R. (1995). What is participatory research? *Social Science and Medicine, 41*(12), 1667–1676.

Daly, J., Kellehear, A., & Gliksman, M. (1997). *The public health researcher: A methodological approach.* Melbourne: Oxford University Press.

Deafax. (2012). *Research findings on how accessible sexual health services and sex education is for Deaf people in the UK.* Retrieved February 9, 2014, from http://www.deafax.org/uploads/linkfiles/Deafax%20E.A.R.S%20Campaigns%20Findings.pdf

Denman, L. (2007). Enhancing the accessibility of public mental health services in Queensland to meet the needs of deaf people from an Indigenous Australian or culturally and linguistically diverse background. *Australasian Psychiatry, 15,* 85–89.

Dew, K., Plumridge, E., Stubbe, M., Dowell, T., Macdonald, L., & Major, G. (2008). "You just got to eat healthy": The topic of CAM in the general practice consultation. *Health Sociology Review, 17,* 396–409.

Dickson, G., & Green, K. L. (2001). Participatory action research: Lessons learned with Aboriginal grandmothers. *Healthcare for Women International, 22*(5), 471–482.

Earis, H., & Reynolds, S. (2009). *Deaf and hard-of-hearing people's access to primary healthcare services in North East Essex: A report for North East Essex Primary Care Trust.* Unpublished research report. London: Deafness, Cognition, and Language Research Centre, University College London/Royal Association for Deaf People. Retrieved March 2, 2012, from http://www.bsluptake.org.uk/info/?p = 560

Feinauer, I., & Lesch, H. M. (2011). Health workers: Idealistic expectations versus interpreters' competence. *Perspectives: Studies in Translatology,* 1–16. Retrieved July 24, 2012, from doi:10.1080/0907676X.2011.634013.

Fellinger, J., Holzinger, D., Dobner, U., Gerich, J., Lehner, R., Lenz, G., & Goldberg, D. (2005a). An innovative and reliable way of measuring health-related quality of life and mental distress in the Deaf community. *Social Psychiatry and Psychiatric Epidemiology, 40,* 245–250.

Fellinger, J., Holzinger, D., Dobner, U., Gerich, J., Lehner, R., Lenz, G., & Goldberg, D. (2005b). Mental distress and quality of life in a Deaf population. *Social Psychiatry and Psychiatric Epidemiology, 40,* 737–742.

Fellinger, J., Holzinger, D., & Pollard, R. (2012). Mental health of Deaf people. *Lancet, 379,* 1037–1044.

Fellinger, J., Holzinger D., Sattel, H., Laught, M., & Goldberg, D. (2008). Correlates of mental health disorders among children with hearing impairments. *Developmental Medicine and Child Neurology, 51,* 635–641.

Ferguson, W. J., & Candib, L. M. (2002). Culture, language, and the doctor-patient relationship. *Family Medicine, 34*(5), 353–361.

Folkins, A., Robins Sadler, G., Ko, C., Branz, P., Marsh, S., & Bovee, M. (2005). Improving the Deaf community's access to prostate and testicular cancer information: A survey study. *BioMed Central, Public Health, 5,* 63, doi:10.1186/1471-2458-5-63. Retrieved March 2, 2012, from http://www.biomedcentral.com/1471-2458/5/63

Frank, R. A. (2000). Medical communication: Non-native English-speaking patients and native English-speaking professionals. *English for Specific Purposes, 19,* 31–62.

Furlonger, B., & Rickards, R. (2011). Understanding the diverse literacy needs of profoundly Deaf sign-dominant adults in Australia. *Reading Psychology, 32*(5), 459–494.

Glaser, B., & Strauss, A. (1977). *The discovery of grounded theory: Strategies for qualitative research.* Chicago: Aldine.

Hadlow, J., and Pitts, M. (1991). The understanding of common health terms by doctors, nurses, and patients. *Social Science and Medicine, 32*(2): 193–196.

Harmer, L. (1999). Healthcare delivery and deaf people: Practice, problems, and recommendations for change. *Journal of Deaf Studies and Deaf Education, 4*(2), 73–110.

Harris, M. (2008). The role of primary healthcare in preventing the onset of chronic disease, with a particular focus on the lifestyle risk factors of obesity, tobacco, and alcohol. Commissioned paper for National Preventative [*sic*] Health Taskforce, Centre for Primary Healthcare and Equity, UNSW, January. Unpublished research report.

Harris, R., Holmes, H., & Mertens, D. (2009). Research ethics in sign language communities. *Sign Language Studies, 9*(2), 104–131.

Hedding, T., & Kaufman, G. (2012). Health literacy and deafness: Implications for interpreter education. In L. Swabey & K. Malcolm (Eds.), *In our hands: Educating healthcare interpreters* (pp. 164–189). Washington, DC: Gallaudet University Press.

Howard, B. (2012). Telehealth trial declared a success. ITPro. *Age.* Retrieved July 25, 2012, from http://www.theage.com.au/it-pro/government-it/telehealth-trial-declared-a-success-20120724-22lu6.html

Howard, D. (2007). Intercultural communications and conductive hearing loss. *First Peoples Child and Family Review, 3*(4), 96–105.

Howard, D. (2009). *Submission to the Senate Committee Inquiry into Hearing Health in Australia, October 2009.* Retrieved April 1, 2012, from http://www.healthinfonet.ecu.edu.au/key-resources/bibliography/?lid = 18394

Iezzoni, L. I., O'Day, B. L., Killeen, M., & Harker, H. (2004). Communicating about health care: Observations from persons who are deaf or hard of hearing. *Annals of Internal Medicine, 140*(5), 356–362.

Jin, E., & Daly, B. (2010). The self-reported oral health status and behaviours of adults who are deaf and blind. *Special Care Dentistry, 30*(1), 8–13.

Johnston, T. (2003). W(h)ither the Deaf community? Population, genetics, and the future of Auslan (Australian Sign Language). *American Annals of the Deaf, 148*(5), 358–375.

Johnston, T., & Napier, J. (2010). Medical Signbank: Bringing deaf people and linguists together in the process of language development. *Sign Language Studies, 10*(2), 258–275.

Johnston, T., & Schembri, A. (2005). The use of ELAN annotation software in the Auslan Archive/Corpus Project. Paper presented at the Ethnographic Research Annotation Conference, University of Melbourne, Melbourne, Australia.

Jones, E. G., Renger, R., & Firestone, R. (2005). Deaf community analysis for health education priorities. *Public Health Nursing, 22*(1), 27–35.

Jordan, J. E., Briggs, A. M., Brand, C. A., & Osborne, R. H. (2008). Enhancing patient engagement in chronic disease self-management support initiatives in Australia: The need for an integrated approach. *Medical Journal of Australia, 189*(10), 9–13.

Jorm, A., Kitchener, B., MacTaggart Lamb, A., & Brand, S. (2007). *The evaluation of mental health first aid in a rural area: Determining its effectiveness in improving mental health literacy, attitudes, and behaviour towards people with mental health problems.* Sydney: NSW Department of Health.

Kaskowitz, S. R., Nakaji, M. C., Clark, K. L., Gunsauls, D. C., & Sadler, G. R. (2006). Bringing prostate cancer education to deaf men. *Cancer Detection and Prevention, 30,* 439–448.

Kitto, S. C., Chesters, J., & Grbich, C. (2008). Quality in qualitative research. *Medical Journal of Australia, 188,* 243–246.

Luff, P., & Heath, C. (2012). Some "technical challenges" of video analysis: Social actions, objects, material realities, and the problems of perspective. *Qualitative Research 12*(3): 255–279.

MacFarlane, A., Dzebisova, Z., Karapish, D., Kovacevic, B., Ogbebor, F., & Okonkwo, E. (2009). Arranging and negotiating the use of informal interpreters in general practice consultations: Experiences of refugees and asylum seekers in the west of Ireland. *Social Science and Medicine, 69*, 210–214.

MacKinney, T. G., Walters, D., Bird, G. L., & Nattinger, A. B. (1995). Improvements in preventive care and communication for Deaf patients: Results of a novel primary healthcare program. *Journal of General Internal Medicine, 10*, 133–137.

Major, G., Napier, J., Ferrara, L., & Johnston, T. (2012). Exploring lexical gaps in Australian Sign Language for the purposes of health communication. *Communication and Medicine, 9*(1), 37–47.

Major, G., Napier, J., & Stubbe, M. (2012). "What happens truly, not text book!": Using authentic interactions in discourse training for healthcare interpreters. In K. Malcolm & L. Swabey (Eds.), *In our hands: Educating healthcare interpreters* (pp. 27–53). Washington, DC: Gallaudet University Press.

Margellos-Anast, H., Estarziau, M., & Kaufman, G. (2006). Cardiovascular disease knowledge among culturally Deaf patients in Chicago. *Preventive Medicine, 42*, 235–239.

Middleton, A. (2010). General themes to consider when working with deaf and hard of hearing clients. In A. Middleton (Ed.), *Working with deaf people: A handbook for healthcare professionals* (pp. 29–83). Cambridge: Cambridge University Press.

Middleton, A., Turner, G. H., Bitner-Glindzicz, M., Lewis, P., Richards, M., Clarke, A., & Stephens, D. (2010). Preferences for communication in clinic from Deaf people: A cross-sectional study. *Journal of Evaluation in Clinical Practice 14*(4), 811–817.

Minkler, M., & Wallerstein, N. (Eds.). (2011). *Community-based participatory research for health: From process to outcomes* (2nd ed.). San Francisco: Jossey-Bass.

Napier, J., Major, G., & Ferrara, L. (2011). Medical Signbank: A cure-all for the aches and pains of medical sign language interpreting? In L. Leeson, S. Wurm, & M. Vermeerbergen (Eds.), *Signed language interpreting: Preparation, practice, and performance* (pp. 110–137). Manchester: St. Jerome.

O'Hearn, A. (2006). Deaf women's experiences and satisfaction with prenatal care: A comparative study. *Family Medicine, 38*(10), 712–716.

Orsi, J. M., Margellos-Anast, H., Perlman, T. S., Giloth, B. E., & Whitman, S. (2007). Cancer screening knowledge, attitudes, and behaviors among culturally Deaf adults: Implications for informed decision making. *Cancer Detection and Prevention, 31*, 474–479.

Patton, M. Q. (2002). *Qualitative research and evaluation methods*. London: Sage.

Pollard, R. Q. (1992). Cross-cultural ethics in the conduct of deafness research. *Rehabilitation Psychology, 37*(2), 87–101.

Pollard, R. Q. (1998). Psychopathology. In M. Marschark & D. Clark (Eds.), *Psychological perspectives on deafness* (Vol. 2, pp. 171–197). Mahwah, NJ: Erlbaum.

Pollard, R. Q., & Barnett, S. (2009). Health-related vocabulary knowledge among Deaf adults. *Rehabilitation Psychology, 54*(2), 182–185.

Pollard, R. Q., Dean, R. K., O'Hearn, A. M., & Haynes, S. L. (2009). Adapting health education material for Deaf audiences. *Rehabilitation Psychology, 54*(2), 232–238.

Quintana, Y., Feightner, J. W., Wathen, C. N., Sangster, L. M., & Marshall, J. N. (2001). Preventive health information on the Internet: Qualitative study of consumers' perspectives. *Canadian Family Physician, 47,* 1759–1765.

Remine, M. D., & Brown, P. M. (2010). Comparison of the prevalence of mental health problems in Deaf and hearing children and adolescents in Australia. *Royal Australian and New Zealand College of Psychiatrists,* 351–357. Retrieved on February 22, 2012, from informahealthcare.com

Rivadeneyra, R., Elderkin-Thompson, V., Silver, R. C., & Waitzkin, H. (2000). Patient centeredness in medical encounters requiring an interpreter. *American Journal of Medicine, 108,* 470–474.

Roberts, B., & Mulgavin, J. (2007). *Alcohol and other drug use in the Australian Deaf community: A needs assessment.* Unpublished research report. Fitzroy, Victoria: Turning Point Alcohol and Drug Centre.

Robertson, L. M., Douglas, F., Ludbrook, A., Reid. G., & van Teijlingen, E. (2008). What works with men? A systematic review of health-promoting interventions targeting men. *BMC Health Services Research, 8*(141), doi:10.1186/1472-6963-8-141. Retrieved March 12, 2012, from http://www.biomedcentral.com/1472-6963/8/141

Royal Children's Hospital Melbourne. (2012). *Telehealth Video-consultation with the Royal Children's Hospital.* Retrieved July 25, 2012, from http://www.rch.org.au/kidsconnect/services.cfm?doc_id = 15364

Royal National Institute for Deaf People (RNID). (2004). *A simple cure: A national report into Deaf and hard of hearing people's experiences of the National Health Service.* Retrieved February 5, 2012, from www.bsmhd.org.uk/simpcure.htm

Shabaik, S., LaHousse, S. F., Branz, P., Gandhi, V., Khan, A. M., & Sadler, G. R. (2010). Colorectal cancer video for the Deaf community: A randomized control trial. *Journal of Cancer Education 25,* 518–523.

Sheppard, K., & Badger, T. (2010). The lived experience of depression among culturally Deaf adults. *Journal of Psychiatric and Mental Nursing, 17,* 783–789.

Silverman, D. (2006). *Interpreting qualitative data: Methods for analysing talk, text and interaction* (3rd ed.). London: Sage.

Singleton, J., Jones, G., & Hanumantha, S. (2012). Deaf friendly research? Toward ethical practice in research involving Deaf participants. *Deaf Studies Digital Journal, 3*(Spring). http://dsdj.gallaudet.edu

Skelton, J. R. (2005). Everything you were afraid to ask about communication skills. *British Journal of General Practice, 55*(510), 40–46.

Smeijers, A., & Pfau, R. (2009) On the communication between general practitioners and their deaf patients. *The Sign Language Translator and Interpreter 3*, 1–14.

Steinberg, A., Barnett, S., Meador, H. E., Wiggins, E. A., & Zazove, P. (2006). Healthcare system accessibility experiences and perceptions of Deaf people. *Journal of General Internal Medicine, 21*, 260–266.

Stone, C., & West, D. (2012). Translation, representation and the Deaf "voice." *Qualitative Research, 12*, 1–21.

Tamaskar, P., Malia, T., Stern, C., Gorenflo, D., Meador, H., & Zazove, P. (2009). Preventive attitudes and beliefs of Deaf and hard-of-hearing individuals. *Arch Family Medicine, 9*, 518–525. Retrieved September 25, 2011, from www.archfammed.com

Thompson, C. L., & Pledger, L. M. (1993) Doctor-patient communication: Is patient knowledge of medical terminology improving? *Health Communication, 5*(2), 89–97.

Turner, O., Windfuhr, K., & Kapur, N. (2007). Suicide in Deaf populations: A literature review. *Annals of General Psychiatry, 6*(26), doi:10.1186/1744-859X-6-26.

Ubido, J., Huntington, J., & Warburton, D. (2002). Inequalities in access to healthcare faced by women who are Deaf. *Health and Social Care in the Community, 10*(4), 247–253.

Wollin, J., & Elder, R. (2003). Mammograms and pap smears for Australian Deaf women. *Cancer Nursing, 26*(5), 405–409.

Woodcock, K., & Pole, J. D. (2007). Health profile of deaf Canadians: Analysis of the Canada Community Health Survey. *Canadian Family Physician, 53*, 2140–2141.

Zazove, P., Meador, H. M., Reed, B. D., Sen, A., & Gorenflo, D. W. (2008). Cancer prevention knowledge of people with profound hearing loss. *Journal of General Internal Medicine, 24*(3), 320–326.

Scientific-Based Translation of Standardized Questionnaires into Sign Language of the Netherlands

Anika S. Smeijers, Beppie van den Bogaerde,
Martina Ens-Dokkum, and Anne Marie Oudesluys-Murphy

ABSTRACT

Specialized psychological and psychiatric health care for deaf and hard of hearing clients has emerged during the last 50 years. It has long been known that deaf and hard of hearing clients are often misdiagnosed with psychiatric disorders, but little scientific attention has been paid to the tests used with this group. Although these clients may have poor spoken-language skills and a different (cultural) background from mainstream clients, regular diagnostic tests are used even in specialized settings.

To enable the use of standardized questionnaires without language barriers, we have developed a guideline for adapting internationally validated questionnaires and translating them into sign language. We used this guideline to adapt and translate four questionnaires into Sign Language of the Netherlands (Nederlandse Gebarentaal, NGT). In this chapter we introduce our guideline and describe the selection and translation process of research instruments for use with deaf and hard of hearing individuals. The problems, dilemmas, and ethical issues encountered are discussed.

One in a thousand people worldwide is born deaf or severely hard of hearing (Kennedy & McCann, 2004), and this number increases with age. These children face many challenges in acquiring the spoken and written language of their environment. Many of them have great difficulty in achieving a literacy level comparable to that of their peers (Musselman, 2005). One of the reasons for a prevalence of low literacy among deaf people is that many Western languages have an alphabetical writing system (consisting of letters or graphemes) that is based on phonemes. Phonemes are the sounds (e.g., vowels, consonants) of a language that change the meaning of words (e.g., *hat* versus *bat* [h/b distinction] versus *hit* [a/i distinction]). When you cannot hear these phonemes, you have to memorize—for all words—which letters/graphemes represent them (e.g., what combination of characters and in which order they are used for a certain concept). An English example would be the verb "know," of which the visual image on the mouth resembles the pronunciation of the word "no"; these two written forms of the sound [no] thus need to be explicitly learned. Deaf people also cannot automatically use vocalizations when reading. This means that deaf people are able to read fluently only those words that they have read before and whose written graphemic construction they have memorized.

For many deaf and hard of hearing individuals a sign language is their natural language because they have full access to it. In the Netherlands, Sign Language of the Netherlands (Nederlandse Gebarentaal, NGT) is used. In contrast to certain other sign languages like American Sign Language and Flemish Sign Language, NGT up to now has not been recognized by the Dutch government as an official language of the Netherlands.

Over the past 25 years there have been discussions about whether deaf people have more in common with each other than just their medical condition (*in casu* their hearing status) plus the fact that many of them are sign language users. Researchers from Great Britain (Ladd, 2003) and the United States (Padden & Humphries, 1988, 2005) have convincingly defended the existence of a Deaf culture. These studies show that the Deaf communities constitute social and linguistic minorities within many Western hearing cultures. Such a Deaf cultural minority is characterized by shared experiences, values, traditions, behavioral rules, and, most important, the use of a sign language as the main mode of communication. Having a cultural identity different from that of the majority in society may have a negative effect on communication and healthcare provision (Van Wieringen, Harmsen, & Bruijnzeels, 2002). To distinguish between the audiological concept of deaf and the cultural Deaf, a capital letter is used for the latter. The designation "Deaf" is used here to include people who see themselves as culturally Deaf and as belonging to a linguistic minority group. The designations "deaf" and "hard of hearing" are used here for people who developed a hearing loss, including Deaf, deaf, and hard of hearing.

In the Netherlands, as in many other Western countries, there are limited facilities for Deaf people to ensure their full participation in the wider society. For instance, sign language support by interpreters is restricted, and medical information in NGT is scarce. In contrast to the United States, we in the Netherlands do not have a disability act. An international UN convention handles the rights of people with a disability, but the Dutch government has not yet ratified this convention. These aspects, together with lack of access to the spoken language (e.g., no incidental learning), explain why deaf and hard of hearing individuals often have less general and medical knowledge than hearing people (Barnett, 1999; Jones, Renger, & Firestone, 2005; Vernon & Andrews, 1990).

MENTAL HEALTH CARE

Little information is available on the impact of cultural and linguistic barriers on the medical care offered to and received by deaf and hard of hearing individuals (Smeijers & Pfau, 2009; Van Wieringen et al., 2002). The incidence of psychological problems is higher among these individuals than among the hearing population (Fellinger et al., 2005b, 2007). This is partially explained by the fact that people with severe hearing impairment often face social barriers due to communication problems. Another explanation is that this might be a result of the two to three times greater prevalence of sexual abuse (possibly due to communication barriers and poorer social skills) in this group than in the hearing population (Hoem Kvam, 2004).

The incidence of psychiatric disorders in deaf and hard of hearing individuals is an important subject of discussion in the medical literature. In the 1950s deaf and hard of hearing individuals in the United States were relatively overrepresented in psychiatric clinics (Pollard, 1994; Stein, Mindel, & Jabaley, 1981). These findings ultimately led to the development of specialized mental health care for deaf and hard of hearing patients. Within these specialized settings extra attention is given to the patients' cultural background and language skills. After the transfer of patients to these specialized facilities, it became evident that many of them had no psychiatric disorder. Some had a mild cognitive impairment, and some had a severe language impairment caused either by weak language skills, first-language deprivation, or a primary language disorder. Although nonspecialized clinics still report a higher incidence of psychiatric disorders within the deaf and hard of hearing population, no evidence for this has been found in specialized settings (Pollard, 1994). Since the emergence of specialized healthcare facilities for deaf and hard of hearing individuals is only recent, the number of research instruments especially developed for or adapted to deaf and hard of hearing individuals is still low.

Psychological Tests

Psychological testing of deaf and hard of hearing sign language users is usually done via written questionnaires. However, as explained earlier, using the written language of the hearing minority may be problematic in this population because its members have an inadequate mastery of the local spoken/written language (Musselman, 2005). More often than not these questionnaires are translated ad hoc by sign language interpreters because very few test instruments are available in sign languages (Munro & Rodwell, 2009). If an interpreter interprets a written questionnaire ad hoc into sign language, the interpreter may make non-standardized linguistic and cultural adaptations. Such adaptations can of course influence the replies to the questionnaire and thus the general outcomes. In most situations the interpreter will also interact with the deaf or hard of hearing test participant who is filling out the questionnaire. A common pitfall is that the results of questionnaires that were administered by ad hoc interpreters are analyzed as if they are standardized questionnaires, while the questionnaire was actually converted into a sort of interview.

Research on ethnic minority groups has demonstrated that the mental and physical well-being of the group members is influenced by their cultural identity (Guillemin, Bombardier, & Beaton, 1993). Therefore, health-related quality of life (HRQoL) questionnaires can be used for people whose linguistic and cultural identity are different from that of the original target group only *after* an accurate process of translation and cultural adaptation (Guillemin et al., 1993; Hocker, 2010). Furthermore, online surveys that use a recorded sign language translation of a written questionnaire are more suited to reach deaf persons (Graybill et al., 2010; Hocker, 2010). However, as far as we know, only one adapted and translated HRQoL questionnaire for deaf people exists, and this instrument is in use in Austria (Fellinger et al., 2005a). A limited guideline is available for translating questionnaires into sign language (Crowe Mason, 2005).

However, we could find no comprehensive guidelines that cover the whole process of translating and adapting the questionnaires for use by deaf and hard of hearing respondents. When we planned to conduct an epidemiological study on the health and healthcare needs of deaf and hard of hearing individuals in the Netherlands, we became aware of the enormous problems posed by the lack of suitable instruments for this group. To help solve these difficulties we developed guidelines that we adapted during the process of translating four questionnaires into NGT for our research project.

METHODOLOGY

Procedures

Founded on current guidelines for translating and adapting HRQoL questionnaires for spoken languages (Hocker, 2010; Pollard, 1994; Ravens-Sieberer et al., 2005; KIDSCREEN Group Europe, 2006) and referring to our own trials and experiences, we have developed guidelines for translating international written questionnaires into a sign language (figure 1). A group of Deaf NGT communication experts, a physician/ NGT linguist, a second NGT linguist, NGT interpreters, and a master's student in Deaf studies translated the selected questionnaires into two different variants of NGT. After backward translations (i.e., from NGT into written Dutch), consultation between experts, and reviews by deaf and hard of hearing test participants, the signed questionnaires were adapted to the cultural and linguistic needs of deaf and hard of hearing individuals.

Besides the two NGT versions, a sign-supported version (spoken Dutch with simultaneously produced NGT signs) and a written Dutch version were also provided. All of the questionnaires were placed in a secure online environment. We used Unipark software, which allowed us to create our own layout and has a direct link to a database (Hocker, 2010; www.unipark.de). The guidelines are presented in appendix 1, while their development is discussed in this chapter.

Instruments

One of our first challenges was to select test instruments that were suited for translation into NGT and that were reliable also when used by

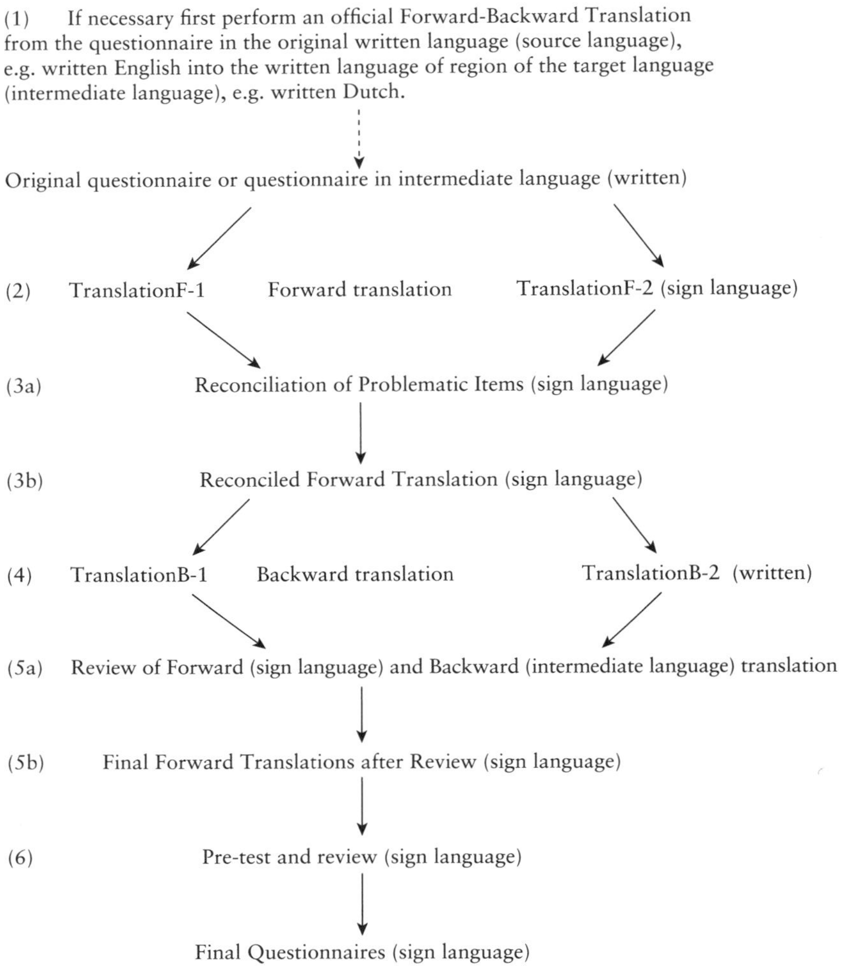

(1)   If necessary first perform an official Forward-Backward Translation from the questionnaire in the original written language (source language), e.g. written English into the written language of region of the target language (intermediate language), e.g. written Dutch.

Original questionnaire or questionnaire in intermediate language (written)

(2)   TranslationF-1   Forward translation   TranslationF-2 (sign language)

(3a)   Reconciliation of Problematic Items (sign language)

(3b)   Reconciled Forward Translation (sign language)

(4)   TranslationB-1   Backward translation   TranslationB-2 (written)

(5a)   Review of Forward (sign language) and Backward (intermediate language) translation

(5b)   Final Forward Translations after Review (sign language)

(6)   Pre-test and review (sign language)

                    Final Questionnaires (sign language)

FIGURE 1. *Guidelines for translating questionnaires into a sign language.*

people who have weak language skills and minority cultural backgrounds. The selected questionnaires for this study are as follows:

- World Health Organization Quality of Life-BREF (WHOQoL-BREF): This is an internationally standardized questionnaire that has been translated and validated in more than a dozen languages and has been widely field-tested, which makes the instrument methodologically strong (WHOQoL Group, 1998). Numerous questionnaires have been designed to measure all sorts of aspects of quality of life. Quality of life questionnaires that explicitly evaluate participants' physical health are less common. We chose the WHOQoL-BREF because it was the only short questionnaire that met both our content demands and our methodological demands.

– General Health Questionnaire (GHQ): This is a screening instrument to identify minor psychiatric disorders. It can be used in the general population or with clients in nonpsychiatric clinical or primary care settings. We have used the GHQ-12, the shortest version, especially designed for research studies (Goldberg & Williams, 1988). One of its strong points is that it is a short, reliable questionnaire.

– KIDSCREEN: This is a generic quality of life instrument that has been designed and normed for (hearing) children and adolescents between the ages of 8 and 18 years. KIDSCREEN can be used as a screening, monitoring, and evaluation tool in health surveys (Ravens-Sieberer et al., 2005; KIDSCREEN Group Europe, 2006). It covers ten health-related quality of life dimensions, whereas many QoL questionnaires for children cover only psychological and schooling domains. It is an internationally standardized questionnaire that does not require a high language level.

– Deaf Acculturation Scale (DAS): This is a 58-item scale that measures deaf and hard of hearing individuals' degree of acculturation to both Deaf and hearing cultures. It consists of two overall acculturation scales: a Deaf acculturation scale (DASd) and a hearing acculturation scale (DASh). Both measure acculturation in five domains (Maxwell-McCaw & Zea, 2011). The DAS is the only validated international scale that provides information about the cultural status of deaf and hard of hearing individuals. Having a cultural identity different from that of the majority in society may have a negative effect on an individual's communication (Van Wieringen et al., 2002). The DAS can be used to evaluate such effects among deaf and hard of hearing individuals.

Issues Encountered during Selection and Translation of Questionnaires

Our project consisted of five phases: 1. choosing the questionnaires; 2. producing the forward translation; 3. producing the backward translation and harmonization; 4. testing; 5. taking the survey. We encountered linguistic, cultural, and technical issues during all phases of selection and translation of questionnaires. Later we describe these issues and how we dealt with them.

Selection Criteria for Questionnaires

It is difficult to perform a validation study on questionnaires to be used by sign language users because of the small number of such persons in the population, as mentioned earlier. Therefore, one has to be very sure of the potential and the characteristics of the questionnaire. We preferred to use only internationally validated questionnaires that had already been successfully translated into a number of languages and have been used in various cultural settings, not questionnaires that were validated in only a limited number of European countries or only the United States. From those we chose the ones that showed the most potential for cultural and linguistic translation. For instance, questionnaires that use a great deal of figurative speech are more difficult to translate into another language, as are questionnaires with many semantic weaknesses (see example 1). We also took the required language level into account. Since the medical knowledge of deaf and hard of hearing individuals is often limited, we excluded questionnaires that use a large proportion of medical jargon or require a high language level.

EXAMPLE 1. *(from GHQ)*
Have you felt capable of making decisions about "things"?
"Things" is semantically weak and therefore a difficult concept to capture in translation.

Selecting Signers

The main but elementary difference between a written questionnaire and a signed one is the need for a signing interviewer on the screen. The person who is recorded signing the questions will automatically function as the interviewer. As with any interviewer, this individual may cause some bias. To minimize the bias, the signers must be carefully selected.

A central point in this is that the respondents to the questionnaire must feel comfortable with the signer, who may be asking very personal questions. Although the respondents will be aware that the signer on the film will not see the answers, the signer will unconsciously exert influence nonetheless. Interviewer bias can also be caused by gender, age, status, cultural and ethnic background, language, and/or linguistic style.

To minimize potential bias, we decided to make different versions. One version was signed by a deaf woman who is a teacher of NGT and Deaf culture and is well known in the Deaf community. The second version was signed by a hearing male NGT interpreter who has much experience in working in psychiatric settings but has no personal attachments to the Deaf community. In the Netherlands the Deaf community is rather small, and most of its members know each other. By choosing one interviewer who was well known in this community we created an opportunity for the participants to be questioned by someone familiar and trusted. By also selecting an NGT interpreter without personal attachments to the Deaf community and who works only in a small, specialized setting, we provided an opportunity for the respondents to be questioned by an unfamiliar, more neutral person. In addition, NGT has five regional variants, all of which are mutually understood by native signers. For educational reasons, a standard version of NGT's most basic lexicon was introduced in the 1990s and is firmly established today. The two signers of the questionnaire came from different parts of the country. They were both instructed to sign in as standard a manner as possible, but they did so with a slightly different NGT accent.

Two-thirds of the participants finally chose the Deaf woman as the sign model. This model also resulted in fewer respondent dropouts than with the male interpreter as the sign model. This supports our hypothesis that the current practice of using ad hoc, noncultural Deaf sign language interpreters to administer nonculturally adapted tests may cause bias and a false sense of feeling that the participants' needs are sufficiently met.

Adaptations in Translating the Questionnaires

While translating the questionnaire, one must understand both the underlying reason for the questions and the frame of reference of the target group related to them. One of the issues that we encountered during translation was that the items on some questionnaires are written in the first person, for example, "I feel sad." This is done to encourage the participant to internalize the item. Since sign language is a visual language, an interviewer will always be present. If a question is written in the first person, the interviewer will always have to use a form of direct speech (i.e., the interviewer will point to himself while asking the question). It is arguable whether with the original purpose of first-person use, more internalization of the question is reached in this situation. We found that second person (e.g., signer points at respondent [= viewer] while asking the question [e.g., "Do you feel sad?"]) is a more direct and more suitable form for sign languages. Therefore we adapted the first-person phrases, for example, in some of the questions in the American DAS questionnaire (see example 2).

EXAMPLE 2. *(from DAS)*

Original question	Adapted question
I call myself Deaf (yes/no) ->	Do you call yourself Deaf? (yes/no)

One of the questions that was adapted for person.

An example of cultural issues during translation was the question "Are you a member of a club or society?" (yes/no). The purpose of this question is to test social involvement, but it was placed between mainly medically oriented questions. Within a hearing population this will not cause any problems, but within the Deaf community, lobby groups and associations of Deaf or hard of hearing persons are often also seen as clubs or societies. We transferred the question to the section where other social questions were asked and added the word "socially" to avoid "yes" answers when the respondent was actually not socially active ("Are you a member of a socially active club or society?").

Technical Issues of Translation

Our questionnaires consisted of 151 questions. This meant that, including formal introduction and instructions, we had to translate 170 items. We estimated that it would take approximately 8 hours to produce the first forward sign language translation (translationF) and 4 hours to film the adaptations. We expected the backward translation (translationB) to take 2 hours. For the production of the sign-supported version we reserved 4 hours. Our estimations for the sign language version turned out to be very accurate.

Although no full translation had to be made, it turned out that it is as time consuming to film a sign-supported version as it is to produce a sign language version. In our case we also used a signer who was not accustomed to being filmed, which possibly caused some extra delay. It took a total of 12 hours to film the first sign-supported version.

For all of the recordings on different filming days, the signer has to wear the same clothes, which should be neutral in color but contrasting with the background. When the camera is positioned, one has to make sure that the whole signing area (picture) is captured. The signer's hands should not go outside the filmed area, not even during breaks between contiguous sentences. Moreover, the signer must always look directly into the camera. Often a helper will be standing next to the camera or a text will be put up next to the camera; alternatively, an autocue can be used. When the signer looks at this person or the text during the filming, the signer's eye direction changes, which may have grammatical consequences in most sign languages. Since "person" in NGT, like in most sign languages, is expressed by pointing at a certain locus (localization[1]), the question will seem to be directed to a third person rather than to the viewer/participant (second person).

Presentation

Since sign language is a visual language and deaf and hard of hearing individuals are visually oriented, it is imperative to pay special attention to the layout of the recordings and how the films are presented online (Baker, van den Bogaerde, & Woll, 2008). The combination of yellow and blue is known to provide the best contrast and be the most comfortable to read; therefore we chose a light yellow background and a dark blue font. We placed the film clip with the NGT question in the center of the screen because this is the most important item. To create a layout that would be familiar we placed the written text below the clips on the screen, as in subtitles. A bar at the top of the screen shows the participants what percentage of the questionnaire they have filled out (figure 2).

When answers were only short phrases (e.g., yes/no/don't know), these could be provided only in writing because, when several clips are placed on one screen, the overall view is reduced, and a great deal of viewing time is required. Although using NGT instead of written text improves Deaf respondents' comprehension, it is also more time consuming to look at movies than to read. When the answers are only short phrases, these side effects compromise the positive effect of NGT on comprehensibility.

Other researchers have tried to compensate for the difficulty of displaying sign language answers by making the answer options more visual in written text (Graybill et al., 2010; Hocker, 2010; Munro & Rodwell, 2009)

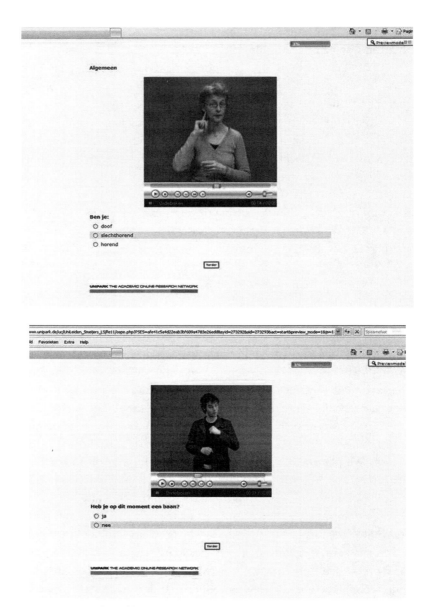

FIGURE 2. *Examples of layout.*

(e.g., color-coding [green for a positive answer, red for a negative one], the use of illustrations such as thumbs up, flat hand, thumbs down for good, moderate, poor, respectively], or smiley faces). However, because colors or illustrations might impart a positive or negative connotation to the answers and thereby possibly add a bias, we decided not to use these.

Some computer-based tests require an answer to every question before the respondent can proceed to the next question. We used this restriction only for the most crucial questions (e.g., "date of birth"). We gave the participants the option of skipping questions because the written questionnaires also have the option of leaving a blank in case the test participant does not understand the question or does not know the answer or does not want to answer the question. Filling out an answer just to be able to continue the test would compromise the reliability. Although it was possible to do so, none of our respondents left blanks while filling out the questionnaires.

Testing the Questionnaires

Pretesting can be done by many different methods. For the questionnaires we used a cognitive interviewing method based on paraphrasing as a variant of the think-aloud method (KIDSCREEN Group Europe, 2006) (asking the respondents to repeat the item in their own words immediately after answering the item). This technique permits the researcher to find out whether a respondent understands the question and interprets it in the manner intended. It may also reveal weak wordings of items.

Additionally, using the general probing method (KIDSCREEN Group Europe, 2006), the participants were asked whether the items were comprehensible and clear and whether they were easy or difficult to answer. During the translation process the review committee (a committee designed to assess the entire forward-backward process in order to provide a final forward translation) noticed a difference in focus of the two forward translation teams. The forward translation team that was producing the Deaf woman sign model was focusing more on comprehensibility and cultural adaptation, whereas the team that was producing the male interpreter model focused more on making the translation as literal as possible. After consultation, the former team was instructed to translate more strictly, and the latter team was instructed to focus more on a conceptual than a literal translation.

During the testing phase differences also surfaced. Testers who were deafened early in life preferred the Deaf woman sign model because they felt that the language used in that version was slightly more accessible. Testers deafened at a later age tended to favor the more literal male interpreter model. Six persons were asked to test all 170 items. They considered only one item to be difficult to understand because there is no proper translation for the concept "leisure activities" in NGT (see example 3). This is because the concept of leisure time seems to be unfamiliar in the Deaf community.

Conducting the Questionnaire

In contrast to written questionnaires, questionnaires in sign language cannot be filled out using paper and pencil. Some sort of visual technical support is needed. We placed our questionnaires in an online environment. Participants filled out our questionnaire at home on their own computer. Several meetings at Deaf clubs and a center for elderly deaf persons were organized. People who did not possess enough computer skills to fill out the questionnaire at home could receive help at these meetings. Assistance was given by three members of our team who were trained to provide only technical assistance; none with regard to content was given.

During the first phase of the study the questionnaire was made available at a secure Internet site. After signing a written consent form participants received a personal login for the questionnaire. During the second phase of the study this was altered because the procedure seemed to hinder both Deaf and hearing people in their study participation. The Dutch Deaf community is a small, close-knit community. Some of its members reported to us that they had doubts about the anonymity because they had to write their name on the informed consent, while some Deaf community members were team participants. In addition, some of the possible candidates for our hearing control group reported that the written informed consent procedure was too time consuming.

During the second phase of our study we tried to overcome these barriers by placing the questionnaire in a secure environment without login authorization, enabling people to give online consent instead of written consent.

Participant Recruitment

We generated much publicity about the project with articles and announcements in patient group newsletters, magazines, national and local newspapers, and websites of Deaf clubs and/or organizations for people with hearing impairment. General information about the study was provided at gatherings of the Deaf community, symposia for people with hearing impairment, and medical symposia. In addition, participants were recruited through snowball sampling and newsletters of hearing aid manufacturers.

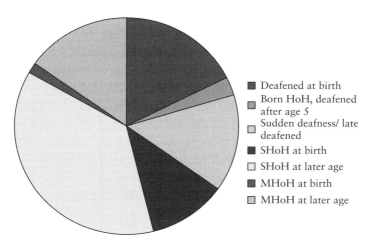

Deafened at birth
Born HoH, deafened after age 5
Sudden deafness/ late deafened
SHoH at birth
SHoH at later age
MHoH at birth
MHoH at later age

FIGURE 3. *Hearing status of our participants based on self-report (SHOH = severe hard of hearing, MHOH = mild hard of hearing).*

Informed consent was obtained by providing information brochures and consent forms both in written Dutch and NGT. All of the information was customized for people with weak language skills.

A total of 274 deaf and hard of hearing individuals filled out our questionnaires. The audiological characteristics based on self-reports are shown in Figure 3. Twenty-eight percent of our participants described themselves as members of the Deaf community; 19.7% had at least one deaf parent; and 15% had a cochlear implant. Of the 76 participants who were deafened at an early age and described themselves members of the Deaf community, 37% filled out one of the sign language versions of the questionnaire; 4% filled out the sign-supported version; and 59% chose the written Dutch questionnaire.

GUIDELINES

The most important differences between guidelines for spoken language translations and translating for deaf and hard of hearing individuals are the following:

- Current guidelines always advise translating the original questionnaire using one native speaker of both languages. However, often no native speakers of both the target sign language and the source language are available. Therefore a full forward and backward translation to the written form of the local spoken language (intermediate) has to be made first, in accordance with international guidelines, before starting the forward translation into the sign language of choice.

- We advise setting up a multidisciplinary team instead of making the translation with one person alone. These teams should include at least the following:

    a) a professionally trained sign language interpreter
    b) a native user of the target sign language, preferably a Deaf communication specialist or Deaf sign language teacher

If possible, the team should also include the following:

    c) a linguistic specialist in sign language (sign linguist)
    d) a psychologist/psychotherapist with experience in the development of psychological tests

All of the team members must be familiar with the target sign language and the cultures of both the region of the source (written) language and the target (sign) language and have experience with psychological testing.

- As prescribed in international guidelines, at least two separate translations should be made, differences discussed, and adaptations made. International guidelines advise proceeding with one version after performing the first forward and backward translation. The experiences of both translators and translation groups are used to improve what is considered to be the stronger translation. Ideally, when adapting to and translating into a sign language, one should start with four translations (two signed by a sign language interpreter, and two by native Deaf signers), choosing the best version of both groups to continue with. Depending on possible local cultural issues, more versions might be necessary. Since resources for carrying out this kind of project are often limited, it will frequently be unfeasible to start with four or more translations. In this context we advise performing two translations using the experiences of the two translation groups to improve both versions. Continuing with at least two versions also serves to minimize the interviewer bias. At least one of the versions should be signed by a Deaf native signer of the target sign language. Other personal characteristics, depending on local culture, should be taken into account.

CONCLUSIONS

Specialized mental health care for deaf and hard of hearing clients has emerged during the last 50 years in many Western countries. The deaf and hard of hearing client group poses additional linguistic and social challenges to (mental) health care providers. This makes the process of diagnosing and treating deaf and hard of hearing clients more challenging than that for hearing clients. Various diagnostic tests have been used for these clients over the years. However, these tests were not specifically developed for this group or were translated only ad hoc. The reliability of such testing is questionable.

We advise the use of internationally validated written questionnaires in this population. However, questionnaires have to be carefully selected, translated, and modified both linguistically and culturally. If this is not properly done, bias can occur, potentially resulting in the misdiagnoses of many clients. With this chapter we hope to raise the awareness of this group's special needs, and we propose a set of guidelines (see Figure 1) for practitioners and researchers who would like to use standardized tests for deaf and hard of hearing sign language users.

NOTES

1. *Localization* refers to pointing to a specific place in space, whereby the pointing acquires semantic meaning (e.g., "first person" is pointing at yourself, while "second person" is pointing at the interlocutor or at the space directly in front of the signer).

REFERENCES

Baker, A., van den Bogaerde, B., & Woll, B. (2008). Methods and procedures in sign language acquisition studies. In A. Baker & B. Woll (Eds.), *Sign Language Acquisition* (Special issue). *Sign Language and Linguistics,* 1–49. Amsterdam: Benjamins.

Barnett, S. (1999). Clinical and cultural issues in caring for deaf people. *Family Medicine 31,* 17–22.

Crowe Mason, T. (2005). Cross-cultural instrument translation: Assessment, translation, and statistical applications. *American annals of the deaf, 150*(1), 67–72.

Fellinger, J., Holzinger, D., Dobner, U., Gerich, J., Lehner, R., Lenz, G., & Goldberg, D. (2005a). An innovative and reliable way of measuring health-related quality of life and mental distress in the Deaf community. *Social Psychiatry and Psychiatric Epidemiology, 40,* 245–250.

Fellinger, J., Holzinger, D., Dobner, U., Gerich, J., Lehner, L., Lenz, G., & Goldberg, D. (2005b). Mental distress and quality of life in a deaf population. *Social Psychiatry and Psychiatric Epidemiology, 40,* 737–742.

Fellinger, J., Holzinger, D., Dobner, U., Gerich, J., Lehner, L., Lenz, G., & Goldberg, D. (2007). Mental distress and quality of life in the hard of hearing. *Acta Psychiatrica Scandinavica, 115,* 243–245.

Goldberg, D. P., & Williams, P. A. (1988). *User's Guide to the GHQ.* Windsor: NFER Nelson.

Graybill, P., Aggas, J., Dean, R. K., Demers, S., Finigan, E. G., & Pollard, R. Q, Jr. (2010). A community-participatory approach to adapting survey items for deaf individuals and American Sign Language. *Fields Methods, 22*(4), 429–448.

Guillemin, F., Bombardier, C., & Beaton, D. (1993). Cross-cultural adaptation of health-related quality of life measures: Literature review and proposed guidelines. *Journal of Clinical Epidemiology, 46*(12), 1417–1432.

Hocker, T. J. (2010). *Sozialmedizinische Aspekte der medizinischen Versorgung gehörloser Menschen in Deutschland Entwicklung und Durchführung einer internetbasierten Umfrage mit Gebärdensprachvideos.* Inauguraldissertation zur Erlangung des Doktorgrades der Medizin der Universitätsmedizin der Johannes Gutenberg-Universität Mainz.

Hoem Kvam, M. (2004, March). Sexual abuse of deaf children: A retrospective analysis of the prevalence and characteristics of childhood sexual abuse among deaf adults in Norway. *Child Abuse and Neglect 28*(3), 241–251. http://www.unipark.de

Jones, E. G., Renger, R., & Firestone, R. (2005). Deaf community analysis for health education priorities. *Public Health Nursing 22,* 27–35.

Kennedy, C., & McCann, D. (2004). Universal neonatal hearing screening moving from evidence to practice. *Archives of Disease in Childhood: Fetal and Neonatal Edition, 89,* 378–383.

KIDSCREEN Group Europe. (2006). *The KIDSCREEN Questionnaires: Quality of life questionnaires for children and adolescents.* Handbook. Lengerich: Pabst Science.

Ladd, P. (2003). *Understanding Deaf culture: In search of Deafhood.* Clevedon: Multilingual Matters.

Maxwell-McCaw, D., & Zea, M. C. (2011, January). The Deaf Acculturation Scale (DAS): Development and validation of a 58-item measure. *Journal of Deaf Studies and Deaf Education.* Advance Access published. DOI:10.1093/deafed/enq061

Munro, L., & Rodwell, J. (2009). Validation of an Australian Sign Language instrument of outcome measurement for adults in mental health settings. *Australian and New Zealand Journal of Psychiatry, 43,* 332–339.

Musselman, C. (2005). How do children who can't hear learn to read an alphabetic script? A review of the literature on reading and deafness. *Journal of Deaf Studies and Deaf Education, 5*(1), 9–31.

Padden, C., & Humphries, T. (1988). *Deaf in America: Voices from a culture.* Cambridge, MA: Harvard University Press.

Padden, C., & Humphries, T. (2005). *Inside Deaf culture.* Cambridge, MA: Harvard University Press.

Pollard, R. (1994). Public mental health services and diagnostic trends regarding individuals who are deaf or hard of hearing. *Rehabilitation Psychology, 39*(3), 147–160.

Ravens-Sieberer, U., Gosch, A., Rajmil, L., Erhart, M., Bruil, J., Duer, W., Auquier, P., Power, M., Abel, T., Czemy, L., Mazur, J., Czimbalmos, A., Tountas, Y., Hagquist, C., Kilroe, J., & European KIDSCREEN Group. (2005). KIDSCREEN-52 quality-of-life measure for children and adolescents. *Expert Review of Pharmacoeconomics and Outcomes Research, 5*(3), 353–364.

Smeijers, A. S., & Pfau, R. (2009). Towards a treatment for treatment: The communication between general practitioners and their deaf patients. *Translator and Interpreter, 3*(1), 1–14.

Stein, L. K., Mindel, E. D., & Jabaley, T. (1981). *Deafness and mental health.* New York: Grune and Stratton.

Van Wieringen, J. C., Harmsen, J. A., & Bruijnzeels, M. A. (2002, March). Intracultural communication in general practice. *European Journal of Public Health, 12*(1), 63–68.

Vernon, M., & Andrews, J. F. (1990). The psychology of deafness: Understanding deaf and hard-of-hearing people. New York: Longman.

WHOQoL Group. (1998). Development of the World Health Organization WHOQoL-BREF quality of life assessment. *Psychological Medicine 28,* 551–558.

Appendix 1.

Translation Methodology for Translating Questionnaires into Sign Language

---

I. INTRODUCTION

This guideline is based on the WHOQoL (WHOQoL Group, 1998) and KIDSCREEN (Ravens-Sieberer et al., 2005; KIDSCREEN Group Europe, 2006) guidelines for translating questionnaires between written languages. Our adaptations conform to these international guidelines for translating into sign languages.

2.1. Overview

The translation process should focus on achieving conceptual equivalence of all versions rather than linguistic/literal equivalence. With regard to the translation methodology the forward-backward-forward technique should be applied.

In Step 1, the translation of the original questionnaire into the local written language (called the "intermediate language") should conform to the international forward-backward translation guidelines.

Step 2: Two independently working translation teams should translate the questionnaire into the local target sign language (TranslationF-1 and TranslationF-2) (cf. Figure 1, step 2).

In Step 3 (the following reconciliation), the two forward translation teams and one member of the research group review the two forward translations into the target sign language in order to create the reconciled forward translation. They identify problematic items, discuss the original formulation and intention of these items in the source language, and consider possible ways of translating them into the target language while meeting all of the demands of conceptual equivalence with the original questionnaire in the source language (cf. Figure 1, steps 3a and 3b).

In step 4, the reconciled forward translation should be translated back into the intermediate language (translationB-1 is the backward translation of translationF-1, and translationB-2 is the backward translation of translationF-2). This should be done by independent professional sign language translators meeting the criteria as described later (cf. Figure 1, step 4).

In step 5 the members of the research group (and, if available, external experts with experience in instrument development and translation) and the forward translation team compare TranslationB-1 and TranslationB-2 with the original, source language version, thus reviewing the reconciled forward translation. If necessary adaptations are made, this version is considered the final forward translation (cf. Figure 1, steps 5a and 5b).

In step 6, subsequent to the generation of the final forward translation all reviews and translation data are sent to the developers of the original questionnaire for documentation and consultation. The objective of the consultation is to resolve both inadequate concepts of translation and all discrepancies between alternative versions (cf. Figure 1, step 6).

2.2. Pretranslation Phase

There are often no native speakers of both the target sign language and the original language available. Therefore a full forward-backward translation, conforming to international guidelines, must be made before starting the forward translation into a sign language.

2.3. Forward Translation

All of the translators working on the project should not only be professional and experienced translators but preferably also have experience with psychological and/or psychiatric testing or even test development.

We recommend that the forward translation team and the review committee be formed as a multidisciplinary team consisting at least of a professionally trained sign language interpreter (often a nonnative signer) and a native user of the target sign language. The team should also include a deaf communication specialist or a deaf sign language teacher, a linguistic specialist in sign linguistics, and a psychologist/psychotherapist with experience in the development of psychological tests.

All of the team members need to be:

- Signers of the target sign language
- Knowledgeable about the source language, the intermediate language, and the target sign language

- Familiar with the cultures of the region of the source language and of the target language/community (e.g., local Deaf culture)
- Experienced in test development and/or psychological testing of deaf and hard of hearing clients

Two translation teams should translate the questionnaire independently from each other into the target sign language. The translators are asked to use natural and acceptable language for the broadest audience and to be simple, clear, and concise in their formulations.

The following guidelines may be given to the translators:

- The translators should always focus on conceptual equivalence rather than on literal word-for-word translation. They should always try to grasp the most relevant meanings of the original terms and translate them accordingly.
- The translators should try to be simple, clear, and concise in their formulations; long sentences with many clauses should be avoided.
- The translators should take into account what typical respondents will understand when they see the items.
- The translators should take the age of the respondents into consideration and thus not use any jargon or terms that would be difficult to understand. The translation has to be clear, simple, and comprehensible. Double negatives should be avoided.

The two forward translators provide two forward translations: TranslationF-1 and TranslationF-2. The two versions are then reconciled in the next step.

2.4. Reconciliation of Items

Participants in the reconciliation procedure review the two forward translations. These participants should include the following:

- The two forward translators
- One member of the research group with good knowledge both of the source language and of the target language

To reconcile the two independent forward versions a reconciliation meeting should be held so that the two translations can be compared and assessed with regard to their conceptual equivalence, comprehensibility, and clarity of signs relative to the original questionnaire.

Participants in the reconciliation procedure should document their assessments item by item and, if neither is adequate, suggest another translation. They should focus on differences in culture and linguistics that may cause difficulties when transforming the source version into the target languages. The reconciled versions are to be derived by means of a subsequent discussion between the participants. In contrast to most international guidelines we advise that, after doing this, the participants proceed with both versions to minimize the interrogator bias. At least one of the versions has to be signed by a Deaf native user of the target sign language.

The reconciliation procedure may also produce valuable clues to differences in culture and/or linguistics that are relevant to the whole translation process.

2.5. Backward Translation

Designed to assess the conceptual equivalence of the reconciled forward translation and the source questionnaire, the backward translation serves as an instrument to measure the quality of the reconciled forward translation. The backward translation and the intermediate language version are supposed to be very similar, and if they are not, discrepancies such as problematically translated items will thus become manifest and can be corrected.

The backward-translator must be a professional sign language interpreter (if possible, a native signer) and should have familiarity with the cultures, both of the original language/ country as well as of the target signers (ecg local Deafculture), have experience in test development and/ or psychological testing of hearing impaired participants.

The reconciled forward translation is translated into the intermediate language by the backward translator, who should not have worked with the questionnaire before. The guidelines as described earlier (guidelines for forward translators) may also be given to the backward translator. The result of the backward-translation process is a translated version of the reconciled forward translation in the intermediate language.

2.6. Review of the Forward and Backward Translation

The review is designed to assess the entire forward-backward process in order to provide a final forward translation. Participants in the review procedure should include the following:

- Two members of the research group with good knowledge of both the source and the target sign language
- One of the forward translators
- If available, external experts with experience in instrument development and translation

Focusing on conceptual differences, the backward translation (in the intermediate language) is to be compared with the original, source language questionnaire. The participants review the translation process item by item by comparing the TranslationB items to the original source language items and suggesting a version for the final forward translation in the target sign language. This is done either by confirming the results of the reconciliation process or by suggesting an alternative translation if necessary. All changes in wording or meaning of the items are to be undertaken while generating the final forward translation.

In this final process, the review board is expected to ensure that the translation is simple, clear, and concise and, most important, that there are no conceptual discrepancies between the original (source language) and the final forward translation (target sign language). The focus should be on achieving conceptual equivalence and clarity as well as on using colloquial language.

2.7. Assessment of Conceptual Equivalence and First Harmonization of Problematic Items with the Developers of the Original Questionnaire

International harmonization is intended to ensure the comparability of the translated questionnaires. The reviews and translation data of problematic items will be sent to the developers of the original questionnaire. The objective of the consultation is to resolve inadequate concepts of translation as well as all discrepancies between alternative versions.

This is done to ensure and, if necessary, generate interconceptual equivalence.

2.8. Pretest (Cognitive Interviews)

The pretest is expected to show whether all of the items are comprehensible and acceptable.

Test participants should be provided with a quiet place for testing. With regard to their contribution to the test development procedure, tested individuals are to be informed of the objective of the pretest.

Pretesting is critical for identifying questionnaire problems such as misunderstandings about the intended meaning of items. Problems with item content, including confusion about the overall meaning of items, as well as misinterpretation of individual terms or concepts, can also be identified. Pretesting incorporates many different methods. We propose a cognitive interviewing method based on paraphrasing as a variant of the "think-aloud method" (asking respondents to repeat the item in their own words immediately after answering it).

This technique permits the researcher to determine whether the respondent understands the question and interprets it in the manner intended. It may also reveal better wordings for items.

Additionally, when using the "general probing method," respondents will be asked whether the items can be considered comprehensible and clear and whether they were difficult to answer.

2.9. International Harmonization

All translation reviews and translation data will be sent to the developers of the original questionnaire for documentation and consultation. The objective of the consultation is to resolve inadequate concepts of translation and all discrepancies between alternative versions.

The international harmonization procedure should be carried out by one or two members of the research group, if possible those who have already been involved in the review procedures. A telephone or Skype conference with one member of the questionnaire group should serve as a platform to discuss all questions about conceptual and cultural aspects of the item translations.

The final questionnaire versions are generated in the process of international harmonization and should preferably be subsequently tested in a validation study.

Remote Possibilities: Trialing Simultaneous Video Interpreting for Austrian Hospitals

Franz Pöchhacker

ABSTRACT

This paper reports on a technology-based initiative to promote healthcare interpreting in a previously underdeveloped institutional context. Amid a persistent lack of policy on reliable communication support services for patients with an insufficient command of German, a project was launched to provide professional interpreting via videoconferencing (VC). Following a review of the policy dimension of the project and of issues such as the choice of technology and interpreting mode, the paper describes a field test involving authentic clinical encounters and remote interpreting in the simultaneous mode. The latter is shown to be viable and effective, though prospects for implementation need to take account of public and professional attitudes.

INTRODUCTION

It is well known that the development of professional interpreting in health care, which is in evidence throughout the world, proceeds at a highly uneven pace in different national contexts. What is common practice in some countries—such as telephone interpreting services—may be a novelty or nonexistent in others, and one state's legal provisions underpinning concerted efforts to ensure equal access to care may be nowhere on the books in another. This has obvious implications for research since progressive institutional practices engender new opportunities and needs for scientific inquiry, whereas a lack of institutionalized (i.e., planned and acknowledged) service provision severely limits the possibility of collecting empirical data and contributing to current debates in the scientific community.

As I explain in more detail later, this chapter on healthcare interpreting is set in an underdeveloped institutional context. It nevertheless reports on a pilot study that innovates on the state of the art. Amid a persistent lack of policy on reliable communication support services for patients with an insufficient command of German, an initiative was undertaken to jump-start professional interpreting service provision by harnessing videoconferencing (VC) technology. What is more, the project was not limited to the standard mode of consecutive interpreting but was designed to explore the feasibility of VC-based simultaneous interpreting in clinical encounters. In the present chapter I therefore cover both the policy dimension of the project, so as to identify the potential for and the constraints of successful implementation, and the more specifically interpreting-related issues, including the technological options for remote interpreting solutions and the choice of interpreting mode for medical encounters. The core of the chapter is nevertheless the description and analysis of the field test carried out in preparation for a pilot project on video interpreting for Austrian healthcare institutions. The discussion of the field test data then links up the various dimensions, highlighting how social forces such as public and professional attitudes and policy considerations are as critical to successful project implementation as human and technological resources.

POLICY

In sketching out the background and policy context of the video interpreting project described in this chapter, I draw on Ozolins's (2000) model of the "spectrum of response" to multilingual communication needs as a point of departure. Along that spectrum from "neglect" to "comprehensiveness," ad hoc provision and generic services appear as steps along the way. In terms of this model, the Austrian healthcare system is essentially in the ad hoc stage, with a few pockets of generic service provision. Despite well-documented interpreting needs arising from the country's sizeable immigrant population, medical service providers routinely rely on family members (children) and bilingual staff (cleaners and nurses) to communicate with non-German-speaking patients (Pöchhacker, 2000).

However, as acknowledged in a subsequent publication (Ozolins, 2010), the spectrum model is deceptively linear and does not explain why different countries are at different points of the spectrum. Ozolins goes on to posit a number of determinants and uses them to categorize 15 countries, including Austria. With reference to two attitudinal and three public-policy dimensions, he sees the Austrian community interpreting scene as characterized by politicized (negative) reactions to immigration, a view of interpreting that is centered on conference interpreting, and a legalist framework favoring court interpreting. In addition, he points to the role of local (municipal and state) authorities in the federalist system of government. Ozolins's account is generally on the mark, with the possible exception of public perceptions of interpreting, which have evolved toward greater awareness, though not necessarily greater appreciation, of interpreters working in community settings.

Status Quo

In a global perspective on healthcare interpreting, Austria, which is home to one of the oldest university-level interpreter-training institutions and an even older professional association of court interpreters, must be regarded as a developing country (Pöchhacker, 2007), and the analysis put forward by Ozolins (2010) goes some way toward explaining why this should be so difficult to change. To begin with, the Federal Ministry of Health has little actual power in matters of healthcare provision, which is squarely in the jurisdiction of the nine federal states—unlike the courts, which have a regional structure but come under federal regulation. Thus, a Court Interpreters Act, which now mandates examination-based certification, dates back to 1975, whereas comparable provisions guaranteeing the right to an interpreter where needed in healthcare settings do not exist. In theory, the health minister could ask Parliament to pass such legislation, but implementation would have to be funded at the state level. What is more, right-wing parties who use antiforeigner sentiment as one of their strongest appeals, control up to a third of the seats in Parliament at the federal and state levels. In this political climate, legislative provisions and budgetary appropriations that, in the public view, benefit immigrants would require exceptional political courage.

Politically and institutionally as well as demographically, the state and capital city of Vienna plays an outstanding role in the field of interpreting in general and healthcare interpreting in particular. Vienna is home to more than a fifth of the foreign nationals residing in the country, whose total population is 8.4 million. Of the 1.54 million residents of immigrant background, two-thirds are first-generation immigrants, mainly from Turkey and the former Yugoslavia. The communication needs of this sizeable immigrant community have made themselves felt, particularly in the health and social service sectors, since the 1980s, but there has been little systematic response. Among the few exceptions is a project dating back to the late 1980s, which provided half a dozen municipal hospitals with a native-Turkish liaison worker/interpreter. Despite growing and more diverse language needs, the measure has seen no expansion in more than two decades.

The Vienna Hospital Association, under the aegis of the municipal government, comprises eleven hospitals and more than a dozen geriatric centers and nursing homes and is one of the largest hospital operators in Europe. Its flagship institution is the Vienna General Hospital, which ranks among the largest in Europe and also serves as the teaching hospital of the Vienna Medical University. Even so, it has no policy or structure for interpreter service provision to speak of, and the efforts of its two lone interpreters for Turkish, who date back to the aforementioned pilot project, are dwarfed by pervasive reliance on ad hoc arrangements. This decade-long stagnation in the country's most important healthcare institution is due to the interrelation between leadership and organizational structure. Although several initiatives have been undertaken at the level of the Vienna Hospital Association, including an in-house interpreter-training course for bilingual staff, hospital management is largely autonomous, and the general manager in question, in place since 1989, has been conspicuous by his lack of support for measures in the area of healthcare interpreting. In short, the prime candidates for championing the advancement of medical interpreting in Vienna, and Austria in general, have either not played this role or not been able to play it and left this a barren field.

In his perceptive analysis of the state of the art in 15 countries, Ozolins (2010) also reflects on how to promote public-authority initiatives in language services. Aside from the search for cross-sectoral solutions, he mentions (1) normative factors and (2) coalition building and alliances, and these two factors are indeed the driving forces behind the initiative described in this chapter. The normative pressures in this case stem not from antidiscrimination or equitable-access provisions but from recent medical liability cases. Concerns about the latter in the legal-affairs section of the Federal Ministry of Health gave rise to a joint initiative with the Austrian Network for Patient Safety (ANetPAS), a national forum of experts founded in 2008 at the initiative of the Health Ministry. It is in this context that an interdisciplinary working group on the management of non-German-speaking patients was set up in May 2011. Significantly, this was the first such initiative at the federal level, giving explicit support—that is, endorsement rather than funds—to a project aimed at improving communication with non-German-speaking patients in the Austrian healthcare system.

Working Group Project

The working group, led by the managing director of the ANetPAS and composed of a variety of stakeholders from the healthcare sector and academics from various fields, met seven times over the course of 2 years. Prompted by the Health Ministry official spearheading the initiative, the group soon directed its attention to a technology-based measure to provide communication support, notwithstanding a keen awareness in the group that the provision of on-site interpreting services in hospitals and doctors' offices would remain a fundamental objective in light of international developments.

With some kind of remote-interpreting solution placed at the top of the agenda, the group first explored the option of telephone interpreting. This had just been piloted as an in-house service by a public hospital in Salzburg (represented in the working group), and a private telephone interpreting company had been set up around the same time in Graz, the country's second largest city. In light of interpreters' concerns about the lack of visual access in this novel (by Austrian standards) working mode and the shared assumption that over-the-phone interpreting would not be suitable for all types of medical encounters, the group decided to aim for a more advanced, twenty-first-century solution based on broadband VC technology with which to provide professional interpreting services to healthcare institutions throughout the country.

Exactly what kind of solution this might be was for group members with a background in interpreting research and practice to consider. The evidence to support the decision ultimately made for the project is reviewed in the following section, which also provides the theoretical underpinning to and rationale for the field test I am reporting on in this chapter.

TECHNOLOGY AND TECHNIQUE

Several studies over the past decade have investigated the viability and suitability of technology-based forms of interpreting in healthcare settings, often in comparison with traditional face-to-face arrangements.

With one exception (Hornberger et al., 1996), the interpreting mode used in these remote interpreting trials was consecutive, whereas the technology of interest in these studies was mainly videoconferencing. A selection of these studies is briefly discussed, as this body of research helped inspire both the technological choice for the Vienna pilot project and the design of the field test.

Video Remote Interpreting

In a systematic review article covering nine studies on the subject of remote interpreting, Azarmina and Wallace (2005) conclude that patients and doctors were as satisfied with remote interpreting as with face-to-face interpreting but that interpreters preferred the latter. They acknowledge higher costs for remote interpreting, especially in the case of videoconferencing, but find remote interpreting to be an "acceptable and accurate alternative to traditional methods" (ibid., p. 140).

In a pilot study that covered 35 interpreter-mediated consultations with Turkish-speaking patients over a 2-month period, two standardized instruments translated into Turkish were used to measure patient enablement/satisfaction with face-to-face (14), video (11), and telephone (10) interpreting arrangements involving a single pair of participants (Jones, Gill, Harrison, Meakin, & Wallace, 2003). Both remote methods were considered feasible and acceptable even though patients seemed reluctant to express a preference and were found to be happy to have an interpreter at all. Despite some lower quantitative scores for the video condition, some qualitative data highlighted the value of video in creating a "social presence"—"as though there was somebody there with you" (ibid., pp. 54–55).

Korak (2010) tested the feasibility of remote medical interpreting via Skype in a hospital in Graz and found, on the basis of semistructured interviews, that some two-thirds of the nine Turkish-, five Russian-, and three Arabic-speaking patients were highly satisfied even though a majority would have preferred to have the interpreters on-site. The 17 doctors involved were even more satisfied with the interpreting provided via Skype, and the seven interpreters gave a rather favorable assessment as well despite some issues with image and sound quality.

A study on a much larger sample that similarly covered all perspectives on the interpreter-mediated encounter was carried out by Locatis et al. (2010) with seven interpreters, two dozen healthcare providers, and a total of 241 Hispanic postpartum patients. Their quasi-experimental design involved 80 cases each of in-person and telephone interpreting as well as 81 encounters interpreted via videoconference. Based on Likert-scale ratings of interview/encounter quality, they found that patients rated interpreting services highly no matter how they were provided. Care providers and interpreters were more critical and, despite some technical problems with audio quality, wireless video signal strength, and equipment positioning, preferred videoconferencing to the telephone as a remote interpreting method. Aside from the poor videoconferencing resources in their study, the authors also acknowledge that it would have been desirable to work with transcripts of the encounters for a more thorough analysis of communication quality.

Focusing solely on the interpreters' perspective, the survey by Price, Pérez-Stable, Nickleach, López, and Karliner (2012) on the suitability of telephone versus video interpreting in different healthcare scenarios yielded an overall preference for the latter, particularly in encounters with "educational or psychosocial dimensions" (ibid., p. 226). While the 52 interpreters in three different medical centers considered telephone interpreting adequate for information exchange, they significantly preferred videoconference-based interpreting for the interpersonal aspects of communication.

Given the evidence in favor of videoconference-based interpreting in the literature, there remains the question of the interpreting technique to be used with such arrangements, that is, the choice between the consecutive or the simultaneous mode of interpreting.

"Going Simul"

In the studies reviewed earlier, the default mode for videoconferencing as well as telephone interpreting is consecutive. Indeed, there seems to be not a single study on video remote interpreting in health care that considers the simultaneous mode—with spoken languages, that is. Looking across language modalities, in contrast, one finds a wealth of established professional practice and experience with video remote interpreting (and video relay service) in signed languages. This shows that, at least in terms of communicative dynamics, simultaneous interpreting in dialogic encounters is feasible. Admittedly, technological requirements are more complex when two spoken languages are involved, as separate audio channels are needed to avoid acoustic overlap. But this, too, has been shown to be perfectly possible in experiments on remote simultaneous conference interpreting (e.g., Roziner & Shlesinger, 2010). Major advances have also been made in videoconference and remote interpreting in criminal proceedings (Braun & Taylor, 2011), and although most remote provision of court interpreting services appears to be in consecutive mode, there are also examples of equipment with dual-channel capacity, allowing for simultaneous interpreting in the courtroom.

The only well-known example of using simultaneous interpreting (SI) in doctor-patient communication dates back to an initiative in California in the mid-1990s, where a provider of conference interpreting equipment supplied the hardware, then analog, for a dual-channel system for interpreting in audio-only mode, and training was provided by staff members of the Monterey Institute of International Studies. This system for what was called remote simultaneous medical interpretation (RSMI) was field-tested with considerable success (Hornberger et al., 1996) and subsequently adopted and developed in a New York hospital. Research focusing on this method was carried out by Francesca Gany and associates, who found RSMI to be superior to remote consecutive (telephone) and on-site interpreting with regard to patient satisfaction (Gany et al., 2007b) as well as time and errors (Gany et al., 2007a). In their controlled trial involving 371 patients requiring interpretation, the 167 who were randomized to RSMI showed higher overall satisfaction with physician communication and care, but no differences in the perceived quality of interpretation (Gany et al., 2007b). In an experimental study comparing time requirements and errors with different interpreting arrangements on the basis of four scripted dialogues interpreted from English into Spanish by six professionals and four ad hoc interpreters, Gany et al. (2007a) found that encounters with RSMI took only roughly half as long on average (12.7 min.) as those using remote consecutive (23.7). Their analysis of the 16 transcribed encounters for linguistic and medical errors showed a distinct advantage of RSMI over other modes: a total of 548 linguistic errors (additions, omissions, substitutions) compared to about 900 each in remote and on-site (professional) consecutive interpreting. Similarly, the number of medical errors (i.e., linguistic errors involving medical information of moderate to greater clinical significance) was seven to ten times higher in the consecutive mode (remote and on-site) than in RSMI. (The finding that ad hoc interpreters performed as well as or better than the trained interpreters in the on-site consecutive mode is intriguing but of no concern for the purpose of this chapter.)

In addition, RSMI had fared much worse in the qualitative comparative study by Saint-Louis, Friedman, Chiasson, Quessa, and Novaes (2003), who found this method, which essentially involved two telephone lines and headsets, to be the most technically complicated and problem ridden, even compared to videoconferencing. The patients using RSMI felt uncomfortable wearing the (light) headsets and hearing the other party speak at the same time. Moreover, the system did not allow for more than two users (headsets). Although the interpreters felt that RSMI allowed for a more direct provider-patient relationship, the care providers commented that the equipment felt like a barrier disconnecting them from the patient.

These problems notwithstanding, the studies on RSMI clearly point to the potential of SI to help achieve time savings as well as greater accuracy in interpreter-mediated medical dialogues. Although the findings from comparative patient-satisfaction studies suggest that users are quite amenable to interpreting in audio-only mode, the distinct preferences for video over audio on the part of care providers and interpreters (e.g., Locatis et al., 2010) render RSMI rather questionable as an interpreting method of choice. Hence the idea of combining the strengths of videoconference-based communication and SI, which we submitted to a field test in Vienna.

FIELD TEST

Once the decision to launch a video interpreting pilot project had been made in the broader interdisciplinary forum, implementation came down essentially to a collaboration between two organizational units of the University of Vienna and a private hospital represented in the working group. Since the managing director of the ANetPAS, Maria Kletecka-Pulker, is a staff member of the University of Vienna Department of Medical Law and Ethics (referred to here by its German acronym, IERM), the project, which encompasses research as well as institutional development, came to be hosted by this academic institution. Expertise regarding interpreting was provided by members of the University's Center for Translation Studies (CTS).

With a view to choosing and trialing the videoconferencing method to be used, a test run was designed and implemented in May 2012 at the CTS. The basic research question therefore related to the viability, acceptability, and usability of the remote interpreting arrangement in both the simultaneous and the consecutive mode of interpreting, and an assessment of these issues was sought from all three perspectives—patients, providers (doctors), and interpreters. While the choice of hard- and software was in the hands of the project leadership, based at the IERM, and constrained by a very limited budget, the interpreting research partners took charge of configuring the setup of the remote interpreting equipment as well as developing the test design and analytical approach, as described in more detail later.

Design

The central goal of comparing video remote interpreting in consecutive and simultaneous mode would suggest a controlled experiment with scripted input and randomized assignment of participants as the design of choice. However, the aspiration to methodological rigor had to be balanced against the need to investigate acceptability under real-life conditions, as was done in most of the studies carried out to date. We therefore opted for a field test involving several consenting patients and care providers in authentic medical encounters. The idea was to have the patients seen by two different provider teams, as if obtaining a second opinion, using video remote interpreting in the consecutive mode in one case and SI in the other. These consultations were to be served by three professional interpreters who volunteered to take part in the test. For considerations of availability and relevance, the choice of working language(s) fell on Bosnian/Croatian/Serbian (BCS). (Immigrants from the former Yugoslavia constitute the largest group of non-German ethnic background.)

Data collection followed a multimethod, essentially qualitative approach. It included semistructured interviews with all participants, various types of recordings (using VC system software, stationary video cameras, and MP3 players), and direct observation by members of the project team at the respective sites—two staff members of the CTS and three of the IERM. Interviews with patients were conducted in BCS by a native-speaker interpreting researcher (Mira Kadrić) and included a prior meeting for orientation and informed consent and the main interview immediately following the consultation. The debriefing interviews with care providers, also at the field site, were conducted by the IERM staff member coordinating the project (Sabine Parrag), and I myself conducted the interviews with the interpreters at the remote site.

Partner

Whereas the remote interpreting workstation was set up in a small meeting room at the CTS, the field site was an outpatient department of St. Anna Children's Hospital in Vienna, a nonprofit institution wholly owned by the Vienna division of the Austrian Red Cross. This choice of partner institution suggested itself not so much (or not only) because the manager of the hospital's interpreter service (set up for the treatment of Russian-speaking cancer victims after the nuclear accident in Chernobyl) was an active member of our working group but also because St. Anna's is engaged in highly specialized transplant treatments with international partners and therefore disposes of very advanced information and communication technology (ICT) infrastructure.

These favorable conditions for the field test were to some extent offset by the special challenges of the pediatric setting, which typically involves multiparty interaction, especially on the patient side.

Two provider teams (pediatrician and pediatric nurse) agreed to take part in the study as part of their regular duties. On the day designated for the field test, the remote interpreting equipment was set up in an examining room of the neuropediatrics department, one of the hospital's nine specialized outpatient clinics.

Equipment

The basic choice with regard to equipment was between installing a dedicated VC system, as available from major suppliers such as Cisco and Polycom, and experimenting with more flexible, PC-based video messaging software. Reference projects in the field of video remote interpreting in health care, such as Martti by Language Access Network and the HCIN system in California, seemed to be based on the former option, at least in their initial phases. Even so, considerations of cost and interoperability for the Austrian project led to the decision to work with VC-platform-independent equipment. Through contacts by the project leadership, an IT company was contracted to implement the VC link with Microsoft's instant messaging software, Lync, using the server infrastructure of the Vienna University Computer Center. This permitted the use of available (Windows-based) endpoint equipment at the field site, ranging from desktop PCs in the examining room to laptops and tablet PCs.

While establishing a point-to-point video link with this VoIP technology did not pose any problems for consecutive interpreting arrangements, the challenge was to configure the system in such a way as to allow for simultaneous interpreting. No models for this were found in the literature. Since SI requires two separate audio channels, it was decided to have two separate VC links, that is, two endpoints with webcam and screen each at the field and the remote site and a custom-built manual switch at the interpreting workstation, with which the interpreter could direct the SI output to the respective channel. The interpreter's image was captured by two webcams placed close together, which delivered a largely identical picture to the two screens at the field site. There, with one webcam filming the doctor and the other the patient/parents, the dual VC setup had the significant advantage of furnishing the remote interpreter with images of both interlocutors, one each on the two PC screens placed side by side on the desk.

Rather surprisingly, it proved at least as challenging as setting up the dual VC link to put in place the necessary audio equipment at the field site. Aside from an omnidirectional microphone, the need to provide for more than two interactants in SI mode made it necessary to connect two or more (wireless) headsets and microphones to the VC equipment. Within the limited timeframe and budget for the test, the IT company ended up fitting the system with infrared receivers of portable SI equipment as well as wireless headset microphones. A few days before the day designated for the field test, this equipment was installed and tested in a simulation involving IERM staff at the field site and me at the interpreting workstation. Sound quality proved problematic for SI when using only the microphone in the room, but it was adequate with the headset microphones. The volume on the PC system was set at about 70% of the maximum to allow for a reserve if needed under more difficult conditions in the examining room. The manual audio switch at the interpreting workstation proved adequate but made a somewhat disturbing clicking noise in the output channel.

Procedure

On the day designated for the field test (May 16, 2012), the three families contacted in advance came to the hospital for their appointments as planned. There were two technicians each at the field site and the remote site and at least two project staff members in either location for observations and interviews.

The following procedure was implemented: At 9 a.m. the first family to arrive was taken to an adjacent room and informed about the project in their native language (BCS) while the equipment setup was being finalized in the examining room. Two interpreters were ready at that time at the remote site at the CTS. After the family (Fam-A) had given their consent to participate and be recorded, they were seen by Provider Team A, and the consultation was interpreted in simultaneous mode by one of the interpreters (Int-A). Interpreter B had been ready to work in consecutive mode, but after a last-minute decision at the field site to use the simultaneous mode, interpreter A decided to start. After the interview and examination, which lasted some 45 minutes, the family proceeded to see Provider Team B, with interpreter B working in consecutive mode. The second family (Fam-B) was meanwhile being prepared for participation and asked for their consent, after which they proceeded to the examining room while the native-BCS CTS staff member conducted the postconsultation interview with Fam-A. Fam-B was seen by Provider Team A, with Int-A working in consecutive mode; their second consultation was with Team B and Int-B providing SI, followed by the postconsultation interview. Fam-C was also prepared for participation, but no interpreted medical consultation took place due to time constraints. Debriefing interviews with the two doctors were conducted by the IERM project coordinator after each had seen a family in both interpreting modes.

Findings

PARTICIPANTS AND INTERACTIONS

Based on the preconsultation interviews, the three cases can briefly be summarized as follows: Fam-A, a Serbian-speaking father, whose wife apparently had a different native language (presumably Romanian), came to see the doctor because of their 2-to-3-year-old son's convulsive attacks. They also brought the boy's older sister along to the examining room. Fam-B was a Serbian-speaking mother, whose very restive 4-year-old son showed signs of retarded neurological development. Fam-C was a Serbian-speaking mother who came to the hospital to have her 6-year-old daughter prepared for surgery.

The first consultation with Fam-A was the longest by far (45 minutes). The other interactions lasted only some 12 minutes. In the case of Fam-A this was due to the fact that the father, as the main interlocutor, found it difficult after the thorough consultation (and examination) with Team A to approach Team B afresh about his son's medical problems. Rather, the medical interview with Doc-B, interpreted consecutively by Int-B, turned into a sort of feedback session, with the father talking mainly about his interaction with Team A (and Int-A) and his wife and children no longer present in the examining room. Although this meant that the original test design of a comparison by interpreting mode had to be abandoned, the unplanned discussion yielded valuable spontaneous data about the father's immediate impression of what the family had just experienced. In the case of Fam-B it was the interaction interpreted in consecutive mode (by Int-A) that proceeded as planned, whereas repeating the consultation in simultaneous mode (with Int-B) was hampered by poor acoustic conditions during the physical examination. The findings reported here therefore focus on Fam-A in the spirit of a case study and are based mainly on the video-recordings of the actual interactions at either site, complemented by interview data.

Fam-A in SI: General Observations
The main consultation under study—Fam-A with Team A and Int-A—could be summarized as a model case of interpreter-mediated dialogue with SI. Judging from the way the interaction unfolded, the two main interlocutors—the young patient's father and the pediatrician—addressed each other directly (with eye contact) and spoke naturally, receiving the interpretation of the other party's utterances with only minimal delay. The fact that the mother, who followed the main dialogue through her headset, did not use her microphone to speak to the doctor was due, regrettably, to her limited language proficiency rather than technical feasibility. The various internal exchanges between the parents were evident as such to the interpreter, thanks to the video image, and were consequently left uninterpreted.

From the video images on the screens at the remote site and the sound as captured by the video camera there, the interaction appears highly fluent, with smoothly alternating turns at talk by the two main interlocutors. Despite the physician's protagonist role in the early part of the consultation, with various questions regarding the patient's current condition to establish the history and prepare for the physical examination, the father has many extended turns and easily manages to introduce new topics. Indeed, the unusual length of the interview is not due to technical or communicative problems; on the contrary, the father seems to take advantage of the efficient interpreting arrangements to raise and discuss his concerns as fully as possible.

PATIENT PERSPECTIVE

The observer's impression of fully functional communicative interaction is confirmed by the father's comments on the simultaneously interpreted consultation in the course of his talk with Doc-B. As rendered by Int-B, working in consecutive mode (and shown here in English translation), the father says, "What has been done here was very good not only for people from Yugoslavia but for all those who do not speak German, especially because they cannot only understand what is said but can also ask questions" (father, remote site video recording at 1:24:00–13).

A persistent lack of understanding in medical consultations transpires also from the father's comments in the preparatory interview, conducted in his native language. He said he had been to hospitals two or three times a month over the past year, relying mostly on his very limited German, but felt he had "never fully understood." He also makes this point during the consecutively interpreted interaction: "If people don't have a strong dialect, then I will understand them, and when—but when they use a lot of medical language, then I will probably, out of five terms I will probably understand only two" (remote site video recording at 1:29:25–38).

With regard to the depth of understanding as well as the opportunity to express his personal concerns, the father clearly comes to a highly positive, even enthusiastic assessment of the (simultaneous) interpreting service he has received. Discussing his experience with Doc-B he concludes: "What's important is that it allows you to really understand everything that is said" (remote site video recording at 1:27:50–53).

The father's very favorable judgment actually follows a point of criticism directed against the use of the audio equipment for SI. But unlike the doctor, the father was not so much dissatisfied with the cumbersome gadgetry as with the voice-over principle, which is at the heart of an SI service:

> Well, for me, that thing with the headset just then was a little strange because you always have in a way your ears plugged up and you always focus, you concentrate—you look at the screen, and you can't take in anything else, you don't hear what the doctor is saying, but other than that it worked fine. (remote site video recording at 1:27:28–49)

While this comment also points to relevant issues of gaze direction, the basic complaint about not being able to hear the other speaker is of course peculiar to the mode of limited-proficiency communication that such speakers are accustomed to in the absence of an interpreter. As he had admitted elsewhere, he would understand only a fraction of the doctor's utterances if listening directly; concentrating on the interpretation instead feels highly unusual to him, but it is precisely this mode that allowed him "to really understand everything that is said." Hence his reply to Doc-B's question about his level of comprehension in the simultaneously interpreted consultation: "Yes, I understood everything very well. So when the neurologist was speaking, I understood everything very well."

The father is in fact fully aware of this when he sums up his assessment: "So, again, this is the only drawback, with the headphones, that I was a bit irritated by the headphones (17 s). But I think if this was done more often I would probably get used to it, to the headphones" (remote site video recording at 1:27:54—1:28:19).

INTERPRETERS' PERSPECTIVE

In the interview I conducted with Int-A right after her 45-minute turn of simultaneous dialogue interpreting, the overall assessment was highly favorable. The interpreter, with decades of professional experience working in conference as well as public-service settings, said she had actually been "skeptical that this could work well." She had no complaint about the length of turn, which was excessive by simultaneous conference interpreting standards (cf. Moser-Mercer et al., 1998), and when asked about the technical working conditions stated that "the image quality was very good." Sound quality, in contrast, was sometimes found to be problematic, especially due to noise coming from the two children and body movement picked up by the microphone. This was most critical during the physical examination.

Int-B had similar complaints about sound quality but, in his turn at SI for Fam-B, had suffered in particular from rather thoughtless behavior on the part of the nurse in Provider Team B. Fitted with a microphone that could not be muted, she spoke on the phone while Doc-B was addressing the patient's mother, forcing the interpreter to intervene. On the whole, though, Int-B, who regularly and mostly interprets in on-site consecutive mode at St. Anna Children's Hospital, coped very well with VC-based SI, including the handling of the manual channel switch. When asked about his work in consecutive mode, he said it had been "unrealistically easy." In his experience, patient/parent–provider interactions in pediatric consultations were normally characterized by multiparty talk and frequent overlaps, whereas the interaction between Fam-A and Doc-B was limited to the father speaking with the doctor.

DOCTOR'S PERSPECTIVE

Of all the participant perspectives covered by the analysis of the various datasets, the most skeptical attitudes by far emerged from the debriefing interviews with the two pediatricians. Their most immediate—and understandable—complaint concerned the rather cumbersome audio equipment used in the simultaneous mode. The rather heavy collar-type infrared receivers of the portable SI system, worn in combination with light-frame wireless headset microphones, were admittedly not only inelegant but also impractical. This poor choice of equipment—the best solution to be found under the circumstances—was a key point of discussion in the team session following the field test, and the contractor in charge of supplying the technical infrastructure indicated that more effective audio equipment could be found, at higher cost, in specialist circles such as military communications.

The participating doctors' skepticism was not limited, however, to the choice of ancillary equipment. Rather, it was the provision of interpreting services as such that they did not seem fully convinced of. As suggested earlier in this chapter by way of sketching out the policy background to healthcare interpreting initiatives in Austria, care providers typically rely on ad hoc arrangements involving accompanying persons and auxiliary bilingual staff. This approach to meeting interpreting needs (when the use of rudimentary language skills is patently impossible) has become established practice in the course of several decades and is by now deeply ingrained in care providers' attitudes. Doc-A, who interacted so extensively and successfully with Fam-A, for the first time giving the Serbian-speaking father the satisfaction that he had fully understood as well as made himself understood, candidly expressed his doubts about the systematic provision of technology-based interpreting services during the debriefing interview with the project coordinator.

Before reproducing a lengthy and highly illustrative excerpt from that interview, which I have translated from the German, I must mention a structural imbalance in outpatient hospital care within Austria's socialized public health system. It appears that immigrants with a Turkish background in particular tend not to be familiar with the institution of general practitioners (GPs) or community/family physicians from their (former) home country. Primary care is therefore sought by many members of this community (as by many native-Austrian patients) directly from hospitals. Such apparently misdirected patient flows in the host country may lead hospital physicians to question the need for treatment in their specialized outpatient department—and all the more so the need to provide inter-preting services for communication support to such patients. Against this background, Doc-A can be heard venting his frustration in the interview about the combined burden of presumably misguided hospital visits and language barriers when asked about his attitude toward calling in a trained interpreter when communication with the mother is difficult:

> In the acute situation, if the child is seriously ill, and I need to get something across to her, it would make sense, yes, definitely sensible, but for simple fever stuff and so on, more or less, you often get, with, you get the parents in here, and I tell them things for about 10 minutes and then they go "speak on the phone, there is papa then," you see? So in most cases like that I usually say, no, I won't do that, I won't say everything again when the PC screen is full and it's a 4-hour wait out there; we don't have the resources for that. (Doc-A, debriefing inter-view at 08:15)

This attitude on the part of Doc-A comes up again in the interview when he is asked about the use of the VC-based interpreting system:

> If I see they're helpless, they're poor, the child has something serious and they haven't got a clue, and it's important that I get this across, it would of course be useful if we had one and could say, "Okay, just wait a moment, 5 minutes, take a seat, we take a microphone here, put it there, and then"—that would be perfect. But that's probably not how it will play out in reality, because—but okay, but it would be useful. (Doc-A, debriefing interview at 09:24)

As one can see, these views have little to do with the novel interpreting arrangement as such, which was found to work quite well. Rather, they reflect a pervasive way of coping out of necessity with a "reality" that this hospital physician, who is relatively young and certainly not burned out, perceives as fairly overwhelming. Nevertheless, he had agreed to partici-pate in the video interpreting field test.

SUMMARY

The findings from this first field test of video remote interpreting in simultaneous mode for medical consultations are, on balance, rather favorable as far as technology and technique are concerned. The main problem at the field site was the quite cumbersome audio equipment con-nected to the dual VC system, whereas the latter proved fully satisfactory.

The makeshift solution for headsets and microphones to enable SI resulted from the need to provide for the reality of multiparty communication typical of pediatric settings. Conducting the field test with prototypical doctor-patient dyads would have avoided the technical complications, but the more challenging setting of pediatrics was instrumental in pointing to the need for further improvements to the audio equipment used at the field site.

With respect to the main research questions, it can safely be claimed that the rather simple off-the-shelf VC solution (two point-to-point video links using Microsoft Lync) proved fully viable in the high-performance IT environment of St. Anna Children's Hospital and the University of Vienna. With the exception of the less than user-friendly audio equipment at the clinical site, acceptance of the VC-based interpreting system and of remote simultaneous interpreting was very high. Whereas the father in Fam-A indicated that the headphones would probably take some getting used to, the interpreters worked in remote video mode without feeling any need for special adjustments. At least none was mentioned during the interviews immediately following the interpreting turns (in consecutive as well as simultaneous mode). Even the extended (45-minute) turn taken by Int-A in simultaneous mode was considered quite acceptable, whereas sound quality, especially during physical examinations, remains an issue that requires special attention.

Although the spontaneous behavior of Fam-A, the father of which was not inclined to begin a lengthy medical consultation from scratch with another doctor, did not allow us to implement the comparative study design, it is fair to say that video remote interpreting in simultaneous mode (VRI-S) is, by and large, as functional as video RI in consecutive mode (VRI-C). As demonstrated in our case study, VRI-S can achieve high user satisfaction on the part of patients. From the perspective of the medical institution, the time savings it allows may well offset the higher cost derived from greater demands on IT infrastructure.

DISCUSSION AND CONCLUSIONS

The present contribution to the literature on healthcare interpreting, which has seen impressive development as a professional domain and a topic of research in many countries, exemplifies the broad range of issues in this field—from social policy at government level to communication technology for patient-provider communication. Whereas the former sphere tends to evolve rather slowly, and even with the risk of some setbacks under more difficult sociopolitical and economic circumstances, the latter has been developing at a fast pace and shows evidence of great potential for innovation. Significantly, the use of ICT in support of communication in health care is a broader trend, with doctors in some areas getting ready to "see" their patients and dispense medical advice in remote mode. Technology-supported interpreting services for healthcare interactions between providers and patients not speaking the same language can be expected to ride on that telemedical wave, often using traditional remote interpreting solutions over telephone networks as a starting point. Recent examples, especially in North America, show how video remote interpreting may be turning into a major growth area within the language services industry.

However, as is characteristic of social practices like healthcare interpreting, and community interpreting in general, the national and sociocultural context plays a major role in shaping institution-bound developments. The present contribution is a case in point and illustrates a case of retarded policy development in an increasingly difficult ideological environment. Among affluent welfare states in the industrialized world, Austria takes its place as a developing country when it comes to providing language access to public services for its sizeable immigrant population. Indeed, little, if any, dedicated infrastructure exists for professional healthcare interpreting in the country despite well-established postgraduate training programs for interpreters. Outside the academic context, repeated small-scale efforts over the years have failed to prosper on such barren ground. The latest such initiative, and perhaps the most promising ever in terms of high-level endorsement, is the video interpreting pilot project that prompted the need for the study reported in this chapter—a field test to investigate the viability, acceptability, and usability of videoconference-based remote interpreting in the simultaneous as well as the consecutive mode. Since the use of SI in spoken-language video remote interpreting of medical consultations has not yet been described, the trial described here links the cutting edge in remote interpreting with a national and institutional policy context that can benevolently be described as lagging behind.

Following a review of recent literature on remote interpreting, the study was inspired by work on authentic interpreter-mediated encounters eliciting feedback on satisfaction from all participant perspectives. Given the widespread use of spoken-language VRI in consecutive mode (VRI-C) as well as the established practice of simultaneous VRI with signed languages and reports on the advantages of audio-only RSMI (Gany et al., 2007a, 2007b), a mode-based comparison, consecutive versus simultaneous, was at the heart of the trial. In this respect the field test described here was a failure, as it proved impossible to implement the repeated-consultation design with authentic patients. The test therefore turned into a case study on the viability and acceptability of VRI-S based on a rich set of qualitative data.

Analysis of selected parts of this dataset, in particular the remote-site video recording and the debriefing interviews conducted at both locations, yielded several valuable insights. The main challenge regarding the technical equipment resulted not from the dual VC setup needed to implement SI but from the multiparty dynamics typical of the pediatric setting. The effort to provide all of the main parties with headsets and microphones for full participation in the interaction made the audio system unwieldy and uncomfortable to wear, though it did allow the mother and the nurse to be fully "connected." Admittedly, the situation was simplified by the fact that the mother's limited proficiency in Serbian did not allow her to speak to the provider team. Her more active participation would likely have posed more challenges to the interpreter's turn management in VRI-S. On the other hand, it is not clear whether or to what extent working in consecutive mode makes it easier to deal with simultaneous talk and overlap in multiparty interaction. This remains to be tested in a more successfully implemented comparative study, presumably with a better controlled experimental design based on scripted dialogues.

A language-proficiency-related problem of the opposite sort arose with the father, who understood some German and would have liked to hear the care provider speak despite his awareness of less than complete understanding in this direct mode of interaction. This could make consecutive the mode of choice for those with a certain proficiency in the host-country language, provided that they can still opt for interpreting services at all.

On a broader level, the phenomenon of semitransparent communication by limited-proficiency speakers is of course at the root of the widespread lack of interpreting service provision in community-based settings. The typical case of the father often managing in German but not quite achieving full understanding highlights the problem of undetected message loss in unmediated communication. From the institutional perspective, this risk may seem worth taking in exchange for avoiding the cost and effort of calling in an interpreter. Whether it should be permissible for the care-providing institution to leave the onus of successful understanding on the limited-proficiency client is another matter. Some recent medical liability cases, which had created much of the impetus for the Austrian Federal Health Ministry to take an interest in launching a video interpreting pilot project, have called this pragmatic institutional approach into question at last.

Aside from this soft and possibly shifting ground in the area of legal provisions to ensure equitable access through communication support, multicultural health care in Austria is also influenced by the long-standing problem of the overutilization of hospital outpatient departments instead of GPs—or pediatricians—in private practice. This problem was identified long ago and has been talked about in the context of health-reform policies for years, with little change for the better. (At one point a special fee system for outpatient department utilization was even introduced to redirect patients toward GPs, whose services are covered by the public health-insurance system.)

The original idea for the VRI pilot project had been to serve precisely the highly utilized outpatient departments and thus relieve some of the pressure arising from the high volume of patients, not least from immigrant communities. It has emerged from the case study, however, that these difficult conditions may actually make hospital physicians less inclined to accept the introduction of institutionalized interpreting services. Therefore, it has meanwhile been agreed to also include some GPs in private practice among the designated service users in the pilot project, with costs to be borne by the medical association.

By way of conclusion, I would like to state that the link between the IERM-led pilot project and the feasibility test to investigate technology and technique as well as acceptance of a VRI system on the part of users and interpreters has become less close as the project leadership has entrusted the videoconferencing solution to a different provider. A new server-based VC platform has been programmed for the project, which will operate only in consecutive mode. As has become evident from the new contractor's site visits at the participating hospitals and outpatient clinics, the existing IT infrastructure is mostly insufficient to ensure consistent bandwidth for the operation of two parallel videoconferences, as required for SI. With the newly developed VC technology and staff costs for a total of eight interpreters hired for the 6-month duration of the pilot project already straining existing resources, upgrading the IT infrastructure in a dozen or so institutions cannot reasonably be part of the project.

It remains to be seen whether St. Anna Children's Hospital, which proved such a potent partner for the field test of VRI in the simultaneous mode, could be persuaded again to conduct a trial with VRI-S in the course of its participation in the pilot project. There is some hope that this could be the case, as the successful interdepartmental partnership between the IERM as the pilot project leader and coordinator, and the University of Vienna Center for Translation Studies seems to have managed the first successful trial of VRI in simultaneous mode to enable real-time communication in two spoken languages in a medical setting.

ACKNOWLEDGMENTS

I wish to express my sincere gratitude to all of the partners in the video interpreting pilot project who have made this study possible: Maria Kletecka-Pulker and Sabine Parrag as project leader and coordinator, respectively, at the Department of Medical Law and Ethics (IERM); my colleague Mira Kadrić at the Center for Translation Studies as well as the technicians there; and Katrin Mahlstedt, whose enthusiastic contribution to the field test was essential even though the related thesis project never materialized.

REFERENCES

Azarmina, P., & Wallace, P. (2009). Remote interpreting in medical encounters: A systematic review. *Journal of Telemedicine and Telecare, 11*, 140–145.

Braun, S., & Taylor, J. L. (Eds.) (2011). *Videoconference and remote interpreting in criminal proceedings*. Guildford: University of Surrey. Retrieved May 20, 2012, from http://www.videoconference-interpreting.net/BraunTaylor2011.html

Gany, F., Kapelusznik, L., Prakash, K., Gonzalez, J., Orta, L. Y., Tseng, C. H., & Changrani, J. (2007a). The impact of medical interpretation method on time and errors. *Journal of General Internal Medicine, 22* (Suppl. 2), 319–323.

Gany, F., Leng, J., Shapiro, E., Abramson, D., Motola, I., Shield, D. C., & Changrani, J. (2007b). Patient satisfaction with different interpreting methods: A randomized controlled trial. *Journal of General Internal Medicine, 22* (Suppl. 2), 312–318.

Hornberger, J. C., Gibson, C. D., Wood, W., De[g]ueldre, C., Corso, I., Palla, B., & Bloch, D. A. (1996). Eliminating language barriers for non-English-speaking patients. *Medical Care, 34*, 845–856.

Jones, D., Gill, P., Harrison, R., Meakin, R., & Wallace, P. (2003). An exploratory study of language interpretation services provided by videoconferencing. *Journal of Telemedicine and Telecare, 9*, 51–56.

Korak, C. (2010). *Remote interpreting via Skype: Anwendungsmöglichkeiten von VoIP-Software im Bereich Community Interpreting: Communicate everywhere?* Berlin: Frank & Timme.

Locatis, C., Williamson, D., Gould-Kabler, C., Zone-Smith, L., Detzler, I., Robertson, J., Maisiak, R., & Ackermann, M. (2010). Comparing in-person, video, and telephonic medical interpretation. *Journal of General Internal Medicine, 25*, 345–350.

Moser-Mercer, B., Künzli, A., & Korac, M. (1998). Prolonged turns in interpreting: Effects on quality, physiological and psychological stress (pilot study). *Interpreting, 3*(1), 47–64.

Ozolins, U. (2000). Communication needs and interpreting in multilingual settings: The international spectrum of response. In R. P. Roberts, S. E. Carr, D. Abraham, & A. Dufour (Eds.), *The Critical Link 2: Interpreters in the community* (pp. 21–33). Amsterdam: Benjamins.

Ozolins, U. (2010). Factors that determine the provision of public service interpreting: Comparative perspectives on government motivation and language service implementation. *JoSTrans: Journal of Specialised Translation, 14*. Retrieved May 20, 2012, from http://www.jostrans.org/issue14/art_ozolins.php

Pöchhacker, F. (2000). Language barriers in Vienna hospitals. *Ethnicity and Health, 5*(2), 113–119.

Pöchhacker, F. (2007). Giving access—or not: A developing-country perspective on healthcare interpreting. In F. Pöchhacker, A.-L. Jakobsen, & I. M. Mees (Eds.), *Interpreting studies and beyond: A tribute to Miriam Shlesinger* (pp. 121–137). Copenhagen: Samfundslitteratur Press.

Price, E. L., Pérez-Stable, E. J., Nickleach, D., López, M., & Karliner, L. S. (2012). Interpreter perspectives of in-person, telephonic, and videoconferencing medical interpretation in clinical encounters. *Patient Education and Counseling, 87*, 226–232.

Roziner, I., & Shlesinger, M. (2010). Much ado about something remote: Stress and performance in remote interpreting. *Interpreting, 12*(2), 214–247.

Saint-Louis, L., Friedman, E., Chiasson, E., Quessa, A., & Novaes, F. (2003). *Testing new technologies in medical interpreting*. Somerville, MA: Cambridge Health Alliance.

Healthcare Accessibility and the Role of Sign Language Interpreters

Beppie van den Bogaerde and Rob de Lange

ABSTRACT

Hearing healthcare professionals do not seem to be aware of the fact that when interacting with deaf and hard of hearing clients they need specific knowledge, skills, and insights for optimal interaction. In an exploratory study we questioned deaf clients (n = 276) as well as medical healthcare workers (n = 445) about their experiences with accessibility to health care for deaf clients. We present the results for a subgroup of eight sign language interpreters (SLIs) and four Deaf communication experts (called the expert group) that participated in the survey and compare them with the answers provided by deaf clients and hearing medical professionals.

We found that only 28% of the deaf clients always ask for a sign language interpreter when visiting a healthcare practitioner, whereas 36% of the hearing professionals said that an SLI was present. The results also indicate that the expert group perceive their knowledge of a client's background as insufficient, whereas the hearing medical professionals believe they know enough to provide sufficient care. This points to a possible unconscious incompetence in the latter group. Subjective evaluations of whether the information provided to deaf clients is sufficient, differ significantly between the expert group members and the hearing healthcare workers. When asked whether the professionals understood the deaf clients, again the expert group differed considerably from the hearing professionals. Our results show, like Alexander, Ladd, and Powell (2012), that deaf-awareness training for all healthcare staff is not only to be recommended but also highly necessary.

In health care, comprehensible communication is a prerequisite (Van Wieringen, Harmsen, & Bruijnzeels, 2002). When patients and healthcare providers do not understand each other because they do not share a language, in a worst-case scenario life-threatening situations can arise (Doof.nl, 2006). Besides language barriers, various cultural references can also influence the experience of health care.

In the Netherlands, an estimated 418,000 people who are 12 years of age and older experience hearing restrictions during a conversation with one other person. About 1,093,000 people have problems when communicating with a group of three or more persons (CBS-POLS, 2009). The number of early (prelingually) deaf and severely hard of hearing persons is about 20,000 (Nationaal Kompas Volksgezondheid, 2013). On average the Dutch (approx. population 16.8 million) visit a healthcare professional about 1.5 times a year. For prelingually deaf persons this would come to approximately 30,000 healthcare visits per annum (De Bruin, 2007). "Adults who are deaf or who experience significant problems hearing were three times as likely to report fair or poor health compared with those who did not have hearing impairments" (National Council on Disability, 2009, p. 10). This implies even more medical visits made by this population than the earlier estimation. However, research shows that deaf people visit physicians less often than hearing people (Barnett & Franks, 2002).

Deaf and hard of hearing clients face communicative difficulties when interacting with hearing healthcare professionals, most of whom have neither the means nor the knowledge to communicate in a comprehensive way with deaf and hard of hearing clients (Smeijers & Pfau, 2009). They are usually not proficient in a signed language and are not aware of the settings necessary for lipreading. As a result, other forms of communication have to be used to facilitate understanding. In practice, people often use pen and paper or gestures to communicate.

The use of discipline-specific language is generally customary for care providers. For healthcare practitioners, too often a gap exists between what the provider is intending to say and how patients interpret and act on that information. Bridging that terminology gap is one goal of the growing field of health literacy, a movement designed to enhance communication and understanding in health care (Ragovin, 2013). However, with deaf people, who often have low general-literacy skills, the content of the messages does not always come across. This can lead to dangerous situations in which the deaf client does not properly understand the prescribed medication, for instance.

Hearing healthcare professionals do not seem to be aware of the fact that when interacting with deaf and hard of hearing clients one needs specific knowledge, skills, and insights for optimal interaction. The main bottlenecks mentioned in the literature (e.g., Harmer, 1999) are language barriers, unfamiliarity with the role of the sign language interpreter/speech-to-text interpreter, lack of awareness of the fact that deaf and hard of hearing clients can have additional cultural references that can influence their view of health care and the fact that deaf and hard of hearing clients often refrain from requesting an interpreter or even from indicating that they have a hearing impairment.

This problem is not unique to the Netherlands. Alexander, Ladd, and Powell (2012) make some very critical remarks about the situation in the United Kingdom:

> Most health-care workers have little experience of sign-language users because few are in the public eye or are health-care professionals. Ignorance leads to negative attitudes, and patients from the Deaf community endure both individual and institutional discrimination. . . . A UK survey showed that 77% of BSL [British Sign Language] users had difficulty communicating with hospital staff. 33% left consultations with their family doctor unsure about medication instructions or subsequently took the wrong doses. . . . Nevertheless, 87% of family doctors feel that they can communicate effectively with their hard of hearing patients and those who use BSL. Most worryingly, however, 30% of BSL users avoid seeing their family doctor because of communication difficulties, thereby risking their health rather than facing another struggle with the health-care system. (pp. 979–980)

The rather cynical title of the article from which this quote is taken is "Deafness Might Damage Your Health."

Parallel to our larger study, we organized a side pilot project (Van Bentum et al., 2009) to determine whether regular healthcare providers (doctors, nurses, other medical professionals) at the University Medical Center in Utrecht, had received any information *during their training* about communicating with deaf and hard of hearing patients. A total of 180 professionals were approached, of whom 110 (61%) responded. A majority of the 110 respondents (68%) stated that they had received no information whatsoever about communicating with deaf or hard of hearing patients when they were students. The almost complete lack of information about deaf patients during training produces professionals who have inadequate knowledge of this group of patients. These

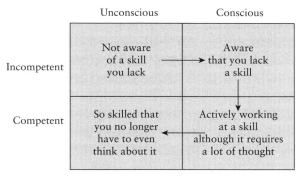

	Unconscious	Conscious
Incompetent	Not aware of a skill you lack ——→	Aware that you lack a skill
Competent	So skilled that you no longer ←— have to even think about it	Actively working at a skill although it requires a lot of thought

FIGURE 1. *The four stages of learning (Adams, GTI website).*

professionals might be termed "unconsciously incompetent" in that they do not even realize they might lack an important skill or valuable knowledge (Adams, n.d., and see figure 1). In addition, while 73% (*n* = 81) of the respondents had at one time encountered a deaf patient, 67 of these (83%) had experienced communication problems with these patients, which made them "consciously incompetent." The website of Gordon Training International provides the following description for this model (Adams, n.d.).

Stage 1. Unconsciously incompetent. We don't know what we don't know. We are inept and unaware of it.

Stage 2. Consciously incompetent. We know what we don't know. We start to learn at this level when sudden awareness of how poorly we do something shows us how much we need to learn.

Stage 3. Consciously competent. Trying the skill out, experimenting, practicing. We now know how to do the skill the right way, but need to think and work hard to do it.

Stage 4. Unconsciously competent. If we continue to practice and apply the new skills, eventually we arrive at a stage where they become easier and, given time, even natural.

Even though we did not ask the hearing professionals who participated in our survey about their training in communicating with deaf clients, the results of the aforementioned pilot study prompt us to be careful about trusting the reliability of the communicative self-evaluation of hearing professionals. This model could be very relevant, and we return to this issue in the discussion of the results.

RESEARCH QUESTIONS ARTICULATED BY PROFESSIONALS IN HEALTH CARE FOR DEAF PEOPLE

Dutch healthcare professionals from de Gelderhorst[1] and de Riethorst,[2] institutions specifically for deaf people, experience various problems every day when assisting deaf and hard of hearing clients in their communications with hearing healthcare professionals in general practice or in hospitals. In 2006, as a result of their request that this problem be addressed, the SIA RAAK[3] project was initiated. Until then, neither the extent of the problem nor the primary underlying factors causing these difficulties in communication were clear.

In conversations and particularly in medical consultations, the various participants may have different views of the interaction. Thus it is important to hear the perspective of both sides with regard to communicating with each other. The first question that guided our research was, How do deaf and hard of hearing clients experience and evaluate their communications with hearing healthcare professionals? The second question was the converse, How do hearing healthcare professionals experience and evaluate their communications with deaf and hard of hearing clients?

In this chapter we analyze the results of an expert group of sign language interpreters (SLIs) ($n = 8$) and deaf signing professionals ($n = 4$) among the respondents and relate their results to the answers provided by deaf clients and hearing medical professionals. We wanted to find an answer to the question, What can we learn from this group of experts ($n = 12$) in Deaf communication and Deaf culture to improve communication between deaf and hard of hearing clients and hearing healthcare providers?

METHOD

The three research questions were broken down into a series of subquestions and eventually operationalized as two separate digital questionnaires: Questionnaire A, with 36 questions for deaf and hard of hearing clients (Appendix A), and Questionnaire B, with 32 questions for (mostly hearing but some deaf) healthcare professionals (Appendix B). Among the latter group were eight sign language interpreters and four deaf signing professionals mentioned earlier, whom we called the "expert group" and whose answers we compared to those of the hearing healthcare providers.

Procedures

We developed the questionnaires ourselves, and feedback on them was provided by several expert professionals from the Riethorst and the Gelderhorst who participated in the project, as well as by other external deaf care professionals and expert researchers in general health care who served as an advisory group for our project. The questionnaire for the deaf and hard of hearing clients (Appendix A) was offered in two ways: online through SurveyMonkey[4] for those who preferred to participate via the Internet and a paper questionnaire for those who did not. We also offered the questionnaire to deaf and hearing participants at Deaf and hard of hearing events, where larger numbers of deaf and hard of hearing people convened, for instance, on World Deaf Day (every year in September) or at specially organized events (e.g., Day for Elderly Deaf People). The results of the paper questionnaire were entered into SurveyMonkey by students[5] of the Institute for Sign, Language, & Deaf Studies at the University of Applied Sciences Utrecht. The link to the online questionnaire for the care providers was sent to a contact person at the participating institutions (*n* = 6; see table 1) and subsequently forwarded to all of their employees via their local intranets.

The outcomes of the questionnaires were processed and analyzed with the help of the *Statistical Package for the Social Sciences* (SPSS). The responses to the open questions were coded after they had been discussed by the research group. The relevant variables were processed into frequency tables, cross tables, and diagrams, and a factor analysis was done on some

TABLE 1. *Information on the Respondents of the Questionnaire for the Care Professionals*

	All n =	%	expert group (n = 12)	%
Hospital *Gelderse Vallei*	304	67.7		
De Gelderhorst	81	18.0	4	33.3
De Riethorst	40	8.9	8	66.7
Pharmacy *De Rietkampen*	13	2.9		
GP post *Ede*	11	2.4		
Subtotal	449	100.0		
Missing	8			
Total	457		12	

of the variables (see details in the section titled "Communication during Contact between Deaf Clients and Hearing Healthcare Providers").

Participants

A total of 276 deaf and hard of hearing people filled out the first questionnaire (Appendix A). The second questionnaire (Appendix B) was offered to the Riethorst (department for Deaf and hard of hearing clients) and the Gelderhorst in Ede (province of Gelderland) as well as to several institutions that operate in their vicinity and cater to their clientele for medical treatment. Table 1 gives information about the various institutions as provided by a total of 449 professional respondents, including the expert group that we highlight in this chapter.

It was interesting—and discouraging—to see that only 304 (15%) of the 2,000 employees of the Gelderse Vallei Hospital filled out questionnaire B (see table 2); again, perhaps this is an indication that communication with deaf clients is not a priority in health care. The two special centers for deaf people, Gelderhorst and Riethorst, mentioned earlier, showed a very high response rate, 55% and 63% (81 out of 146 and 40 out of 64 employees), respectively. Of the employees of the GP (medical) facility called "Ede" (n = 57), 11 filled out the questionnaire (19%). A splendid response rate was provided by the employees of the local pharmacy, Rietkampen, where all of the employees (n = 13) participated in the survey. A second medical facility called "Maandereng" was left out of the data since none of the employees responded. Table 2 presents information about the total number of employees of the different participating institutions and the number and percentages of respondents.

TABLE 2. *Total Number of Employees, and Number and Percentages of Respondents*

Institute	Number of employees	Number of respondents	Percentage of respondents
Hospital *Gelderse Vallei Ziekenhuis*	2000	304	15 %
De Gelderhorst	146	81	55 %
De Riethorst	64	40	63 %
GP Post *Ede*	57	11	19 %
GP Post *Maandereng*	13	0	0 %
Pharmacy *Rietkampen*	13	13	100 %
Total	2293	449	20 %

RESULTS

Background of the Respondents

Deaf and Hard of Hearing Respondents

Questionnaire A was filled out by 276 deaf or hard of hearing respondents. Questions A1, A2, and A3 pertained to their background. Of the respondents, 60% were female; 80% were deaf at birth, 10% became deaf later in life, and 10% were hard of hearing. More than half of the respondents were over 60 years of age (58%). Another 26% were between 40 and 60 years old, and 16% were younger than 40. Partly because of the way we collected the paper questionnaires at the big event for elderly deaf people, the respondents do not seem to form a valid representation of the Deaf community in the Netherlands.

The respondents were asked to answer the questionnaire with respect to one or two particular visits they had made to a healthcare practitioner (question A8). Most persons chose a visit to a general practitioner at a medical facility or a hospital (82%), while other visits included professionals like dentists and physiotherapists.

Hearing Professional Respondents

A total of 457 hearing healthcare professionals filled out questionnaire B (see table 3). Questions B1 through B5 focused on personal information. Of the respondents, 75% were female; 45% were under 40 years of age; 52% were between 40 and 60 years of age; and 2% were over 60. The hearing healthcare providers worked in various functions: most of them were nurses (31%) or worked as assistants or receptionists (25%), social workers (7%), doctors (7%), or analysts (6%) or served in various other capacities (24%), such as teamleaders, activity coordinators, hospital hostesses, and so forth.

Expert Group

The twelve respondents that we called the expert group are all employees of the specialized centers for deaf people (four at the Gelderhorst and eight at the Riethorst) and have many years of experience (see table 3). Questions B1 through B5 revealed that the age range of the nine female and three male employees is 21–55 years. Eight hearing employees have a degree (bachelor's or comparable) as interpreters of NGT (Nederlandse Gebarentaal, Sign Language of the Netherlands), and four deaf professionals hold a bachelor's degree as teachers of NGT.

TABLE 3. *Duration of Employment of Expert Professionals and the Hearing Professionals*

	Experts		All	
	n	%	n	%
<2 yrs	1	8.3	77	16.8
2 - 5 yrs	3	25.0	112	24.5
6 - 10 yrs	5	41.7	99	21.7
11 - 15 yrs	2	16.7	37	8.1
16 - 20 yrs	1	8.3	39	8.5
21 - 25 yrs	-	-	21	4.6
26 - 30 yrs	-	-	11	2.4
31 - 35 yrs	-	-	3	.7
More than 35 yrs	-	-	2	.4

Thus all of the experts (3% of all respondents) have several years of higher education. Of the other healthcare workers 42% have degrees, 33% have completed vocational training at the secondary level, and 22% have completed a general secondary education. They function mainly as nurses (31%), secretaries (25%), physicians (7%), or department heads (7%), the remainder form a miscellaneous group (30%).

How Deaf Clients Make an Appointment

A patient's first contact with a healthcare provider usually takes place when making an appointment. In the United Kingdom, under the Equality Act of 2010, it is a legal requirement that deaf and hard of hearing clients be able to make appointments. There is no such law in the Netherlands, and at the majority of medical institutions, patients must use a telephone to make an appointment. However, Kalb (2010) mentions three alternative ways for deaf clients to make an appointment: go in person, use a mediating telephone facility (with an interpreter via telephone), or use a chat program.

Question A9 asked how the deaf client made such appointments. The results show that they did so in the following ways: 32% actually went to the institution in person, 27% let others make the appointment, 18% used email, 11% used a fax machine, 7% used a text phone, and 5% made a telephone call themselves. In open question A10 the respondents were asked to describe how well the appointment-making process went: 75% rated the process as good, 17% stated that it did not go very well or even went unsatisfactorily, and 8% reported that others made the appointment because they could not do it themselves.

We did not ask the hearing professionals these same questions. Instead, we asked them (question B12) whether they had ever come into contact with a deaf or hard of hearing client; nearly all of the professionals (94%) had done so at least once. This percentage is higher than was found in our pilot project, where 73% out of 110 hearing healthcare providers ($n = 81$) had encountered a deaf client. Based on the 83% ($n = 67$) of those who had communication problems with these deaf clients, we expect that 83% of the hearing healthcare providers in our survey ($n = 333$) will also report communication problems (see the following section). However, taking into account the four stages of learning (figure 1), the percentage of reported communication problems may well be much lower here. In the next section we further discuss this issue as it relates to questions A12 and B13.

Communication during Contact between Deaf Clients and Hearing Healthcare Providers

The deaf participants were asked to describe the quality of communication in two consultations with healthcare providers (question A12). The results for the two situations were relatively similar (figure 2), so we merged the results.

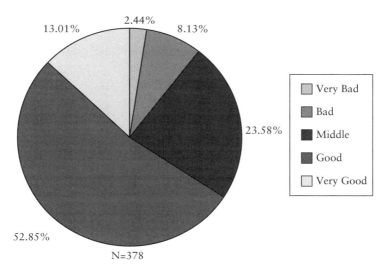

FIGURE 2. *Results for Question A12: Description of communication in situation 1 (n = 254) and situation 2 (n = 124).*

TABLE 4. *Average Evaluations of Different Example Situations Provided by the Deaf and Hard of Hearing Clients*

Visit 1	Mean	N	Std. Deviation
General physician	3.74	110	.809
Physician in hospital	3.52	79	1.060
Dentist	3.55	20	1.050
Physical therapist	3.71	14	.825
Pharmacist	3.25	4	.957
Nurse/doctor's assistant	3.50	4	1.291
Total	3.63	231	.932

This evaluation of the quality of communication differs according to the situation and the professional. Table 4 shows the average number of evaluations per situation/professional, ranked from higher to lower, based on situation 1, as given as an example by the deaf and hard of hearing clients ($n = 231$).

On average, the general practitioner scored the highest on clients' judgments of the communication (3.74 on a 5-point scale); the nurse/doctor's assistant scored the lowest on average (3.50). The standard deviation indicates how much the evaluations vary. Thus the opinions of the nurse/doctor's assistant show the highest variation (SD = 1.291).

When deaf or hard of hearing participants were asked how they would *like* the healthcare professional to act during consultations (question A33), clear enunciation was most often mentioned (29%); establishing eye contact was brought up by 21%; the ability to use sign language, by 31%; writing things down, by 15%; and explaining/drawing, by 4%. Steinberg et al. (2002, p. 733) quote a prototypical example of a deaf woman's experience with a doctor's negative attitude toward people who are deaf: "The doctor had a mask on, so I could not read his lips, but we had this interpreter with us, and [she interpreted when] the doctor said, 'Well, the Deaf woman should tie her tubes so she doesn't get pregnant again.'"

Only 28% of our deaf participants always ask for a sign language interpreter when visiting a healthcare practitioner (question A11), 32% sometimes, and 40% never. When this last group was asked why they never ask for a sign language interpreter, they gave the following reasons: "I bring someone I know to translate" (50%), "I don't need it" (34%), "They are never available" (8%), and "I don't know how to" (8%).

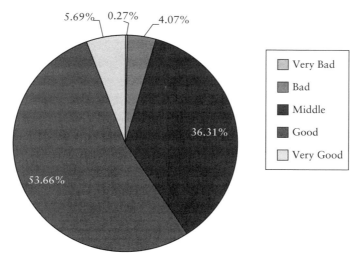

FIGURE 3. *Description of contact with deaf/hoh clients by hearing professionals (n = 371).*

Most deaf persons feel that they received clear information from the healthcare professional (78%) (question A16), that the professional understood them (72%) (question A17), and that there was enough time for the interaction (80%) (question A18). Age and hearing status did not affect these outcomes.

For question B13 the professional hearing respondents (95%) reported that their encounter with a deaf or hard of hearing client went "average" (midpoint of the scale) to "very well," and only 5% said that it went "badly" or "very badly" (see figure 3).

Of the respondents, 79% would like to know whether a client is deaf *before* the actual encounter occurs (question B11). Furthermore, 97% stated that they adjusted their communication to the deaf client (question B14), 87% said that this adjustment was successful (question B17), and 66% believed that they had given sufficient information to the client (question B20). Time needed (92%), understanding the client (90%), making oneself clear (88%), and asking about the client's experiences (82%) were most often mentioned as aspects that differ from a consultation with a hearing client (question B23).

When asked *how* they gave information to the client, 75% say they did so orally (i.e., in spoken language), 56% in writing, and 36% via a sign language interpreter (question B21; multiple answers were possible) (see table 5).

TABLE 5. *Question 21: Means of Conveying Information by Hearing Professionals*

	n	% of responses	% of respondents
Oral (spoken Dutch)	257	44.9	82.6
In writing	191	33.4	61.4
Via an interpreter	124	21.7	39.9
Total	572	100.0	183.9

The overall impression here is that the hearing professionals address the deaf and hard of hearing clients in spoken language or use writing to make themselves understood. Only 40% of the hearing healthcare providers mention the use of sign language interpreters to a lesser extent (22%).

Factor Analysis of Answers by Healthcare Providers

In our search for patterns that might further explain some of the findings, we performed an exploratory factor analysis[6] on 12 variables that seemed theoretically suitable and met the following criteria: measured on an interval scale and sufficient response (De Vellis, 2003). For inclusion in the analysis, we required that factor loadings have an absolute value of at least 0.40. Ten variables met this criterion. We extracted two factors (principal components) with an Eigen value larger than 1. Together these factors explain 42% of the variance (table 6).

These factors are not easy to interpret. The first factor could be called "quality of information about deaf or hard of hearing clients." Female gender shows a positive loading on this factor, indicating that in general the female respondents scored higher on this dimension than the male respondents.[7] This factor explains 24% of the variance and is very reliable (α = .80).

We called the second factor "respondents' own communicative competence." This factor explains 18% of the variance, and the reliability is good (α = .69). The factor scores were retained for further analysis. Figure 4 shows the mean factor scores per institution as a bar chart.

Figure 4 shows that the general hospital (Gelderse Vallei, letter A), Rietkampen pharmacy (letter D), and the medical facility in Ede (letter E) score below average on quality of information and differ greatly from the professionals in the special centers for deaf and hard of hearing clients.

TABLE 6. *Factors with a Value of at Least .40 in the Factor Analysis*

Question	Text of question	Factor 1	Factor 2
10	Do you know something about the client prior to the actual contact?	.527	
13	How did this contact go?		.622
17	In how far was your adjustment successful?		.809
20	Did you give sufficient information?		.754
22	Did you understand the deaf/h-o-h client?		.603
27	Is there information about deaf/h-o-h clients in your department?	.535	
29a	This information about communication is helpful	.867	
29b	This information about communication is useful	.836	
29c	This information about communication is complete	.792	
5	Gender	.439	
	% variance explained	24%	18%
	Cronbach's Alpha	.80	.69

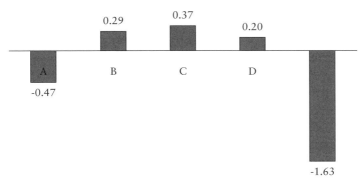

FIGURE 4. Mean scores on factor 1 *Quality of information about deaf or hard-of-hearing clients.*
A = Hospital *Gelderse Vallei*, B = *De Gelderhorst*, C = *De Riethorst*,
D = Pharmacy *Rietkampen* and E = General Physician Post *Ede.*

Comparing Results from the Expert Group to Those from Deaf Respondents and Care Providers

FACTOR 1. QUALITY OF INFORMATION ABOUT DEAF OR HARD OF HEARING CLIENTS

Did you know anything about the patient's background prior to the appointment (e.g., gender, age, cultural background, language)? (question B10)

On a scale of one to five (from "nothing at all" to "a lot") the expert group scored 17% for "a lot," compared to 5% for the hearing professionals. Moreover, the hearing professionals (34%) claimed to know nothing at all or a little bit about the patients, while the expert group (17%) knew "nothing at all" about their client.

Is there information about communicating with deaf or hard of hearing patients in your department? (question B27)

The hearing professionals indicated that they did not to know whether there was information in their department (38%) or said that there was no information (30%). Only one-third of them confirmed that information was available. This is in contrast to the expert group, who all said that information is available; of course, they work in specialized institutions for deaf people, so that is to be expected. We also asked what kind information, if any, was available. The following types of information were mentioned (table 7).

So in some cases information was available or could at least be obtained from the Internet; however, 68% of the hearing care providers ($n = 299$) indicated that they never consulted the available information, in comparison to 42% of the expert group. The latter could indeed look up information and did this more often than the hearing professionals.

TABLE 7. *Type of Information Provided by the Care Providers*

Type of information	n
Communication research (and advice)	16
How to arrange for an Interpreter (tel. no.)	15
Folders	15
Deaf staff	10
On computer or via Internet	10
Sign Language course	9
Care dossier	9
Protocols	8
Sign dictionary	5
List with signs	4
General Information	4
Communication chart	4
DVD's	2
Explanation about sign language	1
Folder with information	1
Pictures for deaf patients, sheet with info	1
Total	114

When the hearing professionals were asked why they did not look up information (question B28), they provided the following answers (*n* = 82) (table 8).

Is this information about communication helpful, useful, and complete? (question B29)

In general the quantity and quality of the information were not rated very highly by the hearing professionals. About 42% rated the information as fairly to very helpful, useful, and complete, in contrast to the expert group, who rated it as fairly/very helpful (55%/45%), fairly/very useful (64%/27%), and fairly complete (55%). The expert group differed here from the hearing professionals in that they often consult the information themselves even though they are already (consciously) competent in communicating. In this they obviously differ from the hearing healthcare providers. When we cluster their answers in table 8 according to consciousness and competence (letters in table 8: b, c, e, f, g, j, k, l = 46%), we find that almost half of the hearing healthcare providers gave no evidence that they even realized that there is something to be informed about. They can be labeled as unconsciously incompetent, according to the model described in section 1.

TABLE 8. *Reasons Mentioned by Hearing Professionals to* Not *Consult Information About the Communication with Deaf or Hard of Hearing Patients*

Why not consult information?	*n*
a Not necessary (no contact with deaf)	27
b Don't know if there is any	26
c Hardly ever needed	10
d Patient can make himself clear (via Interpreter, family member)	5
e No time	4
f I am alright	3
g Never thought of it	2
h I work in a children's department	1
i I don't know beforehand whether or not a deaf patient will come	1
j I know what there is	1
k I don't know	1
l I want to find out for myself	1
Total	82

FACTOR 2. RESPONDENTS' OWN COMMUNICATIVE COMPETENCE

Figure 5 shows that only the institutions for deaf people (Gelderhorst [letter B] and Riethorst [letter C]) score above average on communicative competence.

Later we discuss some of the variables in more detail and compare the results for both groups.

How did this [direct] contact [with the deaf client] go? (question B13)

We have already discussed communication between the deaf participants and the healthcare providers during the consultation (figures 1 and 2). The expert group (75%) rated the contact as having gone "well," and 25% rated it as having gone "very well," compared to 55% and 12%, respectively, for the deaf clients and 54% and 6%, respectively, for the hearing professionals. Apparently the expert group believed they enabled a good encounter between the clients and the healthcare providers, whereas both the hearing professionals and the deaf clients indicated there was much room for improvement.

Did you adjust your communication, and, if you did, how did you do so? (questions B14 and B16)

The twelve experts claimed they fully adjusted their communication to the participants (100%), while 97% of the hearing professionals said they had done so. However, 68% of the deaf clients perceived the communicative adjustment of the hearing professionals to be far less (question A13).

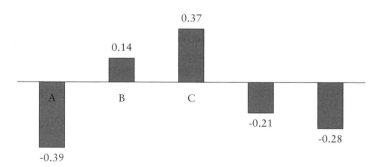

FIGURE 5. Mean scores on factor 2 *Respondents' own communication competence.*

A = Hospital *Gelderse Vallei*, B = *De Gelderhorst*, C = *De Riethorst*, D = Pharmacy *Rietkampen* and E = General Physician Post *Ede*.

The deaf respondents implicitly indicated that they can communicate satisfactorily with mediators like interpreters or deaf supporters.

How successful was your adjustment? (question B17)

In addition, 50% of the expert group answered that their adjustment was quite successful, and 50%, very successful, compared to 61% and 17%, respectively, for the hearing professionals. According to the expert group, this was because they believed they had a great deal of specific communicative knowledge (75%), whereas only 35% of the hearing professionals felt similarly. Of course this is to be expected. What is surprising is that this response was given by only 75% of the expert group: one would expect a higher rate of success evaluation in adjusting to their deaf clientele. Perhaps they are more sensitive to a possible lack of competence than are the other hearing professionals (which would place them in the consciously incompetent corner; see figure 1).

Table 9 lists the indications the hearing professionals considered as to why they perceived their communicative adjustments as successful.

The client's reaction was by far the most useful indication for the hearing professionals, as well as their own subjective impression that the client was understanding what they were saying. However, when deaf clients were asked whether they had received clear information from the hearing care provider 39% answered that the information was fairly clear, and only 14% stated that it was very clear (figure 6). More

TABLE 9. *Question 18. How Did You Know Whether or Not Your Communication Was Successful?*

	All		*12 expert signers*	
	n	%	n	%
Telling back/reaction client	173	54.7	3	33.3
I think client understood	109	34.5		
Communication improved	9	2.8		
Communication did not improve	9	2.8		
Interpreter	7	2.2	6	66.7
Checked via family/accompanying person	4	1.3		
I don't know	3	.9		
I understand client better	2	.6		
Total	316	100.0	9	
Missing	141		3	

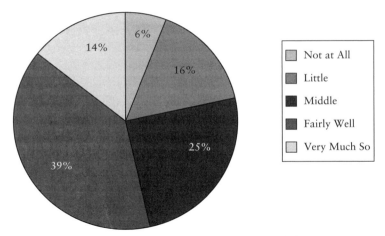

FIGURE 6. *Impression of clarity of information to the deaf clients in situation 1 (n = 253) combined with situation 2 (n = 118), n total = 371.*

important, 22% said that the information was either not very clear or not clear at all.

This is also in contrast to what the hearing professionals thought about the information transfer to their deaf or hard of hearing clients (question B20): 67% believed that they were fairly to very successful, whereas only 54% of the deaf clients felt the same.

The expert group was very confident that they were successful in information transfer: fairly successful (67%) and very successful (25%).

Of the deaf clients, 74% believed they were well understood by the hearing professional, whereas 97% of the latter claimed that they had understood their deaf or hard of hearing client. The expert group was again very confident that they understood the clients (100%). The discrepancy between the deaf clients and the hearing healthcare providers indicates that the hearing professionals overestimate their communication skills with deaf and hard of hearing clients. Table 9 shows that they stated successful communication was due to an interpreter in only 2% of the consultations with a deaf or hard of hearing patient. We conclude that interpreters were only seldomly used.

DISCUSSION

In this study we sought to learn how deaf and hard of hearing clients experience and evaluate their communications with hearing healthcare professionals. The results clearly show that although the respondents' opinions vary quite a bit, about 10% perceived the communications to be bad or very bad; nearly a quarter considered them average; and 66% judged them to be good or very good. However, when asked what could be improved, 31% of the deaf patients expressed a preference for sign language communication rather than spoken language; however, if spoken language were used, it should at least be clearly articulated, and good eye contact should be maintained. We know that hearing care providers in general do not have any signing skills, so a substantial use of interpreting services would be expected of the deaf respondents. Nonetheless, only 28% of them regularly use a sign language interpreter in medical situations. Considering the competency model (figure 1), it would be interesting to see whether the deaf patients could also be described as unconsciously incompetent in their own perceived need for an interpreter. This might be particularly true for this specific group of respondents, in which elderly deaf patients were overrepresented. It would be of interest to overcome the limitations of this study and in new research find out how younger deaf patients would evaluate their contact with the medical profession.

Our second research question focused on how hearing healthcare professionals experience and evaluate their communications with deaf and hard of hearing clients. The hearing professionals believed that the information they supplied was sufficient and well understood. Considering the inaccessibility of speech and the prevalence of low (health) literacy in many deaf clients as well as the hearing professionals' preference for using speech and writing with their clients, it is no wonder that the deaf clients feel they might be missing vital information during interactions with their hearing healthcare provider. The fact that only 66% of the hearing professionals believed that they managed to convey sufficient information to their deaf clients indicates that they have similar doubts as well. This emerging awareness of their own incompetence is partly corroborated by the fact that 97% indicated that they had adjusted their communication to meet the deaf patient's needs. What is more, according to them, they had successfully done so (87%), although fewer (78%) patients concurred.

Hearing professionals have been shown to be unconsciously incompetent in their self-evaluation of their communications with deaf and hard of hearing patients, so we may well wonder whether the estimations in this study are based on solid grounds. The fact that from some institutions only very few people—or none—filled out the questionnaire is both surprising and disturbing and emphasizes the need to raise the hearing healthcare providers' awareness of communication matters with deaf clients. We know from experience that this poses quite a challenge. In general we conclude that communications between deaf and hard of hearing patients and hearing healthcare providers contain too much ambiguity and misunderstanding. The latter do not learn about the specific demands of communicating with deaf patients during their training, and this should be remedied in the curricula of medical educational programs. Also, the findings from the pilot study convey a clear message: although 73% of the respondents had encountered a deaf or hard of hearing client and 83% of these had experienced communication problems in these consultations, two-thirds of them were not prepared for this during their vocational training. If they were able to start their working career with even only basic knowledge and skills, that would already be an improvement over the present situation; as consciously incompetent practitioners they are likely to be more inclined to avail themselves of interpreting services, which would greatly enhance their deaf patients' access. Moreover, if more and good-quality informational and educational materials were available, these practitioners would probably consult them more often, which would support their continued learning.

Among the respondents to the second questionnaire was an expert group of 12 people, consisting of sign language interpreters and deaf signing professionals. We highlighted their responses to the survey questions and found that they differed substantially from those of the hearing care providers. We were curious to find out what we could learn from this expert group in order to improve communications between deaf and hard of hearing clients and hearing healthcare providers. First of all, it was shown that, before the consultation took place, the members of the expert group knew more about their clients than did the hearing care providers. This enabled them to look up relevant information they felt they needed before the sessions. They rated the consulted information as far more useful than did the hearing professionals. Of course, we must take into consideration the fact that they had access to more and better information because they were working in specialized institutions catering to deaf and hard of hearing clients. Nevertheless, this indicates that both keeping abreast of new information and preparing themselves before consultations contribute to their competence. By extension, this would also be true for the hearing care providers. The expert group felt confident that they enabled qualitatively good interactions between the clients and the care providers. By inference, we can thus assume that it would be beneficial for hearing care providers to know beforehand that a deaf patient has made an appointment and what this patient's preferred mode of communication is. Privacy laws in the Netherlands prevent medical staff from entering such a distinctive characteristic of a patient in the (electronic) patient files, which also holds for information about race or ethnicity. However, some patients do tell their general practitioner that they would prefer the information about hearing status to be provided to the specialist, for instance, so that that person can appropriately prepare for the consultation. Time pressure is often mentioned as an excuse for not making such preparation.

Many deaf and hard of hearing clients believe that they do not need an interpreter in their encounters with medical professionals. However, the results of our study show that the cultural and linguistic knowledge that the expert group members have of the communicative skills and needs of deaf and hard of hearing patients extends beyond mere translating or interpreting. The fact that in certain aspects they show a far more critical attitude toward their own competence than do the hearing professionals does not mean that they are not functioning well but indicates that they are more aware of the many potential pitfalls in communication. On the contrary, we propose that their awareness of the unconscious incompetence of many hearing healthcare providers may be of the utmost importance for their deaf and hard of hearing clients and for the quality of their treatment.

Along with Alexander, Ladd, and Powell (2012) we maintain that deaf-awareness training during the education of all healthcare staff is not only to be recommended but is in fact necessary in order to achieve better health care for deaf patients.

ACKNOWLEDGMENTS

This project was made possible by a grant from SIA RAAK Publiek no. 2006-2-1P. The consortium consisted of the Riethorst, the Gelderhorst, the Institute for Sign, Language, & Deaf Studies (ISLD) of Utrecht University of Applied Sciences (UUAS) and the Deaf Studies Research Unit of the Knowledge Center for Education, Faculty of Education, UUAS. First and foremost we would like to express our gratitude to the deaf and hearing participants and to the students and staff of the collaborating institutes. We would also like to convey our gratitude to the people who contributed to this project: Gisela van den Boomen, Sandra van Dulmen, Rick van Dijk, Ellen Enis, Christy Goes, Maaike Hajer, Tineke Holwerda, Noor Huegenin, Helianthe Kort, Marileen Louwerse, Marc van Opstal, Maarten Philipsen, Christiaan Plug, Kees Schipper, Anika Smeijers, Jan Tempelaar, Livienke Vogelaar, Sigrid Vorrink, and Johan Wilterdink. We especially would like to thank Sigrid Vorrink for her contribution to this chapter.

NOTES

1. The Gelderhorst is a special center for elderly deaf people; see http://www .gelderhorst.nl/welcome/.
2. The Riethorst caters to deaf and hard of hearing clients with psychological problems; see http://www.propersona.nl/Home/Ik%20zoek%20een%20 afdeling/?address_category_id=2.
3. SIA RAAK, a program run by the Dutch Ministry of Education, subsidized research done by universities of applied sciences aimed at developing useful innovations for professional practice. We would like to express our thanks to SIA RAAK for funding a grant for the project titled "An Eye for Communication," registration number 2006-2-1P.
4. SurveyMonkey is an online survey instrument; see www.surveymonkey.com.
5. We would like to express our special thanks to the students of the Institute for Sign, Language, & Deaf Studies and the Department of Nursing for their participation in this project. Their eagerness to learn was an inspiration to us all.
6. This was a principal component analysis (PCA), with varimax rotation, part of the standard SPSS software.
7. Gender was transformed into a dummy variable where women were coded as 1 and men as 0.
8. The original questionnaire has been translated into English, and the layout has been adjusted in order to save space.

REFERENCES

Adams, L. (n.d.). *Learning a new skill is easier said than done.* Gordon Training International. Retrieved July 25, 2013, from http://www.gordontraining.com/ free-workplace-articles/learning-a-new-skill-is-easier-said-than-done/
Alexander, A., Ladd, P., & Powell, S. (2012). Deafness might damage your health. *Lancet, 379*(9820), 979–981.

Barnett, S., & Franks, P. (2002). Health care utilization and adults who are deaf: Relationship with age at onset of deafness. *Health Services Research Journal,* 37, 105–120.

CBS-POLS. (2009). *Permanent Onderzoek Leefsituatie: Module Gezondheid en Welzijn* [Permanent study of life situations: Module on health and well-being]. Dutch Ministry of Health, Retrieved July 23, 2013, from http://www.zorggegevens.nl/zorg/eerstelijnszorg/permanent-onderzoek-leefsituatie-module-gezondheid-en-welzijn/

De Bruin, E. (2007). Presentation at "Joining Forces," a conference of the European Society for Mental Health and Deafness, September 2007, Haarlem, the Netherlands.

De Vellis, R. F. (2003). *Scale development: Theory and applications.* Thousand Oaks, CA: Sage.

Doof.nl. (2006). Gebaren op leven en dood [Signing for life or death]. Interview with Anne Baker, chair of psycholinguistics, language pathology, and sign linguistics, University of Amsterdam. Retrieved March 2, 2014, from http://www.doof.nl/nieuws/gebarentaal-op-leven-en-dood/24983

Harmer, L. (1999). Health care delivery and deaf people: Practice, problems, and recommendations for change. *Journal of Deaf Studies and Deaf Education,* 4(2), 73–110.

Kalb, M. (2010). *Vergroten toegankelijkheid huisartsenpost voor doven en slechthorenden* [Increasing deaf and hard of hearing individuals' access to medical facilities]. Centrale Huisartsenpost Rijnmond, May 2010. Retrieved November 2013 from http://vhn.artsennet.nl/web/show/search?searchstring=toegankelijkheid+dove&id=903046&from=0&to=10&googlefilter=&q=toegankelijkheid+dove&domain=VHN

Nationaal Kompas Volksgezondheid [National Compass of Public Health], version 4.4, July 15, 2011. Retrieved June 23, 2013, from http://www.nationaalkompas.nl/gezondheid-en-ziekte/ziekten-en-aandoeningen/zenuwstelsel-en-zintuigen/gehoorstoornissen/hoe-vaak-komen-gehoorstoornissen-voor/

National Council on Disability. (2009). *The current state of health care for people with disabilities.* Report of the U.S. National Council on Disabilities. Retrieved June 24, 2013, from http://www.ncd.gov/publications/2009/Sept302009

Ragovin, H. (2013). When health care is lost in translation. *Tufts Journal.* Retrieved October 15, 2013, from http://tuftsjournal.tufts.edu/archives/1908/when-health-care-is-lost-in-translation

Smeijers, A. S., & Pfau, R. (2009). Towards a treatment for treatment: On the communication between general practitioners and their deaf patients. *Sign Language Translator and Interpreter (SLTI),* 3(1), 1–14.

Steinberg, A. G., Wiggins, E. A., Barmada C. H., & Sullivan, V. J. (2002). Deaf women: Experiences and perceptions of healthcare system access. *Journal of Women's Health* 11(8), 733.

Van Bentum, G., Van den Berg, R., Hullekes, R., Mol, L., Van Vliet, M., Welle, M., et al. (2009). Oog voor communicatie [An eye for communication]. Project research report by the Faculty of Health Care. Utrecht: Faculty of Health, University of Applied Sciences.

Van den Bogaerde, B., & Van Dijk, R. (2006). *Oog voor communicatie* [An eye for communication]. SIA RAAK public project application no. 2006-1-P. October 2006. See also http://www.innovatie-alliantie.nl/projectenbank/raak -project/257-oog-voor-communicatie.html

Van Wieringen, J. C., Harmsen, J. A., & Bruijnzeels, M. A. (2002). Intercultural communication in general practice. *European Journal of Public Health,* March, *12*(1), 63–68.

Appendix A.

Questionnaire for Deaf and Hard of Hearing Clients[8]

1. You are:
   - male
   - female
2. You are:
   - (Early) deaf
   - Suddenly or late deaf
   - Hard of hearing
3. In what year were you born? .... [space for answer]
4. What do you want a hearing healthcare professional to do during communications with you? (you can select more than one answer)
   - Use sign language
   - Use spoken language, supported by signing
   - Speak clearly
   - Look you in the eyes
   - Write
   - Give explanations by drawing
   - Other (please specify) ....
5. Have you ever been to one of the following professionals? (you can select more than one)
   - General practitioner
   - Physiotherapist
   - Dentist
   - Pharmacist
   - Doctor in hospital
   - Nurse/doctor's assistant
   - Other (please specify) ....
6. Do you always book an interpreter for a visit to a healthcare professional?
   - Always
   - Sometimes
   - Never

7. If you selected "never" in the previous question, why did you not book an interpreter?
   - There is never one available.
   - I don't know how to do that.
   - I don't need an interpreter.
   - I always bring a friend/relative.
   - I always use technical equipment (hearing aid, etc).
   - Other (please specify) ....

From here (questions 8 through 19) the respondents were asked to recall a visit to a healthcare professional. They were asked to answer this whole series of questions with this visit in mind. After that, they were asked to recall a second (different) visit to a healthcare professional. They were then asked to answer the same series of questions as earlier (but now numbered 20 through 31).

8. What type of professional did you visit?
   - General practitioner
   - Physiotherapist
   - Dentist
   - Pharmacist
   - Doctor in hospital
   - Nurse/doctor's assistant
   - Other (please specify) ....
9. How did you make this appointment?
   - I made a phone call.
   - I used text phone.
   - Email
   - Fax
   - I went there myself.
   - I asked somebody to assist me (interpreter, relative, etc.)
   - Other (please specify) ....
10. Please describe how you made the appointment ....
    [space for description]
11. Was an interpreter present during this visit to this healthcare professional?
    - Yes, I arranged for an interpreter myself.
    - Yes, the professional had arranged for an interpreter.

- No, but I had brought a friend/partner/relative who translated for/supported me.
- No, I never book an interpreter.
- No, there was no interpreter available.
- No, an interpreter was not necessary in this situation.

12. How would you describe the contact with the professional during this visit?
    - Very poor
    - Poor
    - Average
    - Good
    - Very good

13. Did the professional adjust his or her communication to you?
    - Yes
    - No

14. If you answered "yes" to question 13, please describe how the professional adjusted his or her communication ……………….. [space for description]

15. Did the professional use tools to facilitate the communication?
    - No
    - Yes, pen and paper.
    - Yes, pictures.
    - Other (please specify) ……………………..

16. Do you have the impression that you got clear information from the professional?
    - Not at all
    - A little
    - Average
    - The information was sufficiently clear.
    - The information was quite clear.

17. Do you have the impression that the professional understood you well?
    - Yes
    - No
    - A little bit

18. Did the professional have enough time for you?
    - Yes
    - No

19. If applicable, please describe how the communications went in these locations at the facility.
   - At the reception desk .... [space for description]
   - In the laboratory .... [space for description]
   - In the X-ray department .... [space for description]
   - In a special research department (eye examination, ECG, etc.) .... [space for description]

After this, the same series of questions was asked about a different situation (questions 20 through 31)

32. What can you, as a deaf/hard of hearing client, do to improve the communications next time? .... [space for description]

33. Could you mention three things that would improve a visit to the general practitioner? (you may mention more than three) .... [space for description]

34. Could you mention three practical things that would make the hospital reception and/or admissions procedure more pleasant for a deaf or hard of hearing patient? .... [space for description]

35. Do you ever visit friends or relatives at the hospital? If so, could you mention three things that would make such visits easier/more pleasant for a deaf or hard of hearing person? (you may mention more than three) .... [space for description]

36. This is the end of the questionnaire. If you have anything to add, you can do that here .... [space for description]

Appendix B.

Questionnaire for Healthcare Professionals

1. For which organization do you work?
   - Gelderse Vallei Hospital
   - De Gelderhorst
   - De Riethorst, department for deaf and hard of hearing persons
   - Medical facility Maandereng
   - Pharmacy in Rietkampen
   - Medical facility Ede
2. In which department do you work? .... [space for description]
3. How long have you been working for this institution/ organization? .... years
4. In what year were you born? ....
5. You are
   - Male
   - Female
6. What is the highest level of formal education you have completed? [Respondents could choose from list ranging from elementary school through university.]
7. What vocational/professional training have you had? .... [space for description]
8. What is your job description? .... [space for description]
9. How long have you been working in your present capacity? .... years
10. Did you know anything about the patient's background prior to the appointment (e.g., gender, age, cultural background, language)?
    - Nothing at all
    - A little bit
    - Average knowledge
    - Yes, quite a bit
    - Yes, a lot

11. Would you, prior to an appointment, want to know whether the patient is deaf or hard of hearing?

12. Have you ever, in the course of your duties, had direct contact with a deaf or hard of hearing patient?
    - Yes
    - No

13. How did this encounter go?
    - Very badly
    - Rather badly
    - It was average.
    - Well
    - Very well

14. Did you adjust your communication?
    - Yes
    - No

15. If you answered "yes" to the preceding question, can you describe why you adjusted your communication? .... [space for description]

16. Can you describe how you adjusted your communication? .... [space for description]

17. To what extent was your adjustment successful?
    - Not at all
    - Slightly successful
    - Average
    - Largely successful
    - Very successful

18. How did you determine whether your adjustment was successful? .... [space for description]

19. If you did not adjust your communication, can you explain why not? .... [space for explanation]

20. Do you have the impression that you gave enough information to the deaf or hard of hearing patient?
    - Not at all
    - Hardly
    - Average
    - More than average information
    - Quite a bit of information

21. How did you convey this information? (you can select more than one)
    - Orally (spoken Dutch)
    - In written form
    - Through an interpreter
    - Other (please specify) ....

22. Do you have the impression that the deaf or hard of hearing person understood you well?
    - Yes
    - No

23. Are the following points, according to you, different for deaf/hard of hearing patients and hearing patients?

	More Difficult/More Time Consuming	Not Different
Time needed		
The consultation as a whole		
Making appointments		
Contact outside the appointment		
Asking for the patient's experience		
Empathy for patient		
Making yourself clear		
Hearing the patient		

24. Are you familiar with various tools/methods you can use to facilitate communication with deaf/hard of hearing patients?
    - Yes
    - No

25. If you answered "yes" to the preceding question, could you mention one or more? .... [space for description]

26. Could you indicate which of the following tools/methods you have used in consultations with a deaf or hard of hearing patient? (you can select more than one).
    - Sign language interpreter
    - Typing interpreter
    - Deaf or hard of hearing patient's family
    - Written information (you are writing)
    - A protocol

- Solo equipment
- Circular circuit
- Phone with text and image
- Other (please specify) …………………..

27. Is there any information about communicating with deaf or hard of hearing patients available in your department?
    - I don't know.
    - No
    - Yes
    - If yes, please specify …………………………..

28. If so, do you use this information?
    - Yes
    - No
    - Please specify why …………………………..

29. What do you think about this information on deaf or hard of hearing patients in your practice?

	Not at All	Hardly	Middle	Rather	Very
a. Useful in general					
b. Practically applicable					
c. Complete					

30. Are you familiar with the option of using interpreters for deaf and hard of hearing patients?
    - Yes
    - No

31. What knowledge and skills do you think you need in order to communicate well with deaf and hard of hearing patients next time? ………………….. [space for description]

32. This is the end of the questionnaire. If there is something that you would like to add, you can do so here ……………………
    [space for description]

Index

Figures, notes, and tables are indicated by "f," "n," and "t" following page numbers.

informed consent and, 189, 191–92
for research, 202, 241, 242
European Charter of Fundamental
Rights, 186–87
European Parliament and the Council
of October 20, 2010, 189
European Union, deaf people in,
186–87. *See also specific
countries*
eye contact, 151
eye gaze, 43–44. *See also* gaze
direction

face (social value), 36, 49, 51
face-to-face communication,
preference for, 264, 307
facial expression cues, 48, 51
family members. *See* relatives
fax machines for appointment setting,
334
Federal Ministry of Health (Austria),
304, 305, 323
Felgner, L., 151
filming interview questions in sign
language, 286–87
fingerspelling, 34, 111–12
first harmonization of questionnaires,
300
first-person interview questions,
285–86
Flemish Sign Language, 278
Folkins, A., 260
forward-backward-forward
translation technique, 296–301
four stages of learning, 329, 329*f*
Franks, P., 240
Freedom of Information Acts (Ireland
1997 & 2003), 212
Friedman, E., 310
fund-of-information deficit, 236, 250

Gany, Francesca, 309
gatekeeping behavior of interpreters,
61, 74, 135
gaze direction, 287, 316

Gelderhorst institution, 330, 332,
348*n*1
Gelderse Vallei Hospital, 332, 338
gender differences, 143, 208
General Health Questionnaire (GHQ),
283
general practitioners (GPs). *See*
providers
general probing method, 289, 301
Germany case study, 128–84. *See
also* diagnosing healthcare
assignments
gesturing, 154, 188, 327
goal-oriented nature of interpreting,
83–84, 136
Gordon Training International, 329
Graz, Austria
Skype use for remote medical
interpreting, 307
telephone interpreting company,
306
Greenhalgh, T., 145
Grehan, C., 201
grounded-theory approach, 244
guidelines
for communication, 71. *See also*
codes of ethics
for informed consent, 189, 192–93
for translating questionnaires into
sign language, 280–81, 282*f*,
291–92, 296–301
for working with deaf patients, 256

Hale, S., 61
Harmer, L., 240
harmonization of questionnaires for
international use, 300–301
HCIS (Healthcare Interpreting
Service), 33–34
headset use in video interpreting, 313,
316–17, 321
healthcare access
appointment setting, 138, 193,
238, 334–35. *See also* booking
agencies

Institute for Sign, Language, & Deaf Studies (Utrecht), 331

insurance reimbursing for interpreter cost, 137–38, 169*n*1

interactional skills of interpreters, 35–36

interdependence of participants, 78–81

Interesource Group (Ireland) Limited, 187

International Medical Interpreters Association (IMIA) Code of Ethics, 134

Internet use
  for appointment setting, 334
  for email communication, 147, 157, 211–12, 334
  for health information, 238, 259, 262–64
  for health-related quality of life (HRQoL) questionnaires, 280–81, 290

interpersonal relationships, 92–95, 145–46, 167–68, 222. *See also* relational work

interpreters
  as active participants, 74–78, 91–93, 135
  as advocate for patients, 224–25
  briefing by patients, 150–51
  challenges for, 34, 84–90, 91–92
  clarification requests of, 32–69. *See also* clarification requests
  as co-diagnosticians, 74, 94
  as conduit, 70–103. *See also* bilingual health communication trends
  conversation control of, 81–82
  creating awareness for deaf population, 227
  cultural gap, bridging, 26, 76, 134–36
  as discourse managers, 34–35
  education for. *See* education

emotions of, 82, 88, 91–93

gatekeeping behavior of, 61, 74, 135–36

influence on information exchange, 7–8

as interdependent participants, 78–81

interpersonal relationships and, 92–95, 145–46, 167–68, 222. *See also* relational work

misconduct of, 82, 94

neutrality of, 71–72, 84, 93, 134, 223

nonprofessional vs., 77, 81–82, 85–87. *See also* nonprofessional interpreters

novice, 10, 42–43

outside medical role, 75, 224

payment for, 137–38, 169*n*1, 221, 223, 234–35

proactive behavior of, 159–61

providers and, 93, 134, 221

public perceptions of, 72, 304

relational work of, 35, 50, 149–50, 218–19

requirements for, 10–11, 26, 132. *See also* education

role, defined, 5–6

safety and health of, 209–10

scope of practice of, 209, 224

shortage of, 25–26, 194, 214

of spoken language. *See* spoken language interpreting

strategies used for understanding by, 34–37, 60, 206–7, 207*f*

as support person, 150

survey of, 204–10, 205*f*, 207*f*

types of, 85–90

underutilization of, 87–89, 213–14, 219–20, 237–38, 336

video interpreting and, 8, 216, 302–25. *See also* video interpreting

interrupting. *See* turn-taking

Major, G., 35, 135
Margellos-Anast, H., 240
mass media, health information and,
    236–37, 260, 265
maternity services for deaf patients,
    study on, 196–98
Matthews, P. A., 200
McCaul, E., 196
mediating telephone facility, 334
medical appointments
    of deaf vs. hearing population, 327
    interpreter assignments for, 128–84.
        See also diagnosing healthcare
        assignments
    positioning of participants during,
        75, 133, 151–53, 162
    scheduling, 138, 193, 238, 334–35.
        See also booking agencies
    time allotted for, 193
    video interpreting for, 302–25. *See
        also* video interpreting
medical histories, 81–82
medical interviews in ASL, 104–27
    allergies to medications, 115–17,
        115*f*, 116*t*
    analysis of questions, 110–19
    materials and task, 108–10, 109*t*
    over-the-counter medications,
        110–15, 112–13*t*, 114*f*
    participants, 108
    sexual activity, 117–19, 118*t*
    study overview, 107–8
    transcription and analysis, 110
medical records, 193, 238, 256, 347
medical setting, challenges of,
    132–34
medical specialists, communicative
    needs of, 90–93, 138–41,
    140–41*f*
medical staff. *See* providers; staff,
    medical
"medications," contextualizing in
    ASL, 117, 124–25
Medisigns Project, 186–88, 203–4,
    229*n*2. *See also* Ireland,

interpreted health care in
    mental health care, 277–301
interpreter challenges in, 91–92
psychological problems, 279–80
translating questionnaires into sign
    language, 281–92
    adaptations in, 285–86
    conducting questionnaires, 290
    guidelines for, 280–81, 282*f*,
        291–92, 296–301
    methodology, 288*f*
    participants, 290–91, 291*f*
    presentation, 287–89, 288*f*
    procedures, 281
    psychological tests, 280–81
    questionnaires translated for
        study, 281–84
    technical issues, 286–87
    testing questionnaires, 289–90
    translation methodology, 296–301
    translators selection criteria,
        284–85
Metzger, M., 35, 36–37, 76, 134, 135
microphone use for video interpreting,
    317, 321
Mindless, A., 133
minority, deaf population as, 278, 280
misconduct of interpreters, 82, 94
misplacement markers, 64*n*8
mitigating clarification, 49–54
Monterey Institute of International
    Studies, 309
multifunctionality of clarification,
    54–61

National Auslan Interpreter Booking
    and Payment Service (NABS),
    33–34, 235
National Authority for the
    Accreditation of Translators
    and Interpreters (NAATI), 33
National Health Priority Areas
    (Australia), 234
neonatal screening for deafness, 198
Netherlands

accessing health care in, 326–58, 329f. *See also* healthcare access

mental health questionnaire case study, 277–301. *See also* mental health care

neutrality of interpreters, 71–72, 84, 93, 134, 223

NGT (Sign Language of the Netherlands), 278. *See also* mental health care

Nickleach, D., 308

Nicodemus, B., 107

nodding head, 57

noncompliance of patients, 221–22

nonliteral interpretation, 60–61, 76–77. *See also* conceptual equivalence of translations

nonprofessional interpreters

medical staff as, 8, 87, 88, 140–41, 303, 305

negative impact of, 61

preference for, 257

professional vs., 77, 81–82, 85–87

relatives as, 8–9, 81–82, 85–87, 88, 215–16, 221, 223, 303

types of, 26

nonverbal behaviors. *See also specific behaviors*

for active participating, 75–76

as mitigation devices, 47–48, 51, 53, 54

monitoring of by providers, 82

positioning of participants and, 75, 133, 151–53, 162

Novaes, F., 310

novice interpreters, 10, 42–43

Nuremburg Code (1947), 191

nurses. *See* staff, medical

O'Brien, J., 68

"one-off" signs, 34

ongoing health care

access to interpreter for, 251–53

chronic diseases, 234

qualitative study on. *See* health information

Osborne, R. H., 234

over-the-counter medications (ASL context), 110–15, 112–13t, 114f, 119–20, 124–25

Ozolins, U., 303–5

pain, cultural perception of, 7

parallel conversations, 11–23

paraprofessional interpreters, 33

participatory research, 241–42

"partner," contextualizing in asl, 118–19, 118t

patients

appointment setting by, 138, 193, 238, 334–35. *See also* booking agencies

autonomy of, 189–90

briefing interpreters, 150–51

communication culture of, 159

communication preferences of. *See* communication preferences of patients

deaf people as primary caregivers to, 213

debriefing after examination, 164–67

dissatisfaction of, 157–59

educating on health. *See* health literacy

educating on interpreters, 227–28

equal treatment of, 198, 211

informed consent of, 189–93, 212–13, 219

as interdependent participants, 78–81

interpersonal relationships and, 93–95, 146, 167–68

legal rights of. *See* legal rights

medical histories of, 81–82

medical records of, 238, 256, 347

noncompliance of, 221–22

perceived need for interpreters, 345

positioning of during exam, 75,
133, 151–53, 162
privacy issues of, 133, 198–99, 201,
223, 256–57
procuring interpreters, 138, 145–47,
213
role in health management, 237,
253
state of mind of, 208
trust of, 92, 94, 213–14, 222–23,
285
video interpreting, perspectives on,
316–17
visual aids for, 156–57, 286–88,
288f
Paulini, A., 136
payment for interpreters, 137–38,
169n1, 221, 223, 234–35
Pérez-Stable, E. J., 308
"pharmacy," contextualizing in ASL,
112, 112t, 120
phonemes, 277–78
physicians. See providers
"please," as mitigating device, 53
Pollard, R. Q, 236, 237
positioning of participants during
exam, 75, 133, 151–53, 162
poverty, 201
Powell, S., 326, 328, 347
power differentials, 5–6, 52, 76, 198,
211–12. See also social status
prelingually deafened adults, 240,
289, 327
preparing for interpreting encounter,
208
prescription medication (ASL), 113,
113t, 120
pretesting questionnaires, 289–90,
300–301
preventive health care
access to interpreter for, 251–53
qualitative study on, 233–76. See
also health information
Price, E. L., 308

primary health care, access to
interpreters for, 253–56
print media for health information,
236, 264
privacy issues, 133, 198–99, 201, 223,
256–57. See also confidentiality
privacy laws (Netherlands), 347
private clinics, cost of interpreters
and, 137–38
procuring interpreters, 138, 145–47,
213
professional development of
interpreters, 188
professional vs. ad hoc interpreters,
77, 81–82, 85
providers
attitudes of, 206, 214–15
awareness of patient needs, 217–27,
234, 327–28, 329f, 345–46
bilingual, 104–27. See also medical
interviews in ASL
challenges for, 154–58
communication difficulties of,
130–31
communication skills of, 237,
344–45
control of conversations, 82–83. See
also (mis)understanding
education, on deaf populations, 26,
34, 215, 220, 226–27, 328–29,
346
expectations of interpreters, 93, 134
expectations of patients, 237
as interdependent participants,
78–81
interpersonal relationships and,
93–95
interpreter type, preference for, 88
of mental health care, 91–92
mitigating clarification, 52–54
procuring interpreters, 147
as source of health information,
261–62
specialists, 90–93, 138–41, 141–42f

trust of, 87, 94
underutilizing interpreters, 87–89,
219–20
video interpreting and, 318–19
psychological and psychiatric health
care. *See* mental health care
public-authority initiatives in language
services, 305–6
public perceptions of interpreters, 72,
304

Quessa, A., 310
questionnaires
on access to health care, study of,
302–25. *See also* healthcare
access
translating, 277–301. *See also*
mental health care

rapport, 146, 151
"rash," as symptom example, 116,
120
reading skills, 278. *See also* English
literacy
real-world examples, contextualizing
in ASL, 112, 116–19
receptionists, 147–49. *See also* staff,
medical
reconciliation in questionnaire
translation, 298–99
Red Cross (Austria), 312
referrals, 138
Registry of Interpreters for the Deaf
(RID), 106
reimbursing cost of interpreters,
137–38, 169*n*1. *See also*
payment for interpreters
relational work, 35, 50, 149–50,
218–19
relatives
as deaf primary caregivers of
patients, 213
as interpreters, 8–9, 81–82, 85–87,
88, 215–16, 221, 223, 303

supporting deaf patients, 159,
162–64, 222–23
remote interpreting. *See* video
interpreting
remote simultaneous medical
interpretation (RSMI), 309–10
repair talk, 26, 36. *See also*
clarification requests
research. *See* literature
respect for patients, 89, 94, 156–57,
166, 197
Riethorst institution, 330, 332, 348*n*2
Rietkampen (pharmacy), 332
Robb, N., 145
Robertson, S., 68
role-plays as educational tools, 62
role space model, 135–36
Roman Catholic Order of the
Brothers Hospitallers, 138
Rosenberg, E., 134
Roy, C., 44
Rozanes, I., 136

Sacks, H., 36
St. Anna Children's Hospital (Vienna),
312, 324
St. Catherine University (U.S.), 106
Saint-Louis, L., 310
Salzburg, Austria, public hospital, 306
scheduling appointments, 138, 193,
238, 334–35. *See also* booking
agencies
Schegloff, E., 36
*Schloendorff v. Society of New York
Hospital* (1914), 191–92
second-person interview questions,
286
Seller, R., 134
"sexually active," contextualizing in
ASL, 117–20, 118*t*, 127
Sheikh, A. A., 191
shift-implicative device, 46, 55
shortage of interpreters, 25–26, 194,
214

Vine, B., 68
visibility of interpreters, 74–75
vision of deaf people, 139, 153, 247–48
visual accessibility. *See* positioning of participants during exam
visual aids for patients, 156–57, 286–88, 288*f*
visual health information, 260, 260*t*
voluntary trust, 145

Wadensjö, C., 36, 134
waiting rooms, 149–51, 166
Wallace, P., 307
workshops for health information, 266
World Deaf Day, 331

World Health Organization Quality of Life-BREF (WHOQoLBREF), 282–83, 296
writing, for medical exam communication, 197–98, 206–7, 211–12, 238, 256–58, 327
written health information
Internet use of, 238, 259, 262–64
power dynamic and, 198, 211–12
preference for, 264
questionnaires, translating, 277–301. *See also* mental health care
recommendations for, 236, 239, 248

Yugoslavia, immigrants from, 304–5, 311